Praise ɪ ... rs:

"This is a book lockɛ ... ...an life, heroic stories—written by Terry ... ...ıan life, heroic man to match. These page-turning moɪ ... ɪy ɪales remind us, in harrowing and frightful detail, that often the only thing standing between the public's wildlife heritage and the bad guys who want to despoil it are the brave men and women carrying the game warden's badge. *Wildlife Wars* is the new sportsman's thriller."

—Todd Wilkinson, author of
Science Under Siege: The Politicians' War on Nature and Truth

"This collection of experiences as a young warden in his native California paints a stirring picture of the constant struggle to protect our outdoor resource from a constant assault from lawbreakers. The book gives a brisk, sometimes swashbuckling account of Grosz's running duels with a variety of miscreants from market hunters to garden-variety poachers. A wonderful storyteller, Grosz keeps the reader in an almost constant tingle with lively intrigues and chases that include his being deliberately shot in the back. ... A second book ... should be available by autumn. Grosz promises it'll stir plenty of interest and emotion. I can hardly wait."

—Charlie Meyers, *The Denver Post*

"Because wildlife is important, wildlife law enforcement officers are important, and Terry 'Tiny' Grosz was one good one. He recounts his lively and dangerous career as a wildlife cop in the same exuberant, unpretentious style it was lived—something like Louis L'Amour meets Mike Hammer."

—David Petersen, author of
Heartsblood and *Ghost Grizzlies*

"From the first chapter till the last, the reader will find no dull moments. This is one of those books that are hard to put down once you start. ... After you finish Terry's book, you will be looking forward to the next in the series."

—*International Game Warden*

"We're the top-dog species on this planet. Even the most wily or fearsomely armed critter stands little or no chance against a thoughtful and well-armed human. And when you add malicious amusement and avarice to the mix, entire species quickly find themselves running for their lives—and into the black void of extinction. Or at least that's how it would be if it weren't for a small group of incredibly dedicated wildlife officers who possess the unrelenting spirit (and occasionally, even the mass) of a protective mother grizzly. In Terry Grosz's *Wildlife Wars*, you will meet such an officer—and find out, in very vivid detail, why it's a terribly bad idea to violate the hunting laws regarding one of his treasured creatures."

—Ken Goddard, author of *First Evidence*

"His collection of tales needs to be told, for it helps combat an enormous problem concerning our country's natural wildlife. Grosz is obviously a very committed individual—and also a natural storyteller. This collection consists of stories about his early years as a warden in California. They relate many close calls with mother nature: wild creatures and savage lawbreakers. ... Those who cherish the outdoors for hunting and fishing as well as those involved in environmental studies will benefit from this work."

—*Booklist*

"Ultimately, wildlife will be saved by committed individuals—people like ... Terry Grosz. They wake up every day and go off into the trenches, one step at a time, to face up to the many challenges: poachers discharging automatic weapons into innocent creatures; laws that need reforming or implementing; societal trends and ethics that require discussion and reshaping. ... Such individuals fighting to save America's wildlife marshal a special grace, if you will, in the face of terrible crimes and near overwhelming adversity. They are remarkable not because they are necessarily so courageous, but because their common sense is in tune with their conscience."

—Michael Tobias, in *Nature's Keepers*

For Love of Wildness

For Love of Wildness

The Journal of a
U.S. Game Management Agent

Terry Grosz

JOHNSON BOOKS

Boulder

Published by Johnson Books, a division of Johnson Publishing Company, 1880 South 57th Court, Boulder, Colorado 80301.
E-mail: books@jpcolorado.com.

9 8 7 6 5 4 3 2 1

Cover design: Debra Topping
Cover photograph © Jeffrey Rich Nature Photography. Snow geese, Mount Shasta at sunset, Tule Lake, CA.
Author photograph © James Bludworth

Library of Congress Cataloging-in-Publication Data
Grosz, Terry.
For love of wildness: the journal of a U.S. game management agent / Terry Grosz.
    p.   cm.
ISBN 1-55566-265-X (cloth: alk. paper)—ISBN 1-55566-264-1 (pbk.: alk. paper)
    1. Grosz, Terry. 2. U.S. Fish and Wildlife Service—Officials and employees—Biography. 3. Wildlife management—United States—Anecdotes. I. Title.

SK354.G76 A3 2000
363.28—dc21
[B]   00-044388

Printed in the United States by
Johnson Printing
1880 South 57th Court
Boulder, Colorado 80301

♻ Printed on recycled paper with soy ink

THIS BOOK IS DEDICATED to Larry Davis, the quintessential state Fish and Game warden, conservationist, friend, and human being. A man whose soul is in tune with the history of the times, whose clear eyes are always watching for the next sunrise and what the morning brings, whose understanding smile and friendship is meant for all who truly see, and whose wisdom and gifted counsel is before its time. To the man whom I admire as a wildlife professional possessing a conservation ethic not of this century, respect as a man for all seasons, and love as a brother, I dedicate this book of life's stories from one westering man to another.

Contents

Preface

IN 1966, AFTER GOING THROUGH an extensive written and physical testing program, I accepted a commission as a California state Fish and Game warden just months after graduating from Humboldt State College with my master's degree in wildlife management. My first duty station was in Eureka, Humboldt County, California. A year and a half later I transferred to Colusa in Colusa County, a prime waterfowl district in the heart of the Sacramento Valley. Owing to my hard work over the next several years in that capacity and to my academic background, I was offered a commission in May 1970 as a U.S. game management agent for the U.S. Fish and Wildlife Service. I had wanted to become a game management agent ever since I first read about the duties of that position in a government brochure sent to my college, and now my wildest dreams were about to come true.

However, making that change wasn't without its hatful of hornets. I had truly enjoyed my position as a state Fish and Game warden and, for the most part, the people with whom I worked within that organization. Working in the Sacramento Valley as a conservation officer was a challenge that offered many rewards, including those that came from working with many special people of the land. I also had just helped in the building of our first home, a 3,100-square-foot brick house with all the trimmings just north of the small valley town of Colusa. Suffice it to say that that home was a dream come true for my wife, Donna, and me. With that fly in the ointment, I had little desire now to move from a home just barely lived in to a large city.

My bride, who was a schoolteacher—and a damned good one, I might add—held a teaching position in the small town of Williams, about ten miles west of our home in Colusa. She too enjoyed the people of the area, including their children, and was making a real difference with many of those children as far as their education was concerned. In fact, I can still remember several children in some of her classes who when they first came to school were so shy, or just so plain out of the loop of society, that they wouldn't even speak. However, after several weeks, or months in some cases, those kids were speaking, running, and playing with all the other kids, thanks to her exceptional guiding hand. So those thorns of transfer were not only for me but also for my wife with the loss of her career. In fact, this kind of proposed move to another duty station turned into an all-too-common theme for her, repeated some five more times before I retired. You can imagine what that moving scenario did to her teaching career and professional desires each time.

However, I made the decision to accept the federal position because of its potential for my future and that of my family. I notified my captain and thirty-one days later was sworn in as a U.S. game management agent and sent to Martinez, California, some ninety miles away. The position of game management agent, in addition to wildlife law enforcement, included some duties of a wildlife biologist. Soon I found myself using my college training in wildlife management banding ducks in Canada, conducting dove population counts in the San Joaquin Delta country, banding mourning dove in Colusa County, and in the fall and winter enforcing federal laws as they related to the many species of wildlife the Service was mandated by Congress to protect.

As time went on I found the new position even more exciting than the one I had previously held as a state Fish and Game warden. Instead of working just with those violating the wildlife laws in my assigned district, my "district" now was basically the entire United States. In addition, the everyday operations of an agent were generally directed at the more serious wildlife violator or more serious wildlife crime. Because of this difference, it was not uncommon for me to find myself doing much more complex criminal investigative work than had been required of me as a state officer.

Don't get me wrong—state conservation law enforcement work was and remains terribly vital. In fact it is without a doubt the first line of defense when protecting the resources of this nation. And many times game agents pitched right in and gave our overworked state counterparts a helping hand, especially on the opening weekends of important hunting seasons. However, I began to find myself more and more, with information developed myself or received from my state counterparts, starting to sight in on the really serious wildlife criminals involved in wildlife crime such as baiting, killing marine mammals, taking large over-limits of migratory birds on private shooting preserves, killing eagles, or smuggling wildlife through the Bay area Ports of Entry. I also found myself providing assistance to Service covert operatives on multistate and country investigations and becoming a member of flying squads sent to quell other serious wildlife crime. However, I still found the time, working either alone or with my state counterparts, to revert back to the basics of wildlife law enforcement and pursue those breaking any wildlife laws, state or federal. The beauty in this dualism was that it allowed me to keep a handle on my roots and at the same time undertake new tasks that helped me learn and mature within the profession.

Along with these new and exciting duties on a national scale came a reduction in the quality of my home life because I was almost always on the road on assignment. Keep in mind that there were 178 of us agents in the country during those heady days in the early '70s, and to say the least, we were swamped with illegal activity. Subtract from that number the sick, lame, and lazy, and you can see just how pressured those remaining few of us really were, working to get the job done in the face of increasing illegal activities at the federal level (as human populations grew, so did the requirements for our wide-ranging enforcement services).

It is hard to believe that in 1999 the Service, owing to budgetary neglect, poor leadership at the highest levels, and political pressure, after reaching an authorized agent strength of 250 agents in the early '90s (still nowhere near the number needed), saw fit to again reduce the officer corps through attrition to a number almost as low as it was in the 1970s. That reduction is especially criminal in light of the fact that the laws to be enforced by the Service's Division of Law Enforcement increased almost twofold during that same period! It's a pretty sad testimony to that agency's lack of commitment to the American people. ... But it is a historical fact that the Department of the Interior, the parent agency of the U.S. Fish and Wildlife Service, is a dumping ground for political hacks. In my thirty-two years of public service I have never found that assumption to be inaccurate, and many times the results show.

Getting off my high horse and back to my quality-of-life issue, I remember that in 1971 I was home only seventeen days between January 1 and June 15! Throughout the rest of my career, similar needs often kept me away from home for long periods. It was plain and simply the nature of the beast, and my long-suffering bride had to be Mom, Mr. Mom, schoolteacher, homemaker, and Mr. Fix-It as I roamed the wilds grabbing hold of those who needed their hands slapped. Needless to say, my wife is one tough lady, not to mention still my best friend after thirty-seven years and counting. What else is new? Most good law enforcement wives and husbands send their men and women off to the wildlife wars, patch them up when they come home, listen to their stories, wipe away their tears, and send them right back into battle so that those yet to come will have something in the wildlife world to truly enjoy when it is their turn. They do all that knowing full well that their own quality of life will be diminished as well as that of their children.

After two eventful and educational years in the San Francisco Bay area, I was transferred back to Colusa as the resident game management agent to once again protect the waterfowl from both the sportsmen during the day and the illegal waterfowl shooters plying their trade, be it market hunting or "dragging" for their own use, against the unsuspecting ducks at night. Bear in mind that the Service's Division of Law Enforcement was founded on the Lacey Act, passed in 1900, and the Migratory Bird Treaty Act passed in 1918. The Lacey Act, in addition to importation restrictions on certain species of wildlife to protect American species and agriculture, was designed to stop the illegal taking and transport of wildlife across state, federal, tribal, or international boundaries. Before the act was passed, once the poachers had illegally taken wildlife and crossed state lines, local conservation officers were unable to continue pursuit. The Migratory Bird Treaty Act was implemented to protect migratory birds in order to preserve the environment and agriculture (by protecting insect-eating birds) for the sake of the American people. In time five other nations implemented similar treaties.

These acts are part of the reason why these stories show that as a federal officer I remained involved with the protection of migratory birds and with stopping illegal interstate or foreign trade in wildlife. With thousands of sportsmen hunting waterfowl during the daylight hours at every point on the compass in the Sacramento and San Joaquin Valleys and the illegal night shooters killing the ducks as they fed in huge flocks in the fields at night, I found myself more than busy, many times seven days a week and fourteen to eighteen hours per day for months on end. In addition, my duties as a game management agent included protecting marine mammals, endangered species, eagles, National Wildlife Refuges, and much more. It should be easy to see why the days were long and our mates superhuman.

This book shows a young man starting to mature and develop as a wildlife officer under the demands of these duties, often learning by mistakes but managing to keep a keen eye on the battlefield as it laid itself out before God and everyone. If you read between the lines, especially if you are a wildlife officer or a serious user of our natural resources, you will notice what I call "tips of the trade" — how it was done, or how to do it better. I have not spelled out the best tips because if any readers have a tendency to walk on the dark side, I would just as soon make them work for it, if you get my drift. In these stories you will see wrecks that almost cost lives, and you will see the dark side of your fellow humans manifesting their will over animal species struggling to survive.

In that wildlife war tapestry you will also see the work of corrupt politicians; budgets intentionally designed to restrict officers from the performance of their sworn duties (because such restrictions led to less political pressure on the agency leaders); poor high-level leadership as a constant; officers limited by their worn-out bodies, minds, and emotions; death angels in their many forms in our midst; and the not uncommon sheer joy of success in the face of those tremendous odds. You will see the kind of greed that could only make the devil happy and God sad. In short, you will see man's inhumanity to man through sheer destructive practices against the ever-changing world of wildlife and against humankind as well. You will also see the lengths to which those of us who carry that four ounces of gold or silver on our chests will go to stop the carnage by using every tool known to man and a few others known only to God.

Keep in mind that these stories are only part of my life's experiences and what I have to share as one officer in his world and time. There are ten thousand state, provincial, and federal officers in North America who could tell you like tales. That number demonstrates the magnitude of the problem and our chances of success when you consider the 400 million human beings on the North American continent and the problems many of them create for the wildlife officers spread rather thinly across this great land of ours.

This book, the second in what I hope will be a series, deals with only a small portion of my experiences as a U.S. game management agent. These events are true, but they have been altered so that no one will be able to identify any of the real-life characters or sometimes the exact situations. I have even incorporated some blind alleys into the text to throw off the really astute students of wildlife law enforcement, be they pursuers or pursued.

The places described in the book are very real, but the names of the characters have been changed to protect any who remain living or their families. They have done their time and paid their debts to society as far as I am concerned and should be left alone unless they stray across the line once again. You may find many of these tales sad, disgusting, evil, funny, moralistic, or even plain and simply gross. However, they come from my life's fabric, and many of the events they depict are still going on in new forms and places.

Enjoy the time-honored sports of hunting and fishing. Just realize that our renewable natural resources are limited. Also realize that there are those out there who carry a bit of the devil within their hearts, which is sometimes triggered when the opportunity to kill and not be apprehended rears its ugly head. Revel in happiness when representatives of the "thin green line" are there to meet the thrust of those black-hearted souls head on, and cry along with me and other members of the fraternity when we lose. Because what we lost belonged not to you but to your children and theirs. Our parents and theirs used up our share of the natural resources when they settled this land called North America. If you don't believe that, show me where to find great herds of bison, great flocks of passenger pigeons, the Heath hen, rivers full of salmon, clean drinking water, land free of life-damaging chemicals, or clean air. I rest my case! So as you can see, those resources that remain truly belong to our children and their children! Remember that next time an opportunity carrying the smell of brimstone is served up to you, it may be a *long day* if you take the devil up on the offer. ...

Acknowledgments

ON AN ALMOST FORGOTTEN SHELF in my combination firearms and ammunition-reloading room sat an old wooden cartridge box filled with numerous scraps of paper. These scraps bore titles of hoped-for stories in a series of books, along with torn pieces of lined paper carrying abbreviated texts accumulated from my thirty-two years as a conservation officer in the world of wildlife. If it were not for Stephen Topping, editorial director of Johnson Books, this series of books would never have amounted to more than a forever incomplete endeavor lost among scraps of paper in this old cartridge box. Topping, when asked by an unknown voice on the telephone if he cared to read a few of these stories, had the gift of insight to ascertain that they merited publication. He also had the professional ethic to follow through and *persist* in the development and publishing of the first book, *Wildlife Wars,* and now this second book in the series, continuing those wildlife wars histories, this time as experienced by a game management agent of the U.S. Fish and Wildlife Service.

I am forever indebted to this man of vision for his tireless support in shepherding into print these stories of one man's thirty-two-year battle as a wildlife conservation officer protecting the nation's natural wildlife resources.

I

The Russian Trawler

IT WAS MAY 1970, and I had just gone to work with the U.S. Fish and Wildlife Service as a U.S. game management agent for the Portland office of the Division of Law Enforcement. When I arrived on board as a regional hire (that is, someone hired locally by the agent in charge), it took some time for the Sacramento leaders to get organized as to what they initially wanted me to do. This disorganization was partly because one of the region's game management agents had suddenly been released from service after crossing swords with a judge over a personal domestic legal matter and drawing jail time for contempt of court. Hence, the Service had to quickly hire another officer in order to fill the vacancy in an important waterfowl work station. So my assignments, other than gathering the equipment I needed in the new profession and signing all the paperwork associated with joining another agency, were a little unguided. However, I soon found myself working my tail end off, a situation that didn't change for the next twenty-eight years while I worked for the service in a law enforcement capacity.

My first assignment was on Delevan National Wildlife Refuge, a migratory bird refuge in the heart of California's Sacramento Valley. I was operating an airboat and using a pitchfork to pick up soupy dead ducks that had died from botulism, type C, avian strain (a bacterial poisoning). That year we had a combination of hot weather and low-water conditions on all the national wildlife refuges in the Sacramento Valley. Those conditions, coupled with the alkaline soil types prevalent in much of that area, were a potential recipe for disaster in the world of waterfowl. When those deadly combinants came together to form a rich organic, anaerobic marsh environment, the botulism was off and running, as was the time remaining for many migratory birds. I worked at that task for a solid two weeks and personally picked up and buried over ten thousand dead ducks by actual count! The sad thing was that there were three other airboats working within the small confines of this refuge, doing the same thing and picking up like numbers of dead ducks. Most of what we picked up were pintail and green-winged teal, and we never did get to do the same kind of cleanup work on adjacent Sacramento, Sutter, or Colusa National Wildlife Refuges because of time and manpower shortages.

Botulism is deadly to waterfowl, and other species of water-loving birds, because the bacterium normally found in alkaline soil types (and in dead birds killed by it) produces a nerve toxin that, when ingested, causes the bird to lose control of its nervous system and eventually die. By picking up the many dead birds we removed a source point of the bacterium, the maggot-infested carcasses. The maggots eating the putrid flesh of infected birds magnified the lethal bacteria and their metabolic by-products within the maggots' bodies. Then, as live ducks swam along in the marsh and began feasting on the maggots off their dead buddies, those birds found themselves dead even sooner, having eaten the supercharged maggots.

That fall I patrolled the same areas on foot to check waterfowl hunters and found many thousands of duck skeletons throughout the refuges that had not been cleaned up. In fact, in some parts of Sacramento National Wildlife Refuge I could step from duck skeleton to duck skeleton during my day's patrol activities and never step on just plain muddy ground! The crunching of duck bones every step of the way was sobering. I would bet that more than 400,000 ducks perished on those four refuges because of botulism during that summer and early fall of 1970!

My supervisor, Jack Downs, arrived on site one Friday afternoon and waved me over to the levee where he had parked his patrol vehicle. I worked my airboat over to him and, shutting off the loud engine, said, "What's up, Chief?"

He replied, "The state needs you to go to the north coast and assist the wardens up there on a really low abalone tide in which they anticipate thousands of fishermen hitting the beaches. Can you do it?"

"Hell, yes," I replied. "That would be a great detail."

Jack just grinned, knowing anything had to be better than picking up thousands of rotten duck carcasses, and said, "Get ahold of Elvin Gunderson, the local officer, and make the necessary arrangements. Then you'll be on your own. Also, be aware that there will be a high-ranking state Fish and Game official up there somewhere on the private properties of the Sea Ranch taking abalone as well." (The Sea Ranch was a ritzy private real estate development, beaches included, along the north coast.) The way he left that information hanging told me there was more to that utterance than met the eye.

"And?" I said.

Ignoring my question, Jack asked if I had gotten my California deputy state game warden card signed yet. I replied that I hadn't, and he advised me to take off a day early and drive to Sacramento to get Director Ray Arnett to sign the card before I left for the north coast. As a federal officer, I could enforce only those laws that Congress authorized me to enforce. That authorization did not include state laws. In order for me to enforce California state laws while working investigations within state jurisdiction such as those involving abalone, a state-protected species, and their fishermen, I needed to get deputy state game warden credentials from the director of the Fish and Game department.

There was still something in the way Jack had spoken earlier that continued to pique my interest. "And?" I said again.

"Well, just watch yourself. I don't have any firsthand knowledge, but the word out on the street is that sometimes that high-level state official will stray over the line of legality if the opportunity presents itself," Jack said.

"A state Fish and Game official responsible for upholding the resource laws of his agency breaking his own laws!" I exclaimed.

Jack gave me a look that said, "Ah, youth," and replied, "Just be on your toes and be right on the money with a provable offense if you tangle tail ends with him. He has a bite."

I gave him a know-it-all grin (backed up by a somewhat empty head when it came to matters such as this, as I was soon to discover) and a thumbs-up. Then I turned to finish my smelly, distasteful work in the marsh, and Jack went on to visit another of his men.

Those of you reading these lines who do not know what an abalone is or how it tastes are among the world's unfortunate! The abalone is one of many species of marine gastropods that come in many sizes and colors and at varying ocean depths, depending on the species. It possesses a large edible portion that is highly prized by its collectors. The meat is initially tougher than a boot, but if properly cared for and prepared it is very tender and delicious to the nth degree. I have been removed from that arena for many years now, but the last I heard, abalone was selling on the commercial market for $65 per pound. Need I say more?

The next day I picked up Tim Dennis, my deputy federal agent, at his Maxwell ranch, and the two of us prepared for the forthcoming detail. For anyone wondering what the hell a deputy federal agent is, I should explain that in the old days the Service used to hire untrained civilians for 740-hour appointments to assist the game management agents. Those good folks were credentialed, carried guns, and could do everything a regular agent could do. Things were less hectic and litigation-crazy then, and the agency was a lot less mindful of the potential liability. Those folks made one hell of a contribution toward saving some of our resources and plugged a manpower gap that even today, because of lack of understanding, management acumen, and commitment by the Service leaders, is ever present within the agency. I had known Tim, the deputy assigned to me, for several years. He was a hardworking rice farmer and was totally dedicated to catching anyone who broke the laws of the land. He had many unique talents, one of them being that he was an outstanding cook with cast iron. Since I was always an eager eater, we got along great! Tim was also one hell of an officer and did an excellent job of protecting the resources. Looking back on that time as I write these lines, I find that I really miss him and the opportunities we created on the field of battle as young men.

Since we would be camping out in a secluded area behind locked gates on state park lands with many other officers, which translated into the possibility of many extra mouths "just happening" to be around during chow time, we went full bore in our preparations! We loaded all the cooking and camping gear we could think of. You see, Tim and I enjoyed cooking everything imaginable and, being the good cooks that we were, always cooked enough for a marine regiment after a fifty-mile hike.

Then it was on to Chung Sun's Market in Colusa to shop for gigantic quantities of food. This market was owned and operated by some of the finest folks one could run across in a lifetime. They were always courteous to the extreme, considered every customer a personal friend (most were), and provided goods and services the quality of which I have yet to meet again to this day some thirty years later. They had a butcher named So Han Park, or "Sonny" to his friends, who was to meat what Wagner was to brass. I could give Sonny the details of what cuts of meat I wanted and their exact marbling qualities, and he was uncanny with what he supplied! I still relish in my memory those cuts that my very capable close friend was able to provide.

The next morning, to a clear blue sky and air that was a pleasure to breathe, the two of us, with lit Parodi cigars stinking up the cab of the truck, hammered off down the road to another adventure. We took the freeway to San Francisco and then drove north through wine country (stopping off at various wineries to sample the wares, of course), ultimately reaching the quaint town of Santa Rosa. From there we crossed over to Stewart's Point via the Geyserville turnoff and shortly thereafter turned into the little hiding place behind locked gates furnished to all the conservation "law dogs" by the California State Parks sys-

tem. Other officers, including old friends of mine from my recent game warden days, were already there, lying in wait for the
big opening day of abalone season on Saturday. After the usual
hearty greetings common to this fraternity, everyone fell to
helping Tim and me unload our gear and set up our camp. Tim
and I broke out the chilled wine, cold beer, Italian salami (Molinari, if you please), cheese, sliced onions, crackers, and other
items of interest (smoked venison, smoked eel, cigars, etc.), and
all the lads fell to with appetites close to those of a marine regiment. God, I thought through a huge grin over a mouthful of
salami and cheese, it was hard to believe the government paid us
to do this kind of "work"!

About then I noticed a small house trailer in the trees by itself,
off to one side of the general tent campsite. It had two Fish and
Game patrol cars parked to one side and a green, late-model
Chrysler sedan parked in front.

"Who belongs to those?" I said to Warden Don Harn, pointing to the three vehicles.

Don stepped closer to me and quietly said, "David Robinson,
you know, the governor's close friend and one of our high
muckety-mucks, along with warden Captains Manty and Jones.
They're up here to try their luck for abalone on the Sea Ranch.

"Don't worry, they won't mingle with us plebeians," Don
added with a look framed in disgust.

"Just as long as they don't get in my way, I don't care who
they are," I replied somewhat arrogantly (part of that empty-
headed thing). Then, remembering my early college-days affilia-
tion with Captain Manty, when he was just a warden in the
north coast squad under Captain Gray, I marched off to the
front door of the trailer to renew an old friendship. A knock
produced Captain Manty, and, after shaking hands, we visited
for a few moments about old times in Humboldt County. Then
David Robinson, whom I had met only once before, appeared,
and after shaking his hand and exchanging a few brief words on
the upcoming joint state-federal law enforcement operation, I
excused myself and headed back to my group of friends to finish

setting up our campsite under some nearby pine trees. Then Tim and I spent time with our working game warden teammates enjoying life as it can be enjoyed only on the Pacific north coast of California on a lazy afternoon just before a series of good abalone tides.

Later that afternoon, as the sun set over the ocean, Tim and I fired up the old Dodge and left our hideout to scout out our assigned portion of the marine domain for the morrow's "ab" tide. There were a lot of people camped in some areas, and we decided to avoid those locations because when there are a lot of people in close proximity, they generally tend to control each other, and violations, especially the big over-limits, tend to be scarce. Driving farther up the coast, toward the Sea Ranch property, Tim and I found our ideal work area. It consisted of narrow, curvy mountain-bluff roads, cloaked on the west by steep gorges, and rugged, stony beaches with lots of hidey-holes, or places to take abalone without being seen if one had a violating bent. Brush and trees were everywhere, good cover for a couple of game warden types, and a cape of fog was anticipated in the morning to add that sinister touch of things to come. It was a perfect place to break the law with little chance of being caught, or so the bad guys would think. Tim and I grinned at our good terrain fortune and headed back to camp with visions of violators dancing in our heads.

Daylight found Tim and my large carcass cleverly hidden in deep stands of brush right at the cliff's edge. From our vantage points we could look 150 feet down into two likely-looking coves where four vehicles parked along the highway above and fresh tracks going down the trail to the ocean evidenced abalone action. With our 7x50 binoculars we would be able to look right into their gunnysacks as the lads filled them, counting the abalone as they hurried among the seaweed-draped and wave-covered rocks looking for more before the tide changed, precluding further shallow-water activity.

On that particular day we had nine people working the rocks exposed by the neap tide (the very lowest tide, which occurs at

the first and third quarters of the moon). All of them were wearing wetsuits except two women who were working along the
rocky kelp-, algae-, and barnacle-encrusted shore. That kind of
situation was always a good bet for violations because the men
in wetsuits working the deeper water and flooded rocks would
more than likely take over-limits (in those days the limit was five
red abalone with a width greater than seven inches), bring them
ashore, and give them to the ladies. Once the women had received their "limits," the men would return to the water, take
their own "limits," and return with their spoils to their vehicles,
with way more than the law allowed. This kind of "party fishing" of such a fragile resource would drive the abalone population right into the toilet in short order. Hence the law against
this kind of fishing and the reason for our presence that beautiful, slightly foggy morning.

People flocked to the north coast of California in those halcyon days because the ocean there was a haven for the red and
black abalone. Those good conditions, coupled with the excellent table-fare nature of the abalone, made for an over-limit opportunity if anyone had even a little of the devil in their soul. In
that matter we were not disappointed. As Tim and I lay there on
the damp, good-smelling earth, densely covered by greenery,
with the crashing sound of the waves as background music, we
observed the divers in the water below stepping over the line.
Several of the lads found nice big abalone and, after removing
them from their rocks (no small chore—they have to be found
first, then pried off the rock with a large, flat piece of steel), measured them to make sure they were legal size. They casually
looked around the beach and up the cliff to see whether anyone,
especially a game warden type, had noticed them until they were
satisfied that they were unobserved. Then they slowly moved to
shore as if they were still looking for abalone, and the women,
sensing what was coming, slowly moved toward them as if they
too were still hunting. When they met, the men again looked up
along the steep cliff face and its brushy rim to see whether anyone was watching the activity below. Convinced that they were

alone, they laid the abalone on a rock, one of the women picked it up as if she had just found an ab, and everyone was happy (except the abalone). The diver then moved back into deeper water and continued his search. Tim and I looked at each other and grinned. This kind of work was too easy, I thought as I recorded the events and times in my notebook for later use in court if necessary.

This little illegal drama was played out many times that morning until the lads with the wetsuits had filled everyone's limit. Then several of the divers met out in the open water between two large rocks and appeared to be having a nervous discussion. They all looked landward, examining the cliff side again as if looking for something, probably the likes of Tim and yours truly. We were well hidden, and the lads' intense looks soon dissolved as one of them produced a net bag from beneath the water, which we had not seen before, filled with eleven abalone that had obviously been taken moments before Tim and I arrived. Keep in mind Tim and I had had to wait until the abalone fishermen were on their way down to the fishing area before we moved in behind them. In that time span before we arrived and worked into position, the lads had taken the abalone in the sack and hidden them. With seven wetsuited fishermen, this catch would not have taken much time with the "abbing" as good as it was. The abalone in the bag were plain and simply a gross over-limit, over and above the over-limits they had already taken for the two women.

While five divers watched the cliff side, two others dragged the bag closer to the shoreline. Leaving the bag in the water, all the divers started wading toward the shore and commenced gathering spiny sea urchins, bringing them in and piling them into several heretofore empty gunnysacks. Once these gunnysacks had been partially filled with sea urchins, they brought in the net bag, and while several divers continued their watch along the cliff's edge, the others loaded the gross over-limit of abalone from the net bag into the two partially filled gunnysacks on top of the sea urchins. Then they loaded more sea urchins on top of

the abalone in the sacks. With the abalone cleverly hidden between layers of prickly sea urchins (a place where most game
wardens wouldn't look, or so they thought), the party loaded up
their gear and remaining bounty from the sea and, after a *brief
frolic,* up the steep cliffs they came, struggling along the narrow
dirt trail in single file.

Since Tim and I were between them and their vehicles, we just
waited for our catch to haul their ill-gotten gains up the cliff to
us. It was several minutes before the first heads of those who
were the object of our rapt attention came into view from our
hiding place in the brush above the cove. They were winded, and
they paused at a little flat spot in front of our hiding place to
wait for the rest of their party to arrive. They were in a euphoric
state of glee. They were talking about how good the fishing had
been, how big the abs were, and how good they would taste
when they got back to camp. It was kind of fun lying there unseen, less than ten feet away, listening to a conversation not
meant for our ears. When it appeared they all had their second
wind and were ready to go, Tim and I rose up out of the little
swale we had been hiding in and moved around some heavy
brush, and before the lads knew we were there and from whence
we came, we were upon them.

At first they reacted with complete surprise and astonishment,
but the normal innocent front was quickly presented to us once
I identified myself. I explained that I would like to check everyone's limits and fishing licenses. I continued, "If you all will lay
out the abalone you took in front of yourselves and hand me
your fishing licenses at the same time, we can measure the abs
and be on our way." They all complied, and as they were doing
so one of the lads told me that the two gunnysacks with the
tightly tied tops and purple spines sticking ostentatiously out
through the sides were just full of sea urchins (no limit, no license required in those days). Nodding, Tim and I checked the
abalone laid out in front of us as game wardens normally would.
Then, after a long look at all the questioning faces, I asked, "Do

you want to tell us the real story on who really took what, or do you want us to tell you what actually happened?"

There were blank looks and then instant communal denial of any suggestion of illegal activity on their parts. This reaction was normal, but Tim and I still had an ace in the hole. Looking at the group of "wrongly accused and innocent" men and women, I began, "You lads didn't give me a chance to tell you the whole story." I paused, seeing that I now had their complete attention.

"What do you mean?" the leader of the group cautiously asked.

Looking him dead in the eye, I said, "My partner and I have been here since before daylight. We watched everything you folks did, including hiding the extra abs in the sea-urchin sack, and recorded the same with my movie camera." With that I reached over and produced an old movie camera (with no film) from my "possibles bag," which I carried to hold all my extra field gear. Seeing that they all now had a bad case of the "big eye," I put the camera, with a show of flair, back in my bag. I continued, "Even to the point of capturing the group sex all of you had with these two young ladies, whom I see from the drivers-license and fishing-license examination are not married to any of you lads." (In those days, a woman was almost certain to take her husband's last name—and this event, which I referred to earlier as a "frolic," was a fairly normal occurrence in out-of-the-way places in California. No big deal, just a way of life for some people.)

"Since all of you folks appear to be married to someone else," I said, pointing to the wedding rings on their respective fingers, "I just figured you might want to forfeit bail in lieu of any court appearance and avoid a *very* public trial." My words struck them like a thunderclap. All I saw were eyes as big as dinner plates and the shuffling feet of the two lovely "maidens."

"Where do we pay?" the group leader asked.

"The whole process can be handled very simply through the mail," I told him. With that, Tim and I seized, documented, and

placed evidence tags on the groups of abalone, then emptied out
the gunnysacks full of sea urchins and seized those abalone as
well. When it was over we had seven citations for possession of
over-limits of abalone at $500 each. Not bad for a morning's
work, I thought as I tagged the last of the evidence. As Tim and I
hauled our evidence to the empty ice chests in the truck, we
could only chuckle at the morning's events and how easily those
men had settled up with the game warden. Maybe it was our
good looks, or possibly the contents of the "film" in the camera.
It really didn't matter what was or wasn't in the camera, though,
because I had recorded every event in my notebook, not to mention in my mind, and could have testified to every detail if the
case went to trial. However, it was always good business to let
the bad guys think you knew more or had more evidence than
you really did. Such an approach often kept the fence-sitters
contemplating criminal acts against the environment either sitting on the fence or getting off and out of the dirty business alto-
gether. Any port in a storm, just as long as it is legal, I thought
with a grin as the last of the abalone slid into the waiting ice
chest.

Tim and I worked several other coves that morning until the
high tide returned, and with it a cessation of abalone fishing activity. Another event, though, left us laughing for most of the
rest of the day. Slipping into one cove overlook near our previous location, we saw two divers looking for abalone. One was
standing by a large rock in about two feet of water, measuring an
abalone. Everything looked normal as we slipped into a hiding
place for a better look. All of a sudden the diver near the rock
dropped into the water, thrashing around, and, pulling his sheath
knife, began slashing something around his legs. He was screaming at the top of his lungs, and Tim and I could clearly hear him
even forty yards away over the roar of the incoming surf. This
drama continued as he, still slashing at his legs, tried to get away
from the rock and drag himself onto shore. Tim and I raced
down the cliff and reached him just as he crawled up onto the
rocky beach, wide-eyed, frantic, and out of breath. The man was

absolutely terrified, and I wasn't sure he wasn't having a heart attack as well! He reached for Tim's legs, screaming, "Save me, save me!" Tim and I pulled him up on shore and, looking down at his legs, were startled to see a medium-sized octopus, chopped all to bits by his knife, with several tentacles still clinging to his leg. The damn critter, probably all of eight pounds, could not have killed anything bigger than a pissant! The octopus, probably thinking his movements meant food, had reached out as the lad stood by the rock and wrapped its tentacles around his foot. The rest was history. We got the man calmed down, but he had had enough of the mysteries of the sea and got the hell out of there. The poor little octopus was almost dead, so Tim killed it and took it back to camp for food. I told you Tim and I cooked everything but what a French chef would recognize. By the way, the critter was good—tough and rubbery, but good.

We arrived back in camp late in the morning along with a light fog characteristic of the north coast at that time of the year. As Tim and I unloaded our evidence into ice chests, with ice to keep it from spoiling, other officers who had already returned from the abalone wars sauntered over to see how we had done. As it turned out, Tim and I had done better than anyone, and before long our rather large over-limit of abalone was drawing a lot of attention. Warden Don Harn walked over to our group and gave me the high sign, so I split away from the other lads and we walked a few feet away to converse in private. Don, a damn good officer and friend, told me that the three chaps in the trailer had just returned, and it appeared that they all had their limits of rather large abalone. There was no reason they shouldn't, I thought, taking their abalone off a private, underfished beach. Don said it appeared that all three were going to stay longer and go after abalone during the next day or so as well. Now, in those days, the bag-and-possession limit of abalone was only five. Because of the biologists' concern over the fragile abalone population and the tremendous fishing pressure on this tasty species, you were allowed to take five abalone a day and allowed to legally possess *only* five abalone at a time, no matter how long you stayed along the ocean. This meant you couldn't take more unless you ate or otherwise disposed of your first five.

Don's intense, steely eyes, those of a courageous ex-marine who had experienced many of the brutal island-hopping campaigns and landings in the Pacific theater of World War II, looked hard at me. He said he had heard through the grapevine that Robinson had a tendency to stray across the line every now and then, not to mention the fact that he was hated by just about every game warden in the state for that and his alleged outright disdain for Fish and Game or penal-code laws and those who enforced them. He also had a reputation for thumbing his nose at the California Vehicle Code and made no bones about being a friend of the governor when he was apprehended for speeding. I thought back to Jack's words when he had hailed me on the airboat to give me this assignment.

"Just wanted you to know," Don continued, following these words with another hard look. I knew exactly what that look meant. If Robinson tried to leave with an over-limit of abalone, Don and others like him would be hard-pressed to issue him a citation for the violation if they wanted to keep their jobs because, as state officers, they worked for the governor in a somewhat politically corrupt system. Big Republican fund-raisers in the powerful state of California had that kind of horsepower. Don knew it would be harder to get at a federal officer politically, and because of that immunity, the feds could take on the powerful political giants without a backward glance. Don also knew that my reputation as a California state Fish and Game warden was based on four and a half years of taking on anyone who was wrong and letting the chips fall where they might. He surmised that as a federal officer my enforcement philosophy had not changed; if anything, it might be a degree or so harder than before because of that political protection. Shaking my head, thankful I was now a fed, I thanked Don for the information and returned to our campsite.

Tim and I busied ourselves with the ritual cooking of breakfast, as it turned out, for the whole game warden crew and their families, minus the patricians in the house trailer. Scrambled eggs (forty-eight of them) with freshly chopped onions, celery, green peppers, tomatoes, and fresh garlic, blended with two pounds of fresh shrimp, two pounds of fresh crab meat, and a ton of Monterey Jack cheese, sailed into one sixteen-inch Dutch oven. Next on the menu were Dutch-oven beer biscuits (every three minutes once the Dutch ovens were hot) that were so light I had to hold them down with a cast-iron lid to keep them from drifting off. Last but not least were my Dutch-oven spuds (five pounds), sliced and cooked slowly in mounds of pure butter with more fresh onions, green peppers, and garlic. Boy, talk about good. In fact, it was so good I had to set a plate for God that morning, and He didn't let any go to waste. In short order all was gone except the memory.

Long about noon on the second day, after another full enforcement morning on our parts, Robinson and his two warden captain friends returned to their camp. They all had limits of large abalone (five each, fifteen total), and into their trailer they went so they would not have to associate with the plebeians gathered around camp that fine day. Our feelings were not hurt, though, and the group of us just rested, waiting for the next neap tide the following morning at daylight. Tim and I had done rather well again, with four more over-limits and several short (too small) abalone cases to show for our morning's efforts. However, I had gotten one bad piece of news that day from Gunderson, or "Gundy," the local warden, who told me that the local judge had just changed. I thought I recognized the name of the man who was the new judge: as near as I could tell, I had issued citations to this judge and his father the year before on a duck club in Colusa County for a rather large over-limit of pintail—thirty-two over, to be exact. If that turned out to be the case, I surmised that my citations filed in this state judicial district, no matter how good they were, would not get the consideration commensurate with the offense if the judge were to recognize the name on the citation as the one that had spoiled his illegal duck shoot the previous year. In other words, I would get a $5 fine for an offense for which others would get $500! Damn, talk about bad breaks. Oh well, I said to myself, I would just take the information down on any bad guys I caught during the rest of this trip and turn that information over to "Gundy" to write the citation as if the pinch were his.

The next morning Tim and I were up before daylight and at the abalone tides again. We headed north until we found a likely-looking cove with several cars parked along the highway, and down we went into a hiding area. This time we had fewer divers, but these lads came out with gunnysacks full of sea urchins, sacks of brown kelp, sea slugs, cabazone (a kind of fish), and of course over-limits of abalone. Tim and I dutifully did our duty, dug their extra and short abalone out of the middle of bags of brown kelp, wrote five illegal possession and short ab citations, and went on to check other abalone divers along the shoreline until we finally ran out of favorable abalone tide.

Returning to camp with our usual trailing morning fog, we took care of our evidence and began preparations for another morning's feast. The only thing that marred that morning's events was that damn judge problem, which kept running through my mind. If he was the same fellow I had cited for the waterfowl violation, I knew I would have to turn over my tickets for someone else to sign and process if I wanted any decent adjudication. Damn! It is hard to do such a thing after all the work that goes into producing such cases, but necessary if one is to get a fair result from his day in court. Finally I just drove the issue out of my mind, hoped the judge wasn't the same man, and, figuring I would do what had to be done in that arena, got down to the business of building another memorable breakfast.

After breakfast and the usual "see you next time," the other wardens and their families pulled up camp and headed home, their details over. Tim, Don Harn, and I remained to try our luck one more day and to see if the weekday fishermen would give us even bigger over-limit cases because of lack of competition and oversight by crowds of their fellow abalone fishers. As the three of us sat by the campfire, through for the day and drinking a little wine, Robinson and his two compatriots returned again. They again appeared to have limits of large abalone taken from the Sea Ranch property. Good old Robinson; he could always be depended on to use his position to wrangle a special hunting or fishing trip anytime he could, I thought grimly.

About an hour later Robinson emerged from the trailer with an armload of gear and put it into the trunk of his vehicle. Returning to the trailer, he came out again a few moments later with a small zinc washtub filled with what looked like abalone in the shell. There appeared to be at least seven or eight abalone in that tub. A look at Tim's and Don's eyes betrayed the same suspicion. The thought that the take and possession limit was five raced through my mind. Five, period! Anyone with more than five in his or her possession was routinely cited for a possession over-limit. There were no exceptions! I looked intently at Don Harn, and he just looked back with that same look I had received a day earlier and shrugged. Don was an excellent "catch dog," but there wasn't much he could do here if there was an over-limit in that tub, Robinson being the governor's pet, a high state official, and all.

Robinson loaded the abalone in his trunk, closed it, and stepped around to the driver's side to get in and drive off. Looking at Don to see if he was going to say anything to this chap regarding what appeared to me to be a possession over-limit of abalone, then finally realizing he wasn't, I let my wine take over. "Hey, Dave," I said. "What you are doing with those abalone, if you have more than a legal limit, is illegal. We are citing people for possession of any abalone over five."

He turned and fixed me with an icy "what I do is none of your business" stare and then said, "Screw you," though in somewhat more colorful language than that. With that he got into his car, started the engine, and made his final preparations to leave. Rising from my chair with every intention of trying one more time to get him to comply with the law of the land if he had an over-limit, I decided that if the outcome were not positive, he was going to get a citation, state favorite or not. Then it dawned on me: I might not have a supportive state judge. If the new judge was the one I had pinched the year before, more than likely he wouldn't support me with a conviction after I issued Robinson a citation. I would also have tough sledding within the Fish and Wildlife Service if I issued a citation to a political big-wig and couldn't make it stick. I had been with the Service less than a month and was one of very few officers in the nation left in their state of hire. The Service policy historically had been that the state a lad was hired from would not see him again for some time until after the officer matured and the state agencies basically forgot from whence the man had come. Even in the small wildlife officer fraternity, especially among the state higher ups, some animosity always existed when an officer was pirated away from one agency into another, especially when the latter was the Service. This was very true of the California Department of Fish and Game in those days; hence the political sensitivity surrounding any work performed as a fed by an ex-officer from that agency.

As one of the rare few who were hired and returned directly to their state of origin, I was very aware of the consequences in the eyes of the state agency of any "improper" activity on my part. In fact, the sitting law enforcement chief had allegedly boasted to a bunch of Fish and Game captains, at a meeting to discuss restricting game wardens to an eight-hour day, that "Terry" would not go to work for the feds "because he had just built a big home and could not afford to move." I resigned my state commission two weeks later and went to work for the feds in my home state! Suffice it to say, the chief was somewhat embarrassed. I could just see my appointment to my home state being reconsidered as a bad move and me ending up in Oklahoma or some other godforsaken hole in the wall if I missed on this one.

Fuming because my black-and-white world had suddenly turned gray, I returned heavily to my chair beside Don and Tim and watched the "chosen one" drive off into the fog with what had appeared to me to be an over-limit of abalone—an over-limit I am sure he did not take while fishing with Manty and Jones during a one-day stint in the water. Robinson wasn't that stupid. But more than likely he had been unable to eat all he had caught over their three-day fishing trip and just decided he would take a nice mess of abalone home for later, or for his friends. A nice gesture, but illegal just the same. I noticed that neither Manty nor Jones had accompanied Robinson out to his car to assist him with any of his gear. That would have made it difficult for them to "ignore" the over-limit of abalone (not that they didn't already know) and placed them in an awkward position with the three of us sitting around the campfire just yards away. So much for my subsequent friendship with Manty and Jones, I thought.

Not wanting to look at Don because of my weak position, I just sat there and steamed. I haven't walked away from any fights since that day in my career, and that one on that day in 1970 still sticks in my craw. I should have done my job and let the chips fall where they may. But I didn't, and the American people sure didn't get their money's worth out of my stinking hide that fine day. ... I guess you could say I lived to fight another day.

Manty and Jones left shortly after Robinson, leaving Don, Tim, and me to the fog, good California wine (and lots of it, I might add), and our thoughts. That mixture of ingredients in the folks present around that crackling campfire could lead to mischief every time, and sure as hell, it wasn't long in coming. Sitting there in my chair, looking into the thick fog rolling in from the sea with a quart fruit jar of wine in my hand (and a gallon in my belly), I heard a *clank-clank-clank-clank* sound from the small cove not forty yards away. I looked at Don and Tim and saw that they were listening intently as well. It sounded to me like the anchor chain of a seagoing ship of substantial size being let down into the water. What the hell? There wasn't any harbor there, I thought. All that was there was the California coastline, a rugged cliff, and a small covelike indentation in the shoreline.

Grabbing our drinks as if on cue, and with the rolling walk of a sailor just off his ship, the three of us staggered down the gently sloping cliff face toward the ocean until we could see the water below through the ever-thickening bank of fog.

Damn, there was an oceangoing ship just below us in our little cove! Not a big one, mind you, but an oceangoing vessel just as sure as God made little green apples. It was anchored about seventy-five yards offshore, just at the dense seaward fog line, and was swarming with deck hands. About six or seven of them were in wetsuits and were obviously planning to go over the side of the ship. Another group had gathered at the rail to watch, as did we three semidrunk "musketeers" from our vantage point above, unobserved by the seamen below. We stayed a little back in the trees and brush, watching now with awe as the situation unfolded below us. The vessel looked like a Russian trawler! A quick look into the rigging showed no flag flying at all. If that was what this vessel truly was, it was not supposed to be this close to the U.S. shoreline, but here it was!

Then up from the ocean floor came several heretofore unseen "frogmen" with what appeared to be armloads of abalone. They hurriedly tossed their catch to eagerly waiting hands leaning over the deck rail and dove below for more. As several more divers left the ship for the cold Pacific waters, we couldn't believe our eyes. Those bastards had come into U.S. waters illegally and were now violating state law by taking abalone with scuba outfits, not to mention the fact that they almost certainly didn't have any fishing licenses. This was *war!*

Don growled, "How can we get to them bastards?"

I said, "I don't know; they are out to sea, and we don't have a boat."

Don said, "Let's crack a pistol shot across their bow; bet that will get their damn attention!" As I said earlier, Don was an ex-marine and combat veteran. I should have expected that kind of response from a man with such training and life experiences, not to mention the gallon of wine he now carried in his belly.

"Don," I said, "I have a better idea. Besides, if we start shooting they will too, and we will be outgunned before we know it!"

I turned and, running quickly (if you can imagine a three-hundred-pounder running quickly uphill with a gallon of wine in his gut), opened the utility box of my patrol truck and took out a carton of ten-inch SCRAM rockets and their hand-held launcher. Returning rapidly (downhill now) to my two brave comrades (no pun intended), I handed Tim the box of rockets and told him to start inserting the fuses. Turning to Don, I told him to get out his lighter, and I commenced to connect the launcher handle to the flash guard. There we were, three intrepid patriots standing on a cliff, all "gowed" up with good California grape, with a box of five herding rockets to start and finish a war with the hated Russians for taking American abalone in violation of the law of the land. And taking them, I might add, right under our very noses! The stirring music of Wagner began to run through the inner recesses of my grape-fogged mind, as did the sound of a fife and drum from the battlefield of long ago at Concord on Lexington Green. From the wild, wine-fed looks in the eyes of my two allies, they were marching to their own drummers as well.

Tim placed the first rocket on the end of the launcher rod as I aimed it high over the Russian trawler, directing it so it would land amidships, and Don lit the fuse. *Whoosh* it went, high into the air and out of sight into the fog as the crew on the trawler, upon hearing this new sound, turned to face the "might of the United States." Now, in those days I was damn good when it came to the exact placement of a herding rocket on an intended target. These little rockets had been routinely used in the Sacramento Valley for some time to scare waterfowl out of the rice fields, thereby preventing crop depredations. It was not uncommon for me to use one thousand or even two thousand of these a year in such endeavors, and I had gotten quite good at their placement in order to not waste them. In addition, each rocket had an explosive device on the nose that after a certain amount of burn time would detonate—and with quite a bit of authority!

Wine or no wine, I wasn't going to be more than a foot off once I took aim at these rascals stealing abalone below the high

ground where we stood. Shooting one of these rockets at a
seagoing vessel in an ocean was a hell of a lot easier than aiming
at a duck in a rice field, I thought. Without waiting for our first
shot "heard 'round the world," Tim loaded another rocket on
the launcher and Don set fire to the fuse on our little greeting
card. *Whoosh* into and out of sight in the fog it also went. I had
aimed this one somewhat lower, hoping it would make a direct
hit amidships, where most of the crewmen were now huddled in
wonderment. Then, as if the sun had finally shone on the ma-
nure pile behind the barn, the Russian trawler deck exploded
with activity. They had located the source of the *whoosh* and,
recognizing superior firepower, were falling back to the Stalingrad line on their vessel. As we watched the crew scurrying
around the deck, we saw the frogmen hurriedly climbing back
up the alongside ladder to their ship, reacting to a frantic banging on the outside hull by a seaman with a hammer. We heard
the anchor chain being rapidly brought up.

Just about that time, the first rocket dropped out of the fog
and went off not more than three feet above the trawler's revolv-
ing radar antenna. *Boom*, it went, and if we had thought the
Russian seamen were moving before, they sure got it into gear
now! I could imagine the radarman with his earphones strapped
to his very sensitive ears and ever-vigilant eyes on the radar
screen, watching for any ships of the U.S. Navy that were looking for Russian trawlers such as these lads. Then *wham*, off went
the explosion just over his radar antenna! Damn, I bet that blast
blew him right out of his chair and away from his earphones.

By now we three were *really* full of fight! About that time I
noticed the second rocket dropping out of the fog and ricochet-
ing across the stern deck of the trawler, just behind the superstructure. It hammered right off the deck and sailed toward the
rear ends of several running Russian frogmen who were trying
to get out of sight and below decks. *Boom* went the rocket, not
two feet from one man's hind end, and that Russian, who had
not seen it coming, out of surprise and instant fear ran straight
into a vertical standpipe on the deck. Hitting that pipe at the rate

of speed he was running, he just folded like a sack of wheat, crumpling to the deck, obviously out like a light! He just lay there, and no one lifted a hand to help him as the other deck hands scrambled to places of safety away from the aerial bombardment. In fact, the man running alongside him one moment, and then seeing a brilliant flash within feet of his tail end, hearing an explosion, and seeing his partner fold, just dove down an open door on the vessel's superstructure at a full run to avoid the same treatment.

By now the strains of "the rockets' red glare" were coming through loud and clear in my wine-soaked brain, as was the mirth of the moment. The last frogman got aboard as the ship was rapidly moving out to seaward, all the while dragging a still rewinding anchor chain and anchor up the side of the ship. Talk about funny! Tim was lying on the ground laughing so hard he got the hiccups. Don was doubled over holding his sides, and I had tears running down my cheeks like there was no tomorrow. Not wanting to let well enough alone, I had Tim stick another rocket on the launcher, and Don again lit the fuse. *Whooosh* went that one as I held it low and aimed it at the fleeing Russian ship, using a bit of grape-induced windage this time because of the range of the rapidly moving vessel. At first I thought I was going to miss, but good old American technology saved the day. As luck would have it—and thanks to a somewhat keen eye— that rocket ran right up the stern of the trawler, zipped up over the deck railing, flew across the deck, and disappeared into the open doorway the frogman had just taken his swan dive through. A few seconds transpired, followed by a very loud and deep *boom!*

By now we were all doubled over with laughter. The Russian trawler steamed off into the fog, stern waters just boiling, and out of our lives for the moment as the three of us, through tear-soaked faces, watched it go. But not before I launched another rocket into the fog in the direction in which the ship had vanished to bid it farewell. A final fog-muffled *boom* moments later told me my message had been received by the cream of the Russian fleet. Back to our chairs, the fire, and more wine we staggered to discuss how brave and intrepid we were, and to talk all night "of cabbages and kings." ... Suffice it to say, no more Russian trawlers arrived in our little cove that evening.

Several weeks after our naval engagement, Don told our funny story to a friend who was in the naval reserve. Don's buddy related it to his commanding officer, who didn't find it funny at all. It seemed the faces of the U.S. Coast Guard and Navy would be somewhat red over the Russian trawler incident if it were true. It was the surveillance of the navy that kept us safe and secure from any type of foreign invasion, and that included Russian trawlers, and to have any black spot on that record would not do! As our story worked its way to the top, it was met with disbelief by the navy's top brass. Basically, we were being called liars in official circles. As I recall, Don was asked to identify the so-called Russian trawler from a picture in a book supplied by the navy. He put an end to their disbelief when he identified it as one of the "worst" kinds of trawlers to be discovered in U.S. coastal waters. The trawler he identified, he told us later, was the type responsible for laying navigation buoys along the sea floor to key spots along coastlines so Russian nuclear submarines could follow them right to their targets without betraying their positions to our navy on the sea or aircraft flying overhead!

With that revelation, the navy got really serious with us and some time later asked Tim and me to try to identify the type of trawler as well. The navy wanted us to validate what Don had reported earlier, still not wanting to believe our story. If we confirmed Don's identification, the navy had a major security problem in its patrol and surveillance program, and they knew it, but they had to ask the question! Well, even separated, as we were, Tim and I identified the same make and design of Russian trawler that Don had as the one we had seen earlier that month. Wow—it was a hot time among their ranks for a while as they tried to figure out how the Russian trawler had penetrated their at-sea surveillance patrols. Needless to say, what the three of us had seen became restricted information, and we were instructed that to say any more than we had to anyone other than navy officials would not be wise. So for twenty-plus years our "attack," successful, I might add, on the Russian vessel remained a secret. But we had the satisfaction of knowing that our country was safer as a result of three "patriots" standing somewhat firm on the beach head that foggy afternoon, dueling toe to toe with the Russian trawler. American munitions carried the day—not to mention knocking a Russian radarman from his chair to the floor.

I bet to this day that poor Russian radarman flinches every time he hears a *whoosh*. ... and I wonder what kind of medal they pinned on the frogman who was struck by a post from the front and a rocket from the rear. The rocket that went off below decks had to be even funnier. Just imagine what it might have been like if you were a Russian seaman sitting on the john, minding your business and all, and then all of a sudden an explosion went off outside the toilet door. If you were having any trouble before, I would bet it would have left you in an instant after the blast. Or imagine what it must have been like for the frogman who sprinted through the door and dove down the steps to avoid what his friend had encountered, only to be followed and hammered moments later!

But what was even worse was that the seamen had to eat borscht for dinner again that night instead of good old fresh American abalone. Oh well, sometimes you eat the bear and some times he eats you, but I guess that's the American way. ... It was surely the case that day in May 1970, with the shot heard 'round the cove and across the deck of a Russian trawler.

2

Forty-five Italian Shooters & Plan B

THE COLD OF THE MORNING just before the coming of the dawn made itself felt on my legs, hands, face, and ears. A runny nose also testified to the cool temperature. Off in the distance a ranch-house dog barked several times, and the smell of fresh, moist earth from a nearby field, which had been plowed by Mexican laborers the evening before and into the early morning, hung heavy in the air. A slight breeze from the northwest began to rustle the leaves of the English walnut trees in the orchard where I was hiding as I waited for the day's events to begin.

Glancing down at the luminescent dial on my watch, I could see it was just a little past four A.M. Pulling my coat sleeve back down over my watch to ward off some of the morning's dampness, I impatiently glanced to the east to see if the false dawn was making its appearance yet. Inky blackness was my reward. Reaching into my jacket, I let my fingers slide around a cold Molinari salami and withdrew it from my pocket. Good old game warden fare, I thought, a greasy Italian salami for breakfast. Nothing better to keep out the cold in my boiler room, I said to myself as I bit through the casing and let the juices from my mouth surround the salty, garlicky meat. Slowly chewing, alert to the sounds around me and basically warm in my thick camouflage coat, I let my mind review the past week's events leading up to this moment.

It was September 1970, the month of the start of many hunting seasons, particularly the mourning dove season. In essence it was a ritual time of celebration if one was a sportsman, especially an Italian hunter in the San Joaquin Valley of California. September heralded the rebirth of sorts of the American hunting public. Most sportsmen waited all year for the advent of the dove season, and when that day arrived it found almost everyone who hunted out to sharpen their shooting eyes on the elusive winged target, or "rocket of the sky," the mourning dove. The San Joaquin Valley was where I happened to be quietly standing in the predawn dark in a walnut orchard on the Albert De Noto ranch that fine morning. Albert was a son of old Italy, a hunter, and allegedly, according to the Stockton Fish and Game warden, Buck Del Nero, a bit of an outlaw to boot, especially in relation to the sport of dove hunting. That day it looked like I just might get to confirm that information in spades—but I am getting ahead of my story.

I was a newly appointed U.S. game management agent with only four months' experience on the job under my belt, assigned to the northwestern half of California with an enforcement district running from about Monterey north to the Oregon line. In part because I had had few opportunities that year to work large dove concentrations in much of that northern area because many of the dove had already migrated south owing to cooler weather, and in part because there was no game management agent in the Stockton area, my supervisor had temporarily assigned me to that vacant district. It was loaded with dove staging to migrate farther south and also had a history of numerous migratory bird–hunting violations, hence my presence. The people of the area, which was heavily populated with farmers and other folks of mainly Italian descent, historically had the reputation of taking more than their share from the wildlife horn of plenty—especially dove. With the knowledge of being a U.S. game management agent sent to enforce the federal wildlife laws, I could not help but stand just a little taller that morning.

I reached into my shirt pocket, removed my new gold shield, only months old, and ran my fingers over the cold metal as if to assure myself that this was really happening. I had wanted to be a game management agent since my junior year at Humboldt State College in Arcata, one of the greatest wildlife management training institutions in the nation, especially in the academic and practical instruction of applied science in wildlife management. However, because of federal hiring freezes at the time I graduated from college, I had settled for a job with the California Department of Fish and Game and spent the next four and a half fine learning years as a conservation officer at two very different duty stations. Then, in May 1970, Jack Downs, U.S. Fish and Wildlife Service agent in charge in Sacramento, had offered me a job. So here I was: at just thirty years old I had attained the second of my two most important life goals, the first being to marry Donna Larson, my childhood sweetheart. What a thrill it was to be one of just 178 federal wildlife officers nationwide, with responsibilities as big as the territory.

Several dove noisily leaving their roosts in the walnut orchard near where I stood brought me back to reality and the moment at hand. I slowly scanned the plowed field in front of me, the object of my presence here, and the adjacent orchards for any signs of life. It was still dark and quiet. Snuggling further into my coat to ward off the damp morning chill so common in the Stockton farming area, I again let my mind wander. I was now undertaking enforcement work in the dove roosting and gathering areas of the San Joaquin Valley. According to Jack the Italian people who lived in this entire area were historically prone to closed-season shooting, shooting of over-limits, and shooting over baited fields (an area where feed is put out for the dove, which acts as a lure and attractant so the dove shooter—no hunter in such a case—gains an unfair killing advantage). Because many of these activities were violations of federal law under the Migratory Bird Treaty Act, it was primarily the responsibility of the game management agent to enforce the act and to assist his state counterparts in the apprehension of the errant lads calling themselves dove hunters. I wanted to be a good soldier and was always eager to prove my worth and learn new tricks of the trade, so it wasn't long before I kissed Donna good-bye (an occasion that was to be repeated a zillion times thereafter), and, thanking her for letting me run as I did, off into my new world of wonders I went.

At first, not having worked any baited dove areas as a game warden, I soon found that I was not much of a skilled "catch dog" in that arena. I was not exactly sure what to look for because that problem had not existed (at least not that I was aware of) in the area I had just left as a game warden. I had had some baiting problems with ducks and geese, but that was basically a horse of a different color, as the bait was usually placed underwater. In addition, as a brand-new game management agent, making more money and with a better retirement system than the Fish and Game wardens, I was too damn proud (read *dumb*) and embarrassed by my lack of knowledge to ask the local state officers for assistance in figuring out this new line of work. Also, there were several state officers in the surrounding area I didn't know, and until I learned whether I could trust them I was a little gun-shy of working with them on sensitive and possibly political cases such as those associated with baiting. (Baiting could be politically charged because many times those who set out bait on their lands turned out to be very wealthy or important people, landed gentry, so to speak; a dove hunt over a baited field could also be a way to pay off political debts.) The geographic layout of the central valley farming country was new to me compared to the upper Sacramento Valley with all its rice, and in these unfamiliar surroundings, from vineyards to huge walnut orchards, I was essentially over my head and lost as to what really needed to be done and how best to do it. Finally, I wasn't too good at finding the bait and then getting in and out without being caught in the act by the ever-vigilant landowner in this neck of the woods, who, along with his friends, was usually among the shooters. These landowners, unlike the ones in the Sacramento Valley, were always on their toes regarding the trespass of anyone who didn't belong on their property. It seemed that every way I turned, I ended up with a hand full of crap.

Working that first week before the start of dove season alone in the Stockton area, I made a few cases and then had the opportunity to team up with an old game warden friend from my days at the Fish and Game academy. Buck Del Nero was his name,

and he was a legend in his district. Seldom did much get away
from him, and if it did he was there waiting for it on the next
pass. That first weekend, working as a team, we knocked the bad
guys dead on everything from over-limits to shooting over
baited areas. If I remember correctly, the two of us wrote over
sixty-five citations in just two days, with Buck all the while
teaching me about the area and how to work those baiting the
dove there. But since that first weekend I hadn't been able to
work with Buck because he was busy sorting out other fish and
game problems.

However, after a week of training from Buck I was a big boy
(or so I thought), so off I went. I found myself doing very well
catching the lads early-shooting the dove out of their roosts or
those driving the roads and shooting dove off the power lines
with the aid of their vehicles and the like, but no brass ring for
those shooting over baited areas or placing the bait where the
dove would find it in time for the second big weekend of dove
hunting, which also promised to be good if the number of birds
in the area was any indicator. That second weekend of the season
was coming on with a rush, and I still hadn't figured out how to
do the job like a real game management agent—at least, not the
way I thought it should be done. As was typical, the agency expected you to do the job on your own. There was no formal national training in those days, and because of the low number of
officers in the ranks and a hell of a workload, senior officers just
were not available to break the new lads in. Most of us received
just a badge and a gun and the instruction to "go get 'em."

I was sitting on Road D north of Stockton one day eating
lunch when the exasperation at being ineffective, at least in the
dove-baiting arena, really began to manifest itself on my miserable and still somewhat proud carcass. The way I had been operating, other than my time with Buck on the opening weekend,
was just not getting the job done to my satisfaction. I knew I had
to change my methods or the dove would catch hell again in just
a few more days. As I tried to think through the problem in its
simplest form, little did I actually appreciate that at that very

moment I was taking one of many positive steps I would take down the long road toward becoming a "real agent."

Sitting there by myself on that hot San Joaquin Valley day, bathed in the sound of grasshoppers and the smell of wild sunflowers growing in profusion along the deserted road, I started to put two and two together. First of all, I decided, one had to have a mixture of wildlife and people to have the opportunity for violations. Then you had to have the kind of people capable of getting the "job" done. I had that all right—so I met that element in my mind's equation. Then I had to locate where the dove liked to feed in numbers numerous enough to attract my shooters. There for a moment I seemed to have hit a stall until I remembered my dove-banding experiences. Dove came to areas with lots of grains more than to areas with little food or the wrong kinds of food, which meant I had to locate large concentrations of dove in order to find either the baited areas or the actual food sources themselves. Dove fed primarily in the morning and late afternoon, so those should be the times I looked hardest. However, if the food was really good they would stay at it all day long. Therefore, I would look all day, but with emphasis on the morning and late afternoon.

Feeling better after my self-examination regarding the principles of the problem, I began to cruise the area in my patrol vehicle, looking for concentrations of dove in unusual numbers during oddball times of the day or for certain types of fields (for example, safflower or wheat) to prove or disprove my theories. It wasn't long before I found concentrations of dove on fence lines and telephone wires overlooking weed fields or cultivated fields in numbers sufficient to generate my interest. Knowing the bad guys were probably watching these "honey holes" as well, I just marked the areas in question with a circle on my road maps for later examination during the dark of night. Before long I had located over a dozen fields that looked promising because there were large numbers of dove sitting in high perches around them and loads of dove moving to and from the suspicious areas.

I also noticed that in some of the fields, if I looked closely with my binoculars, I could see large numbers of dove feeding like maggots on the ground and even some dozens of rock dove (barnyard pigeons) feeding in those areas as well. Most of these areas of interest were harvested croplands, a natural gathering place for any seed-eating bird like the dove, but a few were nothing more than fields plowed to fine dust next to rows of trees or orchards. I dutifully marked all of these suspicious areas on my maps for the evening's "shank's mare" (on foot to those readers considerably younger than I) operations. About eight in the evening I started my examinations. I would hide my un-marked vehicle about a mile from the spot marked on the map and then walk that mile or so into the area in question to pre-clude discovery by the landowner or the person who had placed the bait in the first place.

At first no luck. I couldn't find any baited areas because everything looked very different at night, and I was concerned about using a flashlight to locate the actual baited area because I hoped to avoid discovery. I was getting tired from walking a mile or so into each of these areas in the dark and stumbling over every blasted thing imaginable, along with hiding in the ditch from every passing car to avoid detection. I knew if I kept up this pace I would never get the job done because it was taking too much time. So I developed Grosz's Rule Number 1, or a Tip of the Trade: *If the bad guys were not looking for you, they wouldn't see you.* In times past I had crawled through eight-inch-high cheat grass right up to lads violating the law and was never seen because they were looking skyward for the birds and not at the ground for some silly-assed game warden making like a pitcher's-mound-sized aardvark.

So I began parking my unmarked car right next to the areas in question, opening the hood as if I had car trouble, or leaving a note under the windshield wiper saying, "Out of gas—be right back." And off I went. Soon I began to cover a hell of a lot more area and as luck would have it began to find (read *stumble over*) baited areas—not a lot of them at first, but I *was* beginning to find bait scattered throughout some of the fields in question.

Then came my next lesson: After finding seventeen really good baited areas in three days, which one was I going to work come Saturday? It didn't take me long to realize that areas behind locked gates, or recently posted with "No Hunting" signs, or with mounds of bait (or feed) or large enough acreage to hold many hunters should be my targets of choice. But another Grosz's Rule, *If you get too greedy you will end up with a hand full of crap for your efforts,* kept looming large in my mind. Plain and simply, I needed help. I couldn't get Buck until he had his other affairs squared away. That meant I would have to try to get extra agents to help (fat chance with only 178 in the entire nation, five for all of northern California) or, as a last choice, pick out one of the best-looking baited areas or the one with the most potential based on the dove numbers and hope I could successfully go it alone. Well, the "go it alone" ended up being the option I chose.

After two days of homing in on three of my best baited fields—basing my ratings on the amount of bait, the level of dove use, the activity of humans watching the field, and the size of the area—I focused on one in particular, and it looked like a good bet. On the opening day of dove season a week earlier I had heard a lot of shooting coming from this direction, but because there was lots of baiting business elsewhere, Buck and I had not checked this area out. Watching it during different times of the day over the week, I noticed many dove flying into the area at all times of the day—and when I say many dove, I mean like bees! Bear in mind that good wildlife law enforcement is 98 percent luck and 2 percent patience and skill. My work up to that point in San Joaquin County fitted that formula almost exactly, especially with my choice of that field.

The field I finally selected was completely hidden, except from the air, by extensive walnut orchards on four sides, fences, and locked gates. Once past the fences and gates, one had to traverse a private dirt road of at least three-eighths of a mile no matter what side one came in from to get into my field and suspected baited area. The entire area behind those locked gates was covered with brand-new "No Hunting" signs posted every few yards along the fence wire and posts. The orchards made natural roosts, one of the four orchard sides was being flooded at the time (water for the dove), and there were no houses or other signs of habitation near the area in question to interfere with any questionable activity. Last, but not least, the field in question was a flat, fresh, powder-plowed field. It had also been land planed (leveled) and had at least a ton of safflower seed (seed from a commercial member of the thistle family used to make safflower oil) laid in a straight line down the middle of the twenty-acre area. In fact, the safflower seed was so deep in places that I could see where someone had raked it out so it wouldn't be apparent if a Fish and Game or federal officer were to fly over the field looking for baited areas. In addition, when I went out to gather seed samples for any future court action that might transpire, I discovered that the ground was covered with rock dove and mourning dove droppings along with a zillion dove footprints and scads of dropped feathers from the bodies of dove killed during the previous week's shoot. I knew an area baited to this degree ought to be the one with a "law dog" sitting right around the corner in case some of my suspected sons of Old Italy got carried away and forgot to count and the like.

Two more of Grosz's Rules would come into play before this game was over. First, *Always carry a "master key" (a three-foot set of bolt cutters) to get through locked gates.* Not wanting to be stopped by a locked gate before I could spring my trap, I gathered up the names of the locks and their sizes and key numbers from all entrance points into the field. Then I had keys made for each and every lock so I could get in on shooters in a flash if I had to. However, even after going to such lengths to avoid being locked out at a critical time, it is good to have a handy set of bolt cutters, or "master key," as I called them, just in case. The other rule I violated: *When working a baited field, take more officers with you than you think you will need to get the job done and control the situation.* That way you are covered for any unplanned events. Being of Teutonic stock (read hardheaded) and immortal (ah, youth), I planned to take these guys to task (read *federal court*) all by myself. This was my first really outstanding baited-field investigation, and I was going to do this one by myself, forgetting what I had already learned the hard way! There would be no sharing on this one; it was "cowboy" all the way. Over the years I have come to my senses and now realize that as long as justice is done for the critters, who cares how many lads you bring to the "party" to give a hand. Later I would come to appreciate the maxim, "God loves fools, little children, and game wardens." It surely was applicable in this instance, and many times later throughout my storied career, as you will soon see.

O-dark hundred Saturday, the second weekend of dove season, 1970, found me at my first hurdle, a locked gate at the edge of the orchard next to my suspected baited field. When I tried my new key my devious grin quickly changed to a sour frown. The key refused to work in the lock for which it had been made. Upon closer examination I found that the owner had changed the lock, which told me he really had something to hide, more than confirming my suspicions and whetting my appetite to an even greater degree. Getting out my master key, I made fast work of the chain attached to the lock, knowing that the property owner could only civilly sue for the damages caused to his real property—one link of chain. In addition, my cutting only the link attached to the lock might persuade a suspicious landowner or violator that one of his party had unintentionally left the chain off.

With that little chore out of the way I drove into the walnut orchard at a slow speed so I wouldn't raise dust that might be spotted still hanging in the air by the shooters I hoped were soon to follow. I had picked the orchard entrance road farthest from the baited area because I figured it would be the least used. I was following another of Grosz's Rules: *Pick a time to arrive so the bad guys don't suspect you are there, then get there an hour earlier in order to allow for unplanned eventualities such as flat tires.* It was now two-thirty in the morning, and I had plans for the extra time between then and legal shooting hours. I drove my three-quarter-ton tan Dodge pickup to a semiabandoned wooden farm shed in the orchard and, after opening its doors, removed enough of the junk inside (and the accompanying black widow spiders) to make room for the truck. Then, without any fanfare, I parked it in the shed as if I owned the place. With the vehicle out of sight, it was plain and simply out of mind for the landowner and his hunting buddies. I carefully placed the items I had removed from the shed along an outside wall as a farmer would do when he ran out of space. It was a perfect hiding place. There was an old door in the rear of the shed, and I opened it just to make sure that if I had to hide inside I could get in or out without too much fanfare. Then I trotted off toward my baited field, not using the dusty road leading from the shed but going cross country through the orchard so anyone driving down the road wouldn't see my footprints. I arrived shortly at the spot near the edge of the field that I had previously chosen for my hideout, a large pile of scrap lumber, logs, and old walnut-tree stumps.

In a few moments I had a hiding place dug out of the scrap wood and old limbs in which I could either stand or sit and observe the entire twenty-acre field without fear of discovery. If anyone were to come this way to relieve themselves, the woodpile was large enough that I would remain hidden from them and still be able to watch the shooting in the field without interruption. Once I was settled in and the initial adrenaline rush had subsided, I became aware of the cold sweat on my back that I had worked up trotting into my little hidey-hole. This discomfort was soon overridden by the good feeling of knowing I was once again hunting my fellow humans without their knowledge of my presence. Resting against the backdrop of my log pile, I let my romantic mind wander and dreamed of big over-limits of dove, lots of tickets, and many surprised hunters' faces. I sat shivering in the predawn cold as my anticipation of the hunt that was yet to come loomed larger than life. In a short time all the work I had put into this endeavor would soon come to either successful fruition or a handful of the brown stuff normally used for fertilizer. This would be my first really big case as a game agent, and my excitement as well as satisfaction with my efforts to set this one up ran high—feelings typically found in a rookie who needs a hell of a lot more experience in what to expect. ...

Lights sweeping through the walnut orchard and onto the baited field brought me back to reality in a heartbeat. Four sets of headlights pulled into a parking place in the walnut orchard east of where I was hidden, and out tumbled eight or nine men, all talking excitedly. Several times I recognized the soft, beautiful Italian language floating through the damp air. Nine-to-one odds were just about right, I told myself, thinking of the great over-limit cases that would follow with such a small group shooting, not to mention the bait-related citations. Damn, life was great and getting greater, I thought, now unmindful of the cold on my face and the sweat on my back.

Then it happened! Nine more sets of automobile and pickup headlights came toward my field, again from the orchard road to the east. I could faintly see through my binoculars that there were groups of gunners in the backs of some of the pickups in this convoy. God-o'-Friday, this was a bigger chunk of fat than I felt comfortable chewing! This new string of cars and pickups split before it reached the place where the other cars had parked, with four going to the north side of the field and the remaining five to the south. I now had gunners in the far front of me and to the north and south. There was no way I could count the number of birds all these lads would kill, along with recording the numbers of shots and times shot. I would just have to let them shoot and "weigh the piles" later, I thought, chagrined. Damn! Then, to add insult to injury, I saw the reflection of headlights off my log pile, coming in from behind me through "my" orchard. Turning in my woodpile blind, I counted five more vehicles coming to the baited field. Holy buckets—I now had an army of shooters. Grosz's Rule (the one I had arrogantly broken), *When working a baited field, take more officers with you than you think you will need to get the job done and control the situation,* loomed in my mind. You can bet your sweet hind end

I never violated that rule again, even if I had to go to another state to get help! Dawn was now fast breaking, and the lads on all sides of me were heading for their spots of choice around the edges of the orchards surrounding the bare but heavily baited field. Before you knew it I had forty-five people surrounding the field, waiting for shooting time to begin.

My "hoorah" wasn't long in coming. To the north, two shots were fired at nature's speedsters as they began sailing into the baited area for breakfast. Moments later it seemed that the whole field was ablaze with guns trying for the feathered rockets of the air as the dove entering the field for breakfast got a faceful of lead instead of a cropful of seeds. As dawn progressed into day and I could see better, the number of dove entering the baited area was beyond belief. They looked like swarms of bees! They came in by the hundreds, sailing over, through, and around the orchard, trying to locate a place to feed in the middle of the field. They had fed in peace all week long in an area covered with saf-flower seed. Now they had been joined by gunners shooting rapidly, and the dove, confused by the offering of safflower on the one hand and the sound of shooting and the lethal flying lead pellets on the other, blindly kept coming. Many dove landed right alongside a gunner retrieving another just-killed bird, only to die on the ground as a result of a sluice shot (shooting the birds as they walked on the ground) by the "sportsman."

This carnage didn't let up until about nine o'clock. I wasn't even trying to count shots, identify each shooter, and record each one's kills because of the hunters' numbers and scattered positions. Also, many were moving around, trying to get better shooting angles, and soon all were a blur of faces. It was a sheer circus of shooting guns, swirling dove, and hunters running out into the field to pick up their kills, "seasoned" with constantly exploding puffs of dove in the air falling to their deaths on the ground! By now I could see piles of dove in excess of the daily bag limit in front of some of the better gunners. Many others had had to return to their vehicles to get more shells because they had run out owing to the earlier fast and furious shooting caused by the dove's aerial flying display and, thank God, to their inability to hit their hind ends with both hands. They made these trips with gusto and a quick step in order not to miss out on any of the shooting. I watched with amazement, never having observed a shooting field like this before.

As the shooting slacked off I noticed many of the lads hiding little batches of dove all over the place, around the trees in the orchards and in their vehicles, so that if checked they would be under the bag limit and could continue to shoot. In addition, many dove were left where they had fallen in the field to act as decoys for those dove yet to come, and with the intention of picking them up after the hunt. Almost as if on command, out came the beer as the air warmed, and the killing went on at a more relaxed pace for about another half hour as the dove continued to come into the field in great hungry numbers. All I could think of was that this had to be what passenger-pigeon shoots had looked like during the early 1800s. I decided I wouldn't let the gunners shoot greater numbers of dove that day but would step in and stop the shooting before it got completely out of hand and became a slaughter. I immediately began to record when each shooter shot at a dove and then moved on to the next shooter doing the same until I had observed every gunner shoot at least once over a baited area. Under the definition of *take* in the Migratory Bird Treaty Act a shooter does not have to kill a migratory bird in order for a violation to occur. *Take or attempt to take* is how the act is worded in order to preclude the destruction of a resource.

Finished with my new method of documentation on each shooter, I sat back in my log pile and smiled. Then it hit me! How the hell was I going to capture all these lads? I was but one man in a blizzard of armed miscreants. I didn't mind a good challenge, but this was one for the books. I quietly cussed myself for being so damned stupid and territorial and not bringing help, but here I was in the moment I had created with no way to turn except to myself. I knew the moment I grabbed my first lad the entire field of shooters would be off and running for their cars and out of there like a flock of hens threatened by a junkyard dog. There just was no way to corral the entire lot unless I did something spectacular. But what the hell would that be? Damn, I was trapped by my own, stupidity, greed, and ego. It occurred to me that those were the same three qualities that trapped most violators. ... Boy, was I starting to get a lesson I would never forget.

Then the budding game management agent within took over, along with a rising tide of anger. Every one of these lads had to know the bait was here or they would not have found their way to this isolated field. Also, it appeared that many of them had shot more than the legal limit and hidden the dead birds, not to mention the dozens of dove they had just let lie on the field of battle. No way would I let this one go without a fight—and a damn good one at that! Still, there was the reality of the moment. There was only one of me with the still overriding question of how to capture the lot without a whole series of footraces. Then it hit me like a ton of bricks: the bullhorn in my patrol truck. Why in hell anyone would want a bullhorn had been beyond me, but it had been part of my inventory at the Martinez station of property for which I was responsible, and now I was glad I hadn't thrown it away. If I could somehow get everyone's attention, maybe I could grab a few more than just those few I anticipated catching if I was to move in on them by foot and out in the open in front of God and everyone.

First I had to get that damn bullhorn, then Plan B (Grosz's Rule: *Always have a Plan B*)—but what the hell would my Plan B be? Crawling out of my hiding place and using tree trunks and the woodpile as cover, I cut out for my truck and its hiding place in the old shed as fast as I could crawl, and then as fast as my stiff legs would carry me. Quickly digging the bullhorn out of the utility box in the back of the truck, I pressed the audio button and kept my fingers crossed that it would work and the battery wasn't dead. Turning the volume to low, I whispered into the mouthpiece. It worked! Checking the area I had just come from and finding my return route clear, out the door I went, crawling and, when the coast was clear, racing back to the safety of my woodpile haven. I had the bullhorn but no Plan B as yet—but I was working on it. It's amazing what one can do when pressed into a corner that is too small for one's rather large carcass.

Back at the woodpile, I noticed the lads were still killing dove at a pretty fair rate, though not as rapidly as they had earlier. In fact, some of the men were beginning to clean their birds so they could transport them or better hide them from the prying eyes of any game warden who happened to be in the area. By God, I had the bullhorn but no bull to go with it. Come on, mind, where the hell is my Plan B? I thought. How the hell could I round all these lads up by myself? I continued to curse my earlier "go it alone" stupidity, but hell, you can't get anything through a German's thick skull unless you use a board of high-density wood or something that smells or tastes good. By God, that was it! The area was covered with walnut orchards. They sprayed walnut orchards with insecticides to keep the worms out of the walnut meat.

Out from my woodpile I came when no one was really looking my way and then boldly walked toward the center of the baited field as if I owned the place. The shooting held hot and heavy for a moment and then started to diminish as people saw this person walk out into the middle of their shooting field carrying a bullhorn. I walked right out to the middle of the field, totally surrounded by the lads, all the while noticing hundreds of dead dove, feather piles, bright red blood spots in the brown soil, and hundreds of spent casings, not to mention hundreds of pounds of glowing white safflower seed. Drawing myself up to the most imposing figure I could muster, I triggered the bullhorn. What flowed out had to be heaven sent. Remember what I said about fools, little children, and game wardens. ...

"Gentlemen," I began, "please listen carefully. I am Brad Hicks, county agricultural extension agent, and I have very serious and potentially bad news for you. Late yesterday afternoon when the winds were reduced enough so we could spray, the county started a spraying program next to this area using an experimental chemical to kill walnut-meat worms. The pilot, after one spray pass, was overcome by the fumes of the chemical and headed back to the airport, where he landed just before passing out. Unfortunately, he was disoriented and forgot to turn off the sprayer and as near as we can tell flew right over these orchards, spraying this experimental chemical all over everything." Pausing for a breath, I noticed that all of my shooters were still rooted in their tracks, intently listening to what I had to say. God, I thought, don't let me down now. I continued, "Don't worry, though, he is currently all right and recovering in the hospital. However, I will now need all of you to gather up every dove you killed and bring them to me because you cannot eat them without the possibility of getting violently ill." I noticed that everyone was still rooted to the ground for my finale. I soon would see whether God was still my copilot. Triggering the bull-horn mike once again and hoping the battery would last, I added, "Also, I will need everyone's name and address so I can notify the local area hospital in order to authorize shots for you folks to help your bodies offset any toxins absorbed from this chemical sprayed over your hunting area by mistake. The county will pick up all the medical costs associated with these shots and any subsequent illness you might acquire that is related to this mistaken application. However, right now all of you will be within the window of treatment and should not have any aftereffects, especially if you take the antitoxin shots today or tomorrow."

For the longest moment no one moved, and I thought, Uh-oh, this isn't going to work. Then it was like a burst dam. They all moved to their cars and other hiding places and began to pick up and bring me every dove they had killed, including those left in the field. I had them line up when they finished gathering up the birds and get their driver's licenses out and their dove counted before they got to me so I could record the numbers of dead dove on the backs of their licenses (in those days they were made of paper) as quickly as possible before my little charade was discovered. They minded like little tin solders, and each had the same question when he got to me: Would they be all right?

Many even wanted to know if there was some way they could keep and eat the dove regardless of the insecticide once they had gotten the shots! Good old Plan B had worked beyond my wildest expectations. I told them to give me their driver's licenses and head for the shade of the trees, adding that the shade would retard the effects of the poison, so once they had given me their licenses and birds they should move off and rest until I was finished. This worked like a charm, and before long I had damn near checked everyone and had their driver's licenses and dove to prove it.

I was down to my last four or five chaps when one of the lads looked at me closely and said, "Say, aren't you that state Fish and Game warden from Colusa? I think you checked me one time when I was duck hunting up there."

Without missing a beat I said, "Yes, I used to be there, but now I work for the state Agriculture Department."

Nothing more was said until that lad finally got to me and, looking me over again, said, "Are you sure?"

Taking his license and dove, I said, "No, I'm not sure."

He said, "What does that mean?"

I said, "I am a United States game management agent empowered to enforce the Migratory Bird Treaty Act, and from what I have observed here today, you and your buddies are in trouble for not only shooting over a baited field but maybe some over-limits as well."

He just looked at me for a moment in disbelief and then turned and ran from the field, shouting, "It's a trap; this guy is a *fed*—run!"

With that my violators started to move like mercury through my fingers, tossing their lunches and beer every which way and beating a hasty retreat toward their vehicles. I again got on the bullhorn and, turning it up to high to overcome their rush of adrenaline, said, "Lads, he is correct. I am a federal agent, and all of you are in violation of the Migratory Bird Treaty Act for taking migratory game birds over a baited area. Keep in mind that I have every one of your driver's licenses, and anyone not in the field when I come over to issue citations will have an arrest warrant sworn out for him by nightfall."

It was beautiful: with those words and that realization they all stopped running and walking to their vehicles as if on cue. I cranked up the bullhorn once again and told them to meet me in the shade of a large walnut tree at the edge of the field. Then I started hauling the dead dove across the field to get them out of the sun and into the shade of the walnut tree so they wouldn't spoil. It took me a while to move the numbers of dove I had acquired or found on the ground, but it worked out for the best. As the pile grew, the shooters' faces got longer and longer with the realization of what they had done and what it represented. Almost all the bad guys had resigned themselves to apprehension by the time I was done hauling the dove, and they lay or stood around in little groups, talking in hushed tones and waiting for their names to be called.

Once started I would take a driver's license from the pile I had previously acquired; call out a name; and, once the lad appeared, check his gun for a plug, check his hunting license, and then issue him a citation for shooting over a baited field, over-limit of dove (if he had one), and any other infraction I found in the routine check. This activity went on until I finished writing up all forty-five of my men for their little morning of destructive fun. Most of them had more or less calmed down about my little ruse by the time they got to me, but a few were really wound up. It didn't take but a few minutes, though, for them to quiet down when they were confronted with the issue at hand, and the writing went on. I finished with the last chap at about one in the afternoon. God, what a glorious day. Except for a very tired writing hand and a growling gut, I had a happy heart—that is, until I loaded several hundred dove, along with six killdeer and two kestrels (protected migratory birds—no season allowed) that had also been taken, into my patrol vehicle. The thought that it was just like the days of the passenger pigeon shoots swept over me again, leaving me cold inside as I thought, Will we ever win? That was a tough idea for a man who was just starting his federal career in the wildlife law enforcement field of dreams. But, as it turned out, the question arose many times throughout my career.

It was just as Jack had said regarding the people of that area: if it flies, it dies. That was certainly true this momentous day. My morning's investment of time netted 45 lads with a total of 67 violations (use of bait, over-limit, no license, unplugged shotgun, etc.) and 273 evidence doves. Fines in U.S. District Court for that day's efforts, after everyone had paid over the next month or so, ultimately totaled $5,600! But more importantly, the day's events and the time leading up to them allowed a young officer to turn the corner into the real world of wildlife associated with being a U.S. game management agent.

I saw a lot of wildlife die illegally during my career, and I never did get used to it. Days like the one just described are rarer now, except maybe in Texas and the Southeast on opening day of the dove season. Not because the killing does not go on to such a degree anymore—it does—but because it is getting more difficult to catch these chaps. Outlaws are being educated just like officers, so a wildlife officer had better be maturing and developing daily in the ways of the outlaw or the wildlife will pay a very high price. Additionally, the wildlife is disappearing because of a lot of other life-history factors, such as possible legal overharvesting; politics weakening the baiting regulations under the guise of better hunter understanding of the law, which amounts to hogwash allowing even greater killing (such as in the killing field of *legalized* baiting); and destruction of habitat. Last but not least, most land management agencies are experiencing hard fiscal times and often use their conservation officers to close the gap for other things rather than wildlife law enforcement. It doesn't take the outlaws or those willing to take more than their rightful share long to take advantage of a bad situation.

There is only so much of a natural resource to go around, and when that is gone, it is gone forever. Humankind is usually the cause of that process of extinction. I have often wondered over my years in the field if we too will end up as victims of this process.

3

The Tahoe-Truckee Roadblock

LEAVING RENO, NEVADA, in the early afternoon, I headed west on Interstate 80 en route to Sacramento, California. It was the early 1970s, and I had just finished an investigation into the activities of a well-established falconer and migratory-bird-of-prey propagator (one who breeds and raises migratory birds) who lived east of Reno's urban sprawl. The man had not only illegally scooped some red-tailed hawk nestlings from several nests reported to be located in California but had also made the mistake of bragging to his buddies about his coup. In due time, the word got around and elicited a personal call from a friendly U.S. game management agent from Sacramento, namely, me. The bottom line was that to take red-tailed hawks from the wild, one needed both state and federal permits. A review of permit files had revealed that the chap in question had none and therefore had violated state and federal migratory bird laws if he had in fact scooped the nests as reported. I had spent several hours interviewing the folks who had overheard this chap bragging; then I had talked to the man himself. I had him execute an affidavit regarding the illegal facts of the matter, and my part, except for the later follow-up in the courts, was finished.

With that business completed, I was heading back to the Sacramento Valley. Now that the traffic of Reno was behind me, I could sit back in my Dodge 4x4, three-quarter-ton truck and just let it hammer right along the interstate at a Swiss-watch-smooth seventy miles per hour. I miss the ride a pickup can give you when there is a 383-cubic-inch V-8 under the hood, with a four-barrel carburetor attached for good measure. What I wouldn't give for a return to the good old days of big engines and speed! I never lost a chase in the three years I had that truck; in fact, one time I was clocked at 117 miles per hour by the California State Highway Patrol as I assisted in the pursuit of an armed robber. The great thing was that the old Dodge was still slowly gaining speed.

Coming back from my "dreamin' and driftin'," I reran the events of that morning and early afternoon through my mind. With the evidence I had gathered, the lad scooping the red-tailed hawk nests would be paying for his error in judgment for a while to come; he might even lose his current falconry licenses in the process. The illegally taken birds had of course "flown the coop," but I knew that in time his alligator mouth would overload his hummingbird hind end and word of their whereabouts would end up out on the street. When that happened I would be back for the rest of his hide. Unfortunately, this little episode probably wouldn't stop him for long because it would just make him, like other dyed-in-the-wool falconry men, more careful in his illegal activities and less mouthy in the future. Oh well—my job was to bring criminals before the mast, and the courts' mission was to keep them from a return trip through some form of legal education. If that didn't work, all we in law enforcement could ultimately hope for the person stealing eggs or chicks was a long fall from the tree or rock face holding the eyrie. Such accidents were what we in the trade called "Lions one, Christians nothing."

Damn, it felt great to get out of Reno. I was a small-town boy and didn't cotton to any city with a population larger than several thousand. Brother, was I in for a surprise over the span of my career with the Service and all the big cities I eventually had to live in. The smallest city I lived in during all those years working my way up through the ranks had a population of fifty thousand. Oh well; we learn as we grow up—and I did.

That November day was a typical high Sierra afternoon with crisp air and clear skies spotted with a few cumulus clouds, punctuated with the pungent smell of pines and sagebrush as I started my long climb into the Sierras. The scenery as I climbed

through the foothills and eventually into the mountains was typical Sierra landscape: granite rock, and plenty of it, and the
shrubs and trees associated with the different altitudes and soil
types accentuated my ascent. I could feel a touch of winter still
lingering in the air against my arm hanging out the window of
the pickup, which reminded me of the living history of the area.
I was approaching the Donner Pass area and the memory of the
tragedy that had occurred there so many years ago. Letting my
mind wander, as I tended to do when it came to the history of
this country, I thought, If those poor people could only see this
area and the methods of transportation today. Of course, if they
hadn't come when they did, we latter-day historians wouldn't
have that black moment in history to dwell upon.

These thoughts faded away as I approached the Tahoe-
Truckee state agriculture quarantine station. What caught my
eye and erased my self-indulgent history lesson were numerous
hunting rigs gathered in the parking lot while their owners used
the public restrooms. There were about fifteen such hunting vehicles and trailers, and every one sported evidence of successful
hunts: deer antlers of every size and shape, grand elk antlers,
and the occasional massive set of moose antlers. In addition,
many rigs were pulling trailers, homemade and otherwise, that
obviously, because of the way they were sitting on their axles,
were transporting the meat represented by the prominently displayed antler racks.

I slowed out of curiosity, then pulled into the same parking lot
and parked in an area that offered a clear view of this successful
hunter panorama. From where I sat, I could see evidence of
more than sixty animals that had been taken somewhere in the
western states during their respective hunting seasons. Many
were legally taken, I would wager, but being the curious type of
officer I was, I wondered how many had been taken, possessed,
or transported illegally. The federal Lacey Act, passed by Congress in 1900, and its sister the Black Bass Act (long since incorporated into the Lacey Act), which was passed later, were placed
in the federal conservation officers' arsenal to allow them the

ability to address the issue of fish and wildlife (and later plants) taken unlawfully in one state and transported across state lines. As I watched the continuous stream of dead wildlife being transported in plain view rolling into the quarantine station, with the question of legality growing in my mind like a chewed piece of tripe, the idea of a wildlife check station on a major highway like this one, using those two federal acts as the hammer, began to run through my mind. Damn! Why not? We had the wildlife being transported in plain view, a nice area to work here at the quarantine station with its big parking area, a set of federal wildlife laws to back us up, and, if we seized anything, a large metropolitan area nearby in Reno to distribute the meat to needy souls.

Those thoughts began to whirl in my mind like a pound of buckshot rolling around in an iron barrel. I knew that the Service's chief of law enforcement in Washington, D.C., had a policy of not initiating a wildlife roadblock unless a state first requested assistance in such a matter. But, being the type of rash chap I was in those days, I thought, What the hell do those folks three thousand miles away really know about the world of wildlife as it exists here in the outback? Most states in those days could not have cared less what went on in the hunting picture in other states. If an injured state did request assistance, the receiving state would conduct an investigation, but as a general rule state agencies didn't go looking for political trouble in the form of a major wildlife roadblock to check wildlife taken in other states.

Well, just because states didn't go looking under this rock of opportunity, that shouldn't stop me, I mused. My limited knowledge in the conservation law enforcement arena had already shown that folks in any profession or avocation had their "good, bad, and ugly" elements. The hunting community was no exception. I had found that greed and ego ran deep in many segments of the hunting and fishing communities, and the only way to hold that element in check was to burn those fingers reaching illegally into the wildlife cookie jar! Everywhere I looked that afternoon I found myself wondering if that animal had been legally taken. Loving the sport of hunting as I do, I could think of no better gift than to have Christmas come early in the form of a wildlife check station if the agricultural authorities in charge of the quarantine check station would allow it. That way the Service could help the states police those who tended to stray across that green line drawn in the sand and, in one fell swoop, reinforce the ethical side of sport hunting through some good old-fashioned law enforcement education.

I got out of my vehicle and walked over to the quarantine station office to talk to the site supervisor. Laying out my plan to initiate a wildlife check station because of what I had observed in the parking lot, I requested the use of his parking area and assistance from his officers. After thinking my request over for a moment and looking out over the parking lot, as I had, the supervisor said he didn't see any problem cooperating with the Service as long as we didn't interfere with his officers in the performance of their duties. I assured him that that would not be a problem; his lads could just send the obvious hunters over to the Service agents in an out-of-the-way section of the parking lot, and we would conduct our wildlife inspections from there (my, how things have changed from then to now on a roadblock!). A quick phone call to that man's supervisor in Reno confirmed the willingness of the state agriculture department to assist the Fish and Wildlife Service, again, just as long as it didn't interfere with the quarantine station's mission.

Thanking that man for his cooperation, I headed back to my truck, taking the time as I passed several truckloads of game to notice that none of the animal carcasses displayed any tags, as would have been required by the states where they were taken. Taking that realization and the idea of the work needed in this arena to my truck, I sat there and drew up a mental plan as to how we could operate at the agriculture inspection site. With the seed of that idea continuing to germinate, I drove out of the parking lot and continued my trip down toward the Sacramento Valley and the meeting with my fellow officers.

From then on, the trip was not as nice as it had been earlier in the day. It seemed that every third vehicle that passed me was driven by a grimy outdoor-type man with his friends, towing trailerloads of dead wildlife from some far-off state. During the next few hours I became increasingly aware of the vast amount of wildlife moving in interstate commerce as I drove along the interstate. It was enormous! Driving more slowly so most traffic could easily pass me, I counted 2,671 vehicles moving in the same direction I was carrying evidence of wildlife. Man, talk about a potential law enforcement gold mine! This one, if a wildlife roadblock could be successfully executed along that particular highway, certainly began to look like a mother lode!

Excited about my discovery, I shared it and my plan with Dean Tresch, another U.S. game management agent whose district adjoined mine in the Sacramento Valley, during our waterfowl detail meeting that evening. Now, Dean wasn't much of a man physically; in fact, he was a shrimp compared to my six-foot-four, three-hundred-pound frame. But he was a tiger when it came to work, and never once during our working relationship did he ever refuse to give me a hand or let me down when we were on details. I constantly gave him grief for being so small, but he was always willing to back up me on my crazy and not-so-crazy ideas. One reason was because those crazy schemes usually struck pay dirt, and in order to be in on those "hoorahs," Dean good-naturedly tolerated my ribbing. Dean liked this particular idea as well as I did, and that was all it took for me to shift the plan into high gear. With Dean's commitment to support me, I called my deputy federal agent, Tim Dennis, in Maxwell, California. Tim, or the "Dirt Farmer" (he earned a living most of the year as a rice farmer in the Sacramento Valley), as I called him, was always ready for any kind of action and quickly told me he was ready to go. When I returned to my Colusa office after a successful Stockton detail (nineteen individuals cited for over-limits of ducks and shooting over a baited area over a two-day period), I called the chiefs of fish and game agencies in all of the western states and had them send me copies of their hunting regulations for that year. Armed with those regulations at the roadblock, Tim, Dean, and I would be better able to separate the legal from the illegal. A few more telephone calls to Dean, Tim, and the state agriculture chief regarding the date of the event, and we were set. I marvel at the simplicity of thought and deed in those days. We were like Mounties—we just went and did it.

The plan was for Tim, Dean and me to arrive on a Friday evening, stay overnight at Donner Lake in a rented cabin, and the next day operate the roadblock. Brother, if I had had any idea of the adventure we three were in for, I might have thought twice before setting out (but maybe not)! As a last-minute thought, I called a meat locker and processing plant in the Reno area and made arrangements for storage, cutting, and wrapping of any meat we might seize as a result of our efforts. As it turned out, that was one of the best moves I made! With that and the daily arrival of various state regulations, we were almost ready. As our day of reckoning approached, I made arrangements to borrow a quarter-ton Jeep trailer from the Sacramento National Wildlife Refuge that we could use in addition to my truck to haul our wildlife seizures to the meat-processing plant. Then we were set.

I met Tim on the chosen day, then got Dean on the radio and set up a meeting place along the road for lunch. Dean had his sedan (those were the days when most agents *only* drove sedans), Tim had his Jeep 4x4, which was pulling our trailer, and I followed with my Dodge (I guess I wasn't much of an agent, driving a pickup and all). In those days that was an impressive array of strength. Since that time I have seen convoys of Service and state vehicles on major raids stretch for several uninterrupted miles en route to their targets. Now, that's an impressive sight, especially in the dark of night! After finishing our working lunch, off we went to the place we had chosen for our latest adventure. We visited the quarantine station when we arrived in the area that evening, and while Dean and I worked out the operational details and procedures with the state ag people, Tim drove off to familiarize himself with the locker plant in case we had to haul any evidence there for processing. We met later at our little rented cabin on the shore of Donner Lake, and as the wind howled outside and the temperature continued to drop until it was below 10 degrees, I couldn't help but think of those poor people who took the Warner Cutoff and froze themselves into history forever. Several times that night as the wind tried to blow our cabin off its foundations, I imagined I could almost hear their voices crying in despair.

Arriving at the quarantine station shortly after daylight, we set our vehicles up in a parking area near the agriculture inspection station. Tim pulled his rig off to one side but close enough to where Dean and I parked to move any seized wildlife to the trailer he was pulling in case we filled up my pickup. The basic plan was to have the ag people do their plant thing with people as they stopped (all traffic had to stop at the ag station), then, if there was evidence of hunting spoils, those folks would be shunted over to the three of us for a wildlife inspection. Nothing to it, we thought. Damn, were we ever wrong. We laid out our evidence tags, citations, state regulations, and ice chests; turned around, ready for business; and were promptly overwhelmed! Ten zillion people showed up with their loads of wildlife, all heading for home; all in need of a bath, a shave, and sex; and none in too good a mood about this roadblock! Good God almighty, I never saw so many hunters, critters, bad tempers, poorly kept or spoiled meat, evidence of rotten shot placement on the carcasses, sloppily cared-for equipment, attitudes, lack of the sportsman's ethic—you name it. In short, we weren't prepared for the onslaught that hit us. We were just barely able to inspect for marginal compliance with the laws of the states in which people had hunted. We decided early on that if the violations weren't major, we would let them ride with just a damn good hind-end chewing. That worked well, but it seemed as if all I did for the first hour was eat out a lot of unwashed hind ends! Then, as the breakfast traffic arrived from overnight stays in Sparks and Reno, so did the major violations.

I had just finished checking several hunters coming home

from a hunt in Idaho when I noticed—smelled would be a better way to put it—what had to be Wyoming hunters. A new sedan pulled up to the quarantine station pulling a tandem-wheeled rental trailer. As the wind created by its arrival breezed by me, I smelled the unmistakable odor of antelope, and rotting antelope at that! In the sedan were two clean lads, dressed in suits, with no outward appearance of hunting gear or garb. The ag chap was releasing them so they could go on their way when I hailed them with a raised hand, much to the surprise of the ag inspector, identified myself, and asked if they had been hunting. They both hesitated and then responded in an unconvincing way that they had not. Both sets of eyes were like those of trapped rats. Without further ado, I asked the two to move over to my truck for an inspection, which they meekly did. When they stepped out of their car, I beckoned them over to where I stood next to my rig. "Gentlemen," I said, "let's be frank with each other. There are antelope in that trailer; I can smell them, as can you. Now, if you don't mind, I would like to see them if I could?"

They looked at each other as if wondering how I had known. Then the driver reached into his pants pocket, retrieved a set of keys, walked back to the trailer, unlocked it, and stepped back. Taking that as permission to look inside, I opened the doors. A soft *whoosh* of hot, heavy, and stinking-sweet air rushed to meet me. I damn near puked as the dry heaves inspired by that smell came all the way from my feet. Antelope were stacked clear to the ceiling in the front part of the trailer. In the rear of the trailer was all kinds of hunting gear and tents, cooking pots, camping food, and the like. I couldn't believe my eyes. Not only had these lads taken a tremendous over-limit of antelope but they had just stacked them in the trailer as they had killed them, with no thoughts about spoilage. The antelope had not even been skinned. Jesus, what a stinking mess!

Looking at the lads' downcast faces, I said, "I need to see some hunting licenses and driver's licenses, please." Then Tim and I started dragging out the antelope and loading them into my pickup—all twenty-three of them! While loading those critters into the truck, I found the object of my nose's attention in an ungutted, gut-shot doe. Damn, what a smell. It took two days for it to leave my hands, which was a very bad state of affairs for a person who likes to eat as much as I do. Every time I raised a forkful of food to my mouth I would get a whiff of that rotten smell ingrained into my skin and damn near lose it all over again. It was a good thing I always carried thirty days' "rations" around my beltline for the "Great Famine," as the Good Book instructs—and for lesser crises such as this antelope situation! As it turned out, the lads did not have any hunting licenses for Wyoming, where they had taken the antelope. They had just decided to go on the hunt of a lifetime on a private ranch, and I decided it would be the *last* hunt of a lifetime once I had informed the federal judge of the over-limits; wanton waste; and lack of licenses, discipline, and ethic.

Once that bit of work was over, my truck was full of seized wildlife, and Dean and I decided we had better send that batch to the storage plant in Reno before it got any riper. So off Tim went with the first of many loads that day. The wildlife traffic had backed down to a dull roar, so when I had a moment I would pay closer attention to the ag guys to see if I could spot anyone else the way I had picked out the antelope-killing knotheads. A pickup pulled up, and I recognized the driver as a lad I had pinched in Stockton earlier in September for shooting dove over a baited field. I drifted over to where I could hear the conversation without him seeing me. The men in the pickup said they had been hunting but had been skunked. There wasn't any evidence of a successful hunt displayed on their rig, but it was full of hunting gear. The ag lad glanced over to me with a questioning look, and my gut hunch said to go for it. I nodded for the rig to be sent over to us.

The driver stepped out of the truck and said in a surprised voice, "Where the hell did you come from?" Before I could respond, he added, "What the hell is this all about, Terry?"

I said, "Just a wildlife check station, Jimmy; it won't take much of your time."

He said, "Well, make it fast; we didn't get a thing."

"What were you hunting, Jimmy?" I asked.

"Trophy deer in Nevada, and we didn't get any." His constant denial told me something was wrong, and my attention level was up and running as I began to scan his heavily loaded pickup for evidence of any crime. There didn't appear to be anything out of the ordinary: tents, camp stoves, groceries, cartons of beer, cased weapons, and the like filled the back of the pickup. There were three Coleman ice chests, which I opened only to find the usual contents of food, beer, and frozen meats. I also noticed another large ice chest in the front of the pickup bed that appeared to be a rather large homemade job. Reaching under a tarp, dirty clothes, and camping equipment, I started to pull it out so I could examine it more closely. It turned out to be one heavy son of a gun. In that instant all the carping by the lads stopped, and I knew I had a tiger by the tail.

Now, in those days I was one strong lad. In fact, I remember lifting a 450-pound anvil at Buck Del Nero's place from the ground into the back of my pickup after Buck told me that if I could lift it, I could have it. But let me tell you, I was not prepared for the weight of that ice chest. When I lifted it off the tailgate to place it on the ground for a more convenient and thorough inspection, it took me down to the pavement in a heartbeat, almost smashing my feet in the process! What the hell could weigh so much? Lifting the lid, I was amazed at what I saw. The chest was full to the top of picked and cleaned chukar (a type of partridge). The limit on chukar in Nevada was six! I began to count and finished 258 bodies later. A look into the eyes of the lads standing around watching what I was doing said it all. They had gone deer hunting in Nevada and, finding no deer they thought worth shooting but a wonderful concentration of chukar around the freshwater springs in the area, decided to help themselves. I discovered that all of the birds had been shot with a light rifle. A little digging around in their vehicle produced a scoped .22-caliber semiautomatic rifle.

I looked at Jimmy, and he just shrugged as if it was no big deal and began to dig out his wallet. He damn well knew what was coming next, and he surely wasn't disappointed! After I took down the information that would lead to three later citations in federal court, Jimmy and his party drove off without a parting word. Those poor chukar, thirsty and coming to the only water for miles around, had found hot lead instead. Having worked in Nevada one summer for the Bureau of Land Management, I knew how chukar could gang up by the hundreds at the watering holes. It must have been a piece of cake, just sitting there and killing the birds at point-blank range as they came to the watering hole and death. I shook my head and loaded the homemade ice chest and the 258 chukar into the evidence trailer, with Dean's help. I could tell from my partner's bloody arms that he hadn't been idle either. There were four large mule deer bucks in the back of the trailer that he had seized from some lads who had gotten a little too trigger-happy in Idaho. There wasn't a rack of antlers less than twenty-five inches in the bunch, with the largest measuring thirty-nine inches at its widest outside beam!

We returned to the line of waiting hunters, and the fast pace of examining their hunting successes continued, with seizures of illegal wildlife about every fourth or fifth vehicle. Damn, I never worked as hard as I did that day searching vehicles, conducting interviews, seizing wildlife, and recording information for federal complaints until I was blue in the face and sore of hand and foot (try standing on concrete or asphalt for hours on end with a three-hundred-pound carcass on size 14 feet).

And so it went, vehicle after vehicle, hour after hour. Damn, it seemed it would never quit. We had to run to the bathroom and run right back because there was always another hunter's rig ready to be searched and processed. It seemed that we had caught the high tide of hunters as they poured out of the various western states just ahead of a major high-mountain snowstorm. I didn't mind hard work and long hours, but this was dead-run stuff for the entire day, and I was being physically challenged, as were my two fellow officers. What made it nice, though, were the vast number and variety of violations. This was a "cherry patch" of sorts. It seemed that every fourth or fifth hunter was in deep brown stuff of one kind or another: untagged animals, over-limits, killing the wrong species or sex—so it went throughout the day. During a rare pause in the action, Dean and I decided that we needed Tim to stop writing out pink slips and just run the seized wildlife to the storage locker because by this time the three of us were seizing so much that it was lying on the pavement all around the trailer and truck. Tim started on his runs, and Dean and I went back to the grisly work at hand.

Tim wasn't able to return to checking cars and hunters for the whole rest of the day because each time he returned from the plant another pile of meat was waiting to be transported. The flow of illegal wildlife was getting out of hand. It showed me how easy it was for poachers to get around the local state game wardens; once on the highways, they had almost smooth sailing. It wasn't because the state officers weren't doing their jobs but because of the size of the territory they had to cover and the fact that they were always shorthanded. When poachers have those two elements on their side, the wildlife will die in great numbers without making a sound.

I had just finished writing up a lad for taking a black bear during the closed season in Montana when another group of hunters traveling together in two pickups pulled into my check area, and out came four burly, unshaven, grouchy, smelly, and tired chaps. It was obvious that they were annoyed at being held up by our roadblock, and after identifying myself and explaining my mission, I hustled through the inspection. They had limits of elk, deer, antelope, and a moose. Damn good hunters, I thought. The animals were cleanly shot, the meat was well cared for, and I was pleased with the degree of care shown. When I asked to check a cab-over camper on one of the trucks, there was a slight hesitation, but they finally agreed. Opening the door, I discovered four extra mule deer and parts of a six-point bull elk. Before I could say anything, one of the lads said they belonged to other members of their party who had stopped to gamble in Reno and would be along shortly. I was a shade suspicious, to say the least, after discovering the additional animals without any previous mention by the hunters of their presence. All the animals were properly tagged except one, which had a "slick tag" (one not punched out or validated) attached to its antlers. That tag gave me legal grounds to keep the lads for a while, and I decided I would do so.

I sensed a slight discomfort among the men as I examined the additional four deer and elk. I turned back to them and said, "Lads, are these your animals as well?" That shot out of the dark caught them unawares, and for a moment, I thought I saw a look telling me I had a "kill" coming for an over-limit of deer and elk.

The dumpy lad of the group said, "I told you our friends are in Reno gambling and will be along shortly. Them's their critters."

I said, "OK. If they will be along shortly, you certainly won't mind waiting for them, will you?"

What could they do but agree? Somewhat sullenly, they did. I hustled over to Dean with the names of the chaps they told me to look for and the type of rigs they were allegedly driving so we could both watch for them, then returned to my lads. I had them pull their rigs off to one side to await the arrival of their friends and went to work clearing up their tagging violation. In about twenty minutes, as luck would have it, the other four members of the hunting party arrived. Damn, I thought, I was sure these lads had something to hide and had invented the rest of the party in Reno, hoping to wait me out. But here the other fellows were, and now it looked as if my gut instinct was being made out to be a liar.

Getting the second group off to one side, away from their buddies who had come earlier, I began examining their licenses to make sure they matched the tags on the animals I had discovered in the camper. They did. Damn! Then the dam broke. When I inspected my latest arrivals' two rigs, lo and behold, there under tarps lay four more deer, four more elk, and a moose calf. As the story came out, those animals had been shot by an

Indian who had given the animals to them out of the goodness of his heart! It was a good thing I hadn't fallen off any hay wagons recently. Examination of the tags on the newfound animals revealed names of other hunters not with the party, not any Indian hunter, and my hunt was on again!

"Lads," I said, "something smells here, and it is my job to find out what." I turned and pointed to Tim as he loaded up another load of evidence of for its trip to the evidence locker. "If you don't tell me the truth, that may be the plight of your animals as well, not to mention a certain amount of financial burden levied by the federal courts."

They were all damn quiet now. Hardly anyone moved for fear of breaking the spell. My eyes searched the group for a weakling, and I spotted one. He was a younger man who couldn't bring himself to even look at me, much less speak. "You," I said, pointing to the younger lad, "come with me."

Jesus, you would have thought I had just gut-shot the lad. All his buddies looked at him as if he were a sheep going to slaughter. We walked off a few paces, and turning to the scared young man, I said, "Son, I know there are illegal animals in that mess. I will find them, and then all of you lads will have to stand for the error of your ways. Now, I don't feel you are stupid enough to try to lie your way through this, especially if you consider that I do this for a living, have done so for years, and have probably heard every story known to man as to why things like this happened. But I'm willing to listen to your story before I make up my mind on how I am going to handle this situation as far as the courts and seizures of wildlife and equipment go."

I paused and looked hard into his eyes. He broke like an egg. "Mister," he said, "I don't want any trouble, but if I say anything, they will kill me."

I said, "If you don't come clean, it will go a lot harder on you and your buddies. If they understood that, they would probably applaud you for the courage to tell the truth and square this issue away. Otherwise, we are looking at the potential loss of the animals, firearms, vehicles used to transport the animals illegally in interstate commerce, and any other things of evidentiary value."

He looked hard at me for a moment and then said, "We used some buddies' tags who worked with us at the plant who couldn't come. We thought we would take their tags and fill them, and that way they would have some winter meat for their families as well."

I said, "OK, I appreciate your courage and candor and will let your buddies know you just not only saved their hides but spared them the seizure of their hunting equipment and vehicles as well."

"How are you going to do that?" he asked worriedly.

"Just watch me," I said. I turned and walked abruptly back to the lads. "Gentlemen," I said, "I want the names of those of you who shot the extra animals for your friends back at the plant. I also want the name of the lad who shot the extra moose. Roger here just told me everything, and I don't have a lot of time to fool around here today, so let's get cracking."

The lad who had just spilled his guts to me looked absolutely sick. I don't think I ever saw a man with a grayer complexion (except me when I was at sea). This wasn't what he had expected when I told him I would cover for him. If looks could kill, his buddies would have slaughtered the chap I had just grilled. As if on cue, Dean dragged another two seized antelope by me, and the lads began to realize the gravity of the situation.

"Now, gentlemen," I continued, "Roger, after being advised that to lie would get all of you booked in the federal lockup in Reno and your vehicles and guns seized and forfeited to the government, decided to save your collective bacon and tell the truth." I lied about the booking and all—I didn't have time for such foolishness, nor were the violations severe enough to warrant it. In fact, I hadn't planned to arrest anyone during this roadblock unless he took a poke at me or one of the other officers. But the threat made a good impression on the lads, and a good cover story for Roger. "I would suggest that all of you owe him a debt of thanks and a cold beer for realizing how serious illegal interstate transportation of wildlife is and deciding to handle it like a man." I could see their looks change from pure poison to a grudging acceptance that told me Roger was safe among them, so I went on to the business at hand.

Twenty minutes later I had seized eight more deer, eight elk, and one moose and, with the help of the lads, dragged them to our loading spot for Tim when he returned. Pink slips were filled out, and all the lads trooped by and thanked me with meaningful handshakes for not putting them in jail and taking all their personal belongings. I gave all the credit to Roger and noticed as they loaded up that all of them went to Roger to pat him on the back and the like. Good; what they didn't know wouldn't hurt them, I thought. Roger's backward glance as he got into his vehicle clearly said, "Thanks," and I responded with a nod.

I had no sooner dispatched those lads on their way than along came a camper rig driven by a nice-looking old couple. They pulled up and wanted to know what all the fuss was about. I explained what we were doing and asked if they had been hunting or fishing. They answered that they had done a little fishing, and a lot more gambling then they should have, and were now heading back to Sacramento before they ran out of their Social Security money. I asked if I could check their licenses and fish, and they said sure and bailed out of the rig to assist me. What a nice couple! I hoped my bride and I, when we got that old, could enjoy our retirement as much as this couple. The lady walked back to the camper and opened it up and hopped inside. I checked their licenses and then stepped up into the camper. I commented on how nice the camper was as I checked their complete limits of very large trout. They had the fish in an ice chest, covered with lots of ice and well cared for. I started to leave but then thought I might as well as check their camper icebox and asked if I could do so. The old people looked at each other, and the woman said, "No! Some of the food inside might have shifted, and if you open the door it may fall out on the floor."

The alarm bells went off, and I lied, "My in-laws own one just like this, and I know how to open the door without spilling anything." I reached up and opened the icebox door, and out fell tons of stuff right on my feet! Damn, was I embarrassed—until I looked down and realized that the contents were loose trout, dozens of them. The icebox was full of illegal trout!

I turned to look at this "nice" old couple, and all I got in return was two deadly-looking stares. Boy, were they pissed at being caught. Out came the trout, all forty-one of them, into an ice chest I had in my truck. Flagging Tim to come over and give me a hand, I really took that camper apart. There were twelve more trout in the camper crapper and twenty-six more scattered under the seats and in other compartments. By the time all was said and done, this nice old couple had taken seventy-nine trout, or sixty-nine over the limit for the area they had fished. While Tim loaded the fish into the truck for transport to the Reno storage plant, along with another huge load of deer, elk, moose, and the like, I issued the citations. These two people had turned from nice folks to mean as snakes in a heartbeat. They asked how much the tickets would be, and I told them I didn't know, but they would probably be substantial because they had taken so many fish over the limit.

The old man snapped, "How are we supposed to pay for this, being on Social Security and all?" I wanted to tell them they probably should have thought of that before they broke the law, and I suspected this wasn't the first time they had done so. But I just said, "I don't know," and turned and walked away before the tired in me got the better of my mouth. I found out later from a local warden in the area they had fished that it appeared this couple had found a closed-to-fishing stream full of brood stock and basically cleaned it out.

By now my tail end was dragging, and a look at Dean showed that his wasn't too far off the deck either. The hunting lads kept coming, but for the next fifteen minutes or so I didn't have to write a ticket and began to relax. Then a very tired old Ford pickup with a camper was sent my way, and it was full of the grubbiest backwoods "brush Okies" I had ever seen. The pickup looked like something right out of *Grapes of Wrath*. Out piled the lads, and from their body smells, they had to be buffalo hunters! Jesus, what a stink, breath as well as body odor, I thought, all the while trying to be polite. It had to make a pretty picture, me trying to stay upwind of them as we talked. I don't know what the hell these lads had just eaten, but I am sure the coyotes had rejected it earlier! I hurriedly crawled into the dirtiest camper I had ever been inside in my life to examine their five legal deer, then started to get the hell out of there as fast as I could before I got scabies, fleas, or some disease I would have trouble explaining to my wife.

As I crawled out of the camper, which was stuffed full of junk, sleeping bags, camping gear, rifles, and dead deer, I slid my hand over the top of a sleeping bag. It had a hard lump in it! Looking back at the lads, who were watching me, I got a set of hard stares. If it had come down to a gunfight, I would have been hard pressed to know which one to shoot first based on those glares. They all looked to be as hard cases as any I had seen in a long time. Placing my hand back on that dirty sleeping bag, I again felt the lump. There was something inside, all right. Opening the zipper, I was greeted with the sharp, offensive odor of an unclean sleeping bag and a skinned deer leg. I unzipped the bag, and out popped an entire doe. I hollered at Dean, who came right over. He crawled speedily into the camper, then turned around and crawled just as quickly right back out. As he tried to control a dry heave—and his glee that it was me in the camper and not him—he told me he would collect identification from the lads as his share of the work.

"Thanks, Dean," I mumbled to myself and began a really intensive search of the camper. Inside five other sleeping bags were the carcasses of four more does and one antelope. All illegal— and the lads' silence and hard stares showed that they knew it. I seized all their critters and commenced writing up the men for their violations. An idea occurred to me, and I took Dean off to one side and asked him to check to see if any of the men had any priors or "wants." In a few moments Dean came back and gave me the high sign indicating that we had a problem. As I continued to put evidence tags on the animals, he whispered, "Felony warrant, homicide!" That was great, just great, I thought. We really hadn't prepared for this eventuality, but here it was, and we had to act. Dean moved out of earshot as I asked him silently, "Which one is the dude we need to watch out for?" My answer came quickly. Good old Dean had already called the cavalry. Up drove two Nevada Highway Patrol units.

"Which one of you fellows is Tresch?" the first officer asked. I pointed to Dean and continued my work, making sure I could get to the lads' rifles before anyone else. It was a good thought because one of the men made a determined move toward the camper. In an instant I was in front of the door. The chap with the outstanding felony warrant, and bad breath to match, hissed, "Get out of my way, asshole!"

"If you feel froggy, jump," I retorted, and he hesitated. In an instant the two Highway Patrol officers were on him like chickens on a June bug, and on went the iron bracelets. As he was led away cussing and kicking, I finished with the remaining lads, who were now subdued. They responded satisfactorily to all my questions, and I finished up my part of the show and let them get on down the road, minus their critters and with the understanding that they would be in federal court within a month— including their arrested buddy, if possible. I walked into the ag station and washed my hands and arms to try to get rid of the stench I had acquired inside that smelly camper. It's one thing to be poor, but you don't have to be dirty, I thought as I walked back outside to another hunter patiently waiting for me to check him out and let him get on his way. This is the last time I will poke my nose into an operation like this, I thought as I began the routine all over again. Well ... not really.

Several more vehicles moved through my checkpoint, and all was well. I helped Dean move a moose that had been taken in Colorado over to the evidence area, where good old Tim was loading the truck and trailer for the ninth time that day. He turned, covered with dirt, hair, dried blood, and sweat, and said with a large grin, "Ain't we having a grand time?" I could have killed him for still having a sense of humor after so many hours of damn hard work. He was, and I imagine still is, a hell of a man!

A big Ford pickup towing a trailer pulled up, and out jumped the driver, who walked over to me and asked, "What the hell is going on?"

I identified myself and filled him in on what we were doing, and he said, "What you are doing here is in violation of the Fourth Amendment to the Constitution."

I said, "No, it isn't. We have already checked with the U.S. attorney regarding this roadblock. Just as long as we treat everyone the same we don't violate anyone's right to be secure against unreasonable searches and seizures."

"What do you want us to do, asshole? We need to get on down the road," he replied angrily.

I switched to my most professional stance, realizing I had a hard case, probably a cop, on my hands. It turned out that all in his party were California Highway Patrol officers from the San Francisco Bay area. They were hauling their game, four elk and four deer, in the horse trailer they were towing. The driver jumped into the trailer and threw their stuff every which way as he tried to locate all the required tags for the animals. As it turned out, he found the tags for all of the animals except his. He went through the trailer one more time, but to no avail. His tags were not with the meat. Realizing I had an explosion coming, I called Dean over just to keep an eye on things.

"Well, sir," I said, "in light of you not being able to find your carcass tags, I will need your hunting license and driver's license."

"What the hell for, asshole?" was the less-than-polite reply. "As you can see, everything was properly tagged, and mine just happened to be lost. It's not like we were trying to break the law, being officers of the law ourselves."

"Because Montana law requires the animal to be tagged prior to transport, and neither your deer nor elk are tagged, and you seem unable to locate your own licenses and tags. That makes them illegal under Montana law and also a violation of federal law."

"Screw federal law," he said. "And we aren't in Montana, so their goddamned law doesn't mean much." I don't know what law school this lad had graduated from, but he must have slept through most of the classes. Having had a gutful of this lad, I was a little more stern with my second request for identification, and I think he finally got the message: driver's license or jail! Out came the license and his Highway Patrol badge. I ignored the badge and asked him to take his license out of his wallet. This he did, tearing his wallet in the process. Damn, this lad had a bad temper for a cop, I thought as I began filling out the pink slip. He kept his cool until I seized his elk and deer, then confronted me and said I wasn't taking either animal. I advised him about the penalties for obstructing a federal officer in the performance of his duties in such a manner that he knew my next move would be to throw his arrogant hind end to the ground, put on the handcuffs, and take him off to jail. About that time his buddies dragged him away, and I seized the animals and marked them with evidence tags. I thanked the other lads for their cooperation, then saw the irate lad walking briskly back over to me. Thinking this might be the prelude to a "hoorah," I turned to face him. He stopped just inches from my face and said, "Come into my town anytime, asshole, and you won't get out without going to jail, even if I have to drum up the charges."

"Thank you," I said, then turned to finish my work, hoping the lad would let loose on me. If he did, I figured I would throw his ass so far into the jail cell that he would find out the chickens back there had square faces! He stood there for a moment, not getting any satisfaction from me, then whirled and went back to his embarrassed friends. Dean just shrugged, mouthed the word *asshole,* and returned to his post for more vehicle inspection work. As it turned out, 17 percent of the lads we caught that day were police officers of some sort. That is a pretty sad testimony, but the good, bad, and ugly portions of our society are represented at every level, from priests to police.

By now it was getting dark, and the three of us had been working thirteen straight hours without letup or food. But on the lads came with their game, and on into the night we worked. Tim had now completed fifteen trips to the locker plant and told us that by his last trip the locker plant manager had brought in four extra meat cutters to keep ahead of what we were bringing in. I checked a dozen or so more rigs before I was confronted by a bus that had been converted into a luxury mobile home. It was towing a large six-wheeled trailer that had been custom designed for hauling meat and had a portable generator for a cooling system built right into it. I could sure smell money here. The six lads on board were all aerospace moguls from the San Fernando Valley and let me know it the minute they stepped off the bus. They had heard on their CB about the roadblock and were prepared, handing me all their licenses in one packet, including those of their wives. I didn't see any women on board, so my senses went to the on-guard mode. After checking their Wyoming licenses for antelope, deer, and elk, I asked to see their game. They proudly swung open the doors to their meat trailer, and what a sight met my eyes. The cooler was carrying skinned and hanging deer, elk, and antelope for every tag in the party, thirty-six animals in all. The meat had been beautifully cleaned, and every one of the critters was tagged in accordance with the law. After checking all the tags, I noted the wound placement and gender of every animal allegedly taken by the absent wives on the backs of their licenses.

Crawling out of their meat wagon, I asked the lads where the ladies were, expecting to hear that they were gambling in Reno. Instead the owner of the bus told me, "They went home earlier after filling out because they were planning a wedding." I always got suspicious when one lad spoke for all the others. The last time I looked, God had given all of us tongues, I thought. I told the men I would be calling their wives to verify their kills and asked for their home phone numbers. Dean went by, dragging another seized antelope, and I felt that God was working His mental magic on the lads again. It always amazed me how God timed certain actions for their greatest effect. Every set of eyes in that group of apparently stolid men was on that poor speedster of the plains, recently removed from the sagebrush and now being dragged ingloriously across the pavement. I could sense that I probably had a case of hunters using someone else's tags to extend their opportunities.

Recording all their phone numbers, I told the lads to sit tight and I would start calling. The looks I got showed some concern, but certainly not the level I expected. When I called the ladies, I was surprised to find them all home and to hear each one admit to killing an antelope, deer, and elk while hunting with their husbands. However, every one of them, when asked where she had shot the animal, said after some hesitation, "In the head."

Wrong! Every animal tagged with the women's tags had been body-shot. I also asked on what day they had shot their animals, and again every one of them gave a different day than the ones indicated on "their" tags. Last but not least, I asked what type of rifle they had used. Two refused to answer and said I would need to continue this discussion with their husbands. The other four said they had used their husbands' rifles. They were unsure whether the rifles were semiautos, bolt-actions, or pumps. In fact, one lady said she had used a double-barrel! Suffice it to say that the ladies didn't appear to have accompanied the lads on the hunt, much less done a whale of a lot of hunting of any kind. As a parting shot, I asked two of the ladies how the wedding plans were going, and all I drew was a "Huh?"

Walking back, I put on my worst-case-scenario face and made sure they all noticed my body language. Then, aware that every eye in that bus was on me, I stopped to talk to Dean. We discussed how great it would be to have about a dozen hamburgers to eat, all the while pointing to and looking at the bus as if we were in deep discussion on whether we should just eat the lads right there in the parking lot. Humor is an integral part of any law enforcement officer's makeup, especially a wildlife officer. Even if it's dark humor, I've always thought it's better than ulcers.

With that bit of acting done, I walked over to the idling bus, stopping on the way to help Tim throw a particularly large mule deer into the evidence trailer as a final show of the lads' upcoming destiny. When I reached the front steps of the bus, I looked at the men and said, "Well, the ladies tried to cover for you lads, but every one of them missed most of the important questions that would have cleared you folks."

There was a howl of denial from the bus that would have put a pack of wolves to shame. I raised my hand to stop the caterwauling for a moment. "Lads," I continued, "I really don't have the time to argue with you. Suffice it to say, you are in deep trouble as far as federal law is concerned, and I wouldn't counsel you to lie to me anymore and compound the matter. I am in the position of being able to seize not only the game animals transported in interstate commerce but the items associated with the crime as well. That means the guns, equipment used to carry the critters, and the like, which includes this really nice bus and meat trailer."

I let the thought of walking home sink in, then said, "I am going outside for a few moments, and you guys decide how you want to proceed: the easy way or the hard way." I left the bus before they could ask any questions and, walking off a little way, lit a strong Parodi cigar and waited. It took longer than I figured. About twenty minutes later, after much animation among the fellows in that bus, the door opened. The man who had told me that the ladies had gone home to plan for the wedding walked over and said, "What happens if we tell you the truth?"

"Well, I will need the whole truth and not something flavored with 'wedding plans,'" I answered. "Second, the meat will be seized if it is illegal, and personal information will be taken on each and every one of you for a subsequent filing of an information, or complaint, for violation of the federal Lacey Act for illegal interstate transport of wildlife. If you are fully truthful, I will not seize the bus or meat trailer."

"OK," he said and went back to his buddies. More animation followed, including everyone digging out his wallet as if to check what kind of cash they had on hand. Damn, this was more fun than all get-out. If the lads confessed to what I thought they were going to, I was just moments away from seizing thirty-six animals in one fell swoop!

Out of the bus trooped all the lads. The "wedding plans" man said, "All right, we screwed up and would like to set this mess straight."

"OK," I said. "What happened?"

"Well, we just figured if we got the wives to purchase licenses along with us, we would have a better shoot and could hunt longer. After we killed their game for them, we all called our spouses and told them what to say just in case any game wardens tried to break our stories." He gave me a "your turn" stare.

"You know," I said, "we do this for a living. We run across just about every kind of story you could imagine to cover the taking of illegal game. What made you guys think you could break the system?"

"I never thought of it that way, I guess it was pretty stupid of us, huh?"

Nodding, I turned to the others and said, "Are all of you in agreement with this lad? Did all of you fill your wife's license?"

They all either nodded or mumbled that they had. I stared at them for a few moments for effect. "Lads," I said, "you may beat us many times before we catch you, but it is darned sure not worth it being caught even once." They just stared and listened, embarrassed at the turn in events. I continued, "Keep in mind, gentlemen, that we have seen this scenario so many times that we have put a number on it. In case you are interested, this story you just told me is what we call 'Story 3B.'" The story told by their collective eyes was total humiliation. One minute heading down the road with a trailerload of game and a gutful of whiskey and good food; the next minute a face filled with federal agent. "Also, gentlemen, I could file aiding-and-abetting charges against the ladies if I wished." Now it got *really* quiet. The downcast looks told me that these lads were beaten and that to stack charges would not improve the lesson, so I just let that thought hang.

With camera in hand I recorded the event as Tim, Dean, and some off-duty state ag officers assisted in moving thirty-six deer, antelope, and elk from the hunters' trailer to our pickup, trailer, and tarps on the pavement. My pickup and trailer made some kind of a picture as they bulged at the seams with illegal game. Other hunters gathered around and silently passed judgment on the men who had gotten a little too greedy and been caught by the long arm of the law. That sight made a good lesson for those still passing through the check station, so I asked Tim to take a break for a while so others could see and, I hoped, learn from it. I figured each person viewing that mess would talk to at least three other people when he or she got home, and in the long run maybe that story would help curtail future violations. My idea didn't last long, though, because other seized evidence kept piling up, and finally Tim had to make another run to the Reno plant to prevent a huge pile of evidence from getting any larger.

Dean and I tiredly continued into the dark of the night, talking to returning hunters and seizing the game we identified as having been illegally taken and transported. Over-limits and closed-season pheasants, trout, deer, sage hen, sharp-tailed grouse, antelope, ducks, geese, elk, and other wildlife continued to flow through the check station. Animals taken by a shooter on another license, animals taken during the closed season, animals of the wrong sex or species, spoiled animals, animals whose tags were altered or mutilated or that hadn't been tagged at all— Dean and I saw it all that day! By now I needed wheels attached to my tail end to keep it from dragging. We had been at this endeavor since six A.M., and I mean at it full tilt. It was hard to get time to even go to the bathroom, much less eat or drink anything. It was now around nine P.M., and the pace was just beginning to slow a little when I noticed a Chevy pickup with a topper, towing a trailer, moving out of the ag area and starting down the road. I noticed that the three men in the truck were unshaven, with about a week's growth of beard, just like all the hunters I had seen that day. As the pickup pulled slowly by me, I saw that the camper shell was filled to the top with gear. In the front of the bed, next to the cab, was a freezer. As this outfit passed within five feet of where I was standing, I noticed a bloody palm print on the side of the freezer next to the lid. I hollered at the driver to stop, but the truck kept going.

The ag inspector yelled to me, "It's OK, they haven't been hunting." Ignoring that information, I whistled in a fashion that even God could hear and that certainly got the attention of the lad driving the Chevy. He stopped and rolled down his window as I approached. Walking by the pickup, I could see a Coleman stove in the bed of the truck, and now my interest was really up, as was my gut feeling—and not just from not having been fed for more than fifteen hours!

"You lads been camping?" I asked after identifying myself.

There was a little hesitation, and then the driver of the Chevy said, "Uh, yeah." The pause before his answer and the fact that his left hand had a lot of knife nicks on it, such as one would get doing a lot of butchering, increased my level of interest.

"Why don't you lads just pull over here where you are out of the way of other exiting vehicles?" I said. "I have a few questions I need to ask you."

"Why?" came the driver's reply. "We just told the other officer we haven't been hunting."

Ignoring his statement, I said, "You fellows need to pull over here for a moment; this won't take long." I turned and beckoned for the men to follow me. Once the truck was parked out of the traffic stream, I asked the driver to get out, and he did. His body language and tone of voice told me this man was hiding something. Taking him off to one side, I asked, "Where were you lads camping?" He told me in the Pinedale area of Wyoming. He wasn't prepared for my asking why they were camping.

He hesitated and shifted his weight from foot to foot and finally said, "We do this every year, me and my partners."

"Why?"

"We just do, that's all," came his impatient reply.

"What is in the freezer?" was my next question, and that one really hit home, as his body language, lack of eye contact, and hesitation demonstrated.

"Uh, uh, it's empty. I'm just hauling it back for a friend."

"Why the bloody palm print on the side?" was my next question.

"What bloody palm print?" he said, surprised.

"That one," I said pointing to the telltale print.

There was abject silence. Then he said, "I don't think that's blood."

"Do you mind if I take a look?" I asked.

He looked at me and then said, "No, go ahead, but it is buried by a lot of other junk and will be very hard to get to."

I could tell he was hoping that all the other material in front of the freezer would keep me from looking into it. We walked to the rear of his truck, and he opened the topper door and lowered the tailgate. "Go ahead and be my guest," was his not-too-convincing invitation. I started unloading the gear so I could crawl in to inspect the contents of the freezer, and lo and behold, three of the items I took out were cased hunting rifles. I gave him a look that demanded an explanation of the rifles, but he just shrugged and said, "We did some target practice."

By now his two buddies were standing by the rear of the vehicle as well, but they were not saying a word. When I got about halfway through the mess in the truck, I could clearly see the red stain on the side of the freezer. It was blood, no doubt about it! Finally crawling to within reaching distance, I tried to open the freezer lid. It was locked. As I turned to crawl back out, I noticed that the freezer cord was plugged into an extension cord, which was rolled up near the tailgate. There was no reason to have the freezer hooked up in that manner unless they were connecting it to an electrical outlet to keep something inside from spoiling when they stopped at night! I asked the driver for the key to the freezer. He looked at his buddies, and finally one of them reached into his pocket and, without a word, handed me a key. Back into the truck I went and unlocked the freezer. I then crawled out again without opening the lid and, sitting on the tailgate, confronted the men with an all-knowing stare.

"Lads," I said, "before I look into that freezer, is there anything you want to say?" I could tell from the looks on their faces that I was about to uncover something that would leave them standing in crap up to their eyes!

They looked at each other for what seemed an eternity before the man who had handed me the key said, "There's a little camp meat in there."

"What kind?" I asked.

After another long silence he said, "A little antelope."

I asked why they hadn't told the ag inspector they had been hunting. "Because we didn't want to be unloaded and delayed in our trip home," came the reply. I realized my gut hunch was about to prove itself. Crawling back inside the truck, I opened the freezer lid a few inches (the topper wouldn't let me open it any wider than that) and reached in. It was full to the top with what felt like large slabs of wrapped, frozen meat.

I got back out of the truck and said, "Lads, what kind of meat are we talking here again?"

"Antelope," came the hesitant reply.

"How many?"

There was a pregnant pause, and finally the driver said, "I don't know."

I looked at them for a long moment and then said, "Either you folks can unload the rest of your gear so we can drag that freezer out where I can look into it, or we will."

I could see the resignation in their faces. The driver said, "We can pull it out for you."

I said, "Let's go," and they did. In about five minutes their gear was stacked on the pavement and the freezer had been moved to the rear of the truck bed. I called Dean over to assist me, and we opened the lid to the freezer. It was full of what appeared to be hindquarters of some kind of animal—just hindquarters, nothing else! I gave Dean a look that said, Even after a long day like the one we've been having, the world still

has a surprise or two for us! The disgust on Dean's face confirmed my thoughts.

I asked, "What kind of critters, lads?"

"Just antelope," one man answered.

"From what I can see it appears to only be hindquarters; is
that true?"

"Yes," came the dejected reply.

"How many?" I asked.

"About twenty."

I just looked at them and they at me. Then Dean, Tim, and I
began unloading the chunks of meat from the freezer. They were
indeed nothing but the hindquarters from twenty-three antelope! None of us had much more to say because of the disgust
felt on the one side and the embarrassment on the other. As I
wrote out the pink-slip information, learning that the rest of the
animals' bodies had been left for the foxes and coyotes, Tim and
Dean loaded the frozen hindquarters for transport to the locker
plant. It was getting very late, but because of the huge amount of
meat we had been bringing to the plant, the manager had kept a
crew on to meet our continuing needs.

Having finished with the lads who had taken a few too many
antelope, I returned to the line to continue the work we had
started almost eighteen hours earlier. We had decided to end our
operation at midnight, and that magic hour was almost upon us.
My feet felt as if someone had smacked the piss out of them with
a bamboo stick. My big guts had long ago eaten the little guts
and were now hungrily eyeing my gizzard, and my eyes felt like
two holes pissed in the snow. Damn, that's tired!

Fortunately the traffic was also slowing down, and the three
of us could finally get together and compare notes. Tim had
made nineteen trips to the meat locker with the evidence we had
seized throughout the day, and at that point we had written 110
citations for violations of the Lacey Act and the Black Bass Act.

About ten minutes before midnight, as we were cleaning up,
one of the ag inspectors asked if we were still open for business.
I looked over the vehicle he was holding, a large Ford 4x4 with a

cab-over camper. There were three grubby guys inside, all watching for my response. Their eager look told me I should look the lads over, so I signaled to the inspector to run them on over. As they pulled up, I noticed that the vehicle wasn't particularly dirty, and nothing looked out of the ordinary except that it appeared to be heavily loaded in the tail end. But I assumed it was probably the weight of the camper and let that clue pass.

I asked if the men had been hunting. They answered that they had been hunting mountain lion in Idaho but hadn't had any luck. I requested their hunting licenses, which they began to dig out of their wallets, and while I was waiting I looked over the inside of the cab for anything out of place. There were spent .22 shells all over the floor and a spotlight poorly concealed under the passenger side of the seat with the cord still hooked up to the cigarette lighter. By now my interest was up: tired or not, this setup smelled! The men handed me their mountain lion hunting licenses, and I noticed that these were the cheapest licenses a nonresident like these fellows could buy in Idaho.

I asked, "What's with the spotlight?"

There was a pause as if they hadn't thought I would be able to see it the way they had it hidden among their feet. Then the driver said, "Oh, we've been using it to spotlight coons in apple orchards." A quick check of the Idaho regulations revealed that one could lawfully spotlight raccoons in that state during that year, so there was no violation there.

I then asked the driver if I could look in the back of the camper, saying we would let them get on down the road toward home afterward. There was a telling hesitation before he opened the pickup door and stepped out. As he walked to the rear of the truck, he said, "I lost the key to the camper door, so we can't get in." I had heard that story so many times from bad guys that I called it Story Number 6!

I said, "Hand me your car keys and let me try."

He hesitated again and then slowly handed the keys to me. I found one that looked like a key to a camper door and tried it in the lock. Bingo, it worked like a champ. Swinging open the door, I saw why he had "lost his key." Stacked from floor to ceiling of the camper and covered with a canvas tarp were eight large mule deer and white-tail deer bucks. Every one of them had a huge body (some over three hundred pounds), and they had some of the largest antler racks (two of the mule deer exceeded forty inches) I had ever seen! None were tagged in accordance with Idaho law, and I already knew that none of these men had Idaho deer tags. That explained why they had the spotlight. It's easy to kill such large bucks if one uses a spotlight or takes them on their wintering grounds after the open season.

Turning to the man quietly standing beside me, I asked, "I don't suppose these are legal or you have a story for these, do you?" He just gave me a look like that of an animal just before a *T-rex* finishes it off. I beckoned Dean over and got the remaining two lads out of the vehicle.

"Gentlemen," I began, "we have a small problem here—eight small problems, to be exact. I don't suppose any of you have deer licenses or an explanation to cover that rather nice over-limit of deer I just discovered in the back of the camper, do you?" Before they could respond or get their feet under them, I fired another question at them: "Were the deer taken with that spotlight I saw on the floor of your truck?" No response was forthcoming to either of these questions. This interview was getting boring. "Well, gentlemen, in light of your lack of explanation, I have no choice but to record the information for later federal court action and seize the deer." Without a word, all three of them reached into their pockets, withdrew their wallets, and handed me their driver's licenses. Damn, that was too easy, and unusual to say the least. No one just reaches for a wallet and hands you a driver's license before being asked unless that person has been there before. ... Without tipping my hand, I excused myself, took Dean off to one side, and asked him to check to see whether these lads had any "wants."

In a few moments Dean came back and quietly told me that all three had outstanding felony warrants for theft and burglary from the San Francisco Police Department! Without missing a beat, I continued to take information from the men while Dean went for reinforcements. I took my time and was able to hold them up for another fifteen minutes. Then I told them they were under arrest for the illegal transportation of wildlife in violation of federal law. There was instant panic in their eyes, not because of me but because of what would be discovered if they went to jail. But they got control of themselves in an instant and began to plead with me to let them get back to work; after all, they had been very cooperative. About that time two sheriff's deputies arrived, and the lads knew the jig was up. You could just see the stuffing run right out of them. After a few questions to establish their identities, the deputies slipped the bracelets on and arranged for a wrecker to remove the camper rig. It didn't end there because it turned out that the truck they were driving had been stolen in Martinez, California, about two weeks earlier! I don't know when those lads got out of the slammer, but you can bet your sweet tail end it was some time after they chose to saunter through the first Tahoe-Truckee roadblock.

After that last rig with the bad lads and their warrants, we shut down the roadblock and retreated to a quiet place in the parking lot to gather our thoughts and rest our sore feet. We had been at the effort for eighteen straight hours and had written a total of 113 citations, seized over ten thousand pounds of illegal game, opened the eyes of hunters and various state regulatory officials for years to come, and flattened out three perfectly good pairs of feet by standing that long on the pavement! Ultimately we were to garner over $20,000 in fines over the next couple of months' appearances or forfeitures to the federal treasury for our very busy day's work!

Since that day at the Tahoe-Truckee check station, I have initiated and sometimes supervised many other roadblocks throughout the nation. I learned to relish the work associated with them, especially the chance to work with many fine conservation officers and to meet many really good American sportsmen and their families. These operations have all had the same results: a lot of lads were cited for screwing up and a lot of game was seized—to be given to the needy if it were properly utilized. Jack Downs, my boss at the time of this first roadblock, was surprised and somewhat pissed at the rather large meat-processing bill he received for our efforts that day, but he was also very pleased that we had stung so many knotheads. I had made arrangements with the Reno locker plant to charge us only for the meat end-product, that is, by the pound cut and wrapped. The government was charged for 5,140 pounds of cut and wrapped meat! We ended up with 100 percent convictions for our efforts, even for the lads who went to jail for their outstanding felony warrants. It seems that they sold some of their property to raise the money needed to get out from under the federal charges. Oh well, any port in a storm, I guess! After the various convictions the meat was distributed to numerous churches in the Reno, Sparks, Sacramento, and San Francisco areas for needy families to enjoy this treat of a lifetime.

As I think back on that roadblock and how different such an operation is today, I just marvel. Man, you talk about day and night! Today's roadblocks, if done properly, take six months to prepare, employ anywhere from one hundred to three hundred officers, and cost about $50,000 for a three-day operation! A very different kettle of fish from that small first roadblock we ran at the Tahoe-Truckee Agriculture Quarantine Station so long ago (oh well—one ranger, one riot). I guess the difference reflects the change in the times. I have often wondered what would have happened if the Donner party had had access to the thousands of pounds of wildlife we seized instead of having only each other! But it is obvious that though times change, history doesn't. Unfortunately, with the current changes in Service enforcement policies, I doubt that large interstate roadblocks like those of old will ever be run again. It is amazing how negative politics and lack of good leadership can ruin a good thing. It is too bad because the ultimate losers will be the American people and the animals, large and small, not to mention the loss that will be felt by humanity in the days yet to come.

4
Throm-Throm-Throm

THE FOUR MEN HURRIEDLY UNLOADED what appeared to be five one-hundred-pound sacks of whole-kernel corn from the bed of the pickup into their duck boat until, with passengers, freeboard began to become somewhat of an issue. Once that task was finished, the tallest and heaviest of the lads, after looking around the duck-club area one more time to make sure no one was watching, drove the truck about a third of a mile away and parked on the island's levee to watch for intruders and wait for his buddies to finish. The other three men gingerly got into their heavily loaded duck boat and carefully paddled out through a lane previously cut in the standing, flooded corn to their duck blind and designated shooting area. Little did this foursome realize that their little act had gone unnoticed by everyone but the critters in and around the shooting area and one marsh hawk lazily drifting on a microthermal current alongside the levee — except for one set of eyes peering through an old pair of U.S. Navy 7x50 binoculars.

It was December 1970 on Mandeville Island in the San Joaquin Delta marshes, which are located in the north-central valley of California not far from the city of Stockton. It was waterfowl hunting season, and I was in the midst of performing my duties as a U.S. game management agent. I had always enjoyed the life in and around a marsh, especially on windy, overcast days. Maybe it had something to do with my primal nature — I don't know, but I just knew a marsh was the place for a fellow like me to be in the late fall. The San Joaquin Delta marshes were the most unique I had ever been in up to that time in my career, and my level of joy at being alive and on the hunt that December

afternoon was high. Hundreds of skeins of ducks, mostly pintail, and geese, mostly white-fronts, traded back and forth across
the blue sky looking for that special place imprinted eons ago in
their genetic makeup as they ended, for the most part, their migration south. A soft breeze blew from the northwest, carrying
with it the smells of rotting vegetation, wet wood, damp peat
soil, and other substances that make up the very essence of life.
Lying totally hidden on my side in the heavy grasses of the Mandeville Island levee, I was intensely aware of the dry leaves and
stalks rustling quietly around me and the ever-present marsh
wren, unconcerned by my still presence, as it moved around my
shoulders and propped-up arms looking for life forms to con-
sume that would help to sustain its life for another day.

My joy on that fine December day was brought into even
sharper focus by the drama unfolding in my binoculars some
250 yards to the east. Several hundred acres of standing unharvested corn that had been converted to a very expensive duck
club in the northeast quarter of the island had my now undi-
vided attention. From my vantage point high on the side of the
levee, invisible to all but the marsh wren, I was able to watch the
three men in the duck boat as they moved around near their
duck blind. A man in the bow pushed the boat along with a long
oar while the two in the stern opened the burlap sacks and proceeded to dump corn into the waters of the pond no more than
five yards from their decoy set. For an instant in the afternoon's
fading light it appeared that they were dumping liquid gold over
the stern of their boat into the placid, dark-blue waters of the
marsh. If what they were doing hadn't been so wrong, with such
serious consequences for the ducks and geese at a moment yet to
violently come, that scene, just for its colors that beautiful day,
would have been one of those special moments to remember forever. However, this illegal act is called "sweetening the pot" in
the wildlife officer's jargon, and these lads certainly had a corner
on the market. Over the side and into the water went all five
sacks of whole-kernel corn. Most went in around the decoys,
but one sack was emptied in the water around the edges of their

blind as if to decoy the unsuspecting waterfowl even closer to the waiting guns come shoot day.

Man, they already had a natural "honey hole" with their hundreds of acres of flooded, standing unharvested corn and a duck blind right smack dab in the middle of the whole potential killing field, I thought. I shook my head at the greed being played out before me. Adding the five sacks of corn to the rich "duck soup" already naturally in existence in the pond would do nothing but drag every duck and goose for miles around into that shotgunners' delight. ... No matter how many times I observed the same sequence of events, it never made any sense to me. These four lads had all the money in the world (I already knew who they were), a duck club with some of the finest duck hunting in the world, an absolutely incredible number of ducks in the wintering area surrounding and including their island, a limit of eight ducks and six geese per person that year in California (way more than anyone, even a fellow my size, could eat in a day), and the solitude and privacy for an outstanding hunt any day of the week. What more could a man want or need? I thought sadly—sadly because I knew that in order for me to have the best possible case against these politically influential men, I would have to let them kill a sizable number of birds over the baited area before I sprang the trap. Anything less would mean a protracted fight in federal court, with unpredictable results. So no matter how I cut it, I would indeed have a killing field in my lap before it was all over.

Finished with their devil's work, the men took one more long look around to see if anyone had shared in their golden secret. Satisfied that they were alone, they paddled back to where the boat had originally been docked, and one of the men waved his hunting cap back and forth in the air until he got the pickup driver's attention. As the pickup moved back down into this picture, the three men picked up their gear and empty telltale grain sacks and, after one more look around for anything out of place, loaded merrily into the back of the waiting truck and started to leave the shooting area. Then, as an afterthought, the pickup stopped and one lad ran back to the duck boat moored at their little dock. Getting into the boat, he carefully picked up all the dropped kernels of corn that had fallen into the bottom of the boat and tossed them into the standing corn. That way any routine check by a game warden, at least by one who was tired and not really on his toes, would fail to turn up the preliminary evidence of an illegal act.

That act finished, the man took one more look over the boat bottom and rejoined his fellow soon-to-be outlaws. They drove out of the island bottom on a peat farm road, then moved up onto the levee road and drove to the clubhouse, no doubt for several drinks to celebrate their good fortune at not being seen by a pesky game warden—or, even worse, the local federal agent (worse because being tried or appearing in federal court left little room in most situations for political influence to manifest itself).

Waiting until long after dark, when I was satisfied that I would not be seen, I put on my chest-high waders, slipped down off the levee, and walked to the duck-shooting area via the boat channel, wading out into the decoys in question, all the while carefully avoiding any large peat cracks under the water. Peat soil, once flooded, has a tendency to crack open, leaving very deep and sometimes wide chasms for the unsuspecting wader to fatally discover. To counter that hazard, one must learn to shuffle one's feet along the bottom in an attempt to safely discover the cracks with one's toes before stepping into them, then carefully step over Mother Nature's dangerous traps. An additional safety measure is to carry a substantial wooden rod so that if one does fall into a large peat crack, one can throw the rod sideways across the chasm, thereby preventing any further descent into the potential watery grave, and eventually work oneself out of the danger. As a coup de grâce, the water found in peat areas is highly acidic, so if one does fall into such a death trap, it is just a short matter of time before your body is largely no more as it rests under the coffee-colored waters. Now you see why God watches over little children, fools, and game wardens. ...

Corn was everywhere underfoot, as were numerous mallards

and pintail already feeding in their newfound "buffet." Gathering up several scoops of the corn as evidence, I placed it into one of the plastic bags carried by every good game agent and, after drawing a map of the layout, beat a hasty retreat to my original hiding place to avoid discovery. Catching my breath and seeing that all was clear, I sprinted over the top of the levee, keeping my silhouette low, and hastened down the outside bank to where my boat lay hidden from view in an erosion crack at the levee's edge. I grinned to myself as I removed the camouflage netting and plants from my boat and idled away from the levee and back into the main canal. These lads are mine, I thought as my fingers sought out the damp, cold, yet comforting plastic bags of corn in my pocket. There could be no doubt that the lads hunting in this area come shoot day would not only shoot over this baited area but would also more than likely kill large over-limits of ducks and geese. They would make a fine addition to those Buck Del Nero (the local game warden) and I had caught earlier that week breaking the federal wildlife laws on several private islands near the now baited shooting area.

I knew that the men I had just observed would claim that the corn I would identify as bait had come from the surrounding standing corn and had been distributed in the water by masses of feeding birds knocking the heads off the standing corn. I had heard that same story so many times before that I had given it a number, 7c. That was why it was nice to have witnessed the entire operation, not to mention the fact that I had filmed key portions of the event with my personal Super 8 zoom-lens camera. I chuckled, knowing that the source of the "bait" corn would be a sticking point in any subsequent trial, so I would hold out my film until the very last legal minute so as to put the final nail in the lid of my four shooters' coffin. What was even funnier was that this surveillance had not been planned. The island was always home to many ducks and geese because of the land management system of leaving unharvested corn standing and then flooding it. I had been in the area and wanted to take a look at the ducks, so I had parked my boat (camouflaging it just in case something illegal happened or the gamekeeper came along) and crawled up and over the levee. While I was watching the great flocks of ducks purely for my own enjoyment, along with practicing my techniques for identifying ducks at a distance, the four men had driven in and commenced to do their deed right in front of God and everybody. It just so happened that God had put me in the right place at the wrong time for the lads in question. Who knows? In any case, Newton's Law regarding opposite and equal reactions was soon to come into full play.

For the next several days I worked alone by boat near the duck club. I did not expect the club members to shoot until the coming Saturday (the next club shoot day), but I wanted to make sure that if they did shoot, I would be there to stop the carnage and provide a proper greeting. Friday evening found me back at my hiding place on the Mandeville Island levee, watching my suspects' shooting area. The area was alive with thousands of ducks and geese that by now had discovered the extra corn. It looked like a swarm of bees going to and from that area, and no doubt the next day would bring a shoot beyond anyone's wildest dreams—and, if things went wrong, a game management agent to boot.

Satisfied that no one was nearby, I crept into the baited area at dark, much to the alarm of the feeding waterfowl, collected another bait sample, and got the hell out of there. Getting that bait sample was considerably tougher than collecting the first one. These folks were pretty smart. They only baited once, several days before they were to shoot over the area. That way when they came to shoot, the ducks would have cleaned up most of the bait, and any game warden who happened to check that day would more than likely not find enough corn in the bottom of the pond to arouse any suspicion. Pretty smart unless you are a game warden used to working the waterfowl scene who has seen that stunt pulled many times. Hustling back to my base marina, I fueled the boat and made ready for the morrow's adventure. Little did I realize what an adventure that would be—almost my last. ...

The alarm went off at one A.M. The hour didn't matter because I had slept badly anyway, as I was wont to do before any important detail. I strapped on my sidearm, threw a down coat over my shoulders, and went out to meet whatever the day would bring. Leaving the motel and stepping into the darkness, I was greeted with a thick pea-soup fog! Damn, that would slow me down, not to mention make it difficult to find my island or observe my lads as they hunted over the baited area. It would also make the killing of ducks very easy because of their confusion in the fog and their hurry to land to get out of having to fly in it. Keep in mind that birds fly with their eyelids retracted or only partially closed. Any kind of moisture hitting the eyeball at speeds of forty to fifty-five miles per hour gets old fast; hence the easy killing of ducks in the fog as they try to hurry back to Mother Earth—that plus the fact that they can't see you or the blind very well in inclement weather at the speed at which they fly. All in all, flying migratory birds are very vulnerable in rain or fog, and that point was not lost on me as I hurried to get going.

Damn this fog, I thought. Why today? I was still learning the delta marsh area, and this weather would really try my limited expertise. Generally I would have Stockton Warden Buck Del Nero with me, and he would usually be driving the boat. That man was uncanny even in a fog like this. He had a sense of where to go no matter what the weather, and the fog, no matter how bad or thick it got, never seemed to bother him. I thought, Damn, Buck, why did you have to be gone at this time? I could really use you now! Hurrying to my old Dodge patrol truck, I quickly checked my gear, cranked the truck up, threw it into gear, and off I went just as fast as the fog would let me go. It was slow going, but I always prepared for the worst by leaving earlier than necessary on every detail, and that trick of the trade was serving me well now. Thundering down the road with a vengeance, I hammered into the marina where my boat was moored, hurriedly threw my gear into the boat, released the tie-downs, cranked the engine to life, pumped the bilges, and began idling out through the other boats in the marina. Since the boat did not have any windshield wipers, I had a hard time seeing through the heavy fog even with my lights on. The boat was a typical government rig, purchased from the lowest bidder. It was a 19.5-foot, V-hulled, 100-horse monster designed for deep water, not the shallows of the delta. More than once I had had to walk that last few yards in waist-deep water to the shore because of its hull configuration. That problem could have deadly consequences in this area with the deep peat cracks hidden by the coffee-colored water. Oh well, when you're young, you don't worry about things like that. You live forever, don't you?

Entering the main canal, I found it was so foggy that I had to use the boat's handheld searchlight to keep my bearings. I ran the beam along the shores of the various islands as I moved toward Mandeville Island so I could find landmarks that would help keep me on track, island hopping if you will. It was slow going, but I kept the throttle advanced as much as I dared to make up for the fog that was slowing me down. I still couldn't see out the front windshield worth a damn, so I sat on top of the back support of my seat so I could look out over the windshield into the oncoming banks of fog.

When I arrived in the large ship channel, I took a quick look and then advanced the throttle as far as I safely could in order to get through that part of my trip as rapidly as possible. The San Joaquin Delta area is a real treat. There are about one thousand islands ranging from spot size to many hundreds of acres. Intersecting all of these islands and feeding into and creating the delta are the Sacramento, San Joaquin, and Tuolumne Rivers. It just so happens that there is also a major shipping channel through the delta, allowing oceangoing ships access to the port of Stockton. Not wanting to meet a four-hundred-foot oceangoing vessel in the fog, I kept the hammer down as far as I could and kept on my heading for another island channel out of the main shipping lane. The fog continued to roll over the bow and window of the boat as I plowed along, watching the shoreline as best I could with my searchlight while constantly listening for the foghorns on the large ships that might be moving through the main shipping channel. I had on a life vest, but because of my size and the bulk of my down jacket I was unable to zip up the one-size-too-small flotation device. No matter, once out of the channel I would be in marsh backwaters and OK even if I hit something. Besides, in this fog I couldn't go very fast. That was one good thing about the "hog" I was driving, I thought; it could take a hit with the best of them because of its size, double hull, and weight.

Coming to a channel intersection, I veered to the right and began my last long run to Mandeville Island and my shooters. Changing from the main shipping channel came at a good time; I could hear the foghorn of an oceangoing vessel not too far away, and the more distance I kept between myself and those chaps the better, I thought as I wiped the fog off my face for the umpteenth time. Pushing the speed up another notch, I swung my light from side to side, trying to pick up landmarks that would guide me to Mandeville Island and my hiding place. The damned fog was really making it tough. It was getting thicker, and I was having a hard time picking up my landmarks without getting too close to the shore. There were lots of sunken pilings along the shore that had been used years ago to help build the levees around some of the islands. To hit one of them, double hull or not, might send me and the boat to the bottom, so I backed down the speed a little. To top it all off, I was getting really wet sitting up on the back of the seat looking out over the windshield. At least I was dry from my lower chest down because of the brand-new chest-high waders I was wearing.

Losing my bearings momentarily, I moved over toward another of the many islands in the marsh and followed the shoreline until I thought I recognized a landmark. I cursed to myself as I realized that I was now too far to the east, so I had to backtrack and go down another canal to the west to get back on track. I could still hear the oceangoing vessel off to the west occasionally blowing its foghorn, but he was out there in his channel and I was safely in mine, so I paid him no mind. A look at my watch showed that I would have to hustle if I was to get to my destination in time; otherwise I would be discovered by the workers on the island while still trying to hide my boat. On shoot days the landowners would have their farm laborers out and about early to walk the levees looking for trespassers—in essence, game wardens. In order to beat that early-warning system, I would have to be in place before daylight with my boat hidden. I pushed the throttle back up a notch. Zipping around the end of one island, I got a slight break in the fog and increased my speed even more to take advantage of the better visibility. Speeding along, I kept swinging the searchlight back and forth across my bow to look for island landmarks, keeping my left hand on the wheel. The fog began to thicken again, but I knew I was in a wide channel just south of Mandeville Island, so I kept the hammer down, knowing I would have time to slow down if I lost my way again.

I noticed that the fog was getting dense again, and I was going to have to slow down once more. Since I couldn't see more than twenty feet even with my searchlight, I dropped my eyes to my throttle as I began to lower my speed. When I looked back up into the searchlight beam, all I could see was a *Plimsoll line!* For those who haven't taken Oceanography 101, a Plimsoll line, or mark, is a series of marks on the side of an oceangoing vessel indicating the depth to which that ship can legally be loaded, depending on what sea it is sailing in. That recognition went through my mind just as my boat hit the oceangoing vessel with a loud *ka-thump!* The speed at which I was moving drove my boat right up and along the side of the merchant freighter at a high angle, flipping the boat onto its side and tossing me high into the air and at least twenty feet away from my boat into the black water of the shipping canal—which, I now learned the hard way, I had inadvertently reentered.

I did a complete head-over-heels flip as I hurtled over the windshield of my boat and into the darkness. It seemed that I floated for hours before *sploosh,* I hit the cold, dark December waters of the delta. I landed flat on my back, and the delta waters rushed over my head and body with a vengeance. I heard myself go, *"Aughhh,"* as the shock of immersion and the impact of hitting the icy water at twenty miles per hour forced all the air from my lungs. My down coat, which had shed my unsnapped life vest, lost all its air in a rush of bubbles as I knifed down toward the bottom of the channel. The shock was so great that I went clear to the bottom of the channel and almost headfirst into the mud before I could physically react. It was pitch dark, but as I turned to force myself upward, I could distinctly feel the icy bottom slime as my hands plunged into it. It was even colder than the water. Only a goofy biologist would think of such things as temperature differences in such a situation, I thought.

As I struggled to turn over, I became aware that icy cold water was pouring into my normally watertight chest-high waders. One leg had been torn open down the side as I sailed over the windshield of the boat. Reaching for the sheath knife on the belt that I always kept around the waders for emergencies just such as this (if the waders had been intact, the belt would have kept water from penetrating below the belt line), I became aware of another problem. *Throm-throm-throm* came the sound of the engines through the hull of the oceangoing vessel passing over me, in sequence with the *swish-swish-swish* of the slowly turning propellers. I was being slowly dragged under the damn ship almost as if in revenge for hitting it this cold, foggy morning. As if I didn't have enough to worry about, my body was telling me that more oxygen would be nice! Rolling onto my belly, I took my sheath knife and began trying to slice my way out of my new (cost $70 just two days before) chest-high waders. There was no way I could swim with them on; *they had to come off, and fast!* I thought through a rapidly fogging mind.

As I slashed at the waders in the inky darkness, the *swish-swish-swish* of the propellers passed directly over my head. Desperate now for air, I got one leg out of the waders when all of a sudden the propeller turbulence began bouncing me along the bottom, turning me from side to side and tail end over teakettle. Damn, I thought, what else is in store for me? Well, I wished I had never asked that question because I didn't have long to wait. The turbulence from the ship's propellers spun me around, slamming my head and right shoulder into the ooze of the channel bottom. I hit so hard that the knife came out of my hand, along with the last of the oxygen from my lungs! It is amazing how clearly one can think when one is starting to get in a bad sort of way. Turning over and keeping myself on the bottom (which wasn't hard with a million pounds of water in my boots and no oxygen in my lungs to buoy me up), I mentally pictured where I had lost the knife in the pitch black and reached for it. My hand hit the metal handle, and grabbing it for all I was worth, I commenced cutting off the other leg of the wader.

By now my body had had enough of this no-oxygen crap and was letting me know about it big time. I saw all kinds of colors; my head felt like it was starting to enlarge; my eyes felt like they were going to explode; my chest and lungs wanted badly to take in just a little water to relieve the pressure; and I was losing strength like sand pouring out of a sock. I finally got the other leg of the wader off, only to find myself tangled in the suspenders holding the chest portion. Jerking the suspenders off, I tried to roll over on the bottom so I could get my feet under me and push up so I could start my swim out of this situation. The turbulence was still strong, and I had to try twice to get my footing and my bearings. I could not tell up from down, hence my need to find the bottom and push in the opposite direction. God, how I wanted to suck in some air, or even water. ... I saw colors I didn't even know existed in the backs of my eyes, or so it seemed. Everything seemed to be going in slow motion. My arms hardly seemed to be moving and didn't seem to want to respond to my silent commands. And, as if I didn't have enough to worry about, the abject cold on the bottom began to tell on me. Finally I got my legs under me, and with *throm-throm-throm* as a partner I dropped my knife and pushed off with my legs with all the power I could muster.

By now I wasn't sure my arms were really working, but I felt my feet kicking like hell. I swam upward for what felt like at least an hour. My body was flat running out of gas. I was slowing down, and all I wanted to do was kick back and call it quits. I almost did. ... Then the stubborn in me said, No! Not now! I thought, Your lucky number is six. Swim just six more strokes. If that doesn't do it, then suck in the water and end it. With renewed energy from someplace I didn't know I had, I started swimming like hell, all the while *actually counting strokes* ... one ... two ... three ... four ... and on the fifth stroke I felt my arm come out of the water. I must have sounded like a whale breaching when my head broke the surface. I drew in air so forcefully that my chest and lungs actually hurt for a week afterward. I was so exhausted that for a moment I felt as if I might slip beneath the waters again because I just didn't have the energy to keep swimming in order to keep my head above water. Thank God there was still some kick in my legs, and I kept them moving while barely keeping my head above the cold water. But in a few short moments of deep breaths my arms started quickly gaining strength, and I knew I wouldn't drown because now I was aware of the intense cold I felt throughout my body.

I started to swim to a nearby island when off to my right I heard a boat motor running. It was my boat! The boat, after the collision with the merchant freighter, had slid off to one side, righted itself, and driven itself right into the tules alongside another island. It was sitting there, in gear, with the motor running. God, was I happy to hear that sound. Swimming over to my boat, I tried to lift myself over the side, but I didn't have the strength left to do it, and now the cold and my soaked jacket were seriously hampering my effort to survive. Swimming along the boat until I got to the throttle, I reached over the side and advanced it until the boat began plowing through the tules toward the island, dragging me along. Once I got into the shallow water dense with tules, the boat's forward motion stopped and I was able to partially stand up on flattened tules and drag myself over the side, dropping heavily into the bottom of the boat. I lay there for a moment to gather my strength, then pulled myself into the front seat and backed the boat off the mud and out of the tules. Clearing the prop, I headed for the marina and dry clothes as fast as the fog allowed, only to really become aware of my new plight. I could hardly grip the steering wheel, my hands were so damn cold. Hell, because of my size and excellent circulation, I rarely got cold—but I was cold now! Aware of the problems associated with hypothermia and the lack of insulating properties in my soaking-wet down coat, I sat down in the seat behind the now broken windshield to minimize the wind chill and work my way out of this island maze to safety.

Arriving what felt like twelve days later at the marina, I was so cold that I had to have someone else take the truck keys from my pants pockets and open the door of my vehicle. Stripping down to nothing, I put on the extra dry clothes I always carried with me, assisted by several duck hunters who happened to be there getting ready to go hunting. They couldn't believe my story, and neither could I. Starting up the truck, I sat there with the heater going for an hour until I stopped shaking uncontrollably. I had just had a very close call, but it wasn't my time, I forced myself to hiss through tight, blue, chattering lips. I have had very strong feelings for many years that when God wants me, he will let me know. Also, I have felt for a long time that I was being saved for something special. Until I get that chore done, whatever it is, I will be here for the duration. ...

As that thought crossed my mind, I could see that the fog was lifting and I remembered that my lads would be shooting over the baited area. Those fellows had caused me this mess, not to mention the destruction of a brand-new pair of waders that my office could ill afford to replace (or at least I knew that was the message I would hear!). I got out of the cab and walked around to the storage box in the back of my truck. Digging around in the box, I took out an old spare pair of hip boots and decided they would have to do. On they went, and down to the "sea" I went again, back out into the channel toward Mandeville Island and off to the races in the lifting fog. I found where I had missed my turn earlier that morning and even found my float vest lodged in some tules near my collision site. Since the fog was really lifting and it was now daylight, I reached my spot on the island in fine fettle.

The shooting at my baited site was hot and heavy, and that was just how I approached the area. Storming into the erosion cut in the levee, I hurriedly anchored the boat, took the levee just like Teddy Roosevelt at San Juan Hill, brushed aside the farm workers with my badge and the word "Federales" (which made them disappear like a puff of dust in a windstorm), and went right to the boat launch near the baited duck blinds. The hunters saw me beckoning them, and after a little jawboning among themselves, two of them left the blind, got into their boat, and rowed over to me.

"Can we help you?" came the falsely cheerful inquiry.

"Yes, you can," I said. "You can tell your friends to stop shooting and come over here where I am."

"Can we ask why you want them to stop shooting?" the same man asked, still cheerful but now more guarded.

"You bet," I said. "I am a federal agent, and you lads are shooting over a baited area." With those words, their eyes widened to the size of a Chinese gong and they appeared to be having a hard time swallowing or talking. I continued, "Gentlemen, I want the shooting to stop right now."

After some mild objections, the two lads calmly rowed back out and, after a hurried conversation, picked up their buddies and rowed back to where I was standing. In the boat were exactly thirty-two pintail ducks and twelve white-fronted geese, by some chance the exact limits allowed under state law. I identified myself again, this time with my credentials, and requested their driver's licenses, which they quickly produced. Loading their now empty shotguns into the boat, I told them I was going back to the blind and would be right back and asked them to sit down and await my return. Without a murmur all the men took a seat in the grass by their boat dock and expectantly watched my every move. Paddling out to their blind, I could see that the pond area was very muddy, which was typical of an area where many thousands of feeding ducks and geese were roiling up the mud along the bottom as they fed. In addition, the entire pond area, especially the lee side and the cornstalks, was covered with duck and goose feathers, which was also typical of an area where large concentrations of birds are actively feeding in a baited or naturally excellent feeding site.

Sticking the oar deep into the mud alongside the boat by the decoys where I had observed the lads dumping the corn earlier in the week produced a muddy oar with several kernels of corn sticking out of the mud. I repeated this action several times around the decoy area, each time finding the oar covered with kernels. A quick check of the blind produced thirty-nine additional freshly killed ducks of assorted species and another thirteen white-fronts. With my evidence in hand, I silently rowed back to the waiting party while waterfowl of all sorts slipped quickly back into the baited pond to feed. The pond rapidly filling up with waterfowl with me paddling in plain view was more mute testimony to the effectiveness of a baited area. Anyone who supports baiting as a legitimate waterfowl management or moist-soil management tool is either a complete hind end, has zero knowledge about the killing potential of such a practice, doesn't care, or has been bought off. For anyone who has worked baited areas and observed firsthand the migratory birds' reaction to such areas, there can be no other conclusion. To allow legalized baiting or a moist-soil approach managed in such a way as to increase the number of birds in an area for the gun, one has to be morally and ethically corrupt. There is no way to look at it but square in the face, and that face is death for the birds, pure and simple!

When I arrived back at the boat launch, after a few minutes of discussion (mostly mine), the hunters folded. They were all attorneys and just wanted to settle the matter with the least amount of fuss, an approach I had no problem with. Seventy-one ducks, or thirty-nine over the limit, and twenty-five white-fronted geese, or thirteen over the limit, plus the baiting violations, and it was all over. I wrote the lads up and told them their hunting on this area was over for at least ten days past the moment when the last happily feeding duck was observed on the pond. Because they had so much flooded and standing corn in the area, they figured they'd better forgo any hunting in any blind in the immediate vicinity of the now closed blind until the next hunting season. With an indiscernible grin I agreed, and I didn't see anyone hunt that area of the island duck club for the rest of the season, which gave the ducks and geese a real break.

The lads left, somewhat embarrassed, and I spent the next hour hauling birds to my boat for safekeeping and taking new evidence samples in the shooting area in case the hunters changed their minds and wanted a trial. Once away from the island, I sat down where I could relax and drew the birds so they could be donated to some worthy cause in salvageable condition. The warmth of their bodies felt good on my still cold and chilled hands. Even though I loved being in the marsh, I felt I had had enough of it for that day and slowly cruised the miles back to the marina, drinking in the sights and sounds of the delta. It was amazing how keen the eye, how acute the ear and other senses are after an experience such as I had had earlier that morning. God, it was good to be alive. ...

When I got home from Stockton that evening, I pulled into the driveway at my Colusa home, got out of the truck, and stretched my tired frame. I had been working eighteen-hour days seven days a week during that hunting season, trying to hold the human tide in check and trying to keep hunters from crossing over the line. It had been a hard season, but when one works for the world of waterfowl in the wildlife wars, it just naturally calls for long hours if the job is to be done right. That is why so many game wardens won't work waterfowl seasons to any great degree. It is just too hard physically, as well as politically, and takes a really committed officer to do it right. If you have a weak prosecuting attorney or court system, many times all your work may be for naught! Then throw in all the other hunting seasons going on at the same time, and you have a heavy load for even the biggest lad to carry. I don't know if the American people will ever truly appreciate the work wildlife officers do for them so that they can enjoy the whistling wings of a pair of pintail as they drop into a marsh by the side of the hunter and his son or daughter.

About that time, my bride of many years drove in with my two young sons, and they tumbled out of the car like puppies to greet their long-lost dad. Donna, always correct and considerate, waited until the boys had lost interest in their dad in favor of a duck wing the dog had left on the driveway, then walked over to me. "Was your trip worth it?" she gently asked.

"Yes," I said tiredly. "I wrote fifty-three people this week, most for over-limits and shooting over bait."

"Not bad for an old guy," she said as she walked into my arms with her characteristic smile and beautiful blue eyes searching mine for any information they might add about my latest adventure. I held her in my arms longer than I usually did on that day. I don't think she ever really knew why.

5

Lions One, Christians Nothing

FROM OUR VANTAGE POINT on a levee over half a mile away, it was obvious from the number of dove flying into and landing without any sign of caution in the harvested safflower field that something was wrong in the eyes of the law and nature. It just was not natural for dove to fly in to feed in such tremendous numbers during the heat of the day, and the way the dove were bailing into that field without an ounce of caution told me the field had to be well baited. Buck Del Nero and I stood watching the spectacle from our hiding place as literally thousands of dove moved like a constant swarm of bees to and from the eighty-acre safflower field, which was placed smack-dab in the middle of a huge asparagus field to hide its location. Now, a safflower field is an excellent attraction for dove even under normal conditions because of the abundance of seed left behind by the normal harvesting process. But the spectacle unfolding in our binoculars that morning was anything but normal in our practiced observation of wildlife behavior. It was Wednesday, eleven days before the opening of dove season, and, as the old game warden saying went, "Here we go again!"

The farm with the interesting safflower field was owned by a notorious alleged wildlife violator who was also a Fish and Game commissioner for the state of California. In other words, he and others of his kind were responsible for the administration and passing of the state Fish and Game laws. It seemed to me that they, as political appointees with some experience in the hunting and fishing sports of the state (hence their appointments), were expected to obey those laws as well. ...

Buck had spotted the field several evenings earlier when he

was driving around his district looking for things out of place and, like the good officer he was, had investigated the site with the stealthy aid of his motorcycle. He had found the field to be heavily baited and, knowing and trusting me from our academy days, had called to request my assistance in this potentially sensitive matter. Buck was a fighter through and through, but in this case possibly involving one of his agency's own commissioners, with the political game-playing that would follow if the farmer were found to be violating the Fish and Game laws, he recognized the need for a little extra horsepower from Uncle Sam. Being the good friends we were, we had a pact that he would secretly call me for assistance when he found a politically hot situation such as this one because my federal authority would act as a shield. I would act as if I were initiating the investigation and formally request his assistance; as a U.S. deputy game warden (most state Fish and Game wardens carried these credentials after passing a year's probation), he was more or less obliged to comply. That way, if the crap hit the fan—as it always seemed to do in dealings with this particular commissioner—Buck would be shielded from retaliation since it would appear that I had brought him into the matter.

It's hell when you have to work just as hard to keep your own people at bay as the bad guys, I thought when he first called me. I was not surprised, though, having served in the same state agency that he worked for. Crooked politics was a common problem in any of the state and federal land management agencies in those days, particularly under various state or federal Republican administrations because politicians in those administrations had teeth and saw no problem using them when they became exposed by their own greed. That seemed to be especially true if wildlife violations were the issue because these officials considered such violations to be petty stuff, best kept quiet through intimidation and, if possible, swept under the rug. After all, what was the harm and who was the victim other than some damn critter? Being caught shooting over a baited field tended to upset and embarrass these politically powerful men when we did

run across them because the unfair method of take and the usually high numbers of dove killed made them look bad in the
public's eyes. In those days in the San Joaquin Valley of California, as elsewhere across the country, many baited fields were
traced to the handiwork of the rich and famous, and to break
into that type of "shoot fest" with an enforcement action usually
was to invite intervention at the hand of the office of the governor or other high political powers and their minions. If you were
a state wildlife officer, having the governor's office involved,
even if you were in the right, plain and simply meant hard times
ahead, including intimidation tactics such as lost promotional
opportunities or an unrequested move. So when Buck called me,
I said, "I'll head out and meet you in Stockton at our usual meeting place in a couple of hours. When I get there, we'll go out at
night, check out the field, get our bait samples, and then figure
out how best to handle the investigation." Buck agreed. As the
reader can see, even with the protection I had as a federal officer,
I still had to be cautious because of the anticipated political fall-
out.

Several hours later the two of us were patrolling the back
roads north of Stockton in my unmarked truck, apprehending
regular San Joaquin County people who were shooting dove
from their vehicles during the closed season. This routine patrol
gave us time to review the baiting problem—and Buck's earlier
observations demonstrated that it was a major problem, with
that many birds flying into the field and the number of people
(all likely to be politically influential) who appeared to be coming, based on the quantity of shooting stools set up around the
field. This detail would have to be set up like a military operation in order for it to be brought off without a hitch and with a
minimum of political backlash. We left the levee and began planning our method of attack.

About seven in the evening the two of us walked into the field
from the back side of the farm to avoid detection by the
landowner or his laborers, who had been trained to be on the
lookout for anyone suspicious, especially chaps who might be

game wardens. Cleverly surrounding the safflower field were acres of asparagus, all flowered out and an excellent way to conceal an illegally baited dove field from the prying eyes of the local game warden or friendly federal agent. After all, who would look for dove violations in the middle of an asparagus field? We found the safflower field to be baited beyond our wildest imagination. The entire eighty-acre field, crop, weeds, and all, had been bush-hogged (mowed or chopped down) without any attempt to harvest the crop. This approach was unusual because safflower seed was selling for $270 per ton that year and was not usually wasted in such a manner. Suffice it to say, there were many tons of safflower seeds on that field. Buck and I found piles of safflower seeds so deep that we could see where the landowner had had his laborers use rakes to scatter it a bit, probably because he was embarrassed by the amount showing through the chaff. In all my career up to that time and since then, I never saw a field baited so heavily—and I have seen a lot across this great land of ours.

We began taking bait samples from various parts of the field and photographs of that bait for use down the line in federal court in case the lads caught shooting over the baited area contested the charges. At about midnight, an hour or so into our documentation activities, Buck grabbed my shoulder and motioned for me to be still. Off in the distance we could hear the *putt-putt-putt* of a tractor motor, and it sounded as if it were coming our way! We took off, running like the wind for the cover of the asparagus field. It had to be a riot for any creatures of the night that might have seen about six hundred pounds of game wardens scurrying like a couple of large land crabs for the protective cover of the asparagus rows, all the while trying to stay low. Reaching cover, we turned to look back into the safflower field to see what the hell was going on. It didn't take long to solve that mystery; fortunately we had almost a half moon to illuminate the scene before us. A tractor without lights, pulling a small trailer, was driving straight down the middle of the baited field. We could see that there was a man in the trailer shoveling something white out of it with a big scoop shovel and scattering it into the field. The tractor made a horseshoe loop in the field while the lad in the back continued to shovel the contents of the trailer onto the ground. With that done, they drove away. Buck and I mentally marked the location, then went to check it out. We looked between the fresh tractor tracks, with the beams of our flashlights shining through our fingers to avoid detection, and lo and behold, more fresh safflower seeds had been added to the already overloaded field. Damn, whoever was baiting to that degree had one hell of a dove shoot planned for many very important people, I thought.

No one knew his Fish and Game district better than my big Italian friend. I said, "Buck, what the hell is *really* going on here? One doesn't bait a field like this just for the hell of it or out of the goodness of his heart to feed the birds." Buck just looked at me with an impish, knowing grin. Even in the moonlight, I could see that his coal-black eyes were sparkling with his about-to-break-its-seams secret. I said, "Come on, you, come clean with me; what the hell is going on here?"

Buck gave me a trapped look, then said, "You won't believe this, but this is going to be the shoot of the century."

"I can see that, but there's something else going on here, and it may be bigger than the both of us or our agencies. I don't mind a damned good fight, but I would at least like to know the odds so I know how many bullets to bring to the party," I replied. "This almost looks like someone of the stature of the governor or the president of the United States is coming to the shoot from the looks of the ground, the hunting setup, and all the additional bait being sprinkled at night."

He said, "Good eye, Terry. Dante Martinelli is bringing in all his top farm-loan and machinery creditors, bank presidents, presidents of major airlines, politicians, and the like for several days of free drinking, food, the magnitude of which would knock your eyes out at twenty yards, and the dove shoot of a lifetime thrown in as a bonus."

"How long have you known or suspected this?" I asked.

"Since last year," he replied.

"Damn, Buck," I said, "do you have any idea just how big this really is if what you say is true?"

"Terry, I've been told that many of the folks coming to this shoot have visited or entertained presidents," he said quietly.

"Holy buckets!" I said. "With that kind of horsepower breaking the law, I have to let my supervisor know what kind of pickle this might turn into. If we take on this crowd, it will go right to the governor's office or even the White House, and I'm not so sure you and I can shoulder that burden alone!"

Buck continued to look at me in the moonlight with that impish grin and finally said, "Well, are you a man or a mouse?"

"You damn idiot," I said, "you know well enough I am going to put a stop to this. I just haven't figured out the best way to do it where both of us survive and live to old age. If what you say regarding the clientele shooting over this baited field is true, I have to make damn sure that if I grab them for federal court, they can be held. If not, our whole baiting enforcement program could go to hell in a handbasket through liberalization of the regulations, and I don't want to be the one responsible for that." I could see from Buck's serious look that he agreed with me.

We continued to collect bait samples and photographed the new bait between the tractor tracks to show how it had been intentionally spread, all the while keeping an ear cocked for the telltale *putt-putt* of the tractor just in case the men came back with more safflower seed to sweeten the pot. When we finished collecting evidence, we followed the tractor tracks in the pale moonlight to a small grain storage bin not far from the clubhouse but far enough away to be off the curtilage (the enclosed area immediately surrounding the house), which meant we didn't have to worry about Fourth Amendment rights. The U.S. Constitution protects everyone against unreasonable searches and seizure, so we were prohibited from trespassing on a suspected violator's curtilage (except in certain circumstances) without a warrant. But under the Open Fields Doctrine, the landowner has no reasonable expectation of privacy in the farm fields near his house, so it was legal for Buck and me, having identified probable cause (the great numbers of unnaturally feeding migratory game birds), to look for bait and document the evidence.

Sitting alongside the storage bin was the tractor, with a still warm motor, and the trailer, still containing a small amount of safflower seeds. We photographed the tractor and trailer and took additional seeds from the trailer for evidence. Buck opened the door to the storage bin and beckoned me over for a look. Inside the storage bin was about two tons of safflower seed and a shovel that had obviously been used to load the trailer for its trip to the field. I said, "Buck, tomorrow you and I are going to get a can of fingerprint powder and a black light [used to identify the fingerprint powder, which cannot usually be seen by the naked eye], and we are going to lace the seed in this storage bin with it. That way, when these lads put out the bait, we can check it in the field with a black light, and if it glows we will have an even stronger, almost airtight case against these folks, especially as it relates to intent."

Buck said, "Great idea. Now let's get the hell out of here before we get caught." With that, we left the area with visions of opening-day dove-shooting action of unmatched dimensions as a reward for our hard work and headed back to Buck's place for some well-earned sleep.

Early the next day the two of us visited a police supply house and procured a large can of orange fingerprint powder and a black-light kit. I called Jack Downs, my supervisor, and told him what Buck and I thought we had, including the political problems that might ensue. Jack was one tough, experienced officer, and his first statement was, "Good; let's go get the bastards." He continued, "I will bring N710 [our Service aircraft] down and have a look-see from the air. When I finish, I'll hook up with you guys at the airport and we can get our heads together on how best to approach this one." The tone of caution now manifesting itself in Jack's voice, coming from a man who normally was a tiger when it came to enforcing the laws, told me he was concerned about the action we had going. In fact, if the truth be known, it would be one of the hottest in any of our careers!

That afternoon we met Jack for lunch after he had flown over Dante's safflower field. Jack said, "There is no doubt about it, that area is so well baited, I could even see the bait from one thousand feet in the air. If there is one dove on that field, there are at least ten thousand." There was a long pause, and then he added, "There are so many dove in that field they look like maggots on the ground even from as high as I was in the air! Never in my life have I seen so many birds, and if these lads shoot that field and are half good as shooters, we will have a slaughter." Buck and I nodded, but I could sense some concern in Jack's voice as he continued, "I also did some checking on the list of people's names you gave me, Buck, and we have a major problem. These people are really high rollers in the political arenas, and we just won't be able to hit them like regular village people shooting over a baited area." Buck and I both started to object, but Jack raised his hand and held firm. "Guys," he said, "this class of people is powerful enough and possesses the necessary political connections to get all of us moved for cause and maybe even change the baiting laws to allow such a thing as we have witnessed to legally occur."

Jack looked at us to see if we had an unusual plan of attack that might allow us to continue as we normally would. Not wanting to let these bastards go just because they were well connected, I said, "Jack, this isn't right. We don't let the rich and powerful get off in our line of work and just hammer the little guys. It just isn't right!"

Jack took a long look at this youngster to the business and just smiled. I'm sure that smile reflected his feelings from the days when he too was young and full of piss and vinegar. Seeing that his two young gumshoes didn't have a magical answer to the thorny problem at hand, Jack said frankly, "Well, if we can't ticket them, and it's illegal to post their land against hunting, and we don't want to let them get away scot-free, that only leaves one avenue of attack." Seeing that he had both our ears, he went on, "We'll just have to let all of those lads gather at Dante's club-house on the farm, give them time to excuse their drivers and valets so they can't be reached to come back to take them home or to work, and *then* notify Dante that they can't hunt under penalty of law. This would not only serve the law by prohibiting them from killing great numbers of birds illegally, it would also really piss them off big time because they won't have anything to do with their time other than sit on their big fat hind ends and drink whiskey. Additionally, that kind of action on our parts, among other things, would get the message out to adjacent big landowners who might want to try to do the same thing not to bait their fields and screw with the feds."

Buck and I agreed with this plan, realizing it would be the best way to go, as it now appeared that it wouldn't be in the best in-terests of the law or the poor little mourning dove to try to take such an assemblage of bigwigs though the court system and the resulting political furor. I was disappointed that I wouldn't be able to write up the president of one of the largest banks in America or the presidents of several major airlines, not to men-tion several reported state and federal high-level politicians, but that's the way the law or political reality works sometimes. Be-sides, Jack had always provided wise counsel when it came to battles that took on a life of their own, and this one could easily fit that category. Even though my soul was not totally in support of the plan, Jack was the boss and had spoken. I had had my say, and it wasn't good enough, so now the boss took the lead and I would follow. I guess that's why the statue of Justice wears a blindfold. ...

Jack said he would return to Sacramento and, to all appear-ances, stay out of this one unless something went badly wrong, letting the two of us handle it. That way he could lay the defen-sive groundwork for the "hoorah" that was sure to follow, and by virtue of not being there he would be able to provide a seem-ingly objective point of view should the need arise. There was no way these lads were going follow their obvious plan to slaughter the dove over their obscenely baited safflower field, I thought as

the meeting broke up. Maybe we couldn't snap them up into the
state or federal court system because of their clout, but I still
could let them know they had to obey the laws of the land just
like everyone else. That moment was fast approaching—I just
didn't realize how fast.

Before Jack left to fly back to Sacramento, he told me that the
clerk of courts in Williams had called his office earlier looking
for me and had requested that I testify the following day regarding three deer poachers caught by Cliff Fulton, a deputy Fish and
Game warden for the state, and me. It seemed they had gagged
on the $1,000 bail figure (illegal take and possession of doe deer)
the court had suggested when they called to settle out of court.

"Damn," I said, "how the hell can we get additional bait samples off the field if I am in court almost 150 miles away?" There
was a pause, then Jack said he would fill in for me until I finished
in court and could take over again. That way a fed would be
present at all times, which would strengthen the case as well as
protect Buck. His solution was agreeable to all, and the three of
us went our separate ways.

Buck told me later with a smile almost bordering on a laugh
that darkness found him and Jack back at the storage bin, getting
ready to mix the fingerprint powder into the safflower seed. Jack
was inside the bin trying to get the lid off the fingerprint powder
can, and Buck was posted outside as lookout. Buck said he could
hear Jack grunting as he tried to hurry and get the lid off. Then
he heard a loud *whoosh* and Jack cussing a blue streak. Without
turning around from watching the clubhouse, Buck said,
"What's the matter in there?"

Jack replied, "The goddamned lid came off all right—blew up
is a better way to describe it—and I spilled fingerprint powder
all over me."

Buck started to laugh at Jack's luck and then, unable to suppress his curiosity anymore, walked to the door and looked into
the storage bin. The whole area around the doorway and safflower seed pile was glowing a faint, eerie orangish color. The
entire pile of seed also had a ghostly orange glow, and Jack

glowed like there was no tomorrow. Usually a can of fingerprint powder that size would go a long way. This one apparently would not, going only from the seed bin to the field now. Buck roared with laughter at the picture Jack presented, only to have the moment cut short by the telltale *putt-putt* of an approaching tractor coming from the direction of Dante's fuel barn. Buck hissed at Jack to get the hell out of there before they were discovered, and out Jack came like a shot from an orange cannon, glowing from head to toe. Buck ran and hid in the weeds by the grain bin and watched Jack as he also ran to hide in the weeds, a soft phosphorescence trailing him like a gaily clad, brightly colored ghost slipping through the air. Between laughing and being concerned that the laborers would see him, Jack barely made it to the ditch next to the weed patch before the tractor driver and his companion in crime arrived at the storage bin. Jack was steaming when he got there, but Buck said he had to admit he surely looked pretty!

By now both of them were laughing and trying to hold it down so the laborers wouldn't discover them hiding in the weeds. It turned out OK, though, because the men left the tractor motor running while they loaded seed into the trailer. They didn't seem to notice the soft glow in the storage bin or the trailing phosphorescence from the seed pile in the trailer as they drove out into the field. But from the way Buck told it, the two conservation officers did notice and ended up lying face down in the ditch, laughing until their sides hurt! About twenty minutes later the men returned from sweetening the pot, parked the tractor next to the clubhouse, several hundred yards from the storage bin, and went off to bed. Buck and Jack then went out into the safflower field and collected the new evidence under the black light, orange glow and all.

I returned from court after the three lads had pled guilty and been fined $1,000 each anyway (probably for pissing off the judge), and Buck and I continued to update our evidence until two nights before the opening of dove season just in case this killing field ended up being used in spite of our warnings not to hunt the field or regardless of the state and federal laws of the land.

Friday, the day before the opening of dove season, Buck and I hid near Dante's clubhouse, close enough that we could see and hear many of the events of the day unfolding around us. Around noon Dante's high-powered guests began to arrive. Big black or navy-blue limos began to file in and disgorge their VIP passengers. By three P.M., more than thirty guests had arrived for the drinks, good food, elite company, and the anticipated dove shoot of the century scheduled for the next day. We were close enough, on an adjoining public dike under some blackberry bushes, to hear the rich and famous tell their drivers they had the weekend off. God, for those on our side of the law it was perfect—the first part of Jack's plan was working.

As things died down and the entire elite sporting clan went inside to watch what appeared to be a triple-X movie, Buck and I crawled away from the berm near the house and got into a peat ditch, running down it until we could slip out through an adjacent asparagus field to the safety of our hidden patrol vehicle. It was a good feeling to know that the first part of our trap had been sprung, to be followed shortly by what I anticipated would be Dante's explosion—or should I have said "inferno"?

Buck and I called our respective supervisors to update them. Both supervisors concurred with our plan to go in and warn Dante. Buck and I drove into the front yard of Dante's club at exactly four P.M. on this "good" Friday of sorts. Dante, recognizing Buck, came out and with his usual false friendliness invited us in for a few drinks. Sure, anything to put the hooks into an officer for an ethics violation like drinking on duty, I thought. Buck said, "Dan, I need to see you for a second."

Dante said, "Sure," and walked over to the patrol truck, where I stood. Buck introduced me as Federal Agent Terry Grosz, and Dante instantly popped off, with a phony grin, "Damn, Buck, you got to run with these federals now? It must be awful important if this guy is here."

"It is," Buck said. "Terry, why don't you tell him?"

I shook Dante's hand, then said, "Dan, we have a problem with your safflower field located in the middle of that asparagus field." I pointed to the area in question.

"What's the matter with it?" he replied guardedly, his eyes never leaving mine. The tone of his voice and his rapid response told me at once that he knew what the problem was and was instantly (for obvious reasons—thirty of them) worried. I could see the wheels turning in his head as he tried to look unconcerned and simultaneously figure out what was next, all the while expecting no good to come from this encounter.

"Dan" I said, "let's get right to the point. The field is considered baited, and if anyone shoots it tomorrow when dove season opens, I will have no choice but to issue that person a citation and send him into federal court."

Boy, that stung him like a bee, and he erupted. "That is bullshit!" he yelled. "There is no way you or any other son-of-a-bitch federal is going to keep me from shooting that field." Turning to Buck, he said, "Buck, tell this son of a bitch he can't do that, and if he does I will have his job in a heartbeat."

Buck said, "Dan, Terry is the federal government; he speaks for the federal government; and you can do what he says or not—that's up to you and your shooters. But that field is baited beyond belief, there is no doubt about it, and if I were you I would listen to him very carefully. Otherwise you might be heading for a hard and embarrassing fall. I don't have any jurisdiction here once the feds step in. Plain and simply, they are in charge, and he has requested that I assist him, and I have to do that."

Dante exploded, threw his hand-painted whiskey glass, which blew up into a million pieces, across the yard, and started yelling at me, calling me a stinking goddamned fed and other even more colorful names. Keeping my blood pressure down and my metaphorical grip on his throat, not to mention suffocating an urge to break his face with a good right cross, I said in my most professional tone, "Dan, if you would like I will be glad to show you the bait so you can draw your own conclusion, but the field is baited to the nines."

By now people were streaming out of the clubhouse, drawn by Dante's tirade. Once Dante saw he had an audience, especially the magnitude of the one now looking on at the scene, he puffed up even more and commenced to again call me every name in the book as well as a few I didn't think were there. Knowing I had him by the throat, I calmly held my ground while he made a horse's hind end out of himself. I thought that today was a good time to be a federal instead of a state officer because I knew how much trouble Dante could cause, and would if I had still been a California state employee. He screamed out a stream of orders, and he and several other lads jumped into two pickups and roared out to the field. Buck and I let them go and followed at a more leisurely pace after the dust of their explosive exit and drive across the dry road to the field had died down. After all, there was no way they could get rid of or hide that much bait before we got there. They would clearly be in violation of state and federal laws if they chose to shoot the field the next day, but after my damn good public ass-chewing, I was kind of hoping they would. Since we had pointed out the problem in advance, per Jack's advice, the shooters would have no defense in any court of the land if they shot over the baited field the next day. Game, set, match ...

When we arrived at the field, Buck and I found them frantically trying to hide the safflower seed piles with stems, stalks, and leaves of chopped plants or kicking the piles of seed all over the place. It was a real treat watching them trying to hide the evidence; safflower comes from the thistle family, and these lads were getting the hell stuck out of them as they used their bare hands to try to hide the bait! Stepping out of my patrol truck, and calmly watching over the hood, I let them scurry around for a bit, rather enjoying the scene, before I once again approached Dante. All the while this human activity was going on, the dove flew into the field by the thousands, returning after being sent into the air with the screeching arrival of the pickups. They landed not ten feet away from many of the lads as if they were oblivious to the danger. I thought as I walked over to Dante that it would have been the same even if the men had been shooting at the dove. The birds would have kept coming to the feast, many to never leave the table.

This time, caught with the goods and knowing that all his high-powered friends' dove-hunting sport was hanging in the balance, Dante approached me with a little more fuse and a lot less boom. "Terry, is there any way I can clean this mess up and still allow my guests the pleasure of a good dove shoot?"

Without responding to his question, I started to show Dante around his safflower field, pointing out the bait in all its glory. He didn't say a word, just listened, but I could surely tell his jaw was tight as he hoped against hope. I don't think he was very happy about being lectured about the federal baiting laws by an obvious plebeian.

"It looks like the Mexicans didn't do a very good job here and left a little safflower on the ground," was his rather lame defense. That's right, I thought, blame the poor laborers who only did what they were told. Everywhere there were great piles of safflower, some six to ten inches deep and five to ten feet in length and width. Even Dante had to give up in light of the evidence, especially when confronted with rake marks over some of the piles.

"Dan," I said, "I don't know of any way you or your lads will be able to legally shoot this field tomorrow. The bait has to be totally removed, and no one can shoot over this area until a ten-day period has passed after that lure and attractant has been removed and the birds stop using it."

Dante erupted again and, pointing his finger at me, said, "We'll see about this, asshole; your job is history, as is your fat ass. Either you reverse your opinion right this moment, here and now, or I will call Sacramento and you will be looking for work."

"The phone is that way, Dan," I said coldly, pointing toward the clubhouse. "The right to call your public representative is one a lot of men have died for in battle in many wars, and I sure wouldn't want to deprive you of that right," I added with a little tongue in cheek. "Besides, I don't work for anyone in the state organization anymore."

For a moment I could tell he wanted in the worst way to knock my head off, but I guess the look in my eyes warned him off. Off he stormed in one of the pickups, back to the clubhouse in a huge cloud of dust, leaving all the other chaps behind. Buck and I knew he was now calling the governor's office and the fireworks were about to begin. I told the lads remaining in the field, as they picked safflower stickers out of their hands and fingers, that to shoot over that field at any migratory game birds would bring the wrath of the federal courts down on them, and they had best leave it alone. I said I couldn't keep them from hunting over that field but would most certainly issue citations if I caught them. They were a bit cooler than Dante and agreed that they saw the point of my legal wisdom before they returned to the clubhouse in the remaining pickup.

When the field was empty of all witnesses, Buck and I just sat there and grinned. For once the old saying "How sweet it is" was true in the fullest meaning of the phrase. We may not have been able to issue all the lads citations for shooting over a baited area, and more than likely over-limits as well, but we had stopped the senseless slaughter of at least five hundred or six hundred dove. Generally when one baits an area it is because the blood lust has overruled one's common sense and concept of sporting ethic. In most cases, if the birds cooperate and fly, huge over-limits will be taken before the killing lust is satisfied. People who bait do it for two reasons: greed and ego. It's that simple, and Dante was well supplied with both.

Realizing that our moment in the sun was done, Buck and I went to work again just in case Dan's alligator mouth overrode his hummingbird hind end and he and his friends shot the field the next day. We collected more samples of the bait, especially that between the tractor tire marks covered with fingerprint powder, in order to put more nails in the coffin lid. Before we finished Dante drove back out and told Buck his boss was on the phone back at the clubhouse, and if he valued his job and knew what was good for him, he would get his hind end over there and explain what was going on. Ignoring the root of his problems, me, Dante flew away in a rage and cloud of dust. Buck and I let the dust settle to show the expectant crowd at the clubhouse a thing or two, then casually drove back to the main ranch house, where Buck talked to his boss, Captain Jim Wictum, on the telephone.

Jim was an excellent boss, and all he did was tell Buck that the governor was involved, but, knowing what he did about the case, he felt he could handle the governor, the Fish and Game director, and the chief of law enforcement if they chose to get involved. He told Buck to stay near the radio in case Jim needed any more information for the political firefight that was now starting or had to pass on any instructions. Then he told us to get busy and catch someone else, as we were being paid a princely sum to do, and hung up with a knowing chuckle. As I said, Jim Wictum was a real professional and one hell of a man.

Dante then got on the phone to Jack Downs and shortly afterward came out to tell me that Jack wanted to talk to me. I told Jack we still had a good case and had gathered even more bait just that afternoon and as far as I was concerned, if anyone shot over that field I would give them a ticket. Jack agreed with that approach and then asked me to put Dante back on the phone. As I expected, Jack's conversation with Dante did not go well for the "sportsmen." When Dante put down the phone at a rather high rate of velocity, it was apparent that he was really upset. He walked over to me, evidently trying to salvage something of the dove hunt, and asked if his hunters could shoot dove over the asparagus fields next to the baited field. I said that would be all right as long as they made sure the dove were not going to or from the baited safflower field.

Dante said, "How will I know my guys aren't breaking the law?"

"Dan," I said, "I can't give you a distance, but your guys had better stay far away from that baited field and the dove's flight line to it unless you want my intervention with a handful of citations."

He just swore, whirled, and stomped off into the now not-so-happy clubhouse. Boy, by now he had to be feeling the heat from all those folks he had invited up for a dove hunt, I thought.

Buck and I left that heated situation fueled by Dante's ranting and raving and managed to check the safflower field about every two hours during the opening weekend of dove season to make sure compliance was the word of the day. On several of those passes we could see Dante and his high-class visitors trying to hunt dove in his asparagus fields, half a mile away from the safflower field—and what a bust that had to be. As anyone will tell you, dove don't frequent grasslike fields. Needless to say, Dante's weekend plans for his high rollers was totally destroyed. Another truly unique element of this episode was that a fair number of the lads out for a good time in Dante's baited dove fields would be invited for a similar special deer hunt on Dante's Snow Storm Ranch in Modoc County the next year to make up for their September dove-shooting disappointment. As it happened, yours truly located that ranch on Snow Storm Mountain and ended up busting a bunch of those people for illegal deer violations. But that is another story, and on that one you will just have to take an old, cold potato and wait. ...

In the end, Buck and I took a lot of political heat, as did our supervisors. The word was that Dante tried to have me moved, but to no avail, thanks to Jack Downs having the guts to take the political manipulators dead on. Having an airtight case and warning the folks instead of citing them didn't hurt us either. Buck continued to watch that baited field over the rest of dove season, and it remained baited throughout the season because of the high quantity of seed on the ground. Finally, seeing that the field would probable remain baited for the rest of that year, Dante had it plowed under, thereby ending the drama.

A sad epilogue to the story is that, partly as a result of this investigation, political forces in California and elsewhere got the Fish and Wildlife Service to change its baiting regulations for the mourning dove. A year or so later the federal regulations changed to allow the legalized baiting of dove as a "management tool." This action was pure and simply nothing more than legalizing the unfair taking of thousands of migratory game birds to appease those interests dedicated to killing more than what would be allowed through normal sport taking. Today landowners can bush-hog a field of standing safflower or any other seed crop normally consumed by humans and hunt dove over the area with legal impunity, just as Dante tried to do illegally so many years ago. They can't bring any extra feed into the field as Dante's laborers did that night, but they can hunt over an altered, or "managed," area, which makes for a very effective killing field—to an extent that must be seen to be believed. There is no way a true sportsman would be caught shooting over a baited dove field. It is nothing but outright carnage. Yet state and federal agencies now sanction such "opportunities" for those who don't understand the spirit of a fair chase, even though their missions are to protect, preserve, and enhance the wild populations. Greed, ego, and hunter opportunity are the bottom line. It is sad, but it all goes to show that humankind is the ultimate predator.

Wildlife law enforcement is sort of like the days of old in the Roman coliseum. You can appear to win, but ultimately you lose. In the end, the lions eat the Christians. Who knows how many millions of extra dove have been killed as a result of this senseless regulation change through the Fish and Wildlife Service's knowing abrogation of its responsibilities under the Migratory Bird Treaty Act? But time and humankind continue to march right through the passenger pigeons, bison, Pacific salmon, heath hen, and someday maybe the mourning dove. ... When that happens, just watch; there won't be a soul in state or federal government who bowed to political pressure or knowingly weakened the laws who will step forward and admit that he or she was part of that process of wildlife destruction called legalized baiting.

I don't know what happened to Dante, and I have lost track of Buck, who has retired, but I do know one thing. Until the day I retired, I would still bore-sight any son of a bitch shooting migratory game birds over a baited area if it were at all legally possible. The only voice the migratory game birds have is that of the wildlife officer, and without that voice the wildlife will die without making a sound. I am glad I am known as a bigmouth! Justice may be blind, but I know she can still hear.

6

The Airboat and a Cow Named Sue

IN THE SPRING OF 1971 I received information from Tom Ishige of Yuba City that during the past waterfowl hunting season, after the Sacramento River had flooded its banks and created a huge floodplain in the Sacramento Valley, certain individuals from the local Chinese community had shot over flooded grassland pastures on a Yolo County dairy farm and illegally killed numerous arctic swans as they came into the pastures to feed. Tom told me the Chinese would shoot swans only when the Sacramento Valley's tule fog was at its worst, which meant their chance to escape detection and apprehension was at its best. He figured that because the manager of the farm where the shooting had gone on was married to the sister of one of the shooters, he had just looked the other way in order to keep peace in the family. However, Tom said, the dairy-farm owner would skin anyone alive that he caught hunting illegally on his property. In order to get around this hurdle, Tom thought the swan poachers would wait for a call from the sympathetic manager telling them that the law-abiding owner was away from the ranch. Then, if it was foggy, they would hunt.

Tom said the Chinese had been doing this for years when the weather conditions were right and had yet to be caught. I could tell from the way he spoke that he was unhappy over the wildlife violations, and even more so that Chinese people were involved. For some reason Tom, who was Japanese, did not like the Chinese. Over all our years of working together he never said why, but that underlying current of distrust and dislike was always there. According to Tom, the swans were dressed, taken to Chinatown in San Francisco, and sold to people who considered them a delicacy and were willing to pay the price these illegally

taken birds commanded. Tom gave me directions to the dairy
from several entry points and then, as if he had said more than
he should have, abruptly said good-bye and hung up. In the
seven years I had worked from Tom's information, he had never
been wrong, so I kept his tale in mind and waited for the moment I knew was to come. As the fall of 1971 progressed into
November, the winter storms arrived and began to race across
the Sacramento Valley, dumping their moisture on the parched
lands, much to the joy of the wintering waterfowl, local duck
hunters, and resident dirt farmers. After several weeks of hard
rains, noticing the Sacramento River starting to rise and flood its
banks in some of the lower areas of the valley, I journeyed up to
the Sacramento National Wildlife Refuge and made sure the
refuge airboat was in top operating condition.

I was frequently faced with the age-old law enforcement
problem of not having my own equipment and having to borrow someone else's in order to get the job done. For many reasons, the directors of the Service hardly ever saw fit to supply
their small division of law enforcement with adequate funding
or personnel so the officers could do the job Congress mandated. This was not just a one-time abuse of power by whichever
Service director, male or female, was sitting but a basic lack of
understanding of how to use the law enforcement wildlife management tool to the best advantage. For as long as I can remember, this neglect by Service management was woven throughout
the functioning of the law enforcement division. Published word
and documents from as far back as the 1930s show the reluc-
tance of Fish and Wildlife Service leaders to provide adequate
annual funding to enforce the laws of the land protecting trust
wildlife species, and that almost criminal neglect continues to
this day. It was truly a sad state of affairs that I worked almost
thirty years for the Service and of that time had only two years
during which I was fully funded and could do the job as it
needed doing. In fact, I can remember times when I had to call
my boss to get approval to buy a tank of gas for the patrol vehicle or pay for a ruined tire because of a nonexistent budget!

If only the American people truly knew how shaky the federal "thin green line" is because of this shortsighted management approach! They would be amazed at how far we in the law enforcement division could stretch a nickel and, if the truth be known, would be truly incensed at the basic lack of agency support in the protection of their natural heritage. They would also be surprised if they knew just how far we actually did reach into the communities of illegal activity. One can do that when one ignores one's health and family for the benefit of the resource and those yet to come.

Getting back to my story and off my swaybacked horse, fortunately Ed Collins, manager of the Sacramento National Wildlife Refuge, and I were good friends. Like many other refuge managers across the land, Ed worked closely with and supported the law enforcement program even though his agency leaders chose not to do so. After checking out the refuge airboat and requesting that the refuge shop mechanics keep it fueled and ready to go at a moment's notice, I swung by the main office to inform Ed of my intentions. Ed, with his usual good nature, swung his hand and told me to use the airboat until the need was gone but to please bring it back in one piece. Damn, he must have thought law enforcement was hard on equipment or something!

Sometime in December, just before Christmas, the Sacramento River got serious, rolled over its banks, and flooded the numerous Sacramento Valley bypasses and causeways. Soon there were thousands of square miles of flooded lands throughout Colusa, Glenn, Sutter, Butte, Sacramento, and Yolo Counties, all in the heart of the Pacific flyway, home to millions of migratory waterfowl. It didn't take the birds long to discover these flooded wonderlands and all the joys they held.

The information I had been holding in the back of my mind concerning the Chinese swan shooters came to fruition one crisp December morning when I picked up my madly ringing telephone to hear Tom Ishige's familiar voice over the wire.

"Misser Grosz, Misser Grosz, I need to meet with you."

I said, "Sure, Tom, when and where?"

"Misser Grosz, I am in Colusa getting crawler tractor parts; I will come and see you." *Click* went the phone before I could respond. I smiled. Good old Tom, a real man on the move. Waiting for Tom's arrival, which I knew would be very soon, I thought back over the years of our close relationship. Tom was a Japanese American from Yuba County. Although he and his family had been imprisoned by the U.S. government in an internment camp at Tule Lake, California, during World War II, he still had a great love for his country and her resources. We had developed a close friendship, and once Tom found he could trust me to keep my mouth shut he came to me with information about illegal activities concerning wildlife, especially those pursuits that had a commercial ring. Feeding one's family was OK with Tom, but to feed your wallet at the expense of the things he loved to watch and eat himself earned the offender a real enemy. Where or how Tom got his information I never knew or asked, but it was always on the dime with enough for change.

The minute Tom got out of his pickup at my house that morning, it was clear that he was on the warpath. Without any kind of greeting, Tom told me the Chinese poachers were back at it, killing swans in the Yolo bypass area. He gave me approximate directions to their latest killing fields and urgently requested that I stop them. I assured Tom I would get on it as soon as we finished our business. Tom grinned, knowing full well that I was a man of my word, and I could see the visions of what was going to happen to the Chinese going through his head. Then I noticed Tom looking past me toward my garage. Turning, I remembered the limit of field-dressed drake pintail hanging and cooling in my garage in plain view. Tom had a love for duck and striped bass like no man I ever knew. I didn't have any stripers that morning, but I sure had a fine limit of plump, rice-fed pintail, so I walked over to them, removed them from their stringer, tagged them (federal law requires that birds taken by one individual and being transported by another outside the field where taken be tagged with the name and address of the taker, date taken, species of birds taken, and signature of the taker), and gave them to Tom.

Tom's grin told me those ducks would not go to waste, and I was sure that by that afternoon Tom's wife would have them in some stage of preparation for a dinner fit for an emperor. Putting my arm around this large, kindhearted man, I said, "Tom, if those Chinese lads show, they will have a not-so-nice Christmas." Tom flashed a big grin, and off he went as I began formulating a plan of attack.

That afternoon I called my deputy, Tim Dennis, who lived in Maxwell, and asked if he wanted to go for a little ride on the airboat into a flooded area not far from the Sacramento Airport. Tim, or the "Dirt Farmer," a nickname I affectionately gave him because of his rice-farming background, quietly asked, "Why are we going?" I briefly outlined the detail I had in mind, and Tim, not bothering to conceal the excitement in his voice, said, "When do we go?" A typical Tim Dennis reaction. That man was always ready to do battle and piss on any inherent odds or danger. I have worked with many an officer throughout my career, and few, even full-time professionals, came close to the qualities he exhibited. He was hardworking, always totally dedicated to the moment, and I learned much from him over the years we worked together to stop the problem-makers illegally taking wildlife in California.

I told Tim, "See you in two hours; prepare for an overnight."

Two hours later I picked Tim up at his Maxwell ranch and then headed to Willows, the national wildlife refuge headquarters, to pick up our airboat. Collins waved as we passed the refuge office, and I could see in his eyes his desire to go along. I grinned, waved back, and headed out the refuge gate and down the state highway to another adventure.

Upon our arrival at the flooded Yolo bypass area, you would have had to experience it to appreciate what met our eyes: thousands of flooded acres of rich farmlands with millions of waterfowl happily trading back and forth across the waters and mare's tail–filled skies (a sign that a weather change was in the offing). God, what a sight—the air was filled with migratory birds of every kind! It was a pleasure to be alive during a time like this, seeing Mother Nature on one of her better days. Needless to say, the sight was burned into my soul until the day I'm asked to leave this place for good. A look at Tim showed the same intense reaction to what the world of wildlife laid out for us that fine day in the time of our youth. God puts things like that out there for all of us to look at. It is just too bad that most people don't see what is really there, and why.

Putting the three-quarter-ton Dodge in four-wheel drive, I backed the airboat trailer down a shallow slope on the levee and into the water. Tim unhooked the airboat and floated it off the trailer. Once clear, I pulled the pickup back onto the levee, parked it out of the way, and began to unload our gear. Into the airboat went at least a day's food supplies, two sleeping bags, two bales of straw (to lay in the bottom of the boat for us to sleep on), a gas stove, flashlights, water, cooking pots, raingear, and tarps. Note the lack of any kind of float or safety gear. When one is young, foolish, and apparently immortal, things like that just don't compute. Walking back to my truck, I turned on the weather channel and learned that the forecasters were still predicting heavy tule fog for the whole week, starting the next day, throughout that part of the Sacramento Valley.

A Sacramento Valley tule fog is an extremely dense fog that allows visibility for only a few yards, maybe fifty yards at the most. I have seen this type of fog hang in the Sacramento Valley for weeks on end. Its density makes flying very difficult for migratory waterfowl, and this phenomenon offers the best conditions for hunting, especially if one is even half good with a duck or goose call. The flying birds can't see worth a darn and will rapidly decoy to anything that appears to be a haven on the ground, be it feeding ducks or the supposed call of one of their own.

Satisfied, we double-checked our gear, fired up the boat, and roared off into millions of objecting waterfowl and thousands of acres of brown Sacramento River floodwaters. We steamed down the bypass area for several miles with the cool wind passing over us, very much aware of nature's spectacle that surrounded us. Muskrat, beaver, and a few river otter were in evidence. Just about every tree, isolated like an island, was loaded with pheasants and quail trying to figure out where to go next. Deer stepped cautiously about every rapidly shrinking island, and raccoons, skunks, rats, mice, you name it, were all swimming somewhere or nowhere. Mixed into this nature soup was every form of flying water bird known to North American man. God, if only to see those halcyon days again ...

Picking an area that allowed us access to several miles of flooded and partially flooded pasturelands near the dairy farm in question, I slowed to a quiet idle (if there is such a thing for an airboat) and brought the binoculars to my eyes. From the high seat on the airboat, I could see that the area in question was already home to about five thousand feeding and loafing swans. Seeing my affirmative nod, Tim dropped the anchor, and as the airboat swung gently on the end of the rope, we set up shop. A second look around confirmed our choice of stakeout area. There was water everywhere, the airboat was concealed by a large patch of willows and cottonwoods sitting in about six feet of water, and as far as the eye could see were mallards, swans, and a zillion pintail, the original "greyhounds of the sky." No two ways about it, this area had all the right ingredients except the hunters. But tomorrow, a tule-fog Saturday if the weathermen were right, would be another day.

Tim and I broke the strings on our straw bales and laid the straw out on the dry floor of the airboat along the seat and engine mounts. (I had learned that trick on another airboat detail in the Still Water Marshes in Nevada a year earlier. The straw made ideal bedding because as one operated the airboat after using it, the wind rushing past the prop would suck up the straw from the floor of the boat and blow it past the engine and over the stern. In no time all the straw, a biodegradable product, would be scattered over the environment, leaving no mess at all in the bottom of the boat.) Next came a couple of tarpaulins, which were laid on the straw and then folded over the sleeping bags, providing cover on both sides against any moisture or morning dew. Even if it rained a little, we would be dry in our makeshift beds. If it rained a lot, we would be like all the other creatures swimming along looking for a dry port in the storm.

Next we broke out our cooking gear and a fair-sized two-burner gas stove, which we set up on the expansive bow of the boat. On went two twelve-inch cast-iron skillets, a gob of lard in each, and as Tim hooked up the gas I loaded two twenty-ounce, heavily spiced porterhouse steaks into one of the skillets. Into the second skillet went a large mess of previously boiled and sliced spuds liberally mixed with onions, raw garlic, and fresh, thin-sliced and very hot jalapeño peppers. In a few moments the air was filled not only with the sights and sounds of migratory birds trading across the heavens but with the majestic, pungent smell from the cast iron. Shortly thereafter, with the gusto of modern-day mountain men transported back in time, we fell to the vittles until they were no more. Then, while Tim produced two quarts of his homemade buttermilk (the kind with great big globs of butterfat), I whisked out one of my bride's homemade pumpkin pies, and between Tim and me, there soon was nothing left even for the small swimming mice hastily passing our boat. Tim looked at me over a rather large, recently filled gut and said, "That woman of yours sure can make a pumpkin pie."

Nodding, I said, "Her secret is to mix the pumpkin pie mix, let it sit for twenty-four hours, and then cast it into a pie like you had tonight."

Tim, being a good cook as well, digested the information I had given him, and from then on his pies, especially pumpkin, tasted a whole lot better (not as good as my bride's, but close!).

After cleaning up our eating gear, we stretched out in our lawn chairs and sat quietly smoking rank Italian cigars, lost in our thoughts until the sun set and darkness overtook us. Sitting in a scene like that one, with the water gurgling around the airboat while thousands of waterfowl flew back and forth across the darkened skies looking for home, tends to take anyone who is in love with the land and what it has to offer back a few hundred years. Tim and I were no exceptions. We both would have made good mountain men, I thought. Come to think of it, maybe we had been. ... I could feel a knowing smile spreading over my face. Needless to say, we spent a very enjoyable evening, sitting there in the night, surrounded by quietly moving floodwaters, smoking big cigars, and listening to the world of waterfowl practice its travels and traditions across the darkened winter skies. It just doesn't get any better than that, especially on top of fried spuds, a porterhouse steak, a quart of homemade buttermilk, and half a pumpkin pie each.

About ten o'clock, with the damp of the air penetrating our clothes and senses, we checked our anchor and then crawled into our cold but rapidly warming sleeping bags and dropped off to sleep to the gentle rocking of the boat. The last things I heard were the sounds of whistling wings, the soft, fluting calls of pintail, and droppings occasionally hitting the water around our floating "island." The next thing I knew, my biological clock said it was time to get up. It was still dark, and my face, which had been exposed to the air, was covered with moisture, but it wasn't raining. A quick look at my watch proclaimed that it was four A.M. and we were "burning daylight." Crawling out of the sleeping bag and waking Tim, I noticed that we were completely surrounded by a heavy, wet tule fog—so heavy, in fact, that I couldn't see more than twenty yards in any direction, even with the strong-beamed Mag flashlights we routinely carried.

Tim and I hurriedly dressed in the damp clothes we had stuffed under the tarps to keep dry. Slipping into our hip boots and camouflage hunting coats, we instinctively checked and re-holstered our sidearms. We then fired up our gas stove and, in the dim gleam of our flashlights, loaded the cast-iron frying pans with spuds, sausage, eggs, and more hot sliced jalapeño peppers. Soon the air had a smell that made us want to go out and grab the day for all it was worth. Once ready, these items were dished out onto our plates and topped off with iced tea and rather large slices of a second outstanding pie, this time apple, supplied by my long-suffering (thanks to my profession) wife. It was hard to imagine that we got paid to do this, but we did—and very well, I might add, I thought as I shoveled another forkful of sausage into my happy mouth. Finishing our feast among a waking world of waterfowl, as evidenced by the nearby whirring sounds of lost wings, we put the breakfast gear away under the bow of the boat and prepared ourselves for any events that might come our way. The fog continued to ebb and flow around us, moved along by a soft breeze, as the day began. Tim and I sat back in our chairs, snuggled down in our coats to avoid the damp air, lit up cigars, and let our thoughts drift lazily along with the cigar smoke. The waterfowl started to fly back and forth across the heavens and, owing to the fog, filled the air with their plaintive calls as they sought their unseen buddies on the water they knew was just below. Daylight found us still quietly sitting in the airboat, surrounded by very dense fog, listening for those in need of a game warden's attention.

About eight-ten that morning, three or four hundred yards south-southwest, we heard twelve rapid shots that sounded like they came from shotguns. Tim released the anchor without any fanfare, and the gentle floodwater currents began to drift our airboat slowly in the direction of the shooting. We drifted quietly in this fashion for about thirty minutes, getting closer and closer to the shooting, which by now was constant and loud. We finally got close enough to hear the calls of the arctic swans as they plowed heavily across the foggy skies, trying to find their counterparts on the ground. You could hear the heavy, unmistakable *swish-swish-swish* of their wings as they passed directly overhead toward the area dominated by the sound of shooting. Tim and I carefully listened after the swans passed over us. There would be a few quiet moments, then more shots. We could hear loud *whomping* sounds as dead and dying swans returned to Mother Earth for the last time. It didn't take us long to realize that the shooters were probably the Chinese lads that Tom had told me about, and from the sounds of their shooting, they were having the time of their lives.

The airboat drifted to within about fifty yards of our shooters and then began to drift away. That placed us at the point of end-

ing stealth and, with the start of the engine, waking up the whole
world, including God if he was still asleep. In order to avoid
starting up "old thunder" and shaking anything with ears to the
very core, we tried to paddle closer to our suspected swan
shooters. We continued to paddle as we heard more swans passing overhead, more shots, and more *whomps* at an even greater
distance than before. We were not making any headway, if anything just drifting even farther from the action. So we said,
"Enough is enough!" I scrambled up into the seat of the airboat,
fastened my seatbelt, and cleared the switches. Tim quickly put
on his earmuffs and sprayed ether into the carburetor. I hit the
ignition switch, the engine coughed, caught, and the roar of a
165-horsepower Lycoming engine announced to the world that
it was alive and well, and those in the world of wildlife catering
to the call of the devil should grab their hind ends.

Quickly checking the gauges, I swung the bow of the airboat
toward the last shots, following a quick bearing on my dash-
board compass. Now, just imagine what the sudden starting of
an aircraft engine out there on the floodplain, in dense fog, just
yards away from their miserable carcasses on land, would con-
jure up in those folks' minds. They were hunting in the quiet of a
heavy fog near the Sacramento Airport on a protected piece of
property heretofore unsoiled by anyone's interference. All of a
sudden the morning stillness was shattered by the apparent roar
of an aircraft heading their way, though that wasn't even possible
because there wasn't anything in that direction but water! I
could just imagine what was going through our swan shooters'
minds and couldn't help but grin (just a little, mind you). I still
couldn't see more than twenty yards in any direction, so I picked
my way carefully and slowly around the trees, dead cows, logs,
and fences that made up my flotsam water world for the time
being. After a few moments we started to slowly break out of the
fog and into a large area of semiflooded pasture. About that time,
I noticed the unmistakable forms of four humans standing in the
pasture with the comforting fog rapidly burning off around
them, exposing them and their deeds to the eyes of the world and

two crazy game wardens in a rapidly arriving airboat. Imagine their fear and consternation: one minute enjoying a quiet but illegal hunt, the next standing there rooted in terror as a noisy craft came roaring out of the fog right at them. Seeing that all was clear, I put the hammer down, and at 3,000 rpm we were flying, not to mention making enough noise to cause God some concern. The sight of this apparition flying out of the quiet, fog-shrouded swamp and now howling down on them couldn't have done much for their nervous systems, much less their sphincters. They just stood there with their mouths open and their eyes the size of dinner plates. Damn, they sure looked funny, I thought as I rapidly bore down on them. Added to this misery was the fact that they were surrounded by the bodies of nineteen swans, the taking of which was totally prohibited by state and federal wildlife laws.

Finally reality bored through the fear-crazed minds of our chaps, and they realized they were in big trouble. In a flash, as if on cue, they all took off running for what appeared to be a dairy barn located at the edge of the pasture and dimly visible through the still dense but slowly lifting fog. Running up out of the pasture, they tossed their shotguns and hunting coats filled with shells down on the wet ground to lighten their loads and, moving as fast as they could in hip boots, sprinted for the apparent safety of the farmyard and the comforting cover of the dairy barns and corrals.

Airboats can be driven down a dry highway if you have enough horsepower. It so happened that the airboat Tim and I were running that day could have climbed a tree if there weren't too many limbs. Seeing that the chase was on, out from the floodplain and onto the wet pasture we went, all the while gaining on our fleeing swan shooters. They were certainly aware that they were losing the race by virtue of the fact that the noise coming toward their hind ends was getting louder—*a lot* louder. This realization spurred our chaps on to even greater efforts in their vain attempt to gain freedom from that damned thing coming across what had been their private little killing field.

Tim and I ran the lads right up into the area by the dairy barns. Two of them jumped over a fence into a large corral full of Holstein cows. The other two were a little more dense and stopped to open the gate into the corral. Realizing that we were too close for them to close the gate, they took off into the corral and let the gate slowly swing wide open. Well, that opportunity was too good for ye olde airboat and the German Tank Driver at the helm. *Zip*, right into the corral on the two chaps' heels went the airboat, trapping them in a corner by the barn. Tim hit the ground running after the other two fellows, who were heading for the dairy barn and its open doors to our left. Cutting off the ignition switch, I jumped off the airboat while it was still sliding across the yard and chased the two lads who were now trying to escape through an open door into the barn to my right. Collaring the two men as they loudly hit a wall lined with numerous milk and cream cans, I rapidly identified myself. There was instant resignation, and with that, the three of us headed back to the airboat and several waiting citations.

As we emerged from the barn, I met Tim coming out of the other barn with his two chaps, and then it dawned on me. The corral was filled with about 150 Holstein milk cows! Every cow in that corral had her eyes riveted on the previously roaring metal monster that had hammered up out of their meadow and into their corral. Their eyes were as big as garbage-can lids, poop was flying every which way, and all 150 of them were jammed into a corner of the corral that would have been uncomfortable holding just ten of them! In addition, it was obvious that it was milking time. Every cow had a huge, distended udder, and milk was squirting every which way every time they moved. Obviously I had come at the wrong time. ... To make matters worse, here came the ranch manager with a pitchfork in one hand and a scowl on his face as wide as his corral. He was a huge hulk of a man who was trying to figure out what the hell was going on in his formerly quiet little chunk of the world. You can just imagine the pandemonium. What a picture that would have made for Norman Rockwell!

Greetings and identifications were made all around, the cows settled down, and Tim and I issued citations to our four swan shooters as the now quieted-down dairyman, realizing there wasn't much he could do for his friends, began to deal with his suffering cows. The four Asian Americans, now that the field legal work was done, started to leave to go pick up the rest of their previously dropped hunting gear. It was apparent that they were all somewhat the worse for wear and still carrying a case of the "big eye" after being chased and caught by two crazy game wardens and their howlin' airboat.

Tim and I collected the dead swans and shotguns, tagged them as evidence, and prepared to reenter the flooded area to see what else we could stir up among other duck hunters since we were in the area and had a good start on things. However, it quickly became clear that I had a major problem: getting the airboat out of that corral. These machines are very heavy, especially in the stern over which the aircraft engine is mounted. Once you get them moving on land, it is all right, but once stopped, because of their extreme weight, they are a bugger to get going again. To break one loose from wet ground like we were currently sitting on takes a little bit of doing. You can't just take off and go about your business. You have to crank it up, push one rudder pedal down, and let the boat spin in that direction until it builds up sufficient escape speed. Then, with an eye toward which way you wish to go, you let up on that rudder pedal and quickly push the other one down to change the direction of the air flowing over your rudders. This abrupt change from one direction of spin to another provides the momentum to break loose and allows you to proceed on your way ... most of the time.

Sharing my escape plan with the dairy farmer and finding that he had no objection, I crawled up on the airboat, gave it a shot of ether, and started it up. A quick glance at the cows showed me eyes as big as dinner plates, but that was better than the garbage-can lids they had resembled earlier, so I ran up the engine to 2,000 rpm and started the spinning process. The Chinese lads stood there in the corral and gaped. Around and around and around I went, to no avail. Boosting the power to 2,500 rpm really got the airboat spinning around and around, but again, it wasn't fast enough to escape the clutches of the ground under the stern. I just couldn't get off that damn mound of dirt and cow poop I was sitting on! Advancing the throttle further, I ran the rpm up to 3000, and wow, did that do the trick. I was spinning around and around like there was no tomorrow. The engine was roaring, the airboat was shaking, and out of the corner of my dizzy eyes I saw the cows running out of the corral at a high rate of speed. Continuing to roar around and around so all the cows could get through the gate I needed to pass through as well, I saw the ranch manager running, as was Tim. Both appeared to be running for their lives, all the while holding their heads. The Chinese lads were all on their hands and knees, crawling out of the corral like a bunch of scalded cats. I thought, That's strange, but with the one-ton whirling monster in my hands I quickly got back to business.

I had built up enough speed by now, the cows were all through the gate, and I was getting dizzy as hell, so I figured now was the time to kick the rudder the other way. Down went the other rudder pedal and off the mound of dirt and cow poop came the airboat with a vengeance. Not wanting to get stuck again, I kept the power up and stormed out the still open gate and down through running cows and pasture to the water's edge. Once in the water, I spun the boat around and brought it back onto the shore. Killing the engine, I stepped out of the boat, double-checked the anchor to make sure it would hold against the floodwaters, and walked back across the pasture to the infamous corral. Goddamn, what a sight awaited me. In the corral stood only one cow, calmly chewing her cud. The other 149 cows were gone, the ranch manager was gone, Tim was nowhere to be seen, the Chinese were gone, and every goddamned cow flop that had been on the ground in that corral was now gone. They had all been lifted up by the powerful backthrust of the airboat propeller and hurled like Frisbees into the air toward all points of the compass. As the airboat had madly circled around and around, the cow flops had had been picked up and deposited on every square inch of building, fence, and roof within throwing distance. The whole damn area had gone from white barns and fences to cow-flop-covered barns and fences. In the corral, there was nothing but gravel and dirt where once cow flops had ruled supreme.

Hearing a noise to my left, I turned to see the ranch manager emerging from one of the cow barns. He was absolutely covered with cow flop! Tim came out of another building, and he was the brownest person I ever saw. He even had cow flop up his nose! Some of the other 149 Holsteins were starting to come back, still badly needing to be milked, and they were partially covered with cow flop (each with an amount determined by how long they had stayed in the corral while I whirled around). The swan shooters, well, suffice it to say that they were a soaking brown mess. Looking at the one remaining cow in the corral, still chewing her cud, I saw that she was also covered with cow flop, but only on one side. She was the damndest-looking thing I ever saw, all brown on one side and the typical black-and-white Holstein color on the other. Looking at how foolish that cow looked started me laughing; then Tim started to laugh, followed by the ranch manager. Damn, what a sight. Cow poop all over everything, one poor old cow in the middle of the corral covered with poop on one side and all black and white on the other, the rest of the cows having fled the great poop-throwing airboat, all the while leaving white streaks of milk on the ground throughout the corral, and four Chinese poachers all looking like cow flops with legs.

Looking at the ranch manager with tears of laughter streaming down my face, I said, "What is with that cow; why didn't she leave when the flops hit the fan?"

He grinned through a cow-flop-covered face and said, "That is Sue. She is deaf and blind but gives good milk with high fat content, so I just keep her around." So poor old Sue just stayed there the whole time and took the best of what the airboat dished out. I could just imagine how all the other cows laughed at her when they returned.

Tim and I spent the rest of that morning cleaning off the barns, windows, and fences with brushes and water from hoses supplied by the ranch manager. I think we spent at least six hours cleaning off that mess so the owner of the dairy farm wouldn't get mad at us.

A month later our four Chinese friends appeared in federal court and pled guilty. Then they wanted to tell their side of the story, which the judge agreed to hear. They all began chattering at once in broken English until she stopped them and asked that only one person speak at a time. A spokesman was chosen after a heated discussion among the four lads, in Chinese, so none of us had an inkling as to what was going on. Finally a stout fellow stepped forward and said, "Your honor, no amount of fine you give us here today can off set the fear we felt while hunting when out of the fog we hear the roar of an airplane. Out of the fog comes this airplane thing, it came roaring right at us and then the next thing we know we get a ticket and then it starts throwing cow ship at us. I got hit right on the back of my head and smelled rest of day."

It took a little while to explain that one to the judge. Her grin after I told our side of the story told me we were still welcome in her court anytime. It was a funny ending to a unique case but one I will always remember. That damn deaf and blind Holstein cow, totally covered on one side with cow flops, all the while standing at the edge of the corral, contentedly chewing her cud. I could just imagine what was going on in her mind in her black and silent world when the cow flops arrived.

Now I know that according to the Good Book, God loves little children and fools. I'm sure that after this particular "hoorah," there had to be room for all game wardens, big and tall, as well as a cow named Sue.

7

Snow Storm Mountain

During the fall of 1971, while working waterfowl hunters in the San Joaquin Delta, I often teamed up with state Fish and Game Warden Buck Del Nero. I was roaming northwestern California on various details as a new U.S. game management agent, and since the Stockton game management agent position was still essentially vacant (the new agent was on his way), I chose to drift that way off and on during the duck season that year, splitting my duties between Stockton and the Sacramento Valley in an attempt to keep the waterfowl hunters on the straight and narrow in that part of the country. On one such visit, Buck and I planned to go after duck hunters in the area of Venice Island, but our talks during that detail led me into an even bigger adventure later on.

I arrived at Buck's house about four A.M., and we grabbed a quick bite to eat and headed out to observe the activity on Venice Island in preparation for an in-depth surveillance of duck-hunting activities on the following shoot day. After covering Buck's boat with brush so no one would see it, we scrambled up onto the levee and hid in a dense thicket of brush. Then we began our patient work picking out which blinds the club members were using, what shooters were using the blinds, what part of the island the ducks and geese were using, and where we would hide when we returned to count drops during the next club shoot day. "Counting drops" simply means getting into an area before first light; hiding; and then counting the number of shots fired at the critters (in this case ducks), identifying who fired the shots, and recording the numbers of ducks and the species killed by each hunter. That last feat is no small accomplishment when one is anywhere from forty to one hundred yards away, hiding in the brush to avoid detection, and trying to identify a bird as it zips along at fifty-five miles per hour, all the while looking through tall grass or brush! However, officers in waterfowl districts, after some time practicing identifying waterfowl on the wing, get good enough to pick out most duck species just by how they fly, sometimes from a half a mile away, with 100 percent accuracy! The information is then recorded in our field diaries, and if the hunters go over the legal limits, the information is retrieved to refresh the hunters' minds when we make contact in the field as well as to help us testify later on in a court of law if need be.

On this particular trip, as Buck and I began selecting our targets we began to discuss other wildlife problems, as was usual during slow moments, all the while keeping a sharp eye on the blinds we were watching. Buck mentioned in an offhanded way that Dante Martinelli, a reported San Joaquin Delta waterfowl outlaw whom we knew from an earlier episode with a baited field during the dove season, also owned a large ranch in Modoc County in northeastern California. It was called the Snow Storm Ranch because it was located at the base of Snow Storm Mountain and consisted of many acres of high, cool desert country clothed with big sage, ponderosa pine, and western juniper as ground cover. As Buck recalled, the rumor on the street was that tremendous amounts of illegal deer, antelope, and just about anything else that moved, swam, or flew had been taken on this ranch over the years. That would certainly fit the basic local shooters' creed, "If it flies, it dies," I thought. Since the Italians were among the world's best cooks, having the "with enough garlic and butter, it's going to taste good" philosophy, I could see why anything with a heartbeat on the ranch would be harvested.

Apparently Dante's method of operation was to take the most influential and the wealthiest of the bankers, lawyers, doctors, and other power brokers that he knew to hunt on the ranch during the first weekend of the deer season. These folks would get royal treatment at the ranch house, dine on superb Italian cuisine, and then get to be the first to hunt on the ranch, which would not have been hunted since the end of the previous hunting season. This approach would provide an abundance of large-antlered deer in a semitame state, just what the doctor ordered for these once-a-year big-game shooters. Then all the "lesser nobles" would get to hunt on succeeding weekends after the best animals had already been taken. Those on the first trip, honored with unlimited spoils, would brag about their exploits upon their return and then be beholden to Dante for the rest of the year. It was not an unusual story of a time-worn method that never seems to fade in value or use.

As Buck told killing story after story about the Snow Storm Ranch crew and their illegal shooting (notice I don't call them "hunters") exploits, I began to develop a strong internal sense that possibly it was time for the "Romans" to meet the "Huns" once again. True, the shooting activity did not cross any lines under the federal laws I enforced, but I was cross-credentialed by California, so I could enforce the state laws and had the inclination and wherewithal, so why not? Besides, it would be politically easier for me as a fed to do the work than for my state counterparts, Dante being a somewhat powerful politician in the state and a member of the Fish and Game commission. I questioned Buck about to the ranch and its layout as the importance of the Venice Island stakeout began to fade from the forefront of my mind. It became apparent that Snow Storm Ranch, looming bigger and bigger in my craw, sat behind locked gates in the middle of a vast and wonderfully wild, resource-rich area. In short, it would be very difficult to move in on these people and catch them in any kind of wrongdoing because of the ranch's vast geography. Well, that might have been true, but they forgot one thing, to borrow a quotation from Winston Churchill: "They may have created a fortress, but they forgot to put a roof on it."

At the end of our eight-day waterfowl detail on Venice Island and several other islands, we had netted a total of forty-seven state and federal citations for over-limits, no federal duck stamps in possession, unplugged shotguns, and shooting over a baited area. With that, being needed elsewhere, I packed up, bade good-bye to Buck and his wife, Judy, until later, and headed back to Colusa County. All the way home the Snow Storm Ranch challenge was on my mind. For people to have that kind of arrogance and kill at will a resource that belongs to all of us was particularly galling. With a quiet promise to myself, I dedicated several mental moments to the problem and in no time finished with a grin. I had figured out a way to gain the "keys to the kingdom."

In the early summer of 1972, my deputy, Tim Dennis, and I took my old three-quarter-ton Dodge pickup loaded with camping gear, cast-iron pots, several hundred pounds of potatoes, onions, zucchini, garlic, and all the other neat things two cooks like to work with in the outdoors, threw in my two Labrador retrievers, and away we went. Snow Storm Mountain and the secrets you hold, grab your hind end, I thought. Here comes the German Tank Driver and his trusted sidekick, the Dirt Farmer! I could see that Tim was having some of the same thoughts. When the two of us got together on a detail like this, the chemistry we generated meant that someone doing something illegal was going to pay the price. Even my old Dodge patrol truck seemed to sense the urgency of the detail and ran like a Swiss watch, Rolex variety, the whole way.

When we arrived in Modoc County, we found that Snow Storm Ranch had a vastness, quiet beauty, and isolation that easily propelled one back to historical times. Numerous deer and antelope greeted us at every turn in the landscape. It was not overgrazed, and many varieties of prime deer-forage plants grew in abundance, along with numerous coveys of sage grouse. There were mallard ducks in the creeks and ponds, and under those waters swam trout of a size and pink-meated color that made anyone with any culinary appreciation think of a cast-iron skillet and melted butter sizzling around a trout fillet, or a breast of duck smothered with red currant jelly, all cooking slowly over an aromatic sagebrush fire. You can't imagine the feeling of peace that comes to one's soul when an opportunity like this to immerse the body in nature's luxury presents itself. It also steels that same soul against those who abuse this honor of the land.

Tim and I spent four long days driving the currently deserted ranch's external boundaries in order to learn its layout like the backs of our hands. We became familiar with all the roads and gathered a rough idea of the habits of the wildlife, especially the migration patterns of the California mule deer and antelope inhabiting the area, from the local biologists. We examined each locked gate to discover the type of lock, size, and the number of the key combination (conveniently printed on the bottom of the lock) so we could have keys made later. In general, we conducted an in-depth surveillance and information-gathering detail. This type of work is routine if you want to really know and understand the geographic heartbeat of an illegal operation. It's only common sense to eliminate as many unknowns as possible because once you add the human element, it's best to already possess half of the formula. Knowing the lay of the land and its resources often enables a wildlife officer to cut the human element off at the pass once they have done the devil's bidding. If your surveillance time has been spent correctly, you should be able to handle any type of occasion that may arise. That, plus a little common sense and luck, wins many a battle in the wildlife wars.

As a final preparation Tim and I scouted around for a close-in hiding spot that, with the use of binoculars, would enable us to observe the shooting parties as they pursued the wily deer. That site turned out to be a ledge of rock with an overhang that would allow the two of us to be out of the weather and away from prying eyes, yet allow us a clear view of the battlefield, so to speak.

After we had collected as much information as we could, we went back to Colusa and had keys made for all the locked gates at the ranch for which we had the necessary information. Having all the keys made so many miles away from the actual target would keep the location and type of the party we had planned for the fall away from any prying eyes that might give the operation away. Then I telephoned Inspector Ned Dolahite of the California Department of Fish and Game in Redding, California, to let him know that, number one, I would need some help with this particular endeavor, and number two, the help would have to be fairly close to the target area, and number three, the help would have to be the close-mouthed type. The inspector suggested that we meet in Susanville, a medium-sized town in Lassen County, which is adjacent to Modoc County, to finalize the details, and I agreed.

Dante Martinelli, my main target, was a Fish and Game commissioner for the state of California at that time. He was a high-level political appointee of Governor Pat E. Brown, Sr., and his job was to help the other commissioners set the state laws and regulations for the fishing and hunting communities, not to mention upholding the laws himself. On top of the inherent complexities of this situation, a fresh political problem was handed to me by my supervisor, Jack Downs. It seemed that the attention I had given Dante during the previous dove and water-fowl season had borne some bad-tasting political fruit. Pressure was being put on the Fish and Wildlife Service to get that Agent Terry Grosz out of Dante's hair, especially during hunting season. It seemed that the charge of harassment was being thrown around by the Dante faction and appeared to be supported by the higher-ups in the Fish and Game department. It did not seem to matter, as is the case with most political situations, that every time I went onto his dove or duck clubs somebody fell to the long arm of the law for stepping over the line, usually to charges of an over-limit or shooting over a baited area. Plain and simply, in the highest political circles the fact that I generally caught someone breaking the law was viewed as harassment, not me just doing my job.

Now, Jack was a master at keeping the pressure of this type of politics at bay but in such a manner that the bad guys weren't aware of it. His plan was to let me snare Dante but to let others actually remove him from the snare and issue the citations. That way Jack's hardheaded agent got his way, Jack kept the pressure on, the political manipulators were put off until another day, and the critters got a breather. Not being able to actually put the grab on Dante was a disappointment to me, but years later I understood the wisdom of Jack's order, and I in turn as a supervisor protected my men in the same manner over the years. Hence my trip to Susanville to meet with Fish and Game Inspector Dolahite and two of his senior wardens.

When we met, I informed the inspector in more detail of what I was going to attempt, namely, the project of snaring one of his Fish and Game commissioners and his crew of poachers, a political hot potato if you will, in his district, and I needed his help to do it. I also laid out the political interference issues involving Dante and his supporting cast of characters from the Fish and Game department so Ned could examine the entire playing field with a sure set of eyes. Ned Dolahite listened quietly to my plan and then, without hesitation, said he would be more then happy to support my endeavor. He said he would assign the two officers with him at this meeting to the detail and would round up two additional officers to give Tim and me a hand during the surveillance, which we expected to be labor intensive.

The two senior wardens whom he had brought as part of the team didn't inspire me with a whole lot of confidence. My gut feeling was that both of them would have been just as happy to be assigned elsewhere than this political hotbed. But they were the local officers assigned to that area; that was the inspector's call, so I would just have to take a cold potato and wait, if you get my drift. Inspector Dolahite had an excellent reputation statewide as an outstanding officer and supervisor with a superb work ethic. Based on my personal past experience with him, I knew he wouldn't let me down regardless of the heat this operation would generate if it were successful, and ultimately he didn't. This detail had the potential to be a hot one for anyone involved, even if we were in the right, but that didn't stop Ned. He looked squarely at the benefit to the resource and the law of the land and made his decision to join up. He hung in throughout the project and never looked back. During my years as an officer and supervisor, I tried to emulate this man's integrity and professionalism in many ways because of what I learned from him during those rough-and-tumble days. I only hope that he saw it and felt that I was successful in that endeavor.

As the deer season in Modoc County approached, Tim and I again loaded up the old, tired Dodge pickup with the gear we'd need for an extended surveillance and headed north to Snow Storm Mountain for a time of our lives that truly came from beyond the north wind. Wildlife wars will lead many an officer into enforcement realms he or she never dreamed of. This detail would stretch our abilities to the maximum before it was finished. But what a detail it was! Damn, there I go getting ahead of myself again.

On an extended surveillance of this type, there was nothing to do but cold-camp it. That meant no fire, no hot food, staying out of view, withstanding the elements no matter what, no bathing—in short, we would have to sustain ourselves for the duration, no matter what the luck of the draw brought. In addition to tons of ready-to-eat, high-fat food (to keep the winter cold out) and liquid, I brought double sets of walkie-talkies, night-vision gear, binoculars, and spotting scopes. I made sure we had plenty of gear to get the job done, even if some of it broke down.

The hiding place we had picked earlier that summer while going over the ranch with a fine-toothed comb was a big rocky ledge and overhang on Bureau of Land Management ground. This site allowed us, with the binoculars and scopes, to overlook most of Snow Storm Ranch, especially those areas that would be hunted the hardest by our targets, and would allow us to draw back under the narrow confines of the overhang in bad weather and, except during the worst storms, stay somewhat dry. We had to compete with the wood rats, mice, and hantavirus, but Tim and I came prepared for the worst and loved it—that is, except when the wood rats and deer mice jumped on our heads at night, nibbled on our fingers as we slept, or peed on us when we were trying to sleep.

From our vantage point we would be able to see the shooters almost all of the time that they were hunting on the mountain and flats that surrounded most of the ranch. There were a few deep draws into which we could not see, but by and large our position allowed us a free field of fire. In addition, the main road into the ranch, both from the main access gate and from the main hunting access road to the mountain, was under our scrutiny the entire time. With that kind of placement, we could look directly into the shooters' vehicles and examine their game as they passed into our line of sight. In theory, we could see them hunt, see them shoot, see what they killed, and, as they brought their ill-gotten game back to the ranch house to butcher, look down into the backs of their open-air vehicles and confirm our earlier observations. Damn, that was surely going to make our lives simple, or so I thought. ...

Tim and I arrived in Modoc County late on a Tuesday afternoon, four days before the start of deer-hunting season. We camped overnight in unseasonably wet weather and then met our two promised additional game wardens for the first time at a prearranged place and time the following day. Right off the bat, I could visualize a hatful of problems. I was sure glad this was going to be so simple. ... Both officers were young to the Fish and Game organization; in fact, they were *rookies*. One had quite a few years' experience as a chief of police in a small southern California city, but the other was as green as a gourd. With the potentially hot repercussions of this detail, it was no place for a rookie on probation, I thought grimly. However, both appeared to be physically sound and to possess good common sense, not to mention humor, so I dismissed my reservations and was just happy for the extra "heartbeats." At that time and place, what else could I do? I was banking on Ned's understanding of his people's instincts as hunters of humans and their abilities to get the job done, not to mention what the detail needed in the form of human resources. Ned hadn't failed me yet, but things were not looking so good with two rookies assigned to handle the field work, including covering a Fish and Game commissioner, and two senior wardens who would just as soon be somewhere else when the gates of hell slammed shut on the trigger fingers of the Snow Storm Ranch crew. But before this detail was over, I would learn a damn good lesson about what levels a man can rise to when needed, rookie or no rookie.

Forging past my perception of the weakness of the operation, my plan was to keep the two green game wardens fairly close, patrolling around the spot where Tim and I would be staked out overlooking the ranch in question. That way if the detail blew up unexpectedly, we would still have some law west of the Pecos to hold the line. Ned had instructed the two senior officers to work no farther than half an hour away from the ranch so they could be on the scene in short order to back up the rookies in case Tim and I caught the lads on the ranch with the goods before everyone was ready. The two green officers were to drive Tim and me to a wooded area just above our stakeout point, drop us off with our gear, and split, taking my vehicle with them to avoid drawing attention to our presence. Tim and I would sprint (if you could call it a sprint with ten tons of gear) across a ridge, down through the pines, junipers, and sagebrush, over a small hill, and another hundred yards to the ledge that would be our home for the next several days. Tim and I doubled-checked our gear and reloaded it back into my truck. The two officers drove us into the target area, and since we figured nobody was around because it was four days before hunting season even started, we began to casually unload the gear and foodstuffs from my rig.

Boom-boom! All of a sudden we heard several rapid shots coming from the direction of Snow Storm Ranch. Sure glad this is going to be simple, I thought as I spun around, trying to echolocate the shots. No doubt about it, the shots had come from the ranch area proper. Damn, the lads on the ranch had arrived several days earlier than our intelligence had led us to believe, and now we could be losing valuable evidence! Tim and I immediately unloaded our gear and, gathering it all up, sprinted across the rocks and down the hill toward the safety of our overlook.

Needless to say, gear was flying every which way as the two wardens departed rapidly with both vehicles so no one would spot them and suspect that we were there. Down through the brush we went and reached our rocky ledge just in time to see a Jeep containing four men coming back from the hills by the main ranch house with what appeared to be a skinned-out animal carcass in a screened box bolted to the hood. The Jeep moved down the road not far from us, and we were able to confirm that it was the body of a deer or antelope as the Jeep drove on to the large ranch house and disappeared from view.

Realizing that the lads were up and at it and apparently already breaking the law, we hurriedly reassessed our location and began preparations for the long haul. We scraped out the wood-rat droppings, urine balls, and five hundred years' worth of other accumulated debris and laid our sleeping bags down under the ledge, out of the rain, which was now starting in earnest. We stowed our extra clothing and cold-weather gear with the sleeping bags; covered our ice chests with limbs to hide their color (in those days all ice chests were red); and laid out our optics, radio gear, and night-vision gear along the ledge under a tarp. About that time the Jeep that we had seen earlier passed by again, now headed away from the ranch with what appeared to be an animal skeleton strapped to its hood. We assumed that the meat had been stripped off the bones to be used for camp meat to feed the shooting crew. About thirty minutes later, the Jeep returned without the stripped-clean carcass, which more than likely had been tossed into a brushy draw by the road since the big-game hunting season was still closed.

Lying in the shallow red dust of past centuries now slowly turning into the mud of today on our ledge as the rain came down with a purpose, we counted about twenty people staying at the ranch in this first shooting group, and we continued to watch them for the rest of the week. During that period we saw members of the party, safely behind their locked gates (but with no roof, remember!), kill Canada geese with their deer rifles; we counted over-limits of trout being taken from the reservoir behind the ranch house; and we saw several shooting expeditions leave the ranch house and heard shooting in one of the canyons that was concealed from our optics and eyes. Several times we saw a Jeep come out of that canyon and go to the ranch house bearing a skinned-out animal carcass on the hood, ready for use as camp meat. The same Jeep always left within thirty or forty minutes with a skeleton of an animal, which was driven into the brush away from the ranch and disposed of.

We kept our two close-in backup wardens apprised of the ongoing events via a secure channel on our federal walkie-talkies, and all in all we were pleased with everything from our hiding place to the violations unfolding before us. The only problem was the constant, though not hard, rain that had fallen every day since our arrival. We didn't have anything that was totally dry or warm after the first day of the stakeout. It was obvious that God was mad at either Tim or me again. Probably both of us, I mused as a raindrop ran down my long, wet nose and dropped onto the lens of the spotting scope lying on the ground in front of me. God may not have been pissed, but he surely was not happy with either of us as we lay in the mud on that ledge so long ago. Maybe it was our clearing out of His old buddies the wood rats and their nests. ...

Here we go, I thought. It was just before dawn on Saturday morning, the opening day of deer season, somewhere on a wet, muddy ledge in Modoc County, California. The wood rats had gotten into some of our food and had a heyday, and ain't we having a grand time, I thought as it began to snow. Out from the ranch house came a convoy of old-style, four-cylinder military Jeeps hauling expectant shooters to their "fields of glory" while one lone Hun and his Dirt Farmer comrade lay dismally soaked to the hind end in the rocks above. But our eyes were gleaming and alert, for now was the time for the hunters of men.

The shooters went to their chosen spots on Snow Storm Mountain, and all morning long the cold, wet, alternating-rain-and-snow-filled air rang with many crisp shots of heavy rifles. Tim and I saw numerous deer taken, and many appeared to be

illegal, either does or antlered deer not possessing the correct
number of antler points. California law required hunters in
Modoc County to kill only deer with three points or more to a
side; the reason for this law was to allow the bucks time to age
and breed with the does to help repopulate the declining deer
herd in the area. In fact, Dante Martinelli, the Fish and Game
commissioner, had had to approve of and vote for this regulation
in order for it to become the law of the land. How quickly we
forget ...

About midmorning the Jeeps began coming down from the
mountain with their passengers and ill-gotten gains. They passed
by us on the dirt road that ran near our hiding place, and we saw
that they were carrying many big bucks, none of which were
tagged in accordance with the laws of the state (deer had to be
tagged with the state-supplied deer tag prior to transport). Also,
several were carrying forked-horn (two points to a side) deer,
which were illegal in this county.

During a quieter moment when the lads were having lunch at
the ranch house, I let my mind wander through history and examined the ranch as if through a set of eyes from the past. Snow
Storm Ranch was a large, old-time cattle ranch with massive
beamed barns and corrals placed next to good water in a beautiful valley with a ranch house that spoke to the grandeur of days
long ago. Then the ghost of past times faded and the present
manifested itself as the drama unfolded and each report of a rifle
spoke to the truth of the story Buck Del Nero had told me that
fateful day on Venice Island. Toward dusk on the second day of
the so-called hunt, I noticed a Jeep come down off the mountain
and stop about a mile away, almost directly across from us.
Through the spotting scope I saw two men unload two doe deer,
both of which had been killed illegally. They hid the deer under
several old juniper trees, then went on to the ranch house. I figured enough was enough—those folks, along with the others,
had done enough illegal killing. I called my two green wardens
on the walkie-talkie, and they responded immediately. I asked
them to meet us at our hideout; it was time to drop the hammer.

In about thirty minutes they arrived at our rocky home and immediately commented on how crummy we looked. I've got to give them credit; that remark took courage. I could just imagine how we looked, or smelled, for that matter, but regardless of those facts, either Tim or I could still kill a mule with one right-handed punch. Game wardens really are a special breed, I thought; thank the Lord for them and their strong sense of duty to those who have no voice, however questionable that sense may be in many people's eyes.

Overlooking the comments on our beauty with a large grin, I pointed out where the two chaps had earlier dropped off the two doe deer under the junipers across from us. I told the wardens they were going to have to race across that valley below, with very little cover, I might add, and position themselves near those dead deer. I told them to wait until the chaps had loaded the deer in the Jeep and then, and only then, apprehend them. I also explained that on these same fellows' duck club in the delta, the common trick was to come pick up their illegal game with no lights showing on the Jeeps. But if a game warden was around, they would turn on the lights, blink the lights, or honk the horn as they returned to camp to warn the rest to get their acts together before the law arrived. I told them to make sure the occupants of the Jeep understood that if they blinked the lights, turned them on, or honked the horn, they were going to jail, period. In short, nothing but a darkened Jeep was to go back to that ranch house; otherwise we would lose the edge. I gave the lads a quick briefing on what Tim and I had seen over the time we had been on stakeout, especially the numbers and types of deer that had been illegally taken and moved earlier to the ranch house. Those carcasses were now hanging in a barn near the house.

My two lads started off across the valley in what was left of the daylight at the beginning of dusk. In that scramble they had to use every bit of cover because they didn't have the deep cover of darkness. If they were discovered by the eyes at the ranch, the whole plan would turn to slop. After they disappeared out of my sight into the shadows of the bush, I called Inspector Dolahite on my portable radio and requested backup from the two senior officers who were assigned to this detail. I asked that the two chaps meet the rookies at the main gate just off the county road so we could get our final battle plan in order. Ned acknowledged my request and contacted both officers on the radio to ascertain their time of arrival. As Tim and I listened on our radio, both officers indicated that they were too far away to respond at this time. I thought that excuse was no more than a case of pure lack of guts since both officers had been told to be no more than thirty minutes away, but fuming on my part was not going to save the day! However, Inspector Dolahite calmly reminded the two men that he told them to stay within thirty minutes of the ranch in case they were needed. He told them they were both needed now, and they had twenty-nine minutes to get to the gate, or else. They both indicated that they were on their way.

About that time I heard another voice on the radio, that of Fish and Game Captain Harold Carling, far to the north. Without any hesitation, he told me to hang on; he was coming to give us a hand, and he was bringing a federal refuge manager with law enforcement authority as well. I had known Harold when I was in college at Humboldt State in northwestern California. He was one hell of a game warden in that area then, and he was showing more of the same grit now. He knew he was going into the lions' den with a very powerful Fish and Game commissioner, but that didn't slow him down one bit. Men like that are why we still have resources today for everyone to enjoy. That jumping in took a lot of guts on his part. He could have remained a Fish and Game captain for the rest of his career, and no one would have been the wiser if a man as powerful as Dante or the governor had gotten involved in this "hoorah" as a result of Harold's courage and involvement that day.

So here we were with two rookie game wardens running a mile across a sagebrush flat trying not to be discovered so they could apprehend several lads with two illegal deer; a ranch house full of illegal deer and the lads who had taken them; a Fish and Game commissioner in the middle of everything like a queen bee; two regular officers, after being scolded by their inspector, heading slowly into this area, where they expected to run into at the very least a hatful of political flack; a Fish and Game captain racing at breakneck speed to assist (every time he talked on the radio you could hear the patrol vehicle's engine straining); a refuge manager risking his neck on a purely state issue; and a federal agent with his deputy who had set this damn mess up, whose information everyone else had to trust, and who couldn't assist in the takedown because of politics. Damn, I sure was glad this was a simple case.

I sent Tim to my vehicle (now placed out of sight on the road above our outlook) with orders to participate as an extra man but asked him not to go into the ranch, as Jack had ordered. Tim was like a brother to me. He was tough, had good common sense, was not afraid of anything, and could carry out an order to a T. I knew that if any starch was needed once the entire crew got together for the kill, Tim would certainly provide it, and then some.

Picture the next turn of events. Here I was, lying on this rim of rocks on a hillside, covered with mud, trying to get the crew organized so we could apprehend the lads at the ranch house with their illegal deer, all the while trying to remain low key and out of sight in the mud, when all of a sudden I heard a voice behind me say, "What are you doing?" I turned around, and there standing behind me, dressed in hunter orange, were two deer hunters who had wandered into my hideout and were standing there in front of God and everybody looking at all the optics and radio gear spread out on the ledge in front of me. I hissed, "Get down! Federal agent!" They immediately dropped to the ground, and to forestall a list of questions I showed them my credentials and told them they were going to have to get the hell out of there—now! I said there was going to be a big drug drop by aircraft in the valley shortly, and there could be a lot of shooting.

"Get out of here," I ordered, "and don't look back!" The last I saw of those two unfortunates, they were still running. I saw them cross the last ridge about half a mile away; they hadn't looked back once. That was the kind of surprise one couldn't plan for, I thought as I rolled back over to watch the action below. I surely didn't want those two standing up there on my ridge, where the lads at the ranch could see them and maybe even think they were the law. I had had to use a bald-faced lie instead of a little fib, and to be kinda frank, it worked very well.

Just then I saw a Jeep coming from the ranch house without any headlights. It was too soon for my two green officers to have crossed that damn valley and gotten into position so they could stone-cold arrest the chaps who had killed the does, I thought. It made me sick. We needed those deer in the Jeep to really make our charges stick. I watched in agony as the Jeep passed near my hiding place and headed across the valley, turning up the narrow trail that led back to the junipers where the two dead does lay. I watched the drama unfolding through my spotting scope as the two suspects got out, quickly loaded the two deer into the back of their Jeep, and jumped back in to leave. I was thinking, Terry, this is it. You can't let those lads escape. Whether you like it or not, you are now going to have get directly involved, orders or no orders. Damn the bad luck anyway. I figured I would work my way down from the rocks, and when the lads passed my hiding point I would step out and roll the gold on them. But then, just as the two lads in the Jeep started to leave, I saw two most beautiful, plug-ugly game wardens step out of the brush and grab the bad guys. They had made it! They made it across that long valley in time to get the lads with the deer, I yelled to myself! I couldn't believe it. Damn, was I thrilled and proud of those two lads.

There was a little conference between my lads and the men in the Jeep, and then the two game wardens got in back with the deer and the Jeep slowly started to work its way without lights back down the rocky dirt road toward the ranch. About that time the two senior game wardens, Harold Carling, the refuge manager from Modoc National Wildlife Refuge, and Tim arrived at the front gate to the ranch. A few moments went by before Tim called and told me that the locks had been changed and our keys did not fit. Without hesitation I told him to use our "master key" (a three-foot pair of bolt cutters). Since Tim and I were under orders not to participate, he handed the bolt cutters to one of the local game wardens, who instantly refused and backed away as if he had just been handed a live hand grenade. The refuge manager stepped forward and said, "I'm not afraid of Martinelli; give me the cutters." With that, the link of chain next to the lock was cut (that way we would be liable civilly for only one link of chain if this entry went to court) and the officers were within the walls of the "fortress without a roof." They convoyed without lights down the road toward the ranch house and met the waiting Jeep containing the two illegal deer, the two bad guys, who just happened to be high-powered attorneys, and my two "seasoned" rookies.

While they transferred the two doe deer to a patrol pickup, I got Harold on the radio. I told him to let the Jeep drive back to the ranch house with the two shooters and the two game wardens in the back. I again explained the duck club policy of driving back to the club house with lights if the game warden was present and asked Harold to make sure the driver of the Jeep was warned again to drive without any lights, which he did. The other vehicles were to slowly follow about a hundred yards behind the Jeep, also without lights. Last but not least I told Harold which barn the lads had been putting their deer in as they killed them and hung them to cool. With those instructions out of the way, off the officers went, sans Tim, toward the ranch house. By now it was getting dark. There were bonfires at the ranch house main yard, which cast many moving shadows on the barns and the house itself. This sight, coupled with the noises of happy make-believe hunters doing what they do in camp and the excitement of watching a convoy of darkened vehicles move into the arena—wow! All I needed was a few strains of Wagner and I could have soared with the best of them that evening.

Through my binoculars I watched the Jeep roll into the ranch compound, followed moments later by the convoy of law enforcement vehicles. Then all of the vehicles moved out of sight. The happy noise of the compound continued for a few seconds, then died away to the quiet of the evening, interrupted only by the faraway call of a coyote. I waited. Then I waited some more. The moments seemed like hours. Finally I couldn't stand not being able to participate. I tried calling Harold on the walkie-talkie but received no response. Realizing that I was alone on the mountain until we met again, I began to have doubts about the accuracy of the information I had passed on. Would they find everything as I had said? Would they find all the evidence where I had said it would be? Realizing that I had to wait, I began to collect our equipment in the cool dark of the evening, all the while trying to suppress my growing excitement over all the possibilities or political wrecks that might follow.

Soon Tim arrived from out of the dark, and we packed a load of gear up to the truck without using flashlights so the lads at the ranch would not know we had been there. We walked back to our ledge and were collecting the last of our wet and muddy equipment when I noticed the convoy slowly emerging from the ranch house. It proceeded close to the point of rocks where Tim and I were standing and then, rolled to a stop. Harold Carling stepped out of his patrol vehicle, got on the portable radio, and said, "We got the big one plus a handful of others." That was music to my ears! That meant they had caught Dante! Damn, I could hardly contain myself. Tim and I headed back to our truck, again in the dark, and when we arrived all the Fish and Game lads were there. Boy, what a reunion. We all had tales to tell and could not tell them fast enough. The bottom line was that in addition to apprehending the Fish and Game commissioner in the process of skinning out an illegal deer, they had caught six other men with illegal deer. There were other violations, but the lads just took the major ones to avoid extending the political "hoorah." Attorneys, bankers, real estate developers, and other big wheels all found out that justice might be blind, but she is for all of us during the many times in our lives that we get near the edge.

Tim and I loaded up the old Dodge, thanked the lads for their able assistance, and turned south toward Colusa County, our families, and home. We were tired, dirty, unshaven, smelled like wood-rat dung, and were still soaked, but you know, it was a really nice day.

As we were on our way home, Don Horn, a game warden from the west side of the state and a good friend, hearing me go on duty on my radio, called to ask how we had done. I told him we had gotten "the big one." You could hear a big whoop over the radio, and then he told me I had a quart of the finest whiskey coming the next time we got together. Don had known I was going after Dante. Don was also a very close friend of Buck Del Nero and remembered all the problems Dante had caused Buck when he tried to enforce the dove-baiting and other migratory bird laws in the San Joaquin Delta area. It's amazing how game wardens stick together.

It was an end to a rather long six days lying out there in the elements, eating cold food, getting rained and snowed on, and sleeping in wet sleeping bags with dusky-footed wood rats and deer mice jumping on our heads all night long, but by God, I miss moments like that to this day. There is something about the smell of powder, the sound of battle, the kinship of the Dirt Farmer, and the hunting of humans that I can't describe. It's something you just feel and grow to love to the very depths of your soul. If you don't, then you are in the wrong business.

The next day the shooters who had been cited the night before trooped before a justice of the peace, paid $500 for each violation they had committed, and had their hunting privileges suspended along with receiving a lecture on why we have game laws. As the last of the bad lads left the court, one of those convicted, an attorney, turned to some of the Fish and Game wardens (again I was not present) and said, "I don't know how you did it, but you got us good this time, and we have paid our dues." He turned, entered his limo, and left. Standing on the courtroom porch steps were about a half-dozen knowing grins, big ones, I might add, but not as big as the ones Tim and I were wearing, still in the backwater of the action. We were ecstatic. There had been no problems, nobody had gotten hurt except the deer, and a nice joint operation had been carried off, albeit with some occasional bad moments.

Damn, come to think of it, I never did get that bottle of whiskey from Don Horn.

8

Greed Works Both Ways

IN 1972 I WAS AGAIN working waterfowl hunters in the San Joaquin Delta with my old friend Buck Del Nero, a state Fish and Game warden. Buck was a legend in his own time in the San Joaquin Delta country, feared not so much by the masses as by those patricians who owned large tracts of land and treated all the wildlife upon those lands as if it were their chattel, like European royalty of old. Don't get me wrong: Buck would work the masses of the waterfowl-hunting public in his district, making sure they toed the wildlife conservation line. Those who didn't obey the wildlife laws sooner or later got to know him "up close and personal." However, Buck had a very special spot in his heart for those who were in a position to seriously misuse the land's renewable resources, even more so than the common sportsman, and who took advantage of their positions of trust to abuse the conservation laws and wildlife resources at every turn and opportunity. I guess that is one of the reasons why we got along so famously. We both felt that those in a position to really destroy this nation's heritage, such as some of the good folks on the wealthy private hunting clubs, should have to look over their shoulders every time they went forth. It was just a matter of time before we paid each and every one of those folks on the big private hunting preserves in the delta a personal visit. You can do that when you work every day of the hunting season from dawn to dusk and many times even through the night. Such are the advantages of being young, carrying a badge, and really believing that the wildlife wars can be won.

One day we were checking waterfowl hunters on and around Venice Island, which contained the Venice Island and Delta Hermitage Duck Clubs on its private piece of the island. Routine checks of the everyday sportsman hunting the edges of this area yielded little more than the occasional unplugged shotgun or power-boat shooting of resting waterfowl. Those types of violations were not the real reason Buck and I were here. Venice Island, comprising several private farms and the two major hunting clubs, was loaded with thousands of migratory waterfowl, mostly pintail ducks and white-fronted geese. Every time Buck and I passed the island we were greeted with clouds of milling waterfowl flying over the flooded cornfields looking for a place to feed and loaf. If history repeated itself, we knew the island would soon become a killing field of the ugliest proportions, a slaughter carried out by men who were models of the community one day and wildlife outlaws the next. Not all the folks on the club were like that, mind you, but there were enough to make us keep a sharp eye and ear tuned every time they went into the field.

We had decided to spend some time on a surveillance of the Venice Island Duck Club because the word was that some club members were getting a little carried away with a certain baited mallard pond near the club house and, in general, were having trouble counting the actual numbers of waterfowl being taken on shoot days. This club was owned and hunted by some very wealthy people who had a historical reputation for violating the state and federal wildlife regulations, especially as they related to waterfowl. The isolation of the hunting area, including the inaccessibility of the island to outsiders like game wardens, and the wealth and political clout of the individuals hunting on the club led many of them to believe that invincibility to wildlife conservation officers and the laws they enforced was the word of the day.

It never seemed to fail when we worked this club: our problems always seemed to involve large over-limits of waterfowl (ducks and white-fronted geese in particular) and sometimes the use of bait. These lads would usually add whole-kernel corn to an already harvested cornfield, or most likely to a flooded pond, which would quickly, sometimes within a matter of just hours, draw ducks in by the hundreds in such a feeding frenzy that they ignored the gunners. This behavior of course allowed huge kills to illegally take place. The practice of baiting was outlawed in the 1930s because of the killing fields it created, and that was when we had fewer hunters in the United States than we do today. No two ways about it, it was a terribly destructive practice in the hands of people interested in a true blood sport. Unfortunately, political pressure from some Republican members of Congress, urged on by the greedy among American "sportsmen," and weak leadership of the Fish and Wildlife Service has brought baiting back as a legal shooting tool. Current federal migratory bird hunting regulations allow shooting over a baited area through the so-called practice of moist-soil management. The bottom line is that moist-soil management (mowing weedy fields or certain seed crops and flooding them just before the arrival of the southward migrating waterfowl to increase gunning success under the guise of habitat creation) is nothing more than an excuse to allow greater killing of ducks and geese by so-called sportsmen and land managers too damn lazy to protect the heritage of the sport of waterfowl hunting. Sad to say, these politically coerced actions are nothing less than pandering to hunter opportunity by the states in pursuit of the almighty dollar and a blatant abrogation by the Service of its responsibilities under the Migratory Bird Treaty Act.

This area of our current interest was an artificial island of considerable size, planted to corn, which had become a natural migration stopover for thousands of migrating waterfowl. In particular, the island seemed to be a haven for pintail, mallard, and white-fronted geese. These species are primarily seed eaters and are considered excellent table fare by the waterfowling community. They are also birds whose bodies are above average in size and weight, thereby making a limit of such birds a real gift to the hunter and his family members or friends lucky enough to receive them. Hence, they are highly sought-after species. At this time the daily limit on ducks was eight per day and eight in possession; for white-fronts the daily bag limit was three per day and three in possession—more than enough birds for any person to eat over a period of several weeks. However, many of the members of this duck club seemed to have a problem counting; hence our more than usual interest in this duck club on that fine fall day.

In the evening, as Buck and I were working along the back side of Venice Island in our boat, trying to figure out when and how to work the duck hunters on the island again, I heard a noise that sounded like *chugga-chugga-chugga*. I asked Buck to stop the boat's motor so I could concentrate on the unidentified sound without the gurgling sound of our idling outboard. He stopped the motor, and as the boat slowly drifted to a stop, the sound, *chugga-chugga-chugga*, came clearly to us through the cool evening air.

I said, "Buck, what does that sound like to you?"

He listened intently with a scowl on his face and then said, "I don't really know."

I said, "Think about it for a second."

He concentrated on the sound again without success. Listening hard and trying to locate the spot where the sound was coming from on the island, a light went on in my tired brain.

"Buck," I said, "it sounds to me like a compressor motor off a truck-and-trailer rig, like one hears on a reefer going down the highway."

Buck sat quietly in our drifting boat and listened even more intently. I was sure he was trying to identify not only the sound and its location but its reason for being there in that great game warden mind of his. We always suspected the motives of the folks gunning on this island because of their past history in breaking the wildlife laws and the ingenious ways in which they did so. Having a compressor unit here on the island to be used by a duck club conjured up all kinds of ideas, mostly along the lines of vast over-limits of waterfowl taken by errant club members who needed something larger than the "average bear"–sized freezer to prevent the spoiling of their ill-gotten gain. Buck knew that country like the back of his hand, and after a period of intense thought, he said, "Terry, if that's truly a compressor for a freezer unit, its sound is coming from behind that duck club's picking facility, which is located adjacent to a very dense stand of bamboo." Buck waited a few more moments, and I listened because his scrunched-up face told me his mental wheels were working on overtime. "I can't think of a more perfect place to put a large freezer unit than right next to that picking facility," he slowly uttered. "There's only one way in, and that is past the front door of the Mexican laborers or through that dense bamboo thicket in the back. We won't be coming in from the side holding the bamboo thicket unless we get a bulldozer," he added matter-of-factly. "If it's true that it's a commercial freezer unit, since the birds are now on the club in huge numbers, we have our work cut out for us, Terry." He let his voice trail off as his serious, coal-black eyes met mine.

The folks on this club at that time were mostly judges, politicians, real estate moguls and other moneyed types who were commonly known to invite the California State Fish and Game director to hunt on the club as a favor and, though it might be little known or admitted, as a cover against the immediate presence of game wardens. A clash over the wildlife laws with these people always led to some kind of political "hoorah," no matter how well the lads trapped themselves in the field with their over-limits or use of bait. They just didn't have the backbone to stand up and admit they were wrong, so they would always pull political strings in an attempt to justify their criminally errant behavior.

I listened for a few more moments to confirm the presence of a compressor unit in my mind's eye, then said flatly, "Well, let's go check it out. If it's on this club, it's here for a no-good reason."

It was getting pretty dark by now, so Buck restarted the boat motor and we slowly idled over to the edge of the island, where I jumped out onto the berm and anchored our boat among the rocks. The berm around this island was no different than any other in the delta; it was covered with stinging nettle, dried weeds of every kind, and dense layers of the ever-present blackberry bushes. No matter how one cut it, the job of the game warden never seemed easy. If it did, that usually meant something was badly wrong. Crawling carefully through the blackberries so we wouldn't tear holes in our hip waders and trying to be quiet so we wouldn't be discovered by the island's farm laborers, who had been taught to watch out for game wardens, we slowly peeked up and over the levy in the direction of our mystery sound. Below us on the island floor were a couple of run-down, unpainted shacks with their lights on and a number of nearby darkened outbuildings. Buck pointed toward the two shacks and whispered, "Those are where the island's Mexican laborers live." He explained that on shoot days the laborers acted as extra eyes or lookouts for game wardens, acted as runners with the club members' birds, picked and wrapped the wealthy hunters' ducks, and did anything else they were asked to do. "Other than that," he continued, "their duties consist of working as farm laborers on the island, doing the planting and harvesting during season."

Buck pointing to our right, where there was a large, darkened, run-down wooden building that he said was the main picking shed where the laborers picked and processed the club members' ducks, geese, and pheasants during shoot days. Looking intently at that darkened shed, we became aware that the *chugga-chugga-chugga* sound was coming from the rear of the building, next to a thick grove of live bamboo. After listening for a few moments to our mystery sound, I looked at Buck and said, "I need to see what that is all about. Do you want to stay here and provide top cover for me or do you want to go along?" I asked because of his state officer status. If anything went wrong and we got caught snooping, he was a lot more vulnerable than I was when it came to those politics associated with duck hunting in California and possible trespass.

Buck just gave me his "this is my district" look and started to belly-crawl out of our blackberry brush cover and across the levee road toward the noise. I took my cue from him, and we slunk (if you can imagine two six-foot-four-inch, 250-plus pounders slinking) out of the bushes, over the berm, across the levee road, down the mowed back side of the levee, and across the island floor. Once out of sight of the laborers fixing dinner in their houses, we raced to the front door of the picking facility. Standing on the front porch of the darkened building, we caught our breaths and looked to see if anyone had noticed our passage across the property. Everything appeared to be quiet, so we turned our attention to the door of the picking shed. It had been left open by the last user, so, looking around one last time to make sure we had not been observed when we crawled over the top of the levee in plain view, in we went through the invitingly open door.

What met our eyes was unbelievable. On the west side of the building was a large six-burner gas stove whose pilot light cast an eerie, flickering blue glow over the building's interior. The dim light illuminated a huge stainless-steel cleaning table; numerous stainless-steel cleaning sinks; several rubber-fingered duck-picking machines; a large plastic-wrap packaging machine; paper-wrapping machines; and a large open four-burner gas stove, without grates, for singeing the ducks after they were picked. It was absolutely amazing; we were in a duck-picking and -processing factory even Buck didn't know existed! It was more than plain that the lads on this club were very serious about their duck, goose, and pheasant killing and the care taken of the birds after they were killed. It was clear that these folks could handle a *lot* of birds.

We were soon shaken out of our wonderment by the constant and now louder than ever *chugga-chugga-chugga* coming from behind the north wall of the building, the reason for our original mission. I quietly moved closer to take a look while Buck stood guard at the front door to alert me to any outside prying eyes. The north side of the building was not illuminated very well by the soft gas light, so I felt along the wall with my hands and fingers, trying to figure out what that compressor noise was all about. The noise was coming from behind the north wall all right because I could feel the vibration through my fingertips. I continued to feel my way back and forth along the wall for something like a latch to a door when all of a sudden part of the north wall moved. It was a false wall! I slid the moving section off to one side, up and over the immovable remaining portion of the wall, on a set of well-oiled rollers. All at once a light went on, and there in all its glory was a door to a walk-in freezer behind the moveable portion of the wall. Buck about crapped his pants, as did I. I hurriedly unscrewed the light bulb so it wouldn't alert anyone nearby to our presence, then waited a few moments to see if anyone was coming to investigate and to let my night vision readjust.

All remained quiet, so Buck, whose curiosity was killing him, moved over to where I was standing and we opened the door to the walk-in freezer. The inside freezer light went on as soon as we opened the door, so Buck and I hurriedly stepped into the freezer and closed the door behind us just enough to turn out the overhead light. Using our flashlights, we let the beams diffuse through our fingers over the lenses, allowing us to see but letting little light out for the world to see. Damn o'mighty, what a game warden's treasure trove greeted our eyes. Inside that freezer were two or three hundred pheasants in various processing stages: picked, unpicked, bagged, or in piles. There were three or four hundred ducks and geese likewise bagged or lying loose on the floor, without tags identifying their owners. It was absolutely amazing: possible over-limits, untagged birds, you name it and there it was for God and everybody to see! We were stunned and just shook our heads in utter disbelief.

We looked first at all those illegal pheasants, discussing what legal avenue of attack was needed. They were state violations and would have to be handled in a local municipal court. But, alas, we couldn't take those violations to that municipal court because the judge we would have to go before was a member of this duck club and was probably involved in the violations lying before us. We put those violations, serious though they were, aside for obvious reasons and moved on to the issue of the hundreds of waterfowl scattered around the floor and hanging on hooks on the walls of the walk-in freezer. The illegal duck and goose violations were another matter. They would go to federal court in Sacramento, where petty politics weren't a problem under Chief Federal Judge McBride. Judge McBride was a duck hunter and a wealthy landowner, but he had demonstrated beyond a shadow of a doubt that he was honest and above any vestige of suspicion when dealing with any matter before the courts. He especially liked to hear wildlife cases, and I never found him to be anything but fair, objective, and commonsensical in his rulings. Hell, I would go down a lit cannon barrel for that man, I thought.

I examined the dead birds more closely for any sign of tags. There wasn't a legal tag in the bunch. Turning, I said to Buck, "We'd better get rolling; we've got our work cut out for us here tomorrow." We decided we would come back early the next morning, which just happened to be a Saturday shoot day, historically an unusually busy one, I might add, and stake out this place from a vantage point in the blackberry bushes on the island's berm. Then it would be a simple matter to watch the hunters come in with their over-limits, grab them, and have our case. With that masterful, foolproof plan (or so I thought), we shut the freezer door, then screwed the light bulb on the inside wall behind the slider back in. While I held my hands over the bulb to reduce the light, Buck hurriedly slid the false wall back into place. We checked to see if the laborers had seen the brief illumination in the picking facility. But they were now eating dinner and hadn't seen a thing, so back across the island floor, up over the berm, and down into our boat we went. Buck quietly idled the boat off the island so we wouldn't be heard, and we left the place full of thoughts for tomorrow and especially pleased with ourselves at not getting caught in the process of our exploration.

On the way back to the marina I told Buck we would need another hand to remove our boat from the island once we landed. That way no one would know we were there until we "pulled the trigger." He nodded in approval and said, "Who you got in mind at this late date?"

I said, "Jim Sheridan, a new guy who should be in town this afternoon to work the area. I know where he's staying and will call him and make the arrangements."

Buck looked hard at me for a moment and then said, "Can he keep his mouth shut and do the job?" As usual, Buck's distrust of most federal officers came through.

"Well, I don't know about keeping his mouth shut; he does talk a lot, but he will do the job or die trying," I said.

"You got that right," Buck said. "I will drown the knothead if he can't do what is asked of him tomorrow because this has the makings of a good one."

I had met Jim earlier, and though he was a little ol' runt of a lad and a rookie to boot, he appeared to have a pretty big heart and work ethic to match, so I didn't worry too much about my last-minute selection.

At three o'clock the next morning we had Jim drop us off on the island with instructions to remain within half a mile of the place, and Buck and I crawled up onto the levee. We concealed ourselves in the blackberries where we could look right into the picking facility and plainly see everyone who went in or out without being seen ourselves. Jim idled the boat off into a nearby island's channel where he wouldn't be seen, broke out one of Buck's fishing poles so it would look like he was fishing, and waited for us to call him on the radio if we connected. There were several reasons why we needed to get into position so early. First, it allowed extra time in case of emergencies. Many an operation has gone bad because of a flat tire on the way or the like. In addition, we knew most of our targets would still be sleeping heavily at that hour of the morning. If we got in early, chances were they would never hear us even if we had to make a few adjustments getting into place. Last but not least, it allowed the waterfowl who were frightened away when we arrived time to return. That way when the targets came out just before shooting time, they would scare away the usual quantity of ducks themselves and wouldn't suspect the presence of game wardens on the hunting club. Bottom line: if you are going to sacrifice yourself and your family life, you should do it right to ensure a successful connection with the outlaws you're pursuing. In short, don't waste your time. You don't have it to waste, and neither does the resource.

Once in position we did what most game wardens do on stakeout: we patiently waited. Just before daylight about five women left their shack homes and walked over to the picking facility. Pretty soon the inside lights came on, and Buck and I could see them through the windows beginning to process and bag some birds from the freezer. Daylight came, and with it the sounds of shotguns from the hunting club proper. That island was purely covered with standing flooded corn, pintail, mallards, and a zillion white-fronted geese. Throw into that mix a bunch of chaps calling themselves sportsmen with the opportunity for unlimited shooting, and you have the makings of a stew called a game warden's delight. As the shooting picked up in intensity, so did the numbers of birds that had been disturbed from their places of rest. There were birds in the air everywhere, and the lads were having one hell of a duck shoot! Knowing what was going on and essentially powerless to stop it, I just shook my head in resignation for the loss that would be felt by all those folks yet to come.

Pretty soon here came Robert, the head gamekeeper, in a red military Jeep. Through our binoculars we could clearly see a large metal basket welded onto the hood of the Jeep, filled to overflowing with freshly killed ducks, mostly mallards and pintail. A quick sweep of the binoculars showed that the back of the Jeep was filled with more ducks and geese. It was a huge overlimit, and Buck and I were already starting to count our scalps. Then it dawned on us at almost the same time: the gamekeeper had apparently been directed to make the rounds of the shooting area every half hour or so, collecting the birds killed from every blind. This practice allowed the lads in the blinds to continue killing because unless a game warden was staked out counting their individual kills, they would have "no" birds to be counted against their daily bag limit if a warden came along to check. This "sportsmanlike" process was to be repeated many times that morning, allowing the shooters to shoot the constantly circling waterfowl to their hearts' content, killing far in excess of the daily bag limit.

"Buck," I whispered, "that sure as hell shoots our plan to nab these guys with their over-limits as they bring them to the picking facility. With Robert running their birds as fast as they kill them, all we will get them for is untagged birds."

Plain and simply, with Robert removing the ducks and geese just as fast as the lads killed them, we couldn't nail the direct shooters, and the requirements of the federal court system for a criminal prosecution meant that we were out of luck on the over-limit angle because we couldn't prove who had taken what beyond a reasonable doubt. Damn, I thought, so much for my foolproof plan. But Buck's hard gaze told me we were still in the fight. We still had the birds coming to a "constriction" point in large numbers without being properly tagged as required by federal law. That would eventually allow us to seize all those untagged birds and write at least the duck club a citation for the offense (the definition of person under the Migratory Bird Treaty Act regulations includes a duck club). The fine wouldn't be much in that situation, but the loss of ducks and invasion their heretofore private sanctuary by the law would be. So we settled for that change in our plan and readjusted our sights accordingly.

Just as we finished this discussion, Robert came along again, driving on a small service road off the levee, which led him down and across in front of our hiding place. He stopped by the picking shed and took a long, hard look around to make sure no one was observing what he was doing or what he carried. I suspect that if Buck and I had stepped forth at that instant, he would have fled with the still running Jeep and birds, never to be seen again. Satisfied that all was clear, Robert shouted something in

Spanish to the people inside the shed. The women tumbled out and down the steps to Robert's waiting Jeep. While Robert nervously kept a lookout, the ladies removed the birds by the handful, taking them back up the steps and into the building. As near as Buck and I could tell, they took about forty birds out of the Jeep that time. Off went Robert, presumably for another load. It had been raining off and on all week, and about that time it started to rain again. With the rain came the wind, and as it picked up in velocity, the intensity of shooting out on the club picked up to an even higher level. Damn, I thought, I hope they leave something for brood stock.

Robert continued to make passes through the hunting area, constantly collecting ducks from the members. The success of this grab-and-run program manifested itself in the volume of shooting, which continued unabated. There was nothing to stop these lads unless they ran out of shells or ducks and geese, and they sure as hell weren't going to run out of birds! That kind of behavior by game hogs is just one of the reasons why we don't have the number of ducks today that we had years ago, I thought grimly. Hoping against hope, Buck and I decided to take a long shot: if we let the lads shoot to their hearts' content, the kill might be so great that no matter how they cut it we could issue the club an additional citation for possession of over-limits of ducks and geese. Plain and simply, we would have to wait until such a large number of ducks and geese had been deposited at the picking facility that the club would be in possession of over-limits no matter who had done the shooting. So the two of us just sat there with our grim looks and waited like a couple of oversized vultures.

Robert made four more trips hauling out the club members' illegal ducks and geese, and my eagerness to move in and stop the killing mounted each time. When he came by for a fifth time I started to get antsy. There was one hell of a pile of birds in that picking shed, and I wanted to get going and grab the lot. I had just started to turn to Buck to speak to him when I heard an automobile fast approaching on our levee. Ducking back down into our covering blackberry bushes, we watched. A panel truck drove up, and the pickers and cleaners, as if on cue, started streaming out of the picking shed with paper bags more than likely full of killed, picked, and cleaned birds. I told Buck, "Let's go!" Starting to get up, I said, "It's time to grab these guys; they've done enough damage."

Buck grabbed me by the shoulder and said, "No, let's hold tight; there's supposed to be a big pheasant feed in Los Angeles tomorrow and I think those are the pheasants we saw last night."

I was a little nervous about this, but Buck was one hell of a warden and no one know his people better than he, so I settled back down and waited. The panel truck was filled to the brim with about eighty sacks, and off it went to the airstrip on the island. Shortly afterward we heard a club member's Lear jet start up, and after running for a time to warm up, it finally took off. The plane circled low over the island and illegally hazed many thousands of resting and feeding waterfowl up into the air so the men still hunting on the club would have even greater numbers of ducks and geese to shoot at, then headed south toward Los Angeles, just as Buck had said. Owing to the now even larger number of ducks and geese in the air, the shooting really got intense as the birds attempted to work their way back to earth. About that time Robert brought in another Jeep load of ducks and geese, and I told Buck, "That's it; let's go and stop the killing."

We quickly ran to Robert and the Jeep as he and the ladies began to unload the most recent batch of ducks. Seeing us running toward him, Robert started to get back into the Jeep, and Buck told him in no uncertain terms, with a volume to match, "Stay right there!" Now, when Buck told you to do something, only those willing to die, or those who were as fleet as an antelope of the plains, would consider doing otherwise. Robert stood as if rooted to that spot on the ground when he heard Buck bellow out the command to stop. We approached the Jeep and quickly observed that there were at least thirty ducks and geese on board, way over the limit for any single person. Robert was very nervous, knowing that he was in violation of the law, not a good position for someone in the United States on a work visa. Buck knew that and being bighearted, as he always was, told Robert to relax, we wanted the shooters, not him. Robert calmed down a little, and we asked him to take us into the picking shed so we could look at the day's take. As we walked over to the picking facility we called Jim on our portable radio and asked him to bring the boat in because we now had a load of soon-to-be-seized ducks and geese that needed transport.

Robert led us inside the picking facility, and there on the floor and scattered on the cleaning tables were several hundred untagged ducks and geese. Under federal law, anyone killing and allowing another to transport one's ducks and geese must tag them, and the tag must have the date of kill, number and species of birds, name of the person taking the birds, and that person's valid signature. Failure to tag the birds is a criminal violation under many state laws and the Migratory Bird Treaty Act. The very reason that law was passed was to preclude this kind of gang shooting and to provide a tool to help a conservation officer control the illegal take of migratory game birds without having to identify all the guilty parties, which was often impossible. As a matter of fairness, it also allowed another person to transport a hunter's birds while the hunter tended to other business or continued hunting the next day or whatever.

Even we two seasoned officers were amazed at the killing that had taken place that morning, as evidenced by the pile of birds on the floor. As Buck began separating the ducks into piles of ten, I went over to the wall hiding the walk-in freezer and sort of leaned against it to keep the pickers from suspecting that I had previous knowledge of the freezer. Since nothing happened on my first lean, I tried again, only harder this time, with all my weight. Suddenly the wall moved, throwing me to the floor. I jumped up and in a surprised, booming voice asked Robert, "What the hell is this?" as I examined the door leading to the freezer. He said, "A freezer." Without a moment's hesitation, I asked if I could look in it. He said, "Yes," and I entered in a flash before he realized what he had just done and changed his mind, thinking better of letting the fox into the hen house.

What a surprise met my eyes. There was not a single duck or goose left from the night before, just those damn stinking pheasants! Dadburn it, we had lost a large portion of our case by letting those sacks of birds go out the door and onto that Lear jet. Damn! I fumed. I didn't even know which airport the plane was going to so I could warn someone in the southern end of the state and they could make the grab. Plain and simply, these lads had gotten away because I had been so damn greedy. Hell, it never failed: get greedy and you end up with a handful of crap every time! The look on Buck's expectant face when he looked into the freezer told it all. He was not a happy camper either.

At that moment a light dawned, and Buck and I became aware of the fast and furious shooting taking place on the north end of the island on the other duck club. It sounded like the Delta Hermitage, allegedly owned and run by the Mafia, was having a shoot fest that matched the day the folks on the Venice Island Duck Club were having. Our eyes met and instantly spelled out our thoughts: "Let's hit their picking facility as well since our greed let most of our birds in this case get away from us here." There was no use going out into the duck club blinds here because Robert had just cleaned out their birds. So, not being able to grab our guys on the Venice Island Duck Club for over-limits, we switched gears. The Delta Hermitage allegedly had a list of shady characters, and since they didn't have a clue that we were on the island, what better time to hit them than right now? They almost certainly had large over-limits as well.

We still had what appeared to be a huge possession over-limit of untagged ducks and geese, so I quickly started to inventory the birds Buck and Jim were running to our boat as evidence. The laborers stood by in awe as we raced through the legal process, watching their huge pile of ducks and geese rapidly disappear. We hurried because it was just a matter of time before some one would "Paul Revere" the information that the feds were on the island, and then the "duck" would be out of the bag and out of sight. The only way to preclude such a disappearing act was for the law to occupy a front seat in the house, namely, the picking facility. And you could bet your last part over the fence that Buck and I enjoyed wrecking disappearing acts.

Once we had removed our evidence, I left the Venice Island Duck Club pickers with a receipt for 243 untagged ducks and geese, told them to let the club president know who we were and that we would be back to issue their club citations once we had visited the other duck club. Then we hot-footed it out the door for the Delta Hermitage picking shed, aiming for their "soft un-derbelly," as Winston Churchill would have put it.

I took off running down the muddy road leading toward the Delta Hermitage Duck Club picking shed, which was about 150 yards to the north. Buck and Jim raced over the levee and, taking our boat with all the seized ducks and geese, motored down to the Delta Hermitage's dock in order to prevent any boats from leaving that club with their illegal birds, as by now the hunters were more than likely aware of our presence on the island. I was about halfway down the road, struggling through the ankle-deep peat mud, when a Jeep driven by a hunter came toward me. I kept my head down as I ran, hoping the lad might think I was just another club member. Once I got close to the Jeep I looked up. The driver, struggling with driving in the deep mud, took a quick look at my face, then another look as he recognized me, and tried to turn the slipping and sliding jeep off the road into a weed field to escape. No deal. In that mud he could not go very fast, and I ran the Jeep down on foot.

The driver turned out to be an old "friend," one I had pinched before for shooting over a baited dove field. He tried to ignore me as I ran along on the driver's side of the Jeep, just kept his head lowered as if I didn't exist, all the while keeping the gas pedal floored and throwing mud every which way in his attempt to escape. After being ignored when I told him for the second time to stop the Jeep, I took Mr. Buccioto forcefully out of the still running Jeep and placed his fat hind end forcefully in the mud. With a loud *ooopb,* he flattened out in the mud at my feet, as did his will to escape. The Jeep came to a stop without its "driving force," and I discovered the reason for "Baby Fat" (as I called him) Buccioto's behavior in the form of thirty-eight mallards and pintail piled into the rear compartment of the vehicle.

Realizing that he was caught, Buccioto settled down and began to banter with me about his disappointment at being caught again by the same officer, this time with a rather gross over-limit of ducks. He and I took the ducks and walked over to the Delta Hermitage picking facility. Buck had already arrived, identified himself, and entered the building by the time we arrived on the scene. The same game-hog crime scene that we had seen at the other picking facility greeted us here. Scattered all over the floor and on cleaning tables were dozens of untagged ducks and geese. In addition, they also had a walk-in glass-fronted freezer, which in this case was loaded with picked and cleaned ducks and geese from a previous day's hunt. Since many were also untagged in violation of federal law, all those birds were seized and hauled out to our waiting eighteen-foot Chrysler inboard-outboard boat, which by now was starting to bulge at the seams. Again I left the pickers a receipt for the 148 ducks and geese we had seized with instructions to let the club officials know we had been there, had found them in violation, and would return to settle accounts once we were finished with the Venice Island Duck Club.

I turned to Buccioto and asked for and received his hunting license and driver's license. He was issued a federal citation for being in illegal possession of thirty ducks over the limit, and the thirty-eight ducks found in his possession were seized and placed in our boat by my two hardworking sidekicks. When I finished I asked him if he had any questions. He said, "Yes; who is going to pay to have my muddy pants cleaned as a result of being dragged from my Jeep and hitting the ground?" The look he received from my already tired eyes told him to ask his washing machine, and we parted company.

Jim idled the boat down to the Venice Island dock, and Buck

and I walked to the duck club, putting our heads together on what we would say regarding the 243 untagged ducks and geese. As we had suspected, the word was out that the state and federal wardens were on the island; a hunter sped by who was alerting everyone. I guess he figured we were part of the hunting community on the island, and we let him continue to think so, thanking him for the "information." By the time our little party of officers got to the main clubhouse, all that morning's shooters had fled like the rats they were, leaving a sinking ship. When we knocked on the front door of this rather pricey duck club, all that remained was one poor chap, president or vice president of the club, who had been appointed to accept the ticket, and that was it. Everyone else had left for home to avoid the embarrassment of being caught and identified as the game hogs they were.

After identification all around and discussion of the events Buck and I had observed, I inquired about who else had been hunting on the club that morning. As expected, the code of the duck poacher took over, and the remaining lad was unable to remember any of the names of members or guests who had been there. We weren't surprised at this sudden loss of memory, and he was issued a federal citation in the name of the Venice Island Duck Club for 243 untagged ducks and geese. Without the actual shooters, that was the only way I could go with a citation under the Migratory Bird Treaty Act; the judge would sort out the penalty in a court of law. As I executed the paperwork I noticed that the interior of this very expensive duck club was replete with what appeared to be fresh mounts of every migratory bird under the sun, most of which were protected. Some of the larger marsh birds still had cheesecloth wrapped around their bodies to hold them in place until they dried. It is illegal to possess protected migratory birds without the appropriate state and federal permits, and then only for public uses such as display in a school or museum. I looked over at Buck, but he gave me the high sign to "cool it." When we left for our next business session with the Delta Hermitage, I asked Buck what the hell was going on with all the mounted protected birds. It seemed that another

local game warden was a part-time taxidermist and had been giving the duck club the mounts in exchange for whatever benefits
he could glean from the club and its members, a duck shoot or
whatever. I just shook my head as we continued on our way.

Buck and I walked back to the Delta Hermitage Duck Club
while Jim slowly motored the overloaded boat back to their
main dock. On the way we met Robert and again calmed his
fears that he would be sent back to Mexico for his part in this
mess. I couldn't see prosecuting him for what he had been directed to do by the wealthy club members. Sure, they would
have paid his fine, but the criminal matter might have gotten him
deported, so we let the issue drop. Besides, we now had someone on the inside who owed us one.

As we approached the Delta Hermitage clubhouse, I thought
one would have to see the beauty of that place to believe it. The
clubhouse had cost over $250,000 to build in those days, and it
was built on leased ground at that. But since the Mafia group
Murder Incorporated allegedly held the lease, I had the feeling
the lease would be renewed as often as they liked. Buck and I
went to the front door, knocked, identified ourselves, and were
invited in. The beautiful interior matched the grandeur of the
outside, and we saw several bodyguards scattered throughout
the main room and thirteen beautifully dressed, gorgeous
women standing around. They were obviously not duck hunters
but high-class hookers brought along for the duck club members' enjoyment.

We stayed in the entryway because we were so muddy and
watched a man coming toward us from the back of the club. He
introduced himself as Mr. De Napoli and asked me in a gentle
tone, "Officer, what is the problem?" He was a dapper-looking
chap, middle aged with graying hair, but he had a set of eyes that
clearly stated, "Don't mess." I explained that there was the small
matter of 148 untagged ducks and geese in his club's picking facility, all of which were in violation of federal law. His cold eyes
studied me for a moment while his face betrayed little or no
emotion. Very slowly he said, "That is not a problem, officer,

not a problem at all even though you might think it." Looking at me for another long second, he reached into his rear pants pocket and drew out his wallet. Holding up the wallet, he opened up the bill portion and displayed at least an inch of tightly packed $100 bills. Looking me right in the eye, he said, "All or part, officer, your call."

I said, "Pardon me?"

He said, "It's yours, all or part. That should take care of our little problem."

Without missing a heartbeat, I said, "No, sir, it won't. There have been state and federal violations committed here, and they are going to be handled accordingly."

My response seemed to take him aback as he quickly replaced his wallet. Quickly regaining his steely composure, he got a little huffy and said, "We have a way of taking care of problems like this."

"Mr. De Napoli, is that a threat?" I asked.

He quickly responded, "You can take it any way you like."

I turned to Buck, who was standing by the door, glowering at the two obvious bodyguards who were watching this exchange intently, and said, "Buck, when we get off this island, remind me to call the FBI and let them know that an attempt was made by Mr. De Napoli to bribe and then threaten a federal officer."

With that Mr. De Napoli whirled and walked back into the bowels of the duck club. I never saw him again.

We stood there for a moment, not quite sure what was coming next. Then a wimpy-looking fellow came from the area where Mr. De Napoli had disappeared. He handed me thirteen brand-new hunting licenses with duck stamps and said these folks had taken all the ducks in the picking facility, and since they were properly licensed, perhaps this matter was now settled. It was easy to see who the "hunters" were. Every license was issued to a female; my guess was the "ladies of the night" we had noticed when we first entered the clubhouse. But I ignored the obvious and explained to the chap that the club was going to have to set-tle up with the federal government over the untagged ducks and geese regardless of who had taken the birds. Without missing a beat, the lad said he was prepared to accept the citation. I asked him if he represented the club and he said yes, he was the club's legal counsel. With that, he was issued a citation in the club's name for the 148 untagged birds, with an appearance date in federal court, just like the previously cited Venice Island Duck Club representative.

Our business over, Buck and I left the club for our boat, and then new problems begin. Buck was a big man of about 250 pounds; I weighed about 300; and Jim Sheridan was just a half-pint son of a bitch who weighed maybe 130, soaking wet. Our boat was clear full of seized ducks and geese and was sporting not a whole lot of freeboard. It was clear that if we all got in, this boat was going to the bottom! We finally decided that Jim would slowly motor over to the marina, unload half of the birds, and get someone there to watch them. He would then come back for Buck and the two of them would motor back, unload the rest of the birds, and leave Jim at the marina; then Buck would come back for me. We carried out this plan and then spent the rest of the day cleaning and preserving the evidence.

Several weeks later Juanita Hobbs, our division secretary, told me that the two clubs had requested a court trial in district court in Sacramento. Following the usual course of action, I prepared a full case report for the U.S. attorney's office. Before the trial Buck and I met with the assistant U.S. attorney and laid out the case in our own words, which helped the attorney put together his battle plan. Neither Buck or I could figure out why the clubs wanted a trial in district court. The case was open and shut as far as we were concerned. But we soon found out.

On the day of the trial Buck and I, along with our attorney, sat at the front table opposite four high-powered and well-dressed attorneys representing the two duck clubs. We were pleasantly surprised when it came time for the clubs to enter their pleas because they entered guilty pleas, with a request to speak to the judge in open court regarding the circumstances of the case. Their request was granted. One after another, a lead attorney for each club got up and presented their side of the story. Both told the same tale of a few regular club members and a lot of guests who had shot only their legal limits and let Robert, *at his request,* take the birds for processing as they continued to hunt. The attorneys indicated that in no way was the limit exceeded and that it had just been a simple misunderstanding between the new hunters and Robert, aggressively acting on his own, that had caused the untagged-birds mess. Both attorneys then asked that the two club citations be dismissed and that only one citation be awarded to Robert for his carelessness. They said that if the court agreed to act along those lines, they were prepared to settle up regarding Robert's behavior right then and there. Otherwise they would have to look at the specter of dual court trials regarding these matters, which they were sure the court was aware were very time consuming and expensive to the American people.

Buck and I turned to our assistant U.S. attorney and told him that we had been able to see the Delta Hermitage Duck Club picking facility from where we were hidden and that during that entire morning we had never seen Robert run ducks and geese to that picking facility, only to the Venice Island Duck Club picking shed, and we were prepared to testify to that fact. We knew that the duck club attorneys were plain and simply lying. Our attorney asked the judge if the attorneys could approach the bench, and his request was granted. After a few moments at the bench I could see a cloud cross the district judge's face as he gave an icy stare to the two duck club attorneys. With that, all the attorneys returned to their respective benches. The judge, leaning forward over his desk, asked the duck club attorneys if they wanted to address the bench. One of the attorneys, obviously speaking for all the duck clubs now, said that in light of new information they would plead guilty to one count each of tagging violations. The judge's tight-lipped smile told all concerned that something bad was about to happen.

"Gentlemen, in light of this new information, I find both duck clubs guilty and fine each a total of $500 for the untagged migratory waterfowl offense." The amount of the fine was the maximum in those days and no big deal to the high rollers we were dealing with. That was very apparent when the two lead attorneys dug into their suits, produced checkbooks, and smilingly told the judge they would pay the amount on the spot. "I'm not finished, gentlemen," came the rather curt reply. Both attorneys froze, fearing that jail time or some other form of punishment for their clients was about to follow. "Gentlemen, I find the behavior of both of your clubs to be the worst I have seen in some time. I think we all know that the law of the land, as well as the spirit of fair chase, was violated by your members, and in rather gross fashion, I might add. What *really* bothers me, though, is the loss of innocence of the fair chase suffered by the offspring of those club members who at some point down the road introduce their children to the blood sport they so greedily participated in just recently." There was a long, sad pause; then, lifting his eyes and riveting them on the attorneys for the duck clubs, the judge went on, "Gentlemen, if I ever find you or your kind from those duck clubs in this courtroom again for a like kind of violation, there will be a lot of time to reflect over those deeds in the quiet control of a government facility. Do I make myself clear?"

The attorneys, surprised at the sting in the judge's voice, responded with nods. "Additionally, gentlemen, if you can't control your folks in this sport of kings, I will do everything in my power to encourage the U.S. Fish and Wildlife Service to use their injunctive powers to shut your entire operation down. Do I make myself clear again?"

One attorney, not used to being lectured to by a district judge, said, "Your Honor, we can't possibly control the hunting behavior of all our club members."

There was a moment of silence in the courtroom before the judge answered. "I suggest that you rethink my earlier statements, sir, unless you personally wish to have some down time courtesy of this court."

The attorney rose to speak, then, thinking better of that action, replied, "Yes, sir," and sat down. Then he jumped back up and said, "Your Honor, we still have the matter of Mr. Buccioto and his over-limit problem on the Delta Hermitage."

The judge stared coldly at the attorney and replied, "Yes."

"We would like to plead him guilty as well, Your Honor."

It took a few moments for the clerk of court to find my citation because no one had realized that Mr. Buccioto wanted to clear up his matter on that date as well, but soon it was found and processed. "That will be $500 as well, gentlemen," said the judge, "and I would caution that you request that Mr. Buccioto never appear in my court again as well."

"Yes, Your Honor," was the rapid, "I'm glad to get out of here with my life" reply from the Delta Hermitage attorney.

Most of you reading these lines will look at that figure of 391 dead ducks and geese and sadly shake your heads. Most of you will never kill that many in your lifetime. Keep in mind that half that number probably represented females of the species. For geese the average clutch runs about four to six per bird; for ducks eight to ten per bird. Now think about what we *really* lost if those birds could have survived and begun their life cycle all over again the following year.

It was probably during that case that I realized deep inside that humankind will ultimately destroy itself, but not until we have destroyed everything else around us that we unknowingly hold dear to our hearts and souls. Buck, Jim, and I won the battle that day, but we, along with our hard-pressed and undersupported counterparts, are currently losing the wildlife war. And, unfortunately, it will not get any better.

9
Save Me!

THE RINGING OF THE PHONE finally broke through to the sleep-filled and tired recesses of my mind. Looking from the bed to the clock and realizing that I had only gotten about two hours' sleep after working nineteen straight hours, I reached for that piece of despised technology in a less than peaches-and-cream mood. The voice on the other end responded to my curt greeting with a damned good hind-end chewing for being a "sorry-assed" game warden who slept most of the time while the outlaws shot the hell out of everything in my district. Normally a greeting like that at that time of the morning and under those circumstances would have drawn a like hind-end chewing in response, but the recognition of Buck Del Nero's strident voice on the other end of the line somewhat tempered my tired reaction.

"Buck, you son of a gun, I have been out all night chasing goddamned duck draggers through these stinking rice fields and just got in about two hours ago. I've got to sleep a little bit once in a while."

"Getting too old to handle the rigors of the job, eh?" he answered sarcastically.

I accepted this shot only because he was 130 miles away and I couldn't reach him in order to break his legs. "What's up, Buck?" I asked instead, knowing he would not be calling unless he had a good case going and needed the long supporting arm of federal assistance.

Buck said, "Terry, I have the makings of a good baiting and possible over-limit case on one of my islands but can't work it without help from you damn feds. Since Arnett put that restriction on me and others against working some of the duck clubs in the delta unless we have a violation in progress, it's obvious that his stop-work order has become common knowledge among the wealthy shooting public. As a result, and I hate to say it after the hind-end chewing I just gave you, some of my killing son of a guns have gotten out of hand in a few places. Additionally, the birds have moved into the delta from the upper Sacramento Valley like there is no tomorrow, and for many of them, especially on the Delta Hermitage Duck Club, there isn't. Terry, I would bet you I have at least a million birds down here right now, and most of them are mallards and pintail, which as you know are high-class ducks waiting to be killed by these boneheads." His tone told me he would continue to have a wholehearted go at the lads breaking the law but would certainly appreciate not only the helping hand but the protection the federal government could offer as he tried to enforce the wildlife laws against the wealthy on their private duck clubs in the face of blatant political cronyism.

The person Buck spoke of was none other than G. Ray Arnett, director of the California Department of Fish and Game and a big duck shooter himself. His reputation as a "sportsman" was such among his own game warden rank and file that I always kept a clear eye out for his presence in the fields just in case I ran across him and he was having trouble counting. Arnett's "stop-work" order was, according to the game warden grapevine, based on several recent investigations that had been brought to his attention by several of his aggrieved political friends, in particular a Fish and Game commissioner named Dante Martinelli. It seemed that the commissioner had objected to having a manipulated and clearly baited safflower field closed to dove hunting by the feds and had also groused about being issued a citation for being in possession of an illegal deer on his Snow Storm Ranch in Modoc County. I had been involved in both cases, and it had been just a matter of time before word of my activities made it to Arnett's office. Apparently Dante had made it known to his friend Arnett that too much attention was being paid to Dante's hunting operations, for no apparent reason. The straw that broke the camel's back, though, was Buck's and my recent gross seizure of illegal ducks and geese killed by rich and politically influential waterfowl shooters (I don't call them *hunters* because they were nothing more than greedy, spoiled killers for the most part) on Venice Island. The resulting grousing seemed to spur Arnett into action. In my eyes his actions were nothing less than a ploy to take some of the enforcement pressure off a few of his favorite hunting places on some of the delta duck clubs and to give carte blanche to his buddies' violating ways. My guess is that those club members who had earlier invited Arnett down for free duck hunts on their exclusive clubs were now calling in their chits.

What Arnett was essentially trying to halt was the precursor work officers might do before actually staking out and striking at a duck club. Buck and I would routinely scout the clubs, the blinds in the major shooting areas within those clubs (lots of spent shotgun shells meant lots of shooting), the numbers of ducks feeding and loafing in those areas during the nonshoot days, and any sites that looked like they might be baited based on the feeding waterfowl's behavior. Then, having selected several potential targets based on such reconnaissance and on the reputations of the shooters known to use the area, we would be on the site before daylight come shoot day, usually near a blind that had shown potential for violating the law. After observing and usually apprehending the offending shooters, we would then systematically walk through the club, checking all the other members before the word got out that we were there. Seldom did we leave the duck club with fewer than four to ten citations, 40 percent or more of which would be for over-bags of ducks and geese. We had had a number of these kinds of successes, including our gross duck seizure on Venice Island earlier that fall, and it was clear that members of the duck clubs in which Arnett had hunted had complained of the smothering law enforcement presence in the hope that he would somehow eliminate or reduce that pressure.

It seemed that, regular as clockwork, after a week's work in the delta by Buck and me a meeting would be held in Sacramento the following Monday in response to the complaints of those cited to review our enforcement behavior. Usually included in these meetings were Director Arnett; E. C. Fullerton, chief of law enforcement; Captain Jim Wictum, Buck's boss; and Jack Downs, agent in charge for northern California, my boss. We heard through the grapevine that during one of these sessions, after Arnett found that he could not badger Jack into reassigning me or at least backing down from or lessening our delta work efforts, he boiled over. Using the power of his office as director, he forbade Buck and other state Fish and Game wardens to go on the wealthy island duck clubs in the delta unless they had observed serious violations in progress firsthand. All casual state officer explorations were off, as were joint routine explorations by state and federal officers unless a federal officer specifically requested assistance from a state warden. Arnett considered these activities a form of harassment, even though they were legally supported, and wanted them to cease immediately. He realized that the real strength of a good operation against those seriously violating the conservation laws depended on good intelligence, which could be gained only from hard footwork several days before a suspected event.

Needless to say, it didn't take Buck and me more than two minutes to figure a way around Arnett's order. We did what we knew needed doing and carefully thought out how we did it so Buck wouldn't get into trouble, or get Jim Wictum in trouble, with the powers that be in Sacramento. We continued to work just as we had in the past, and when we zeroed in on a bunch of wealthy delta island hunting-club knotheads killing too many ducks or geese, or suspected the same, I would turn to Buck and say, "I am officially requesting your assistance under your U.S. deputy game management agent credentials to help me work these lads the next shoot day" (most clubs would shoot only on Saturdays, Sundays and Wednesdays). Buck would grin and accept my request for assistance, and off we would go into another dynamite adventure, much to the chagrin of the wealthy violators and the resulting happiness of the ducks and geese as well as two rather large crazies in green.

So Buck and I continued to rack up impressive scores apprehending illegal duck and goose shooters and seizing illegal waterfowl (over 230 ducks and geese seized and twenty-four citations issued in just one two-day period, for example), much, I suspected, to Arnett's continuing dismay. On one club alone we seized an entire freezer chock-full of frozen, picked, and cleaned ducks along with all the fresh ones killed that day owing to large collective over-limits by ten club members. We unloaded the freezer, put it in my truck, and then reloaded it with all the previously picked and cleaned ducks as well as that day's kill. After issuing the citations for possession over-limits, off Buck and I went to his freezer facility to deposit our evidence. I don't remember the name of the island we were on, but I do remember that Pacific Gas and Electric owned a huge gas dome under the island. In fact, we got onto the island and past the ferry operator by posing as PG&E repairmen going there to fix a gas leak. Any port in a storm in order to protect the natural resources—and Buck and I spent a lot of time in various ports, if you get my drift.

Getting back to the story and all these high-powered meetings about Buck and his federal sidekick's delta activities, I had a boss in Jack Downs who was one of the very best, if not *the* best, in the wildlife law enforcement business. He was a seasoned veteran of the wildlife wars, skillful in dealing with any situation and very dedicated to the profession of U.S. game management agents and their protection of the world of wildlife. After several hell-raising sessions with the state powers-that-be over our cooperative work on duck hunters in the delta (bear in mind that prosecutions were running at the 100 percent level in federal court), Jack finally got a snootful of this scarcely veiled political interference and advised Fullerton and Arnett that the U.S. Fish and Wildlife Service would do the job laid before it, and if they had a problem, in essence they could go piss up a rope. This was done very professionally, mind you!

When Jack had his red up, he was a gifted force to be reckoned with. He was unusually smart; he was a damn good infighter; and he possessed a skill many never learn throughout their entire careers: knowing exactly when to "pull the trigger" and hit the target dead on. He backed Arnett and other state officials off from interfering with legitimate law enforcement operations and did so in such a manner that the stop-work order basically died a quiet natural death within a few weeks. Jack then took his reckless, hardheaded officer off to one side and told me to catch every one of those knotheads stepping over the line and to bring them before the federal court system every chance I got. Jack also said he would pave the way for me with Chief Federal Judge McBride and provide the needed "top cover" with the office of the U.S. attorney in Sacramento. He quietly told me that my job was to catch and run every duck club son of a gun illegally killing ducks through the federal system until the problems in the delta stopped. He warned me to be very careful in my peregrinations in the delta and to make sure that I protected Buck in everything I did that might bring him under scrutiny. There were plenty of people with teeth who would cause damage for us if they could, he said, so I should be always on the alert. I guess he figured that if Ray or some of the politically influential targets I was apprehending ever got a clean shot at me, they would try to have me moved from the area or even removed from the Service. That thought was not lost on me as I redoubled my efforts to catch every violator in the valley.

With this green light from Jack and our battle plan on how to dodge the infamous Arnett order, Buck and I made Attila the Hun look like a wimp in the delta marshes. We rode through the San Joaquin Delta seven days a week, sixteen to eighteen hours a day, basically living with the ducks and geese and those of the hunting fraternity who seemed to be having trouble counting what they killed. Needless to say, with the high population levels of pintail and mallards wintering in the delta that year, the hunting was good, and the catching was great. Keep in mind that in those days the limit on ducks was eight and on geese six, more than enough for anyone and his family to eat. Yet there were those who felt above the law who continued to kill more than the limit and then smuggle their ill-gotten gains home. It was fortunate that Buck and I had a lot of youthful exuberance and divine aid in those days. Without it we would have worn out our bodies long before their time. I miss those halcyon days as I sit here writing these words. It was a lot of hard work, and the days were long and muddy, but the looks on the faces of those with a few too many over the limit were very rewarding. That was especially true when Buck and I rose up out of a thousand years' worth of goose crap and tule roots right at the shooters' feet with a grin, a greeting, and a citation. That moment always fueled our tired bodies for even greater efforts. There really is something addictive about hunting your fellow humans! No wonder the bodies of my kind, after thirty years in the profession, are worn out by the time we hang it up—so much so that statistically we live only 2.7 years after retirement.

Buck's and my phone conversation brought me back from my mental wanderings to the moment at hand, namely, the issue of a duck club he had discovered *really* stepping over the legal line the Migratory Bird Treaty Act had drawn in the sand since 1918. It seems that in the two weeks I had been absent from the delta since our big cases on the Venice Island and Delta Hermitage Duck Clubs, the Delta Hermitage had really gone hog wild in its killing. Buck said he had sneaked into the club property after hearing of the members' questionable hunting habits and found drainpipe ends on two peat ditches near their shooting area chock-full of freshly killed ducks. Closer examination of these ducks revealed that they all had been shot by shotguns, and their crops were jammed with fresh, hard, whole-kernel corn, which indicated that they had probably been feeding in a recently baited area. The ducks in the ditches consisted of every species in the delta except mallards and pintail, the biggest-bodied. Buck deduced that the shooters had skimmed off the best eating ducks killed in their "shoot everything that flies" outing and then tossed the "junk ducks" they considered not worth eating into the peat ditches to drift away through the drain pipe little by little and rot in the delta's many miles of waterways. Buck said he had discovered dozens more wasted redheads, shovelers, ringnecks, ruddy ducks, and other species in many other drainage ditches when he checked out the rest of the club.

I was no longer angry about being wakened. The energy that comes from a source deep in a wildlife enforcement officer's soul when he or she hears of a great injustice was welling up inside me until all my recent fatigue vanished. Two hours later I was pounding down the highway in the old Dodge en route to Stockton, Buck's house, and another adventure.

Three-and-a-half hours later I pulled up in front of Buck's farm-style home and was met by Judy, his tiny wife, as she came bounding out the back door of the porch and into my arms to give me a hug. Putting her arm around my somewhat expansive waist, she said, "Come on, I have a hot lunch all ready for you and Buck." Boy, those were good words to hear because I had not eaten since the evening before. Judy was Italian and had the love, heart, and cooking skill her heritage implied. As I entered the house the numerous great smells of homemade Italian food brought on the realization that I was *really* hungry. Hurriedly washing my hands on the back porch and walking into the dining room, I met Buck as he came down the stairs from the bedroom, where he had been resting after working most of the night to prepare for this operation. Buck was a big man in his prime. He had large hands like mine, and it was always a pleasure to shake his hand because of the strength and truth it projected.

Buck said, "I know you're hungry; let's eat what Judy has fixed and I will fill you in on the details that I have dug up in between bites." I didn't need a whole lot of coaxing, and we both fell to a wonderful homemade meal while Judy fussed around us, refilling bowls and dishes and making sure we had everything we wanted. Between great, delicious mouthfuls of food, Buck laid out what he had seen in the kind of detail that only a great game warden was capable of showcasing. It seemed that the Delta Hermitage, located on Venice Island, had planted several hundred acres of field corn in the middle of the club's main duck-hunting area. Once the corn had matured they had taken a tractor-drawn chopper and pulverized the cornstalks, leaves, cobs, and all, in the decoy area and then flooded the site, making it a great illegally baited "supermarket" for the hungry migrating waterfowl. The waterfowl had not disappointed the lads on the club and had arrived by the thousands at this newfound table of plenty.

Putting a third helping of food on his plate (one helping behind me), Buck continued, "Terry, I think the area, in addition to being baited with the mowed corn, has had extra corn dumped in the pond because everywhere I walked in this pond I was kicking up heaping piles of corn with my hip boots. On Tuesday I saw over ten thousand ducks feeding in that area, with more on the way. There is no way that will be hunted by anyone without large over-limits being taken. With that kind of opportunity, it's no wonder every duck in the world is heading to the corn buffet on the Hermitage." It was also painfully obvious that with that kind of food source and the feeding frenzy that naturally followed, every duck and his buddy from every species would be there; hence the reason for all the ducks of less popular species being killed and wasted.

Finishing lunch and getting run out of Judy's kitchen after an offer to help her with the dishes, Buck and I loaded into my unmarked pickup and headed for the marina where he kept his state patrol boat. An hour later we were in the boat watching the duck club and the swirling masses of waterfowl funneling into the hunting area like a huge living tornado. It was a nonshoot day, so our observations were not disturbed by club members killing ducks. But the specter of the next shoot day and what it would bring, based on the myriad of birds dropping into the area, didn't do much to settle the wonderful lunch I had just eaten. After dark Buck idled the boat up to the island's berm looking for a place to tie up and hide our craft. Minutes later we were looking at a five-acre flooded and mowed cornfield covered with about fifteen thousand madly feeding ducks and geese of every kind. The area surrounding the baited hunting pond was covered with acres and acres of standing, unharvested cornfields. It was as if this planting pattern had been planned to shield the offending field in the middle from unwanted eyes. It didn't take anyone with an IQ greater than 50 to realize that we had a wildlife disaster in the making with the right kind of shooters. Since the folks who owned the Delta Hermitage were reputed to be Mafia, I suspected they weren't going to worry too much about breaking the law.

For the next several hours, in the cool of the night, I moved around the area setting up a game plan and memorizing landmarks so I could find my way around in the dark of the morning at a later date. There was only one road to the area of the duck blinds around the baited pond; it came from the clubhouse, and the fields on either side had been plowed right up to the road bed. Walking in from that direction, either on the muddy road or through the plowed fields, would leave footprints, so we ruled out that entry point as an approach option. Because of the political horsepower the club members more than likely had, taking Buck along was also not a good option. I finally settled on taking Jack Downs as my partner and having Buck get his own boss to work with him. That way, if someone got pissed at us and wanted to know the names of our supervisors, we could just introduce them right then and there! I decided that Jack and I would walk in from the back of the club through several standing cornfields in order to get into position off to one side of the blinds doing the shooting. That would mean crossing several peat ditches, but they appeared to be fairly narrow and looked as if they could be crossed with little difficulty.

Leaving Buck on the levee to watch for anyone who might discover the island's two uninvited guests and thereby ruin our little surprise, I made a dry run over my planned approach path to see whether the scheme was sound. Everything worked fine, and I even crossed the peat ditches easily. There was a farm road that crossed both ditches farther down, but if we used it we would have to walk in plain view of the clubhouse and duck blinds, so those crossing points weren't an option. Also, people walking into that area in the wee hours would alarm all the feeding waterfowl, and when their many thousands of wings got them airborne, it couldn't help but warn those in the duck club that there might be a game warden or two on the property. Given those factors, I decided it would be best to tough it out and cross the ditches where we should be able to remain unseen.

Satisfied that I had worked out a good plan of attack, I moved back to where Buck was hiding in the grass on the edge of the levee. We both knelt in the grass and for about an hour silently watched the feeding spectacle that continued unabated over the heavily baited duck club shooting area. The continued arrival of waterfowl, cheerfully announced by their whistling wings, and the sounds of the continued excited feeding frenzy emitted by fifteen thousand clattering bills made clear the potential disaster that awaited the critters the next day if the cavalry didn't arrive. Anyone supporting legalized baiting of waterfowl has only to spend several moments watching a spectacle like this to understand the slaughter inherent in such a practice. Yet there are many in high positions in state and federal government, including certain members of the U.S. House and Senate as well as those standing on their own land, who support a weakening of the laws and the resultant blood sport that would occur at the drop of a hat. I sometimes wonder if these folks might be part of the wildlife world's Antichrist. ...

Returning to the boat, we pushed off the levee surrounding the Delta Hermitage and slowly motored our way into the canal and away from the island. Once clear of the possibility of being overheard, I laid out my game plan to Buck. After a few moments of study, Buck acknowledged the plan with a nod, followed by an increased throttle for the boat because we had a lot to get done before tomorrow. On the way home both Buck and I were lost in our thoughts. We had just busted this club for a rather large number of illegal birds a few weeks earlier, and now here we were again. They must have figured that since we had just left their club with a hatful of ducks and a fistful of citations, maybe we wouldn't be back for a while. They had not figured on Buck's sharp eye and the thousands of migratory waterfowl wildly milling over their club, giving away their dirty little secret. Sometimes the wildlife in this land of ours will try to foil or even kill you as you try to help, but other times it will send a spectacular signal that can't be misunderstood in its request for some life-giving aid. In this instance a living tornado of ducks and geese slamming into a small area certainly advertised to the trained eye of the law that something was out of place and that a look-see was in order. More than a quick look would be taken before all was said and done, I promised myself as I suddenly became aware of the cold, damp delta winter wind cutting over the bow and knifing across my legs and face. Pulling my head and neck further into the comfort of my heavy down coat, I let the sugarplums of a baited field and the morrow dance in my head. I didn't notice that one of the sugarplums wasn't really dancing.

My plan was to have Buck and Jim Wictum take Jack Downs and me to the island early in the morning. They would drop us off and let the feds do the necessary work; when we were ready to spring the trap, a call on our portable radio to request assistance from Buck and Jim would complete the circle. That plan would more than accommodate Arnett's already weakening stop-work order. Buck and I made the appropriate calls and laid out the details, and both supervisors agreed to participate without a moment's hesitation.

The next day around two A.M., Jack, Jim, Buck, and I were in Judy's kitchen enjoying a breakfast fit for wildlife combatants such as ourselves. Today would be a long and dangerous day, politically as well as physically, and none of us wanted to fall short because of lack of staying power. With that flimsy excuse, no one was ashamed to go back for seconds of steaming hot coffee, spuds mixed with onions and garlic, eggs, sausage, and thick, peppery sausage gravy. As we enjoyed Judy's breakfast, none of us suspected how dangerous that day would really be.

By three A.M. we had gathered around Buck's patrol boat and

were hurriedly loading equipment into it for the day's adventure. A light fog greeted us as we pulled slowly out of the marina and into the main canal. Advancing the throttle, we picked up speed until the boat was up on step and flying toward Venice Island, thousands of feeding waterfowl, and maybe a few short-sighted and greedy shooters. A short time later Buck dropped off his federal passengers at the base of the levee surrounding Venice Island, with any noise from the unloading process muffled by the activity of thousands of feeding waterfowl a few hundred yards away. Jack and I checked our portable radios with Buck, set the channels we would be using with each other, leaped the levee road to avoid leaving any tracks, and hurried a few dozen yards into the dew-laden standing cornfield next to our landing place. Buck and Jim moved their boat about half a mile away to await our expected request for assistance while Jack and I listened to ascertain whether we had been spotted.

Because there were four blinds surrounding the shooting area, Jack and I would have to wait until daylight to see which ones were being used by the club members. There was no easy way to easily set up on all of the blinds because of the distance that separated them. Besides, to meet federal criminal guidelines we would have to observe the shooters shooting at or killing and retrieving their game in order to gain successful prosecutions for any hunting over bait or individual over-limits charges to be valid. To do that we would have to crawl close enough to see the lads shoot, identify the species killed along with the number of shots fired, and make sure all charged in the blind had fired that day to prove the taking of migratory waterfowl over a baited area. We also wanted to be close enough to the shooters to identify them in case they spotted Buck and Jim in time to flee the blind. If that happened Jack and I would have to be able to pick them out later if they got away into the cornfields or made it to the clubhouse and mingled with the other members.

Once Jack and I had the information we needed to convict our shooters, we would radio Buck and Jim and they were to motor by the shooting area as if nothing was wrong and go to the Delta

Hermitage boat dock, which was out of sight of the blind. Then they were to walk right out on the road that led to the shooting area and nab the offenders. That way no one from the club could drive down to warn the shooters because the wardens would be blocking the road, plus the shooters would all be facing the other way as they shot at the ducks and geese coming in over their decoys. Buck and Jim's position would also keep any shooters from fleeing to the clubhouse. Jack and I would continue to count the number and species of ducks and geese killed right up to the last minute, and then, once the lads in the blind were apprehended, we would rise up from the mud near the hunting area when no one was looking our way and walk over to help with the arrests and seizures. By staying out of sight in our hiding place, we would be able to see if the lads tried to hide any of their over-limit birds if they were somehow warned of the wardens' approach from behind. If they did, there would be additional untagged bird violations for the club. Also, if any of the shooters attempted to escape into the cornfields around them, Jack and I would intercept those runners and return them to the scene of the crime. Simple enough, or so it seemed. ... Damn, that sugarplum from my earlier dream still wasn't dancing.

A few minutes before daylight headlights from the clubhouse told Jack and me that the lads were on their way to the shooting area. I quickly passed that information over the radio to Buck and Jim. A single *click* indicated that they had quietly received the transmission. The headlights moved to a muddy parking area by a standing cornfield fifty or so yards from the shooting area loaded with feeding waterfowl and then went out. A few moments later four hunters appeared at the edge of the shooting area, sending at least ten thousand assorted ducks into pandemonium and high into the air. The hunters ignored the fleeing ducks and hurriedly moved to a blind north of us by the flooded field. Quickly entering a pit blind, they watched with expectation as thousands of ducks, quickly at ease with the situation (as there were no hunters in sight) and still hungry, began filtering back into the decoy area of the baited pond.

Soon the shooting began, shells flying into the massed bodies of frantically feeding and landing waterfowl. The shooters' pre-occupation was our cue to get moving to a position from which we could collect the necessary evidence and then put a stop to this affair and any subsequent escape by the illegal gunners before their actions reached gross levels of killing. Jack led and I followed as we trotted through our protective standing cornfield until we came to a mowed area between our field and the next one to the north. Jack knelt in the soft peat mud, looked both ways to make sure none of the shooters could see us, and then sprinted across the thirty-five-yard mowed area into the protection of the other field's standing corn. Waiting until Jack was safely hidden and we were sure no one had seen him, I too sped across the mowed area.

We both gathered our wind and then raced through the standing corn toward our now wildly shooting prey. At the edge of the second cornfield we encountered another mowed area before the next available cover, another standing cornfield. However, there was an additional obstacle: a peat ditch that ran lengthwise through the mowed area before us. Peat ditches can be dangerous because they are ten to fifteen feet deep, six to eight feet wide, and the peat soil is very granular, somewhat like sugar. This can make it very difficult to climb out because it's hard to get a good foothold on the banks. The water that drains from artificially created islands like the one we were on is as dark as coffee and so acidic that a human body would simply dissolve and disappear in several days if left in the water. However, I had successfully navigated this obstacle the night before, and since Jack was a hell of a lot more nimble than I, we anticipated no trouble from this challenge.

Undaunted, Jack sped across the open area, entered the peat ditch carefully, held for a moment to make sure the coast was clear on the other side, lunged across the ditch to the far side of the bank, checked again, then leaped from the ditch and raced across the last twenty yards of open space into the haven of the standing cornfield. He motioned for me to follow, and as he kept a lookout off I went across the opening and down into the peat ditch. What greeted my eyes was unreal. I had seen it the night before in dimming light, but it was still shocking! Hundreds of dead ducks lay next to the siphon portion of the ditch, which was an apparent dumping ground for the ducks considered less than desirable by the miserable knotheads shooting on this club. The birds were scattered for about twenty-five yards all along the ditch, stacking up in the weeds by the underground drain-pipe for their final trip out into the delta's thousands of miles of waterways and out of view forever. Sights like this burn forever into the souls of those of us who prey on our fellow humans, and rightfully so, for just such acts as these.

Quickly refocusing my attention on the mission at hand, I checked for a safe place to land on the far bank. Since I weighed in at just slightly over three hundred pounds, I did not consider myself a member of the Flying Wallendas with their ability to leap a great space at a single bound. Seeing hundreds of dead ducks thickly massed at the foot of the ditch, I tested them carefully to see if they would hold my weight. They did, and I sped across them, holding my breath. To slip beneath these waters with chest-highs and all the gear I was carrying was asking to meet my maker. After looking over the top of the ditch to make sure the coast was clear on the other side, I scrambled up the crumbly bank and lumbered across the mowed section to where Jack was standing in the unharvested corn. While we collected our breath, Jack exclaimed, "Can you believe that? There must have been several hundred ducks there. That will just be another charge we will lodge against these boneheads when this is all said and done!"

Nodding in winded agreement, I rose to finish our footrace across the duck club toward our still rapidly shooting lads. We trotted as quickly as we could through the unharvested corn and soft, damp peat soil, hindered by our bulky clothes, chest-high waders, optics, radio gear, and madly clutching cornstalks, to-ward the last mowed area that we needed to cross before we could dig in and watch the blind. Pausing at the edge of the last cornfield, Jack looked both ways and, seeing that the coast was clear, sped for the second and last of the peat ditches running through the mowed cornfield strip before us. Jumping into the ditch, he disappeared from sight as he began to work his way along the steep bank, looking for a safe crossing.

Without waiting for Jack to gain the safety of the standing cornfield on the other side of the ditch, I checked both ways and ran for the ditch as well. I was again sickened by the sight of numerous dead and rotting ducks lying in the coffee-colored water. They had not yet gone down a furiously swirling whirlpool drain at the end of the ditch, as the club members had probably expected, but had hung up on the weeds that grew from the bank's edge. Jack was just starting across the ditch, using a small projection from the bank on his side and the pile of dead and rotting ducks for a foothold, when the dirt point and mass of duck bodies he was crossing over to avenge *gave way!* Realizing that he was going into the water at the deep end of the ditch near the drain, he used his momentum to hurl himself across the water and floating dead ducks toward the bank on the far side, hoping for better traction or a handhold. Desperately he grabbed at the far bank as he began to sink past his stomach, only to discover that the granular soil offered no life-saving grip.

Realizing he was going under, Jack had the presence of mind to use the last of his momentum to thrust his torso back across the ditch toward me. Turning in the water, he stretched out his hand, seeing me almost there, and said, "Save me!" His tone was almost matter-of-fact, but I could sense the fear behind it.

Still running forward, I dove toward Jack as his chest-high waders began to fill with water and drag him under. Landing with a thump on my belly at a high rate of speed, right on top of my 7x50 binoculars and the portable radio, I had the wind flat knocked out of me. Even so, by the grace of God I still had the presence of mind to reach out and grab Jack's outstretched hand, just catching the tips of his four fingers. His weight, combined with the water slowly spilling into his waders, my forward velocity, and the suck of the underwater drainpipe on his legs, started to drag me off the bank headfirst into the ditch along with Jack! I hollered to Jack that I had to lower him even farther into the water (now up to his armpits) in order to scoot my belly back over the bank to anchor myself better. But Jack was no longer calmly discussing this situation. His frantic eyes told me the whole story. He knew that if my grip failed he would be sucked down and through at least a one-hundred-yard underground drainpipe, coming out into the waters of the delta forty feet below the surface. It was all I could do to hang on to my fellow officer's and dear friend's fingers. If there ever was a time for strength, it was now!

I quickly lowered Jack into the murky waters and scooted my potbelly back over the lip of the ditch to gain more traction, so to speak. When I lowered Jack into the murky, ice-cold water his eyes were pleading, and the cold water, at shoulder level now, caused him to exhale loudly in shock. Scooting back also slid my binoculars and portable radio out from under my chest, which allowed me to reach even deeper into the ditch. Quickly but carefully I pulled Jack's body higher and told him, "Goddamnit, don't wiggle, I just barely have a hold on you." I hissed that I was going to try to lift him out of the water with my right hand (my left was braced against the bank to prevent me from falling headfirst into the ditch), and he was to grab me by the back of the neck with his free hand when he got close enough. Without waiting for his input, I continued, "When you grab me I will let go of your left hand and try to grab you by the crotch and lift you out of the ditch with my right hand and arm." I knew this would be my best bet because my right arm and shoulder were the strongest. I had been injured at birth by instruments and as a result had a weakened, smaller left arm and shoulder. I knew that arm would not do the trick. However, since I was right-handed and used that hand for anything heavy or tough, I had a right arm like Popeye and the strength to match. I had better have that kind of strength, I thought, because I was placing every egg, not to mention possibly my friend's life, in this basket—and it had better work.

With real fear in his voice, Jack said, "No, I don't want you to let go. Don't let go of me, just pull me up! Terry, if you let go I will be sucked under and drown!"

I said, "Jack, I am losing strength in my arm just holding you against the suck of the drain and your weight. I have to do something else." Losing strength was a concern, but even worse was the fact that I was slowly beginning to lose my grip on his fingers. Now, in those days I had at least a 220-pound grip with my right hand. In fact, when I had played college football my teammates used to complain during scrimmage that I left black-and-blue fingerprints on their skin when I grabbed or tackled them because of my unique hand strength. However, that was then; this was now. I was losing my grip partly because Jack's fingers were wet, but a larger part of my dilemma was that he was getting heavier with the additional water weight in his waders, and the constant suck of the drain's current and my unnatural position were beginning to take their toll on my strength.

"Jack, I am losing my grip on your fingers. We have to do it now ..." My voice trailed off as Jack's eyes again told it all. He knew that if I couldn't do what I proposed, he would soon be in the act of drowning. I gathered up everything inside me and sent a quick request skyward for a little consideration. Then I started to slowly lift him out of the swirling waters by his fingertips. Up he came, closer and closer, to the point where he could grab me by the neck with his free right hand. But this lift was not without penalty. I could feel the muscle bundles and fibers actually starting to give way and separate in my right shoulder as I tried to lift more than two hundred pounds of man and water, one-handed, head down, and horribly off balance. The terror was still in Jack's eyes as they met mine from about eighteen inches away.

"Now, Jack, grab my neck!" I gave him a split second to react, let go of his fingers, exhaled to reduce the mass of my gut, and, reaching deep, scooped my right hand quickly under his crotch. Thank God he was still able to reason through the fear that gripped him, I thought. The impact when he grabbed the back of my neck and I grabbed his crotch again almost pulled me over the bank. But I had a strong grip on him and, with my left hand pushing back on the bank and with the last of my strength, along with my three hundred plus pounds of dead weight as ballast, lifted him clear up and onto the bank, dropping him beside me.

For the next five minutes neither of us moved except to breathe. My exhaustion was matched only by Jack's fear, which had to be complete if he was reviewing those last few moments. During that time I didn't hear a sound except my beating heart and our panting. Finally I struggled to my knees and helped Jack to his. He gave me a very strange look and said, "Terry, my feet never touched bottom!"

We just looked at each other, forgetting why we were on this duck club in the first place. Finally Jack said, "Let's get out of here." Lowering his waders, he emptied the remaining water that had not drained as he lay on the ground, and with that we trudged back over our earlier trail, both lost in our thoughts. I took that precious moment of time to thank God for the extra strength and resolve he had given me, and for making me aware of whom to call in times of *real* need.

When we reached the first peat ditch we had crossed, Jack stopped and then, without a word, turned and walked about three-eighths of a mile down it to the farm road bridge in front of God and everybody, crossed, and then walked back up the other side to our original point of crossing. We walked through the cornfields and headed for the levee in plain view. The shooters soon became aware of our presence, and the shooting stopped immediately as they hurriedly left the area until they could find out who the uninvited guests were. By this time the pain in my shoulder was unreal, but we were both alive and I thanked God again for that. When we arrived at the edge of the levee, I called Buck on the radio and told him to come get us. He radioed back, "Do you want us to come in and walk in on the shooters? Do you have them?"

I again told Buck to come get us at the spot where he had left us that morning. Buck hesitated, his voice betraying the unasked question of why, and then said, "All right." A few moments later the sound of his outboard came to us over the calm, icy waters from a short distance away.

It is very strange what the senses can do when the body has just gone through an experience such as Jack and I had just had. At that moment I noticed that my down coat and the shirts underneath were soaked clear through, and it was not raining.

We quickly loaded into Buck's boat, and I quietly explained what had happened. Jack's silence told Buck to take us back to the marina. During the ride back, there was no conversation. When we arrived at the marina where our vehicles were parked, Jack got out of the boat, walked alone to his vehicle, and without a word quietly changed into some dry clothes and after a rather short good-bye left for home. In all the years I had known him, I had never seen him act like that. He was always upbeat, even when the cannonballs were raining down around his head. It was obvious that his mortality was on his mind. After he left Buck, Jim, and I talked over the morning's events as only those can do who live on the edge and occasionally go into that zone where they do not belong—not just yet, that is. We all realized that but for several guardian angels and a large right arm. ... Like fighter pilots who have survived a wreck, the three of us went back to work that fine day happy to be alive and looking for those unfortunate souls who were our usual prey. They were easy to find that day, for some reason.

The next day Jack telephoned and asked me to come into the Sacramento office. When I walked into his office, I noticed that he was standing behind his desk looking out the window. I sat down, and when he turned he held out his left hand. The four fingers I had held on to so desperately the day before were swollen and black and blue. Looking intently at me, Jack said, "If you had been any other of my agents, small as they are, with me out there ..." His voice trailed off. He turned back and continued to stare out the window. After waiting for several minutes I realized he wanted to be alone, so I quietly left.

Buck and I went back to the Delta Hermitage a week later and busted five club members with a total of seventy-eight ducks in their possession. This time we didn't fuss around with some grand stakeout plan. We gave them time to shoot about one hundred rounds of ammunition, then headed for the boat dock at high speed. Once up on the road leading into the shooting area, we jogged the entire way to our shooters. They were amazed at our unheralded arrival. That action stopped all hunting over their little honey hole for the better part of the month, or until the lure and attraction of the corn was long gone for the ducks and geese.

Since none of us had seen anyone from the club throw those ducks into the peat canals earlier, no citation was forthcoming for that particular injustice. You can't just grab the rascals even when you know they did it unless you actually see them commit an offense. We knew, and they knew we knew, and wanton waste of lesser ducks didn't happen again while I worked that area as a federal.

Jack never did thank me for saving his life. It was OK, though—that's what friends are for, and thanks were not needed. However, I didn't forget to thank the person who was really responsible numerous times for my strong right arm and hand that caught those four fingers that foggy day so long ago on the Delta Hermitage Duck Club.

That sugarplum is dancing now ...

10

The Butte Sink

STANDING ON THE TARMAC at the Colusa County Airport, I waited for Al Weinrich, our agent pilot, and N710, our Fish and Wildlife Service aircraft, which was currently en route from Sacramento. Sweeping the scene around me, I noticed that the sky to the east was beginning to lighten and show the brilliant fall colors of another day. I could see skeins of ducks and geese, which were especially numerous over their ancestral home, the Butte Sink, already trading back and forth across those lightening skies like swarms of bees. A breeze from the northwest spoke of a weather change to come, and my eyes, searching the dawning sky, confirmed that prediction with the sight of the telltale wispy clouds called mare's tails. A weather change within twenty-four hours, I thought. Good; that made for better duck hunting, and good duck hunting made for better catching of the human element pursuing the critters outside the scope of the law.

The faraway drone of a light-aircraft engine brought me back to the present as my eyes scanned the still dark sky to the southwest. A flashing strobe light about a thousand feet in the air confirmed the presence of an aircraft coming toward the airport. Good old N710 and Al, I thought. As usual, right on time and ready to go. A glance at my wristwatch told me Al would touch down about six A.M., and that would work out fine for what I needed him to do today.

Two minutes after six Al made a perfect three-point landing, braked, and turned in to where I was standing next to my patrol vehicle. Grabbing my camera and binoculars, I walked to the plane, stooped under the wing, opened the door, and got into the Cessna 185. After a handshake and some friendly teasing about his being two minutes late, we taxied to the end of the airstrip. Al rechecked his instruments and "mags," looked up and out the front window for any other aircraft that might be in the area, and advanced the throttle; down the runway we hammered. After gaining altitude, I directed Al easterly toward the Butte Sink for a look-see. With daylight coming upon us shortly, we would be over the marsh before most of the waterfowl headed for the rice fields to eat. The timing couldn't be better, I thought. With the ducks basically in place, I would get a good reading on which hunting clubs were loaded with birds and might need the assistance of the world's largest game agent in keeping them honest—a job, it seemed, without end.

As the resident U.S. game management agent in Colusa, California, I was responsible for federal wildlife law enforcement for the entire western half of northern California, north from Monterey to the Oregon line. That area and those duties included the western part of the Sacramento Valley and protection of its migratory bird resources. Within the larger ancestral wintering area of the Sacramento Valley was a geological anomaly called the Butte Sink, an area in Butte, Colusa, and Sutter Counties, lying north and west of the Sutter Buttes, which was generally lower than the surrounding landscape. This natural land depression historically collected water and the associated plant life that endeared it to the hordes of wintering waterfowl commonly found in the Sacramento Valley in those days. Because of the fantastic duck hunting it offered, it also collected the ultimate predator: man. The waterfowl shooting in the Butte Sink in those days of ducks was unquestionably the finest in all the United States. Some people may think Louisiana was the number one spot for wintering waterfowl. Well, over the years I worked both areas many times, and the Butte Sink is truly the only place I have been where ducks really did blacken the skies—and when I say blacken the skies I don't mean one time but day after day during the fall and winter seasons.

Once the shooting began on the hunting clubs in the Sink, the air would literally be filled with frantic waterfowl trying to figure out what had happened to their once quiet marsh. Many made the final mistake, lured by the decoys below, and set down forever. However, in those days there were always more birds over the next line of flooded brush and timber, and the shooting continued as if one's life were at stake—as for some it was.

The Butte Sink, in addition to the myriad ducks and geese, was home to about forty high-class, exclusive duck clubs. Since the days of explorer Charles Fremont in the early 1800s the Butte Sink had hosted millions of migrating wintering waterfowl, and this fact was not lost on those with an interest in hunting. Some clubs had very few members, and some had a hatful. However, all were expensive to join, and many had a membership waiting list as long as your arm because of the outstanding waterfowl hunting to be found in the area. Many a politician, movie star, millionaire, or wanna-be frequented these clubs for the companionship, good food, chance to get away, chance to enter another world for a day, and opportunity for a return to the primeval struggle of humankind against nature.

Because of the isolation of the marsh and the opportunity to kill to one's heart's content on a prime hunting area, hunters were ethically challenged, and many succumbed to that clarion call of blood lust that perpetually runs barely under the surface in all our veins. That urge to kill in a field of plenty without considering the limited resource or the legality of his actions plain and simply, often without warning, overtook many a good man. The artificial conservation laws established by humans for humankind, including those yet to come, were hardly considered in the race for whatever glory came in killing large numbers of waterfowl. Ten to twenty over the already generous daily limit of eight ducks and six geese was not an uncommon kill, and men of my ilk profited greatly as a result. In the seven years I was stationed in the area, I never went into the Butte Sink without catching at least four to six hunters with over-limits of ducks, geese, or both in their possession. They just couldn't control one of their most primitive and basic urges: the compulsion to kill. Those of us holding the "thin green line" didn't stick to a "bag limit" of such people either! When we went into this area, it was with a grim determination to confront the shooters in such a manner that from that day forward they might think twice before pulling the trigger on any number of waterfowl above what the law allowed.

Most officers were hunters and fishermen themselves in those days and clearly understood what was at stake in our limited resource base. Armed with that knowledge and with determination, we lived in that marsh as avengers for those critters facing the challenges of life. Lord, how the odds always seemed to be stacked against us! Time, distance, luck, weather, cranky equipment, not enough help, you name it, there always seemed to be a stumbling block. At times it even seemed that God must be a poacher for all the hurdles he placed in front of us. I now know that He did so as a form of preparing us for the challenges ultimately to come, and in retrospect, that preparation was much needed.

Bumpy air and Al's voice brought me back from daydreaming to what I was there to do. Below us in all its magnificence was the Bean Field, a 430-acre field of lima beans planted every year by the surrounding Butte Sink duck clubs, then flooded and left for the waterfowl feast that was to follow. The ducks and geese flocked to that area as if there was none other like it in the world, and there probably wasn't. It was a feast beyond compare until the field was gleaned; then the area became a safe haven for the birds—once they got there. The Bean Field was located within the boundaries of all the Butte Sink duck clubs, and in those days it was hunted only on the last two days of the season. It was a refuge of sorts for the waterfowl, but in order to get in and out the ducks had to fly the gauntlet of lead thrown skyward by the lads in the numerous blinds below. As Al and I approached, the spectacle of the sheer number of birds before us on that bean field aroused the deepest feelings within me, as it always did. Stretching out before us was every duck in the world, or so it seemed. The entire field was literally blackish-brown from all the bodies floating gently on its waters.

"Quick," I said, "where is your aerial camera, Al?" He pointed to a carry bag in the back seat of the plane, and a quick look produced the camera. After getting a few instructions on how to use it, I had Al tip the wing down so I could get a flat shot of what God had laid out for us to witness that day. Centering the field within the frame, I took two pictures. God, what a mess of waterfowl! The snow geese, at the sound of our approach, immediately took to the air in great white-and-black clouds beneath us. It made a spectacular picture that is forever burned into the my mind: literally hundreds of thousands of waterfowl quietly lying on the water surrounded by a pristine marsh, with snow geese lazily floating in many layers and crossing patterns in the air above the resting waterfowl but below man's noisy flying machine. Such moments really defined what my job was all about and showed the magnitude of the task was that laid out for me. They also steeled me for what was yet to come in a career of missed family events, missed meals, abuse of my body, and missed opportunities within the assigned field of duties. A fair trade, I would say ...

It was a nonshoot day (shoot days were Saturday, Sunday, and Wednesday) in the Butte Sink, and the two of us in the plane had a good opportunity to see what kind of hunting pressure the clubs were putting on the area, as demonstrated by the number of blinds brushed up (surrounded by freshly cut brush to make them look more natural) and the quantity and size of decoy sets in place. It was amazing. Just about every blind in a ten-square-mile area was set up and ready to go. Ducks were scattered everywhere among the blinds, in addition to those at the Bean Field. I looked over at Al, and he acknowledged my thoughts with a shrug. It was a prospective killing field when we considered the number of birds this area already held, with more arriving daily from the cold, freezing reaches of the north. It was obvious that during the next several shoot days a lot of killing would take place, with a good percentage of it being illegal.

I never had a problem with hunting and never will. My entire family was raised to appreciate and participate in what the outdoors had to offer, and over the years we have grown together in many ways because of our love for such things. But the killing in this restful marsh area was not going to be pretty on the coming Saturday. The birds had flocked into the Sink from their other usual feeding and loafing areas in numbers beyond belief. I found out later that the picture I had taken with Al's camera, when statistically analyzed by our lab at Patuxent, had registered almost one million pintail in that field! They didn't even count all the other species!

After we flew over the length and width of the Butte Sink and I gained the work information I needed, I asked Al to head home. As we headed back to the Colusa County Airport, I began to develop a battle plan on how to work this area during the next couple of shoot days and throughout the following week. It was November, basically the front end of a 107-day duck season in California, and everyone representing the "thin green line" was more than committed in the protection of its wildlife resources in that great rift called the Sacramento Valley. I knew, like all the rest of that fraternity carrying a badge and wearing hip boots for 107 straight days, that we could expect little help because of the season's length and the hard, wet work associated with waterfowl law enforcement. But, I thought with a slight grin on my tired and already windburned face, that had never stopped me yet! Since I was basically on my own, I would have to make a sound, all-encompassing impression on the lads hunting in the Butte Sink or a lot of ducks would be killed illegally over the next several weeks. If I could hit the area hard and successfully for a solid week, I should make the impression needed to take the gilding off their lilies, I thought. What a week it would be!

Back at the airport, Al set N710 down as if it belonged to him (which I guess it did since he was a taxpayer and all). I thanked Al for his time and hopped out, and with a wave he lifted off and headed back toward Sacramento County. Cranking up my truck, I got on the radio and called Warden Bob Hawks, my old friend from Fish and Game academy days. Bob was a little old short fellow with California Indian blood proudly coursing through his veins. He was not only a close friend but a damn good "catch dog" as well. Bob responded to my call and after a short, more or less coded transmission (I didn't want to alert anyone listening about my plans) agreed to meet me on Butte Creek, not far from the Bean Field. We met about thirty minutes later by a milo field containing about ten thousand noisy feeding sandhill cranes, and after exchanging pleasantries amidst the continual sound of their melodious croaking, Bob, in his usual diplomatic way, said, "Now what kind of crap do you have planned for the two of us to get into?" It never seemed to fail: once we teamed up, an adventure was in the offing. It was obvious that thought had already crossed his mind. Grinning over my thoughts, which more than likely paralleled his, I told Bob what I had just seen over the Butte Sink and let that statement sink in for a few moments. I could tell from Bob's stone-cold stare that he was ready to set aside some time to give me a hand. He was just as much a hunter of men as I, and I really enjoyed the chase with him as my friend and equal.

With a lead pencil and the hood of my pickup as paper, I drew a plot of the external boundaries of the Sink and then laid out eight different duck clubs that looked particularly promising because of the numbers of birds covering their flooded real estate, including one right next to the Sutter Buttes in Bob's warden district. I told him I had observed a four-man tank blind in a remote corner of the Senator Duck Club. Bob just looked at me steadily with those coal-black eyes. I knew he thought the folks on this duck club were pretty good people, so I had to make my point well.

"Bob," I said, "the thing that caught my eye was that the water in and around the decoys by this blind was muddy as all get-out, and the lee side of the duck pond was covered with a line of feathers clearly visible from the air."

That was all it took. Bob immediately recognized the probability of a baited pond. The muddy water was a good indicator of many feeding waterfowl stirring up the bottom, as was the line of feathers on the lee side of the pond. In places where a lot of feeding and squalling or a lot of killing takes place, a line of feathers will soon develop as a natural result of the feather loss caused by these activities. Bob was a very busy man, but he knew that when I had something to say he could take it to the bank, so I knew he would give my request serious consideration.

After a few moments of thought, Bob said, "What time do you want me to meet you on Saturday, and where?"

"How about three-thirty A.M. at my place?" I said. "That way we can get in and settled and let the ducks do the same."

Bob nodded, and after a crude epithet in regard to my German heritage, we went out separate ways to the areas we needed to work.

What seemed like the middle of the night the next shoot day found us safely hidden in a small grove of trees and brush, in a direct line of sight southwest from the suspected duck blind. Using our "if they don't expect you they won't see you" guidance system after meeting at my house, Bob and I had driven right to the area we wanted to work and pulled my truck into the grass alongside the county road. I then pulled up the hood on my unmarked truck and left a note on the windshield proclaiming that the truck had broken down and I would be right back with a tow. Then Bob and I had only about a three-hundred-yard walk to our hiding place on the suspected baited pond rather than the mile we would have had to hoof it from the nearest hidden parking place.

Just before legal shooting time, it appeared that Bob and I were to have some company. A sedan drove from the Senator Gun Club clubhouse down the county highway to the same area Bob and I had just walked through, stopping in front of the gate leading from the road into the hunting area. We could see through the binoculars, with the car's headlights for illumination, that a hurried conference was being held regarding my "broken-down" truck just down the highway. Finally the car backed out of the driveway and motored the fifty or so yards to my vehicle. We could see one of the party get out of the sedan and walk up to the truck, take the note out from under my windshield wiper, and read it. The man carefully put the note back and got back into the automobile, and the car backed down the highway and returned to the gate. The men unlocked and then locked the gate behind them and drove toward us, parking a short distance from where we lay in wait under the trees. In a few moments three fellows walked by us on their way to the blind we had staked out, scaring up about three hundred feeding ducks in the process.

I smiled at Bob in the darkness. I was sure he had the same kind of smile on his face. There is no greater thrill than stalking your fellow human, except maybe that moment just before you leave this world to travel to the next one! You could just bet that the shivers Bob and I felt at that moment were not only because of the cold.

It took the lads some time to adjust their decoys and add more brush to their blind to aid their place of concealment. Finally satisfied, they sat there in the darkness as it turned to light and smoked cigarettes, totally unaware of the two sets of eyes trained on them.

Whistling wings told us we had aerial company, and eight shots from the hunters' shotguns confirmed those suspicions, which were validated by the flops of three large ducks into the water. Before the lads could retrieve those birds, others attracted by the water movement around the decoys from the ripples of their fallen comrades and by the thought of breakfast ventured in. They met the same fate as their buddies, only this time five more quickly hit the water.

"Damn, those guys can really shoot," I whispered to Bob as I recorded the kills in the predawn darkness in my notebook.

During the next half hour before the occurrence of daylight, a total of twenty-six ducks hit the water for their last time. It didn't seem to matter to the three lads that the limit was eight each, for a total of twenty-four! They were now in the trap, and I knew where two of the "catchin'est" son of a guns were sitting, ready to let them know all was not well!

From where Bob and I sat, we could look directly into their blind and readily identify the men pulling the triggers. They were some of the best shots I had seen in a long time. It seemed that every time a gun barrel went up, a duck came down. Before long they had a new total of thirty-eight ducks down on the water in front of their blind. The limit hadn't changed; it was still twenty-four, yet these lads continued to shoot their way deeper and deeper into the forthcoming legal morass.

During a pause in the flying the shooters got up and collected their ducks. I could tell that for the most part the bodies on the water represented pintail, a numerous species of wintering duck in that area in those days. What a way for that little graceful greyhound of the sky with the beautiful fluting call to die, I thought. They deserved a better ending than they had just received at the hands of our three poachers. I could feel my eyes hardening as I counted the broken bodies on the water. A look at Bob revealed the same emotion in his eyes. So much for Bob's friendship with some of the members of this club, I thought. These lads would have to pay the price for their shortsighted greed, and it would not be long in coming!

Two of the lads rose from the blind, looked carefully all around, then picked up a legal limit of eight ducks apiece from the water and headed for their parked automobile. Bob and I let them go. We still had one fellow in the blind, and we knew the other two weren't going to leave him there alone for long. The ducks went into the trunk of their car, and the lads left for parts unknown. The other fellow picked up the remaining ducks from the pond and placed them in the blind. Then, as if in awe of the numbers of birds starting to move in the air again, he just sat in the blind and let the ducks swarm in around him without firing a shot.

About ten minutes later the other two lads returned to the blind, emerged again with another limit of eight ducks each, and headed for the car. Once in what they thought was the safety of the vehicle, they headed out to what Bob and I suspected was the clubhouse to hide their over-limits. This little maneuver was repeated once more so that all of the ducks previously killed had been removed from the area. After the last trip the two lads returned to their partner in the blind and, instead of leaving, as Bob and I expected them to do, hunkered down and killed nine more pintail that had drifted through the trees surrounding their blind and into their decoys. The lads never missed a shot. The entire flock of pintail had been killed in some of the finest shooting I had seen in a long time. Bob gave me a look asking, How many more? Just then twelve more graceful pintail floating over the blind for a look-see took my mind off Bob's question. Their effortless flight and fluting calls were pure heaven until they realized that the decoys below were death. Six of the twelve called no more as the remaining six fled in utter terror, their little world shattered by the hard truth of decoys and flying lead.

I turned to Bob and mouthed, "These guys are really killers." He looked hard at me, not pleased at the carnage going on on "his" duck club but realizing that what we were seeing was an instinct to kill that at this moment was totally uncontrolled. We also realized that more than likely this was not the first time this trio had gone over to the "dark side." Such activity would certainly account for the muddy water in the duck pond—not bait but just the constant walking in the area to recover all the dead birds. Without a word, we agreed to let the lads have all the rope they wanted, figuring we would stop their fall just before their feet hit the ground.

The mallards began to fly now, moving back and forth through the flooded timber, and it appeared they would eventually suffer the same fate as their pintail counterparts. However, for the moment the mallards worked the areas outside shotgun range of our blind, and for a fleeting second I thought maybe this would be all the killing in this blind for the day. But then the general flight of ducks at this end of the marsh let up and the lads began their familiar run to what was probably their duck club with the latest batch of ducks killed. Again they did this until all the ducks were gone and all that remained was the muddy water caused by numerous retrievals and the resultant feathers silently floating across the pond to the lee side, mute testimony to the earlier violence. Fifty-three ducks had fallen that morning, seen only by the three shooters, God, and two game wardens in a brush pile.

About that time a large flock of mallards circled and circled as if something was wrong and then decided to take the plunge. With wings set, tails making adjustments for just the right spot to land, loud calls to the "brethren" already on the water, and necks tossed back in the spirit of flight, in they came. As their feet came down in preparation for the water landing, up rose the three gunners, and in moments the lights of life had gone out on fourteen mallards. I was stunned! The lads had shot only three times each at the most all morning. That was the law: no more than three shells per shotgun while hunting migratory water-fowl. Then, when the large flock of mallards had ridden the wind to their hoped-for haven, the lads had erupted with a vol-ley of shots that told Bob and me that their guns were un-plugged. Fourteen dead and dying ducks on the water told me that was the end of the line for these three lads. In my eyes, the rope was now tight!

I rose from my hiding place in the brush without telling Bob my intentions, but I noticed out of the corner of my eye that he was doing the same. No more of this kind of raw killing, we must have thought at the same time! These lads had unknow-ingly hit the end of their rope and were now going to find that their feet were not quite touching the ground! Striding out of our cover, I noticed the lads in the blind staring in disbelief and then dropping down out of sight in a vain attempt to hide their bigger-than-life secret. I walked through the decoy area picking up the dead and dying mallards while Bob walked over to their blind, identified the two lads ruining their hunt, and took their shotguns for safekeeping.

We had a total of sixty-seven ducks in one hour and twenty-three minutes of shooting. Even someone as bad at math as I could tell these lads had a way to go, in the legal arena, that is. All of us marched quietly to their vehicle, and while Bob held them there I went for my truck. When I arrived back on the scene, Bob gave me the high sign that he wanted to talk to me. It seemed that the lads steadfastly denied killing any more ducks than the ones they had in their possession. Without a word, I strode over to the lads and told them that I was a federal game warden, and if they continued to lie we were all going to jail right then and there. Looking them in the eye, I let that statement gather some dust in their minds and then said that the club would be cited for violations as well, and I would make every effort to close it down for the remainder of duck season if this horse-pucky, tight-lipped crap continued. By now I had their rapt attention because they stood to bring the entire club down through the stupidity of their actions if they were not cooperative.

Not wanting them to get their sea legs under them, I continued more in a telling than an asking tone, "Let's go back to the duck club and get the rest of the ducks, lads." I was sure hoping that was where the birds had gone; otherwise my bluff might just hit the rocks. But it seemed they realized that their little lie was exposed, and one, who turned out to be a local businessman, said, "OK." We followed them out of the field in our vehicle and back to the Senator Duck Club hanging facility (a small enclosed or screened room where the hanging waterfowl would remain cool and free from flies after being gutted). There, hanging in "legal" bunches, were all the rest of the birds killed earlier that morning. As I started to remove them for seizure, assuming they were the ducks killed earlier, I noticed that all the bunches were tagged in accordance with state and federal laws. Federal law requires that anytime migratory waterfowl are left in temporary storage, they must be tagged with the date, species, number of birds killed, address of the hunter, name of the hunter, and his signature. These bunches of ducks were conveniently "tagged" with previously filled-out tags by other members of the duck club, dated for *that specific day*. As it turned out, none of the lads whose names were on the tags were even on the club that day!

It was obvious that this whole illegal episode had been planned from the beginning, and planned well. If Bob and I hadn't been right on top of these chaps and watched them breaking the law, we might never have caught them in their little charade. They had taken over-limits, tagged them with someone else's tags, and hoped to smuggle their ill-gotten gains home and into the freezer. I leveled my gaze at each of them as I stood there with several bunches of their illegally tagged birds held conspicuously in my hands. One at a time, as my knowing gaze crossed their eyes, they lowered theirs.

"Gentlemen," I said, "this is not going to look good in any court of law. Taking over-limits, unplugged guns, illegal tagging, illegal possession; in short, fellows, this is going to cost most of the hide off of your collective hind ends." They continued to look down at something apparently more important than looking me in the eye. "I will need hunting licenses, driver's licenses, and duck stamps, gentlemen," I said, and they quickly complied. Bob and I issued them citations for their little act of stupidity, and as the morning wore on the lads began to lighten up, as did Bob and I. They had gotten over the fright of first contact and turned out to be pretty good chaps in spite of their gross actions in the morning. One was a municipal judge, one a certified public accountant, and the other a banker. None had any explanation for their actions except to say that they were guests of the club and they had never seen ducks like that; they just couldn't stop the act of killing once they had started. I asked if they had any kids. They all said yes, they had; in fact all had sons they hoped to get out with them on the club someday. The magnitude of what they had just said hit all of them at the same instant and with the degree of force that I had intended. It got very quiet, and I could read the shame in their eyes.

"Gentlemen," I said, "you just took a bunch of birds that belonged to your kids. I will bet you that when those boys get to the age where they can hunt with you, the bird numbers you saw today will not be here because someone took more than their share. I only hope it wasn't their dads." I let that sink in for a moment, then gave Bob the sign to move on. Before we left I told the lads that their hunting, except for geese, was over for the day and asked if they had any questions. Silence was the only response. Shaking all their hands and noting three sets of downcast eyes, we seized all sixty-seven ducks and departed.

Bob and I returned to my home, where we gutted and stored the seized ducks in the evidence freezer. Then we left for other fields of battle, Bob going his way and I mine.

Today, many years later, a framed print of a portion of the Butte Sink marshes hangs on my office wall. There are huge numbers of pintail flying with the Sutter Buttes framed in the background, the scene punctuated by billowy clouds and a robin's-egg-blue sky. In the lower right-hand corner is an old duck blind. The painter is Harry Adamson, and the blind, pictured in disrepair, is the one on the Senator Gun Club that yielded $3,200 in fines for that morning's work. The pintail numbers have declined by about 80 percent over the last five years, and they no longer fill the Bean Field as they used to. I wonder if those three dads realize that they were part of the demise of these graceful birds. I certainly hope that at least their sons do. If so, maybe there won't be another repetition down the road with their kin ... and the kin of those in the air.

After leaving Bob, not wanting to waste any daylight, I headed for the White Mallard Duck Club on the northeast side of Colusa County. This club sat on the northwest corner of the Butte Sink and had been full of outlaws since my arrival in the county as a game warden in 1967. I offloaded the Grumman Sport boat (a stable, wide-beam work canoe) from the truck into Butte Creek about half a mile below the club and hurriedly loaded my gear for the next venture. I was spurred on by the constant thump of shotguns in the Sink area along with the ever-present flocks of ducks flying over the flooded trees in every direction. Mounting my 9.5-horsepower Evinrude motor and fastening the safety chain, I gave the starter cord a pull and it coughed to life.

I quietly motored down the canal past the clubhouse located on the west bank levee and turned off into a canal that led into the flooded timber maze leading to the main duck club shooting area. I hadn't gone one hundred yards at an idle, trying to sort out where the heaviest shooting was coming from, when I became aware of the sound of an outboard motor coming my way. Putting my motor into neutral, I sat there to see which way the boat leaving the marsh was going. Likely the person running the oncoming boat had finished his duck hunt and was heading for the duck club. It was always a good bet to check the lads as they left the marsh, and that was my intention if I got the opportunity. Sure as God made little green apples, the boat ended up coming my way. I waited patiently. In a few moments I saw a heavily laden duck boat turn off from a side canal leading from a duck blind into the main canal, where a game management agent sat in his canoe (with a grin, I might add). When the lad in the boat first saw me, he hesitated for a moment to consider the unknown entity in his way. I noticed he had his left hand on the steering arm of his outboard and the right hand hanging over the transom of the boat. Once he realized I might not be friendly, the hand over the transom appeared to let something go, and sure as hell, an instant later, I saw five mallards bob to the surface in his wake.

Raising my hand and blocking the canal with my boat, I hailed the lad. He slowed down, and I reached out and pulled our two boats together. By his actions and the look on his face, I could tell he had a problem. A quick scan of his boat revealed a large mesh bag of decoys, a shotgun, and a limit of drake mallards lying on the boat seat in front of him. I introduced myself, showing him the badge, all the while watching for any telltale signs or out-of-the-ordinary reactions to my presence. They were there all right. His eyes never left me, just like those of some cornered prey. After requesting his hunting license and duck stamp, I asked to check the plug in his shotgun. All the while I kept an eye on the floating mallards behind his boat. He also kept an eye on me, hoping I had not seen the ducks now starting to gently drift against the stern of his boat. Boy, talk about the dead coming back to haunt your very doorstep! Those five mallards were really getting their revenge.

I continued going through the motions of my check of the lad and his boat, all the while formulating my attack plan. When I finished I could see the light of hope go on in his eyes and then completely go out with the words, "Why don't you pick up those five mallards you dropped over the stern when you approached me." Jesus, you could see the desperate look slide across his face in anguish.

"Those aren't my ducks," he replied rather weakly.

"Look," I said, "I don't have any time to fool around. I saw you drop those ducks from your right hand, which was hanging over the stern of the boat as you approached me, so why don't you just hand them here." He reached over resignedly, picked the ducks up out of the water, and quietly handed them to me. I then said, "Hand me all the other ducks in your boat as well, please."

He said, "Why?"

"Because you have an over-limit in your possession, and that means all the ducks will be seized as evidence. That means the five in the water and the eight on the seat of your boat. The limit is eight, and you have thirteen."

He meekly complied, but he still had an edge of nervousness that telegraphed that there was more to come. Gathering his ducks into a pile in the bottom of my boat, I leveled a gaze at him that would have stopped a German Panzer in full stride and asked, "Do you have any more ducks in your boat?"

The lad froze and quietly replied, "No," which really said "yes" in game warden "sign language."

Looking him right in the eyes, I said quietly, "You know if I find any more illegal birds in your boat, it will not go well for you in a court of law."

"That is all I have, officer," he replied unconvincingly in a voice now an octave higher.

"What is in the decoy bag?" I asked.

He hesitated for a second, and that moment told me what I already knew, especially when he said, "Nothing." Wrong answer, because there sure as hell was a pile of decoys in the bag—plus I would bet a pile of more dead ducks.

Reaching over the side and into his boat, I lifted the decoy bag. It was too damn heavy for just decoys. Another look confirmed that my prey was trapped, and he knew it. I grabbed the decoy bag with both hands and, lifting it as high as I could from my sitting position, dumped the contents into the bottom of his boat. Out poured three dozen cheap decoys and eighteen additional dead mallards and pintail. My eyes slowly lifted from the broken, wet bodies to his eyes. My look said it all. The lad meekly said, "You can't blame a person for trying."

I said, "No, and you can't blame a person for catching that lad trying to outsmart the law either." He shrugged as I took out my cite book and wrote out a pink slip for later presentation in federal court in Sacramento. The whole time I was writing out the ticket, I could tell something was really bothering this man. He was a fifty-eight-year-old doctor who had been a member of the duck club for years. Something just wasn't sitting right, but I couldn't put my finger on it, so for the moment I had to let it go, even if the sweat was pouring off his bald head in 38 degree winter weather.

After a short talk about the laws of the land, I let the man go back to the clubhouse minus his thirty-one ducks. As I watched him go, my gut feeling told me something was rotten in this henhouse, but damned if I could catch the scent of that trail. I later reviewed our federal case files to see if the fellow had a previous record, but no soap. I then tried the state Fish and Game files and went through seven years' worth of old citations in Sacramento; again no dice. My gut feeling was borne out a year or so later when I was rereading the book *Hunting the Lawless* by Hugh Worchester, an old-time U.S. game management agent who had worked the Sacramento Valley during the 1940s and 1950s. There in print was my baldheaded doctor friend's name.

Apparently, he had been caught as a young adult and had served six months in the "bucket" for being involved in the commercial market hunting of ducks. It is amazing how one human can sense something regarding another human's character, especially regarding the commission of an illegal act. There really is something to say about being a "traveler in time," as many of us in this line of business are! I was always happy to catch those who had crossed the edge of the law before and have probably crossed it many times since. It didn't do the wildlife he killed any good, but it was good for that man's soul to know that the long arm of the law could appear at any time.

The day was still young in the Sink, and I felt there was still money to be made, so off I went. The shooting was dying down as the morning progressed, but the marsh still had ducks and a few die-hard hunters at large. I checked several other blinds without detecting any problems, and as the day's warmth and my long hours began to take their toll on me, I headed for a small clump of out-of-the-way trees in the vast surrounding water. Sliding into the trees, I got out on the small dry levee and sat down with my back to a tree to rest my eyes for a moment. The next thing I knew it was late afternoon, and the marsh was quiet. Checking my watch to the surprised clatter of a pair of wood ducks frightened off the levee not five feet from me, I could see that there were still a couple hours of daylight left. Thinking I would use the remaining daylight in the deserted marsh to check out blinds on other duck clubs, I shoved off in the Grumman.

As I moved out into an area where the water was about six feet deep and surrounded by trees, I noticed a small duck boat gliding slowly along the treeline on the south end. Sliding into some bushes for cover, I got out my binoculars to see what the lad was doing. He was creeping toward a bunch of Canada geese sitting on the water in front of him as if he was preparing to use his motorboat and run up on them so he could get close enough to shoot. If that occurred, that action would be a violation of federal law. With that, I decided to just sit in the bushes and capture another unfortunate lad if he crossed the line in the sand the laws had drawn. For some reason the man just sort of herded the geese toward a single tree standing alone in the middle of the flooded marsh. That was odd behavior, I thought. If he wanted to motorboat the geese, he'd better get with it before they flew. But the man just kept moving the geese toward that lone, flooded tree at a pace that kept the geese busily swimming in front of him, just out of range of his shotgun but not alarmed yet. Finally the geese had a gutful of this lad idling along behind them and lifted off the water amidst the noisy clamor typical of Canada geese. Their flight path carried them past the tree while the boatman chugged along far behind them. Then by damn, it happened! Two shots rang out from the tree, and two geese folded and dropped deader than a stone into the water.

What the hell? I thought. I quickly gave the flooded tree a once-over with the binoculars, and be damned, there was a hunter lodged in the crotch of that tree fully ten feet above the flood waters. I was floored! The man in the boat had apparently dropped the other fellow off and then herded the geese into shooting range of the lad in the tree. How clever, and also illegal. One can't use a boat and motor as a use or aid to take migratory game birds, and these lads sure as shooting (no pun intended) had crossed that line, one for rallying waterfowl (use and aid of a motor-driven conveyance) and the other for aiding and abetting, which carried the same fine as the principal violation. Brother, I had seen it all now.

The lad in the boat picked up the two geese and started to head for his partner in the tree. So did the local federal. Intercepting the hunters, I shook my head after identifying myself and said, "Lads, do you know what you just did was illegal?"

One of them said, "Well, I guess we do now." They had just screwed up, and their lack of knowledge of the laws of the sport cost each of them $50 plus the loss of their hard-won gains in the form of the geese. Citing the two lads, I tagged the geese with evidence tags and we parted company, they wiser for the experience and I shaking my head at how I was constantly being surprised by human antics. If that man had fallen out of the tree, he probably would have drowned because of the chest-highs he was wearing. Brother, what some people will do to kill a critter.

It was getting dark now, and I began to realize I hadn't eaten for about fourteen hours. It seemed the big guts had eaten all the little guts, and I thought I had better take care of that growling issue before any further damage was done to my being. Besides that, I felt it was appropriate that I spend a little time with my poor wife, who had little opportunity to see me during this time of the year. With that, I headed out of the marsh for home with the thought in mind of what the Butte Sink would bring me on the morrow.

At three in the morning the next day my dog Shadow and I quietly unloaded my Grumman Sport canoe in a small canal next to the Butte Creek Lodge duck club. With all my gear loaded, both of us relieved ourselves one more time before we went off into a world of dark, narrow canals and objecting, resting waterfowl that had been sleeping in the marsh moments before. Motoring slowly so as to make as little noise and disturbance as possible, the dog and I moved to the east side of the south end of the Butte Sink. Finding the levee where I wanted to hide next to Bob Stack's duck club and unique tree blind, I settled in for the morning's events. My boss had told me that he had pinched Bob for an over-limit of ducks in years past, and I was hoping I would have the opportunity to do the same that fine day. Bob was reported to be a very good shot, especially with birds on the wing. If that was true, the number of birds in the marsh plus his unusual tree blind should lend my chances a positive lean if he showed up. The marsh settled down, and except for the occasional quack of a disturbed mallard, the quiet plop of a muskrat, or the squeal of the ever-present wood ducks, all was at peace in my world.

Dawn was still a short while away when Shadow caught a far-away sound. Looking in the direction of her nose with my hands cupped over my ears, I too picked up the sound of an outboard motor. The marsh started to wake up as a boat worked its way across from the east to a point near where I lay concealed. Soon I discovered there were two men in that boat coming over to Bob Stack's cottonwood blind. This blind consisted of a single large cottonwood tree about seventy feet tall. Below it and all around were about one hundred decoys. Directly under the tree was a small enclosed area in which one parked and hid the boat. A set of wooden steps going up the tree from the hidden boat dock led first to a boxed-in toilet sticking out from the tree in such a manner that one using it could hang his fanny out over the water below the wooden seat and let go into the duck pond. The crapper was placed in such a way that the poop missed the boat and provided a feast for the crawdads. Another ten steps up the tree one could stop in a little kitchen area to warm up coffee or cook something light on a small two-burner white-gas stove. The area was roomy enough that it contained cupboards and even a place to sit and eat. The steps continued to a large platform blind that had been built into the sawed-off top of the cottonwood about thirty feet above the kitchen. Below it lay the decoys, and all one had to do was call the ducks and, when they arrived to check it out, shoot them from an eyeball-to-eyeball vantage point or from above as they swirled into the decoys below. Either way, the hunt had to be top drawer with the crapper, kitchen, element of surprise, and all-around great view making for a unique experience.

I had hoped to set up on Bob Stack himself but was disappointed in my haul that day. Both men were fairly tall, and since Stack was a stump of a fellow, I knew he wasn't there and just settled for whatever the good Lord provided. The two unloaded their gear, climbed the tree as if they had been there before, and set up in the blind area to await what the day would bring them. As the sun arrived for another day in the marsh, so did the awakening of thousands of ducks. Other boats entered the area and headed for their respective duck blinds around us, the shooting started in earnest, and the air filled with waterfowl as I imagined it would have in the days of old. The birds are greatly reduced in some quarters now, but they will fly forever in my mind until my flight ends as well. God really is something else. He opens the doors of opportunity and lets us look in many times and then closes them, sometimes forever. This was one sight I was to witness through His partially open door many times during my career. I never tired of looking, and He never tired of letting me look. God, how I miss it today.

Looking at my watch, I could see that shooting time was upon me and my two unsuspecting chaps in the treetop. About that time a group of six ducks came in low; I didn't see them in time to identify their species from my hidden position, but the lads in the treetop did, and a pair of plops into the water told me they had killed two of the ducks. Leaving the ducks in the water, the lads continued to have the shoot of a lifetime. Ducks came into the blind from every point of the compass and in such numbers I had a tough time identifying them for my field notes. It was handy that if I didn't have the chance to identify them in the air, when they fell they were right in front of where I lay hidden on a small levee, so an accurate species count was fairly easy.

When the hunters had killed their legal limit, there was a hurried conversation and one of the men came down out of the tree, got into the boat, and poled himself around the decoy area to pick up the dead ducks. After gathering them, including one that lay just six or seven feet in front of me, he poled back to the boat blind, tied the ducks together by their necks with a short length of parachute cord, and started up the tree with them. How odd, I thought; why take them up into the tree blind? Why not just leave them in the boat? My curiosity and patience were soon rewarded. The lad carried the ducks up to the crapper and lowered them down inside the hole. With a quick movement he hung the ducks by the cord around their necks from a nail on the inside wall of the latrine hole. Since side boards hung down around the toilet seat, the ducks were invisible unless you got directly under the hole and looked up. I don't know many people who will look up into a crapper hole from underneath; hence it was a super hidey-hole! (Again, no pun intended.)

With that task completed, the man lowered the crapper lid and climbed back up the tree to the duck blind. A few moments went by, and with the arrival of a small flock of teal the shooting started all over again. After all, the lads "didn't have a limit yet"—or at least one you could see! I always loved it when someone stepped into my arena not even knowing it *was* an arena. These hunters had just done so big time, and I wasn't going to disappoint them when the time came for the finale. The birds flew into this area like there was no tomorrow, and for many there wasn't. Down they came, mallards, pintail, ringneck, and spoonbills. These lads weren't picky about what they shot, that was pretty damn obvious, I thought. But by damn, they were on a killing spree that was not pretty to watch! Twenty-one more ducks fell to the deadly hail of lead before the same lad came down the tree to pick up the dead and dying. This time, since the crapper hideout was full, after picking up all the ducks he poled his boat over to the levee where I was hiding. Damn, I thought, the jig is up; but he turned once he landed on the levee and went to the opposite side from where I lay hidden. He walked about ten feet from where I was hiding half in the water, looked around to make sure the coast was clear, and lifted up part of the levee! Jesus, was I surprised! He actually lifted up part of the levee, exposing a buried ice chest that had dirt and plants growing on the lid. Into the ice chest went the ducks, and the lid was again carefully closed so as not to disturb the dirt-and-marsh-plant covering. Then the lad reached over with a small board, picked up an old "dump," toilet paper and all, and gently placed it on top of the sunken ice chest.

That rascal! I thought. He knew most people wouldn't look around where someone had taken a dump. A perfect crime, except for one thing: the large figure silently watching the activity from about ten feet away. Sometimes God is good to us lads of the green cloth, and other times He is spectacular. That day He matched his beautiful sunrise with the rise of an ice-chest lid that would lead to another rise in the blood pressure of the two chaps having such a hell of a good shoot at the expense of God's critters! Back up the tree the lad went, and the "hunt" recommenced as if nothing was wrong. This time I quietly rose from my hiding place and carefully and silently walked very slowly from the levee under their treehouse blind to their boat. Dead ducks continued to rain down around me, but at this point in the adventure I had a plan and was in the process of carrying it out. Very slowly, so I wouldn't make a ripple, I crawled into their boat and lay down on my back, covering my rather large carcass with their decoy bags so they wouldn't see me if they came down the tree again. Twelve more plops told me they had again more than exceeded their legal limit of eight apiece and this would be a fun morning before it was over. Peeking up out of my hiding place, I noticed my well-trained dog Shadow watching from the camouflaged Grumman Sport boat and not making a sound. She knew what her master was doing, and in a way I think she enjoyed it as much as I did.

Someone was coming down the tree, so I lay back down in the boat, which was partially concealed under the small covered boat dock. The man coming down the tree waded out to the end of the boat, pulled it out from its place of concealment, and without looking in at his passenger started to drag it around behind him as he picked up the most recent crop of dead ducks. Without looking backward, the lad just threw the ducks into the boat on top of me as he searched the decoy area. Damn, let me tell you, if they aren't looking for you, they won't ever see you. Picking up five ducks lying on the pond, the lad headed over to the levee and placed those birds in the buried ice chest. Leaving the rest of the ducks in the boat, he returned and, without giving it a thought, began to push the boat back toward the tree blind.

I was lying there right under his nose, not more than six or seven feet away, looking up at him, half buried by dead ducks and the burlap decoy sacks I had dragged over my ample frame. This was too good to be true. Hardly moving, I said, "Good morning." I thought I was going to lose him. He jumped back about three steps in the three-foot-deep water and, losing his balance, fell flat on his back into the icy water, going clear out of sight. He came up out of the water, blowing hard, rolled over, and tried to crawl toward the levee bank, still making grunting sounds but no words. When he hit the levee, the lad was so shaken up that all he could was flail around at the edge. His legs were flying around so fast he couldn't get any traction, but he sure was a pretty sight lying there thrashing the water up into a froth. Even Shadow, whose head was now up poking over the side of our boat, seemed to be enjoying the "hoorah."

Getting up and stepping out of their boat, I just stood there watching this poor bastard trying to get back into his skin without breaking his zipper. His partner hollered down from the treetop, "What the hell is the matter with you? Keep it quiet, Ted, or you'll scare the ducks. We don't want anyone to know we don't belong here." Well, that was a nice bit of news. It seemed I had a couple of trespass violations as well as shooters of over-limits of ducks. Why they were trying to keep it quiet was a mystery to me, especially in light of all the previous shooting they had done. (In later conversations with the lads, I discovered that they had trespassed on Bob's club many times, which explained why they knew the features of this blind so well.) Oh well; sometimes it is hard for these chaps to make sense of what they do or say, and this was just one of those times.

My grunter finally got his wind and, with a stream of muddy water running off his nose and from his fingertips, bellowed, "Who the hell are you? You scared the crap right out of me lying in our boat like that. Answer me; where the hell did you come from?"

All of a sudden he had his voice. I came to the conclusion that I liked him better when all he could do was grunt. I very softly said, "Federal agent, and it appears you lads have a few ducks too many." He continued to look at me in utter disbelief. A few moments before he and his buddy had been enjoying a hunt of unreal dimensions. Now he had a wet hind end, mud on his head, and a legal problem facing him wearing a four-ounce gold badge.

Without taking his eyes off me, Ted yelled, "Dan, you better come on down here; we have a real problem."

In a few moments I could hear the other lad coming down the

tree, grumbling about his "clumsy" damn partner. When he got to the bottom and saw me, he asked, "Who the hell are you?"

Damn, these guys sure thought alike, I thought. "Federal agent," I said, "and it appears you lads have killed a few too many."

The man who had just arrived looked long and hard at his partner, and the look was so easy to read all he lacked was paper and a pen. Did you get all the ducks hidden? it meant. His wet partner said, "What do you mean?" I could tell it was his hope-against-hope tone. "We have less than a limit apiece." I could see that his mind was moving fast and he thought that if I had been lying on my back in the boat, I could not have seen him hide the ducks in the ice chest or crapper.

I thought, This lad is either a cop or a real poacher. No one in this situation can think so fast unless he is one of the above and used to thinking that way on a routine basis. Not wanting to waste my day or let these chaps get the upper hand, which many times ends up as a pissing contest, I figured I would pull the wool over their eyes.

"Shadow," I yelled over my shoulder. Out from her place of concealment she came in a beeline for where I was now standing near their boat dock. As she raced along the levee and neared the buried ice chest, I pointed "down," and her tail end hit the dirt as if a magnet had sucked it down. She sat there waiting for further orders. "Gentlemen," I said, "I have been hearing a lot of shooting from this area, and that generally means a lot of ducks have been taken. So I brought my canoe over to take a look-see for myself." I lied, of course, but this was a good opportunity to pull the wool over their eyes in fine style, and I was bound and determined not to let this opportunity pass. I continued, "Now, where are the ducks you folks have shot to date?" They just looked at me as if I was a ghost. "Surely you lads aren't that bad of shooters," I said. I waited, and I could just see the confidence building in the two men as they figured their chances of escape were pretty good if I had not seen anything other than the ducks in the boat.

Ted said, "These are the only ducks we have, and if you don't mind we are ready to leave, especially with me as wet as I am and all." With that he grabbed the boat, shoved it over to his partner, still waiting on the boat dock, and told him to get in. I loved it! This was the moment all game wardens look forward to and enjoy: that moment when we are holding four of a kind and the lads who are our objects of attention are holding aces and eights!

"Shadow," I said, "find the ducks." Boy, that was all it took for that dog. Up she came from her position in the mud and straight down the levee she ran toward me, right past the ice chest. Then, with a whirl in midair, she reversed course and put her nose to the ground right on the ice chest. You should have seen the lads' looks as they watched this "magic" dog do her thing. Hell, they hadn't seen anything yet, I thought. Shadow smelled the ground one more time and then looked over at me as if to say, "Here they are, boss." Damn, I could have hugged her. She had a rotten nose but had also been watching the lads hide the ducks, and when it came time for her debut, she brought down the house (their house of cards, that is). I walked over and pretended to read sign on the ground (footprints and all), then lifted up a muddy rope handle, exposing the buried ice chest. I turned and looked at the lads. Neither said a thing. They didn't have to; their eyes said it all!

Hauling out the ducks and laying them on the levee, I walked over to their boat and lifted out all the birds lying in it. I placed those on the levee as well and then said, "Gentlemen, please move over here on the levee next to me." They both complied with questioning looks on their faces. I sat down and invited them to do the same. They did, and then I said, "Shadow, find the ducks." At first she seemed confused. She had already found the ducks. In her mind the work was done, but she also knew that if I said, "Find the ducks," there were ducks to be found, and off she went. She ran out the levee and plunged into the pond, swimming around and through the decoys. Finding nothing, she stopped and looked back to me for more instruction. By now I had the hunters' full attention. "Find the ducks," I said again, and knowing she had just checked the decoy area to no avail, she moved over near the boat dock. She was a big old dog (110 pounds) and made quite a sight as she plowed around and through the area looking for more ducks. She passed under the tree-mounted crapper and paused long enough to sample some previously left wares, getting her butt chewed by me in the process, but in that moment she caught the odor of ducks from the water dripping off their hanging bodies. Around and around she went below the crapper looking for the ducks attached to that smell. I smiled at the thought of how the two lads' hearts must be racing at the thought of my dog working in that area.

Shadow stuck her head under water and walked around like that for a few moments. Satisfied that the object of her attention wasn't there, she brought her head up and shook off the water. Then she looked up and spotted the ducks hanging inside the crapper. Bingo, I thought as Shadow whirled around in the water, all the while looking up at the bottom of the crapper in her attempt to let me know where the her attention was directed. Those two lads were sure getting their money's worth! Looking over at them, I said, "Dog says there are ducks hanging in the crapper. Are there?" Neither man moved; they just looked at me in the sinking hope that I wouldn't go look. I said, "Would one of you go and get the ducks, please?"

The wet one said, "That dog doesn't know ducks from beans; there aren't any ducks there. All she wants is to eat some of the crap in the water underneath; that is what has her attention."

Looking him right in the eye, I said, "If I go look and there are ducks hanging inside that crapper, both of you will go to jail. Any takers?" I really wasn't going to take anyone to jail because it would ruin the rest of my work day, but they didn't know that. That kind of tactic usually loosened up those hanging on to their lies and made the event end more quickly. In fact, when I said, "Any takers?" their eyes told it all. Right now they would have swapped a trip on the *Titanic* for what they were going through.

There was a pause, and then Dan rose from his seated position on the levee and waded over to the boat dock. He walked up the steps to the crapper, lifted the lid, and retrieved the two limits of ducks hanging from the nail, lobbing them over to the levee below.

"I thought you would see it my way, lads," I said. "Thanks for the cooperation."

Ted said, "Want to sell that dog?" I couldn't believe what he had just asked and quickly assured him that the dog would never be for sale; otherwise how could I catch the really serious violators? He just looked at me and then handed me his wet hunting and driver's licenses, knowing what was coming next. Dan did likewise, and I issued them citations for taking over-limits of waterfowl. After that was done I asked them if they had permission to hunt on Bob Stack's duck club. Neither man moved, not even their eyes. I think they had hoped I would overlook that little problem. Finally one of them said, "Look, mister, we lied about our occupations on the citations. Both of us are sheriff's officers for Sutter County and can't afford to get into trouble with the local landowners." I had figured as much when I had asked them what their occupations were and both responded that they were truck drivers. These guys looked like cops (trim, athletic) and acted too damn smart and sure of themselves to be anything but.

"Lads," I said, "you knew what you might get into when you started this little venture. I would suggest you just pay your fines and hope your boss doesn't find out. Violations under our administrative system are erased after three years, and I have no intention of telling your supervisors." That was not the answer they were looking for, but in their position that was all the water their boat would draw. They picked up their gear and left the area, and I did the same. Good old Shadow. I gave her a hug, which was all right, but she preferred the deer-meat sandwich that followed. As she sat on the levee munching her reward, I wondered if she was aware of the legend she was building among the outlaws as a real "catch dog." You could bet those two lads never came back to poach in the Butte Sink again. Especially when they knew they had to pit their wits against a game war-den and his wonder dog, "Crapper."

The shooting, as far as the ear could hear, was reaching a crescendo, so I slid the Grumman over the levee and headed for the Green Head Duck Club, which was located about half a mile north of Bob Stack's tree blind. With Shadow in the bow and me and all my gear in the stern, the Grumman plowed right along. We moved through many watery trails in the flooded under-brush and saw about every kind of wildlife moving through the swamp that morning, including a pair of river otters, which Shadow thought were wonderful. Man, it was a great day to be alive.

Finally arriving near the boundary of the Green Head, I hid in a brush patch about one hundred yards from several blinds that were really having a shoot fest and just listened. One blind to the northeast was going great guns, to say the least. It seemed that every few minutes there was a barrage of five to six shots, si-lence, some excellent duck calling, and then a repetition of the scenario. Those would be my next targets, I said to myself as I lifted my motor out of the water, grabbed my paddle, and started moving slowly toward their blind. The area I was in was nothing but flooded marsh intersected by small boat canals de-noting different club boundaries. As long as you had a boat, you could go from club to club unhindered.

Keeping to a small line of trees and flooded brush, I continued my trek by water toward the shooters I was interested in. The air continued to fill with ducks, in bunches and alone, moving from place to place looking for shelter. Every time they thought they had found that shelter, a few shots told otherwise and fewer ducks than before continued to search. Damn, eight birds was too many for a daily bag limit, I said to myself as I watched this story of the world of waterfowl unfold before me. On many of these clubs the guiding principle seemed to be, "I paid thousands of dollars to hunt here, and I want my money back in a match-ing number of ducks killed."

As the suspected blind moved into my view from my place of

concealment along the trees, I stopped paddling, came back from my judgmental world, and started to function as I had been trained. Picking up my binoculars, I spotted two lads in a stilt blind (a duck blind built on stilts that sat several feet above the water). They were the fellows I wanted all right; I could tell by the duck call I had heard earlier. I took a quick look around with my binoculars for the ever-vigilant resident duck club game-keeper whose main job on a shoot day was to protect his club members from being caught by the game warden; finding none, I returned to my examination of the men in the blind. Five pintail sideslipped into their decoy spread, threw their heads back slightly to aid in landing, dropped their feet, and with wings flaring to slow their speed folded methodically to six quick shots from the gunners. Not a bird survived. There was no doubt that these lads would justify my interest if they routinely shot like that.

One of the men pushed off in a boat that had been concealed under the raised blind, picked up the floating ducks, and returned the boat to its hiding place. In a few moments his head reappeared above the side of the blind, and the familiar mallard call enticing any who would listen could again be heard searching the skies for takers. Presently a pair of mallards responded, and both fell to the same fate as their brethren a few moments earlier. One of the ducks had been head-shot, and after he fell into the water among the decoys he continued to paddle slowly in circles as death closed its grip on the last of his migratory peregrinations. The hunters left the birds in the water, especially the one creating ripples around the decoys as real ducks will do. What better decoy than one of your own, even if he really wasn't an active part of the deception? That little maneuver told me a lot about the fellows I was stalking. They had some of the best duck hunting in the country right at the front door of their blind, yet they were using the swimming, dying bird as a ruse to lure in even more ducks. I smelled killers in this blind and decided to let them do the same rope trick as the men I had caught earlier.

Just then a dozen speedy green-winged teal roared over the water just above the decoys like nature's F-15s and then, seeing the hunters rise to the occasion, shot straight up in a vertical climb just yards in front of the blind. For four birds the afterburners had not cut in on time, and their lifeless bodies lost their built-in air speed, sailed over the blind, and fell almost simultaneously into the weeds at the far edge of the duck pond. Laughter rang from the blind, and no attempt was made to retrieve these little speedsters, the smallest puddle duck in North America. The eyes witnessing this event through binoculars narrowed and hardened, supported by the thought that those birds' deaths would not go unnoticed. They would "speak" from the grave before this day ended! Wanton waste was also a federal violation and would be invoked if these lads chose not to make a reasonable effort to retrieve those four little speedsters of the air. They had not come from the back of the north wind only to die needlessly here, I thought. There would be a reckoning paid in this county, you could bet your sweet hind end!

Both lads hurriedly got down, and soon the direction Shadow was looking told me ducks were coming from behind us toward our shooters. I held still in the canoe, and soon eight or nine ducks effortlessly made a half circle over the decoys and then sailed straight into the decoys, landing without so much as a splash. The lads in the blind just sat there, and soon the air was filled with ducks swarming over the live ones in the decoy set, looking for their spot to land in this obvious safe haven. In about twenty minutes there must have been sixty ducks happily bobbing among the decoys, relieved at having found a place to sit without getting a faceful of shot. Then the happiness of the moment was broken by the ducks' disbelief as two lads stood up in front of them and fired into the flock on the water. Those not killed outright desperately climbed for altitude and safety, only to crumple and spin out of control from a load of number 4 shot. As near as I could tell, about twenty ducks lay on the water as testimony to humankind's inability to let anything live around them in the same neighborhood.

In moments both lads emerged from the blind and hurriedly picked up every duck lying in view. Back to their blind they went, and for a few minutes not a head could be seen. Then I noticed ripples coming from the placid water under the stilt blind where the boat was tethered. Well, I had heard the rope snap taut during that last episode and began to paddle my canoe toward the blind. I deliberately approached from the rear of their boat so that if they tried to flee a few quick paddles would put me within grabbing distance, and you could bet a chicken dinner, once my right hand took hold anywhere on their boat, it was mine. And I don't lose chicken-dinner bets!

The two men were so engrossed in what they were doing that they didn't even realize I was there until I was about twenty yards away. Then one of the lads stood up and looked out over the side of the blind, saw me, said something to his partner, and then disappeared. In just a few moments more ripples came circling out from beneath their stilt blind to flatten out on the bow of my oncoming canoe.

"Morning, gentlemen, federal game warden. How you doing?"

"We got a few," came the guarded reply as both men stood and looked over the side of their blind at the intruder. "Who are you?" the short, fat man asked.

"Federal game warden," I said again, which seemed to go in one ear and out the other of the two confident-appearing chaps in the blind. I thought that cocky look a little strange in light of all the dead birds they had gathered up but let the matter pass for now, figuring they had dumped the extra birds into the water under the blind next to their boat. I checked their shotguns and licenses, and their facade of righteousness remained uncracked. "Mind if I check your birds, lads?" I asked, and they said that would be fine. They also asked if I could hurry, as I was ruining their duck hunting. I said, "Sure," all the while thinking that after what I had seen them do, they hadn't even begun to see "ruin" yet! They laid out fourteen ducks for me to see, exactly two shy of the legal daily bag limit. Looking over the ducks and knowing they had at least thirteen over the limit, counting the teal, I said, "Gentlemen, where are the rest of the ducks you just shot?" Before they could respond, the thought ran through my mind that these chaps had been shooting long before I had arrived. There was no telling how many birds they had downed and had in their possession unless the gamekeeper had made a run and removed their earlier kills.

I was brought back from my figuring by the grouching coming from the blind, which was instantly full of denials and veiled threats. I said, "Gentlemen, I don't have a lot of time for game playing. I just saw the two of you shoot and pick up fourteen ducks. And prior to that, I watched the two of you shoot another thirteen ducks. Where are they?"

"This is all we have, and if you think we have any more, then you show us," one man replied arrogantly.

"OK," I said, and with that I pushed back my canoe so I could pull out the ducks I suspected had been tossed into the water under the blind, causing the ripples I had seen earlier. But when I looked under the blind, which had been covered with brush down to the water level, I saw nothing! That wasn't possible, I said to myself; they had to be there! I looked again, especially around the brush outlining the blind, but still saw nothing. Hauling my carcass out of the Grumman and into the three-foot-deep pond, I walked around to the rear of their blind in my chest-highs. The water was almost four feet deep at that point, so I had to be careful to avoid filling my boots with icy November water. Nothing! Damnit, I was not blind, and the watchful silence told me the lads in the blind were holding tight like a covey of quail when a hawk passes overhead. These fellows were dirty, but I could not figure out what the hell was keeping me from discovering their duck-hiding trick. There weren't any ducks under that blind or in the brush around it; it was just that simple. There weren't any hanging from the floor underneath. Damn, I thought, nothing to go on and a trail that just wasn't there, or at least one that couldn't be seen.

By now the lads were really getting on my tail end about ruining their hunt and demanding that I prove it if I thought they were wrong. Well, I don't know what kind of a heart I had, but I sure as hell had excellent eyes and the stubbornness of my German stock. If that had gotten my kinfolk to Stalingrad, it sure as hell could carry the day here. Moving back to where my canoe was tied, I slid it off to one side and, grabbing the stern of their boat, moved it out of its place of concealment under the blind. There was nothing in the boat except a gas can, an oar, a push pole–boat hook combination, and some tools to repair shear pins. *Boat hook!* Why would these lads need a boat hook? I thought. Taking it out and going on a hunch, I slid it under the blind and, letting it settle to the muddy bottom, dragged it back toward me. Nothing. I repeated this maneuver several times, still with no result.

Now the lads were hot and, in terms anyone could understand, let me know that Ray Arnett, the director of the California Department of Fish and Game, would hear about this. I smiled. You're too late, knotheads, I thought. I no longer worked for Ray; I now worked for Uncle Sam, and in those days he had the guts to take anyone on (or at least Jack Downs, my supervisor, did!). Swinging the boot hook farther off to the side under the blind, I dragged it across the bottom again. That time it hung up solidly on something. Keeping downward pressure on the hook so I wouldn't lose what I had, I dragged it across the bottom of the pond toward me. As it got closer, I began to raise the hook up and out of the water. Finally a fishnet made into a sack and weighted with a concrete block broke the water's surface. Within the sack were the prettiest wet mallards and pintail you ever saw! It was amazing how quickly the two staring lads lost all interest in calling Arnett. Putting the sack of ducks into my canoe, I continued to drag the boat hook along the bushy sides of the blind projecting into the water until it hooked another mystery package, which turned out not to be a mystery once it broke the surface. More dead ducks!

Looking up into the men's now distraught faces for a moment, I could sense even more apprehension than that inspired by the thought of a ticket, so back into the water went the boat hook, and one more fishnet sack with a concrete block emerged. Fifty-seven mallards and pintail were my reward for a good set of eyes, German stubbornness, and the support of God, who just happened to be a game warden that morning. The lads had been shooting all morning and, given the evidence lying in the bottom of my canoe, had done quite well. It was obvious they had planned this and probably similar outings, and if I hadn't been right on top of them when their moment of truth arrived, they would probably have walked away with me none the wiser about their lethal secret. I have often wondered just how many ducks they had killed and hidden in this fashion over the years. Only the game warden in the sky knows that one. I wonder what His fines are?

While writing a citation for one of the lads, I sent the other one after the four teal they had killed earlier. About that time the gamekeeper came by to check on his charges. Not seeing my canoe, which was hidden behind the blind, he came right to the blind. His mistake. He had been out collecting the extra birds some of his other club members had illegally killed and had taken these extras off their hands. His plan was to take them to the clubhouse and tag them with tags bearing the names of the cook and other workers. Then when the club member who was responsible for taking the birds returned to the clubhouse, he could take the whole illegal mess home with none the wiser on the side of the law. Well, guess what? Into my clutches he came with his sixteen ill-gotten gains in the form of every type of duck known to man and that marsh. Damn, was he ever surprised to see me!

"Hi, Terry," he said as he nonchalantly tried to throw a burlap bag over the pile of ducks lying in the bottom of his boat.

"Hello, Charlie," I said. "Looks like you got too many there."

"These are just cripples the dog and I picked up to take back to the club so they wouldn't go to waste," came the standard weak reply.

"You know the regulations, Charlie," I said. "A legal limit in possession in the field, that is all." He just shrugged and sat there, knowing what was coming next, and it sure as hell wasn't Christmas. Throwing the just retrieved green-winged teal into my boat along with the birds from the nets, I finished citing both hunters for their over-limits. Letting them go with a professional, "Thank you, fellows," I turned back to Charlie. "Charlie," I said, "I know those birds in the bottom of your boat are over-limits someone on the club shot, and so do you!" This crap has got to stop because if it doesn't, the ducks will." I could tell that statement went right in one ear and out the other. Man, damn his hide, just hasn't learned that his resources are limited. About 2050 he will find out what life is really all about without hardly anything left to sustain the good life. We will see if humankind is so arrogant and tough then. My guess is it will be. ...

Seeing that I was going nowhere with the lecture and wanting to work other hunters in the marsh, I wrote Charlie a ticket (which the club would pay), seized the birds, and let him go on his way. I knew he would go straight to every other blind on the club and warn the members I was there. Then he would go to the clubhouse and start calling around on the telephone to let other clubs know I was working the Sink area. Knowing I would have to hustle if I wanted to make any more money, I cranked up my Evinrude and headed about a mile northeast, hoping to find someone else who had strayed across the line and hadn't gotten the news of my presence yet. As I moved, surveying other clubs for the fast and furious shooting that gave me a good chance to catch someone with an over-limit, I began to hear what I expected: the soft whir of outboard motors running and stopping, running and stopping. Charlie had done his job well, and it appeared that most of the duck club gamekeepers had moved their dead butts from in front of the televisions at the clubhouses to the seats of their boats and were now busily letting their club members know I was in the vicinity. That was OK; it would make the chase a little harder but the rewards even greater, I thought with a large hunter's grin.

I sat quietly bobbing in the water until I noticed that shooters in the six blinds on the Black Jack Club were still banging away at the ducks. The air was full of mallards and pintail going every which way, including down when they passed too close to an occupied duck blind. With that kind of shooting someone was sure to err, and I decided that would be my next area to have a look-see. As I slowly paddled my way through a flooded row of trees toward a duck blind at the south end of the club, seeking a better vantage point, I heard an outboard motor coming toward the blind. Waiting in a clump of brush and trees, I saw two lads in the blind stand up and look in the direction of the oncoming boat. Pretty soon the boat and gamekeeper, Bob Days, hove into view, moving rapidly. Bob slowed and docked at the blind, and I heard a hurried conversation, after which the men in the blind ducked out of view and appeared to be preparing to leave. Bob pushed his boat off and left, en route to the next blind in his circuit to notify the club members that the law was in town.

Realizing that my chances of making an over-limit case in the field were now not too good, I sat there trying to formulate a Plan B. It wasn't long in coming. The lads in the blind were loading up their boat, and through my binoculars I watched them throw what appeared to be an over-limit of ducks into the bottom. Then they hurriedly pushed off from the blind and began picking up their decoys, throwing them on top of the ducks in an attempt to hide their illegal birds. I thought, OK, here I come, lads. Then I thought again—I had an even better plan!

With the gamekeeper alerting everyone, the hunters, especially those who had broken the law, would probably leave the marsh with their illegal birds. All of them had to return to the clubhouse by boat. Why not see if I couldn't catch the lads at the constriction point, namely, the boat dock and duck club? Looking the lads over one more time so I could identify them back at the clubhouse, I paddled like blazes to get farther out of sight, then covered my outboard motor with a tarp draped clear to the water so the engine noise would be muffled. Starting up my motor and satisfied with the low sound (gamekeepers could sometimes identify strange visitors by the sound of their outboards), I took a short cut to the Black Jack clubhouse, hid my Grumman about forty yards away, and sneaked up to the edge of the clubhouse and dock area.

What a fire drill was going on around the dock! Guys were coming in from the hunting areas as speedily as they could. Some came in at such high speeds that they thumped other boats or rocketed into the dock itself. Everyone was unloading their ducks and yelling for others standing on the dock to get them into the hanging facility before the wardens arrived. Talk about confusion; it was amazing what consternation one officer of the law could cause among the hunters. You would have thought I was Doc Holliday on the prowl for all the hell-raising going on, and it was going to get better if I had anything to do with it.

Because these lads were new members to the Butte Sink and didn't know me, I circled around the duck club and walked in from the rear as if I belonged. Stepping out into the dock area like a rube, I was promptly pressed into service running extra limits of ducks to the hanging room. Taking three limits of ducks, I walked quickly into the hanging facility to find the club members hurriedly forging tags to cover the birds they were going to place for all to view. One man, a gray-haired fellow and club officer of some sort, said, "We have too many ducks to hang and don't have the time to make up a bunch of new tags to cover them. You guys grab all those birds on the floor and follow me!" I grabbed some more ducks and followed three other fellows carrying equally large loads into the basement of the clubhouse. There under a large tarp was a large chest-type freezer. The old guy threw back the tarp, opened the lid, and told us to throw in the extra ducks. As I moved forward, I noticed that the freezer was not running; it looked like this was just an extra place to hide ducks until they could be "laundered."

Throwing my ducks into the freezer, I hurried back to the hanging room for another load. I noticed that most of the boats now seemed to be in, and everyone was bringing their ducks to the basement freezer for safekeeping until the expected the long arm of the law arrived, did its thing, and then moved on. Trying to get a rough idea of the number of ducks in that freezer, I moved upstairs into the clubhouse with the members and guests. From that second-story vantage point, everyone looked marsh-ward to see if the game warden was coming. There were four-teen men eagerly looking out the window for the arrival of the law and lots of smug talk, such as "Let's see if the bastard can find the ducks now."

I just stood there as if I belonged, and the happiness of the moment was not broken until Bob Days arrived. He came in and without really looking around walked over to the window overlooking the Butte Sink and said, "Damn, that was close. That shit-ass Grosz would nail you in a heartbeat if he caught any of you with those extra ducks." It was obvious that the new lads in the clubhouse were very grateful to their experienced gamekeeper for keeping their new-to-the-duck-hunting-busi-ness hind ends out of trouble, and many had nice words for his "Paul Revere" success. "Did all of you get your extra ducks and geese all squared away where they won't be a problem?" Bob asked without taking his eyes away from the view out the win-dow.

"Yes," came the group response.

"Good" he said, still keeping his eyes on the marsh.

Seeing that the game warden was not going to show up at that moment, someone suggested that they all get drinks and act as if nothing unusual had happened so as not to arouse his suspicions when he did arrive. Many agreed, and the entire group, except for Bob, who stayed to keep a lookout, shuffled off to the bar and began to open beers or pour themselves hard drinks. The talk about how close that call had been turned lively. When my turn for a drink came, I said I wanted nothing. The bartender said, "Ah, come on. We have plenty; one won't hurt you." I told him I couldn't drink because I was on duty. He got a funny look, as did others within earshot, and the barkeep said, "What do you mean you are on duty? What kind of duty is that?"

"Law enforcement," I said.

"Law enforcement, hell; you're away from that now and supposed to be having a good time. What can I fix you?" I think he thought I was a guest of a club member and a police officer of some sort.

"Nothing in the way of a drink," I repeated. "But I do need your driver's license."

"My driver's license?" said the barkeep. "What the hell for?"

"Ask the lad by the window," I said. Bob, who was still intently watching the swamp, whirled around after finally tuning in to the conversation behind him. He could not believe his eyes. I could just see the wheels turning as he asked himself, How did that bastard get in here? How much did he hear?

"Hi, Bob; long time no see," I said with a stare that told him he and his lads were in trouble: Bob for aiding and abetting and the rest of the lads for possession of over-limits and tagging violations. The other men just stood there trying to figure out what the hell was happening. Most were from the San Francisco Bay area and didn't know the local law from the back end of a horse. That had worked to my advantage; that and the fact that I had not worked this area as a state game warden because it was in another officer's district. However, as a federal officer my district did include this area. Right now seeing was believing, and poor old Bob just couldn't believe his tired eyes.

Looking around the room at all the questioning faces, I said, "Gentlemen, my name is Terry Grosz, and I am your local federal agent. As such, my job is to enforce the laws associated with the hunting of waterfowl, and what I have seen here in the last ten or fifteen minutes tells me I arrived not a minute too soon." Other than the clanking of ice cubes in glasses, there was abject silence. You could have heard a mallard feather hit the floor. I continued, "I think most of you now realize the large lad who helped you illegally tag some bunches of ducks and helped you load extra ducks into the freezer downstairs was none other than your friendly federal! All that activity in violation of state and federal laws, I might add." There still wasn't a sound to be heard. I could tell the whole picture was just now being understood by my captive audience, and they were not sure they wanted to be part of it.

Moving over to the door I said, "Lads, I need all of you to file by and hand me your driver's licenses and hunting licenses, please." For a moment no one moved. The disbelief still had hold of them. "Bob," I said, "how about starting with you?" The other men looked at Bob as if he were a sheep going to slaughter. Damn, you would have thought they were all being led out to be shot. It is not often that one can infiltrate a group as I had had the luck to do, and now these fellows' reaction was almost crushing. They had felt themselves immune to the law, only to find the law in their midst. Damn, that was a good feeling (for me at least). I could just imagine what tall tales they would tell their acquaintances once this was over, and throughout the years to follow. Bob meekly surrendered his licenses and broke the ice. The rest of the lads did the same and waited for my next instructions. "Gentlemen," I said, "I need for all of us to go down and get those ducks from the freezer and put them out on the boat dock." This was quietly done, and then I told them to go get the ducks from the hanging room that had been illegally taken. They hesitated for a moment, and I said, "Those of you who took an over-limit, bring those ducks to me."

Once that was done and I had everyone's ear, I said, "Now, there are other agents posted throughout the club shooting area, and they have been there since three A.M. today. They can identify not only you personally but the number and species of ducks you shot." I could see the physical change of uncertainty in every one of them. Of course there was no one out there but me, but what they didn't know wouldn't hurt them. I went on, "We know who shot what and have photographed your actions with our long-range movie cameras, so don't attempt to hide the truth from me because to do so will invite a mandatory appearance in front of the federal judge in Sacramento. Keep in mind, lads, that lying to a federal judge is not a real good move, so make sure you have the right ducks and geese when I come by. Bob," I said, "will you help them get who shot what so I don't have to write the club an additional citation if some are left over?"

With that, Bob began to iron out the number of ducks per hunter. Pretty soon I had even more ducks on the dock than I had expected. Not huge over-limits, mind you, but it seemed that everyone had an over-limit of from two to nine birds over the daily bag limit of eight. I had to move fast before they had time to get their stories together. I said, "Every man place the ducks he personally killed in front of him, and I will settle up with each of you once that is done." In short order, with a little remaining confusion over who had shot what, the lads did as instructed, and most just sat down behind their own piles and waited for me to finish the business at hand.

This was almost too easy, and later I found out why. Most experienced duck club members in that neck of the Sink were wily enough to know it was very difficult to control a group that size, let alone with over-limits of ducks. A savvier group would have been going every which way and denying everything. As it turned out, this club had just been sold upon the death of the original owner, and most of these lads were first-time members and guests. This group had apparently gotten together when they became aware the club was for sale and had outbid most of the remaining members. Because this was their first outing in "duck heaven," they had no idea how the game was played, but I would bet they did after this "hoorah," I thought. Finishing the tickets, I explained the process through the federal court system, and I could tell by the generally meek attitude that all would pay rather than choosing to appear. As it happened, I was right.

Leaving the ducks in a big pile on the dock for effect, all 175 of them (63 over the limit), I signaled to Bob that I wanted to talk to him. I could tell Bob was still smarting over my coup and was anticipating still more smarting when the club members got to his backside after I left. "Bob," I said, "this has got to stop. If you lads want to break the law, be my guest. But you need to know it is going to bring down the wrath of my agency on you folks."

"I know, Terry," he said. "But it was these guys' first real time at a good duck shoot, and I was trying to give them a good hunt in light of all the money they paid for the club and all."

"Well, you did," I said. "But probably not the show they really wanted."

Bob stuck out his hand and said, "All right, as long as I am here, which may not be long after today, you can rest assured I will try to keep them on the straight and narrow."

"That's all I can ask for, Bob, and I will treat you accordingly," I said. With that, I walked back to my concealed Grumman, cranked up the motor, and headed for the Black Jack Duck Club docks and my evidence ducks. There wasn't a soul in sight when I got there, so I loaded the evidence in the Grumman, now very much overloaded with the several hundred ducks seized that morning. Because I had very little freeboard, I began a long idle across the Sink to my patrol vehicle. I don't know what Grumman Sport boats were certified to safely haul, but I would bet that day, between a one-hundred-pound dog, a three-hundred-pound game warden, miscellaneous gear, and about four hundred pounds of ducks, that canoe had the most it could carry. It just goes to show that God really loves fools, children, and game wardens!

The air was still full of ducks, and with the shooting for the day beginning to subside they were landing everywhere out of relief. Soon my trip across the Sink turned from work to wonder. Ducks and geese were everywhere. Fluting calls from the pintail, hoarse quacking of hen mallards, whistles from the rapidly beating wings of the goldeneye, and clarion calls from the Canada geese made for a memory I would take to my grave. With all that life around me, it took only a glance at the pile of dead ducks in my boat to emphasize how fragile this world of waterfowl really was.

My daydreaming was brought to a halt when I noticed another duck boat working slowly along a partially flooded levee about one hundred yards northwest of me. Stopping my motor so I could hear better, I sat and watched the single lad in the boat. He had on hunting gear and appeared to be looking for a cripple along the levee. Soon he turned from his east-west direction and made directly for the spot where I was sitting. It was obvious he had not seen me, so I just waited and watched him. When he was about forty yards away the lad spotted me and for an instant took a very hard look, as if he just couldn't believe his eyes. I didn't recognize him, so I was sure he didn't know me from Adam. Without a moment's hesitation, the fellow took something brownish out of his boat and slid it under a pile of floating rice straw. He continued to move toward me and repeated this action twice more before he started to move away.

When someone acts like that, it only piques the interest of the local law. Starting my outboard, I headed toward the man after memorizing where he had hidden the three objects. In just a few moments I caught up to the mystery chap, who was just moving slowly along as if nothing had happened. I identified myself and called him over to my boat, then identified myself with my badge and credentials and asked to check his shotgun and hunting license. He complied without any fanfare, and while he was digging those items out of his wallet I checked the ducks lying in the bottom of the boat, which were legal. Then I noticed it! There were two wet pheasant feathers in the bottom of the boat. I didn't say anything, and when the lad handed me his open wallet, I noticed his driver's license on one side and his Butte County deputy sheriff's commission on the other. Without any ado, I asked him to remove the driver's license, which he did. Looking him right in the eye, I said, "Now, why don't you go back to those three floating piles of rice straw and retrieve those hen pheasants for me."

Jesus, you would have thought I had shot him in the groin. He looked like he was going to get sick. He said, "I didn't put any pheasants under any rice straw."

Using my well-worn ruse, I said, "If I go back there and find pheasants, guess who goes to the Butte County jail?" Boy, talk about lighting a fire under someone—I had a real bonfire going in this lad! Off he went with his boat while I sat there gently bobbing in the floodwaters of the Sink, holding his driver's license and watching his every move with my binoculars. In about ten minutes he returned with three hen pheasants and a look that said it all. He was sick, a law enforcement officer being caught breaking the law and all.

His slow movement along the levee should have told me what he was hunting. The pheasants always headed for any remaining high ground within their home range when the floodwaters came and basically became trapped until they got hungry enough to move into another area, or got poached off their little piece of habitat. Damn, it never quits, I thought. Without a word, I took the hen pheasants from the lad and commenced to write him a state citation for taking a closed-season species of wildlife. He didn't say another word. What could he say when I had caught him red-handed? I handed him the cite book, had him sign, and then tagged the evidence. He asked, "Could you tell me what the fine is in this matter?"

I said, "One hundred dollars per bird is what the bail schedule reads."

He nodded and then asked, "Is anyone going to contact my boss about this matter?"

"I don't plan on it, but you need to realize sometimes things like this get out, so you might want to tell the boss yourself," I answered. He gave me that trapped look and we parted company, I to head for home and he to look within himself over the thirty or so miles before he reached home.

After my successes during those few days in the Sink, things seemed to straighten out and quiet down. Subsequent trips into that area failed to produce anything more than small over-limits of ducks and the knowing looks of those being checked. It seemed that the word had gotten out that one should plan on keeping to the rules of the road or the law would appear, sometimes right in their midst.

The framed print of the Butte Sink marsh hanging on my office wall really takes me back to those days. My youthful body was still holding up well under the wear and tear of the job, the birds were everywhere, and times seemed good. Today, for the most part, many of the bird species, especially the pintail and scaup, are struggling. In the world of the geese things are better, especially for the Canada geese and lesser snow geese. I hope the duck species will come back, but who knows? My body is tired, and Shadow is gone. But the light in my soul and the look in my eyes is still the same, as is my hope for the future. If not, I have wasted thirty-two years of my life putting those in the business of extinction *out* of business.

I I

One-Two-Three-Four

IN THE SACRAMENTO VALLEY OF CALIFORNIA, adjacent to the Sutter Buttes (the smallest mountain range in the United States), lies an ancient geological depression in the form of a natural marsh known as the Butte Sink. For thousands of years this marsh, especially in the wintertime when the floodwaters from the Sacramento River rolled over the banks and inundated the valley, has been home to millions of migratory game and nongame birds and other endemic wildlife species, ranging from the mighty California grizzly bear to the little-known and smallest race of North American elk, the tule elk.

In the days of old, when explorer, topographical engineer, and U.S. Army officer James C. Fremont traveled across the United States and the Utah Territory to help the Californians in the rebellion of 1848 against Mexico, he camped in the Sutter Buttes next to the Butte Sink to allow his men time to rest from their long trek over the Sierra Nevada Mountains and gather strength for the anticipated battle. Fremont wrote in his journal that the roar of the grizzly bear, the crashing horns of the fighting bighorn sheep, and the bugling of the tule elk along with the constant noisy din of the waterfowl feeding in the Butte Sink kept his men from getting the rest they needed. After three days of these unappreciated songs of nature, they had to move on in search of a quieter spot.

Years later, as the rich lands in the Sacramento Valley were being tamed and settled, much of the great Butte Sink marsh was drained for agricultural purposes. However, the high water table created drainage problems that, coupled with the annual flooding of the mighty Sacramento River, led the fledgling agriculture industry to conclude that it could not compete for the heart of the Sink, and as a result parts of it were gradually restored to their original state. With that restoration, both natural and man-made, the great marsh began to return to its original splendor. Lands that had recently felt the plow and baking sun again saw abundant vegetation and aquatic life emerging as the gradually spreading waters returned. Aquatic plant seeds, long dormant, sprang from the rich soils to welcome the winged winter visitors from the north, and all was well again. People began to realize the Butte Sink's historical value as a food source and, in more recent times, a recreational area for the age-old honorable sport of hunting. At first slowly and then more rapidly as time passed and recreational opportunities increased for the landed gentry and new rich, the sport of hunting waterfowl emerged in full. Almost all of the remaining Butte Sink marsh lands ended up being purchased by hunting folks and fashioned for the time-honored sport of hunting the Sink's migratory game birds, with agriculture now a secondary, tax-related consideration. Today, in addition to state and federal waterfowl management units, the Butte Sink is managed with the use and aid of numerous private water-control structures (small dams or other methods of regulating the amount of water allotments) and as a result has been converted into a moderate number of rich farms, which with the advent of the winter season are quickly flooded and converted into high-value deep- or shallow-water hunting clubs.

One of these, the Zarrelli Duck Club, which was established around the end of Prohibition, used to give me wildlife law enforcement problems both as a California state Fish and Game warden and later as a game management agent with the U.S. Fish and Wildlife Service. The Zarrelli was not at the real center of the Butte Sink but was positioned on the northwest margin of the great marsh, which, with land and water manipulation in the fall, became a sportsman's paradise like all the rest.

Problems routinely encountered on any given shoot day during the hunting season included the illegal taking of restricted waterfowl species, taking over-limits of waterfowl, late shooting of ducks, unplugged shotguns, untagged birds, and taking pheasants during the closed season. During the rest of the year members who stayed at their club lodgings considered snagging fish, illegal fish traps, drop lines, over-limits of bullfrogs, and other such activities standard fare. Basically, it seemed that every member of the club got into the act of breaking the conservation laws without an ounce of remorse or concern for the wildlife or the laws of the land protecting those critters. It was almost as if the Zarrelli recruited the most black-hearted lads it could find so that everyone could violate to his utmost desire without fear of any fellow member turning him in.

It seemed that every time I set foot on that hunting club, everyone within eyesight worked to keep the lawbreakers free from my clutches by holding me up with some inane, lame-brained request for "assistance." They knew that as a public servant I would have to at least stop and by so doing allow their poaching kinfolk time to get the evidence of their wrongdoing squared away. During these early times some of the men, after stopping me, would actually hang on to my arm, trying to get me to stay for a drink or whatever, while a friend of theirs was hiding birds or hot-footing it across the wilds with his ill-gotten gains, many times in plain view. More than once I jerked some lad off his feet with a quick burst of speed, going from zero to sixty in an explosive standing start when I spotted a game hog heading for the high country.

After a few such early stick-poked-in-my-eye visits, I realized that I could routinely expect this kind of behavior and made a point of visiting these fine, God-fearing folks on the Zarrelli every time I was in the area. Having caught on to their distraction technique, when someone tried to stop me I just steamed on by, telling the lad with the urgent question that I would be right back. Hence, those hunters at hand found freedom wanting and escape not an option. It seemed that it didn't make any difference what time of year it was, I always ended up making money for the state and federal governments for some damn-fool game law violation. In the summertime I would catch various chaps running set or drop lines for the various species of game fish that inhabited the Butte Creek drainage. Or I would catch them live-trapping pheasants or shooting them from their vehicles as they drove the club's many farm roads with their .22 rifles. Bullfrogs, when the Sacramento Valley still had great concentrations of them before the misuse of agricultural chemicals wiped them out, were regularly taken by these folks at every turn of the waterways in numbers far in excess of the limit of twenty-five. I nabbed several chaps taking gross over-limits of frogs more than once, usually with at least one hundred frogs in their possession that I suspected were destined to be sold in the Italian and Chinese markets of San Francisco. Valley quail were baited and live-trapped, and the beaver, muskrats, and few river otter playing around were shotgunned and left to rot. No matter how you looked at it, this club was a nest of snakes that needed skinning.

I remember one old fellow who looked a lot like Gabby Hayes who would do just about anything to catch some of the "hog" black bass that used to inhabit the backwaters and ponds in the natural area of the Sink. Every time I checked him he would have a limit of five- to ten-pound black bass; I never checked another person in my seven years in the valley who caught bass like that. Maybe one or possibly two big bass, but never a limit of five, each weighing in at no less than five pounds and most closer to the ten-pound mark. Knowing that I was being had by this man but unable to find any net marks on the fish, I made a point of spending some summer "mosquito time" going after him whenever I noticed his automobile parked at the clubhouse. That meant lying out on a bank or other observation spot and waiting for him to err, no matter how many hours or days it took. It took the mosquitoes only a moment to find me because I sweated a lot in the Colusa County heat, but I was determined to discover this lad's bass-catching secret because I was sure that whatever he was doing, it had to be wrong.

After staking out his trailer house parked on the duck club off and on for about a week, I finally got lucky one weekend. His dog, who always made it almost impossible to sneak up on my

bearded target, had died, and I discovered "Gabby" alone one
fine early summer day. I noticed that he spent a lot of time going
in and out of his house trailer to work on something on the
ground in the back yard next to a large thicket of blackberries.
Crawling closer, I noticed that he had baited an area with wheat
and had a very fine mesh figure-eight trap set over the seed. I
watched through the spotting scope and a couple of hours and a
zillion mosquito bites later saw several baby pheasants, three to
four weeks old, go into the trap for the seed buffet. The female
with the rest of her brood nervously circled the trap, all the
while calling to her young inside. A few more of the young went
after the seed, and pretty soon all were in the trap except the
hen. Out of his trailer came "Gabby," who had been watching
this scenario as well, and in a matter of moments he had most of
the chicks in an old wicker fishing creel. Knowing I had him at
least for closed-season pheasants, I was astonished to see him
quickly leave his house trailer with his fishing pole, the creel of
pheasants, a small tote sack half full of something, and a metal
fish stringer. Taking a careful look around, including at the trees
hiding yours truly, he headed for a little-known pond off Butte
Creek, not far from his trailer, that I knew contained some monster bass. I let him get a good head start and followed him a few
moments later, figuring he would be all set up fishing and not
looking for me in the humidity and mosquitoes.

It took me some time to crawl up on him, dodging the poison
ivy, but once in position I was amazed at what I saw through my
binoculars. "Gabby" would take one of those pretty good-sized
pheasant chicks, put a small rubber band around its leg as it
struggled, and then pass a number 2 Eagle Claw hook and line
under the rubber band. Then he would put the chick on a small
wooden block, which he took from his tote sack, and shove it
out into the bass pond with the tip of his fishing pole. Once they
were over water, it was almost as if the young pheasants realized
their danger, and they just hunkered down and froze on the
block of wood while "Gabby" played out his fishing line so the
chick would not be dragged off the block. Most of the time the

chick stayed on the bobbing block of wood and "Gabby" would just let it drift out into the pond until he saw a large, dark form in the water nearby. It didn't usually take long before he would either jerk the chick off the block with a light pull on his fishing line or the block of wood would "explode" and the chick would be gone in an eruption of water, flying feathers, eyeballs, and false teeth. Soon the black bass, if big enough, was on "Gabby's" stringer, and I had solved the mystery of his always taking a limit of large fish. My thoughts on his process and inhumanity to the critters I will keep to myself, but suffice it to say that fishing trip cost "Gabby" $1,000 right off his last part over the fence (use of prohibited live bait, illegal taking of wildlife, and closed-season pheasants), and I never checked him after that with anything larger than a crappie on his stringer.

"Gabby" wasn't the only one at this level of evil when it came to filling the freezer with ill-gotten wildlife at every opportunity. There were at least five other members of that duck club whom I had branded as hard cases. All of these men were college educated, leaders in their communities, and the last people you would suspect unless you were one of the "green." They may have been the good guys at home, but in my arena they were some of the very worst when it came to violating the wildlife laws. There were also several investigations over the years that I was never able to bring to fruition involving the use of gill nets, use of live fish traps capable of taking up to fifteen-pound fish, and the poisoning of several main canals, killing many hundreds of fish and frogs, which I suspected originated with some of my favorite five people botching an attempt to get large messes of fish and frogs.

The other thorn in my foot on this duck club proved to be the gamekeeper. He was a country boy from Oklahoma, and to him taking wildlife in any way, shape, or form was legitimate just as long as you didn't waste the catch. He was a tall, thin drink of water and had the eyes and instincts of a natural-born predator. I think in all the years I pursued the folks on his club, I spent more time avoiding him than any other gamekeeper I ever ran across. He was as good at hunting me as I was at hunting his wildlife-killing members. It was almost as if he had a special instinct that let him know every time I was within a light year of the Zarrelli. More than once I would see him through my optics almost sniffing the air as if to check for the presence of the law. But there is always a silver lining in every cloud, I have found over the years, and he was one of them when it came to honing my stalking skills. It got so I could sneak up on God (well, almost) and check His list to see if my name was on it. Maybe He had misspelled it. ...

On several occasions, after parking at a distance and walking in on the Zarrelli to see if the chaps needed some attention, I had to change a tire or two when I returned to find a slash across the sidewall. There was always the same tire tread of a vehicle nearby that could have been driven by the knife-wielding culprit, but it was a kind of tire used by nearly every farmer in the county. I wasn't able to zero in on my gamekeeper "friend" until I put a distinctive cut mark across his right front tire and then discovered that modified tire tread in the dirt next to my vehicle after another tire-slashing episode. With that, I decided that anything I could do to make those club members' lives more interesting would be the word of the day, and, surprisingly, it was. Knowing what I was up against, I used to enjoy regularly visiting these fine folks, creating whatever kind of havoc I could through the liberal application of state and federal citations for individuals stepping across the line but not stepping quickly enough.

But all in all, it was a tough club to work successfully because of the lay of its boundaries. It was pretty inaccessible on three sides because of deep canals and wide-open spaces that had to be traversed on foot before I could reach the shooting area. If I used that avenue of attack, essentially out in the open, I would find that all violations had been cleaned up long before my arrival as I plodded across a wide expanse of flooded rice fields whose dikes and ditches had been burned clean. There was no way to hide a carcass the size of mine with what was left for ground cover. Besides, the gamekeeper would drive the boundary of the club numerous times on a shoot day, using his binoculars in an attempt to foil trespassers and the local game warden. This vigilance made it very hard to set up on some lads in the front, only to be spotted from behind. If he did discover me, he would radio the cook at the clubhouse, who would raise a red flag on the second-story porch and turn on a huge light on the overhang of the main clubhouse roof. Both of these warning signs were clearly visible to all in the field blinds and were heeded religiously. If I tried to approach from the remaining side, the north side, of the club, I found myself on the main road into the clubhouse, which was slightly elevated and exposed for half a mile before it even reached the first blind in the shooting area. If the chaps in the fields observed an unknown vehicle entering the grounds, everything would be cleaned up and the evidence hidden before my arrival.

Then one fine winter day, it all came together for me and the critters. For years there hadn't been a gate across the end of this road leading into the club's hunting area, and I tried to make frequent use of this "open-door policy," much to the chagrin of the club members who were slow walkers on the "dark side" of the law. I would watch for violations from afar and out of sight on another farmer's property, using my sixty-power spotting scope. The violations I spotted would usually be over-limits that involved those doing the deed being dumb enough to take all their birds to the clubhouse. I would wait until they were in an area of the club where they couldn't hide the birds once they saw me, or wait until they were behind a structure in the clubhouse complex, and then make my run, hoping the building would block me from view until I was upon them. My mad dash down the road leading into the club would scatter members every which way as they hurried to hide whatever I had missed until I sailed into the group of hunters I had seen breaking the law in an attempt to catch them before they destroyed or hid the evidence. But that method of attacking like a cheetah really wasn't the best approach and certainly didn't allow me to get at the root of the problem. There just didn't seem to be any way to get at these

knotheads without help from the inside or a general turnaround
of ethics by the shooters. Fat chance of either of those situations
occurring within the century!

One Wednesday morning that winter, the wind was really
raising hell and a storm was dropping rain horizontally by the
bucketful. When that type of weather manifested itself in the
Sacramento Valley, the waterfowl had to almost walk from one
place to another. Just to give one an idea of how tough it was, the
ducks and geese, in order to make any headway, had to fly almost touching the ground and behind the rice checks (systems
of dikes with inserted rice boxes that allowed the farmer to adjust the water level across an entire rice field), using the natural
eddy created by these ground forms to make any headway! In
short, their flying was low and slow, difficult at best. Everything
else in the critter world just walked on days like those, especially
the coots. However, for the hunters, conditions couldn't be better, and the shooting on the Zarrelli Duck Club that day was fast
and furious. When I chanced to hear that much shooting activity
and knew there were several million wintering ducks and geese
in the Sacramento Valley, I could bet my bottom dollar there
would also be numerous waterfowl violations, especially over-
limits.

Parking my truck in a friend's nearby barn and setting up my
trusty spotting scope so I could look out the barn door at the
Zarrelli, I watched three fellows exceed the limit of ducks in
short order, killing all drake pintail in the process. After a long,
careful look around, they took all their ducks and walked
twenty yards or so behind their duck blind, where they hid them
in an old rice check box. Then they tore up what few clumps of
weeds remained on the rice check, roots and all, and placed those
over the ducks, cleverly making the area look like an old rice box
partially buried in weeds. With that, they moved back to their
duck blind and recommenced shooting ducks like there was no
tomorrow. It was apparent that these lads would stay until they
ran out of shells or ducks, whichever came first, and I knew it
wouldn't be the ducks. I let the lads take a few more ducks each

and then decided it was time to make my move before they killed the entire pintail population. Moving out of my hiding place, I drove down the levee road for a quarter of a mile and then turned off the levee onto the Zarrelli Duck Club road, intending to speed down the entrance road until I reached a position where the offending lads were blocked off, then walk directly to them and do what needed doing. I knew that once they saw me there was no escape unless they were prepared to swim across a thirty-five-yard-wide canal located directly behind their duck blind. But as I roared in from the levee road, with mud flying every which way as I slid through the turn onto the club road, I found myself confronted by a new locked gate totally blocking my access and my plans to ruin those hunters' day! Bringing my growling metal steed to a muddy, sliding halt, I opened the door and stepped out to examine this new challenge.

As gates went, this one would have made any Teutonic knight proud. Plain and simply, if I was going through this gate I would need a Tiger tank and not a flimsy pickup purchased by the U.S. government from the lowest bidder. The support posts were twelve-inch steel pipe sunk at least four feet into the ground. The main frame was six-inch steel pipe, heavily welded, extending from one side of the road to the other and down to the road's surface. Looped around the main support post and through the gate was a chain of sufficient size and dimension to pull a battleship across a creek riffle, precluding the game warden's routine tactic of just cutting the offending chain. To add insult to injury, on the chain was a massive Sesame combination lock of proportions such as I had never seen before. The lock loop appeared to be made of case-hardened steel and was at least three-fourths of an inch thick. No two ways about it: they had installed this gate in my "honor"!

What made it really impossible was that on one side of the gate loomed a twenty-foot-wide, ten-foot-deep canal. On the other side was the start of a large feeder canal into Butte Creek, not as wide as the other canal but just as deep. As I didn't have an amphibious tank, it appeared that I was going to be foiled that morning as far as entering the club with my vehicle and checking out the fast and furious waterfowl activities of the three-man crew I was after. I could have walked in, but that would alert those chaps to my presence, allowing them to cut over to the clubhouse and hide the birds, replug their shotguns, or stomp the over-limits or lesser species into the mud in the flooded rice.

I stared at that gate with chagrin, running like sixty through my mind all my options on how to tackle this new problem. My chagrin intensified as the sound of shooting from the corner of the club where my targets were located continued unabated. Obviously this gate had been put in on a nonshoot day so I couldn't come around in time to discover its presence and attempt to get the combination from the gamekeeper—*if* he were so inclined. Further observation revealed that the main support posts were sunk in deep cement in order to foil a chap as strong as me from just pulling up the posts, laying the gate on its side, and strolling into the club. Whoever had designed and installed this gate had to be an evil genius, like the gamekeeper, I mused. But that was OK because I could be evil also and, being twice the size of most people, could be twice as evil. ...

Picking up the Sesame lock for closer inspection, I noticed that the last two digits on the four-digit combination read, "3-4." I thought, No, this is really too good to be true. Ain't no way, Jack, that this combination could possibly be what I think it is! A slow grin began to develop on my face as I took the lock in my left hand and rolled the number "1" into the first tumbler slot and the number "2" into the second slot. I left the "3" and "4" as I had found them. With that little chore done, I held my breath, hoping against hope, and pushed the lock against the lock strap. Sure as God made little green apples, the lock popped open. The last fellow through the gate apparently had not fully erased the combination on the lock, which was simply 1-2-3-4. By his carelessness he had allowed the club nemesis, the game warden, easy entry, at least this time.

Opening the gate, I pulled the old Dodge through and then

carefully closed the gate behind me, as I had found it. Getting back into my truck, I had a hard time suppressing the large, cat-like grin on my mud-covered, windburned face. Humming a little Wagner, I nosed my modern-day tank out of the trees and into full view of the club members, whose happy day was quickly starting to go sour. Down the road I thundered and into the clubhouse picking facility, thereby cutting off all escape avenues in that direction. From there I lumbered out into the shooting area like a steam engine of old, plowing through the mud and the flooded rice fields, intercepting everyone who looked like he needed a once-over, all the while keeping a sharp eye on my main over-limit chaps.

Before the smoke cleared I had gathered up, and later cited, eleven people for wildlife violations, and I mean good ones. The largest over-limit that day was fifty-eight pintail over the limit, killed by a municipal judge from the San Francisco Bay area and his college-age son. As I gathered up the chaps' hunting licenses, I would write on the back what the violation was and then have them lug the evidence back to the club for me to seize later while I kept their licenses and moved on to the next offender. I continued this action across the main shooting area, noticing that my original three lads had ducked down in their blind and were sitting silently, hoping I would think no one was there and overlook them. Finally finished with the others, I made a beeline to the blind that had started this "hoorah," thinking these lads weren't ready for me this day. It was almost as if the new gate had given them an additional license to kill without fear of the law. I smiled as I continued my tromp across the flooded rice field.

Heads didn't pop up until I got within ten feet of the blind, and then, realizing that the jig was up, three heads appeared. "Morning, gentlemen, federal agent. Would you please go back to that rice box and retrieve all the birds you hid there at nine-thirty-seven this morning?" The three faces all went blank as if on the same emotional string. Nothing like a killing shot right out of the box, I thought as I walked to the edge of their blind.

Looking inside, I discovered another nine ducks and six geese lying on the floor. "I will need these as well, gentlemen," I said. "Now, will someone go and get those ducks in the rice box?" This time I gave them a look of impatience, whereupon two of the lads laid down their shotguns and without a word walked resignedly to the rice box and retrieved thirty-three more ducks. With all of us carrying a load from the morning's hunt, we walked to the main clubhouse complex with hardly a word said. I found that really strange. Usually folks who kill and hide the birds will argue with you about who did the killing. Usually they say the birds belong to someone else or the like. In this case, all the way across the three hundred or so yards of flooded rice field, no one said anything.

Back at the clubhouse, I gathered up the lads caught earlier and commenced to write out pink slips for their violations. There was a lot of grumbling but no outright hell being raised. Once a ticket was written, I would throw their birds into the back of my truck on the end of a seizure tag and say, "Next." This went on for about an hour before I finally got to my three lads. Two county assistant district attorneys and one justice of the peace later, I had the answer to my "why are they being so quiet" mystery. Not making a big deal out of their occupations, they were treated like all the rest, with their birds also being seized and ingloriously dumped into the back of my pickup truck. During this entire time I kept an eye on my "friend" from Oklahoma. He had a tight-lipped grimness about him. To say the least, he was more than pissed! This became more understandable as I wrote ticket after ticket and caught the looks between the recently cited club members and the gamekeeper. It was obvious that the gamekeeper had bragged about his gate, and the shooters had gotten all caught up in the safety it guaranteed and had let it all hang out, so to speak, only to have it taken off at the shank. Good, I thought; maybe this will teach all of these fellows a damn good lesson on being good, bad, or ugly with my ducks! Finishing my work, I explained the federal court process to them all, answered the few questions they had, thanked them, and drove off slowly as if blowing smoke off the end of my gun barrel.

You talk about excited; I was really pleased with myself over the damage I had just spread through a bunch of egos who just moments before were thinking they were protected. The club members were very tight jawed, not to mention a muscle in another part of their anatomy that had tightened up when I arrived on the scene that wonderful duck-shooting morning. It is OK, fellows, I laughed to myself, the sphincter will loosen up in about thirty minutes, and you can breathe again. ... I could just see the wheels turning in all their heads as they quietly questioned how I had gotten into their grounds that fine shoot day when they had just built this massive gate to keep me, my vehicle, and my "catch dog" ways out. When I left them to their thoughts and tickets I didn't tell them about figuring out their lock because I knew they would check with the gamekeeper to see how I had gotten in.

I had expected to have a run-in with the gamekeeper back at the clubhouse and receive a ration of the usual garbage about harassment, but I was surprised that he had mysteriously remained silent. That was good, I smiled, because he was now going to get a ration of what I usually got, only this time from his own. I figured that when the dust had settled over the matter of my unannounced arrival on the duck club, the gamekeeper would be leaving puddles along his legs and around his feet, aside from the rain, which had slackened and was now quietly falling as if in awe of the day's events.

Leaving the club with all of my citations in hand and a truckload of seized ducks and closed-season pheasants, I looked back and saw the usual gesture of goodwill being given to the game warden by several of those recently cited—not the high five that you see in successful basketball games but the high one usually seen by the member of the opposing team who has just slam-dunked the ball. With that parting gesture in mind, when I passed through the new gate and went back to lock it behind me the devil intervened, and without a moment's hesitation I took out my combination-lock tool and changed the combination. I figured since the folks on the Zarrelli had taken it upon themselves to block me from getting in, I was going to be a whole lot more obstructive to those who had to get out and return home or go to work. The lock had to be open in order for the combination to be changed again; I would leave it locked and effectively shut them all inside. When I finished with the work of setting a new combination, off I went and spent the remainder of this great day working other waterfowl areas on foot, out of earshot of my radio and what eventually had to be a rather frantic gamekeeper.

Upon my return to the land of the living about ten o'clock that evening, I swung by the Teutonic gate with the notion of resetting the lock to its original combination, being the nice fellow I was. I figured I had given these chaps enough time to reflect on their lawless ways and the law of physics that for every action there is an equal and opposite reaction. I chuckled to myself, first for having such a good idea, second for having the guts to do it, and third for the trouble I had caused these lawless folks. Little did I realize that trouble came with a lot of capital T's in this club because most of the members were very wealthy businessmen who had to get to work sometime during the day in Colusa and the surrounding valley towns and counties.

Behold, as I approached the gate, I found that the entire massive structure had been bulldozed to the ground so the club members could get out and do what they had to do. Roaring with laughter at the sight, I could just imagine the chagrin of the lawless-turned-honest-businessmen as they approached the gate and tried the old 1-2-3-4 combination, only to have it fail to work. There had to have been panic in the ranks, so much so that a D7 bulldozer still sitting there had been employed by the gamekeeper to "open" their expensive anti–game warden gate. With great glee, after surveying the damage, I opened the Sesame lock using the new combination I had earlier coded it to, promptly reset it back to 1-2-3-4, and shut the lock. Then I carefully laid the lock back on what was left of the gate and fled the scene with a lightness of foot that I thought came with youth, but more likely it was the wind of the devil behind me. Driving home, even as tired as I was from the long, wet, and exhausting day, there was a smile on my face and in my heart. Sometimes you can dance with the devil even in this line of work, I mused.

Donna, my lovely bride of many years of trials and tribulations, awoke as I climbed into bed and said, "The gamekeeper on the Zarrelli Duck Club wants you to call him just as soon as you get home. He is really mad; he says you broke his gate." Even though it was dark in the bedroom, I could almost see her looking right through me. What a woman! Even though she had just awakened, she knew me well enough to know that I had been up to no damn good. Denial would have done me no good, so I remained motionless in the hope that she wouldn't look any further into my sometimes black-hearted soul. I was due to get up at three in the morning anyway, so I waited until then, knowing full well that the next day was not a shoot day and the poor tired gamekeeper would be trying to sleep in.

At three A.M., after showering and finishing a great breakfast of side pork, fried spuds, eggs, and some of Donna's always present, freshly homemade bread, I gave him a call. He sleepily answered the phone. I identified myself and said I'd just gotten back from the fields and my wife had told me to give him a call immediately. He was awake now and really huffy. He said, "Terry you broke our damn gate."

"What do you mean I broke your gate?"

He told me that the club members had been unable to get out after I had left the club, and he had had to take their bulldozer and plow down their new gate. "That gate cost the club members over $1,000 to build," he hissed through clenched teeth. "Terry, that gate worked fine in the morning; what the hell did you do to it?"

Sensing that part of the clenched-teeth discussion taking place was a reflection of his rear end having been snapped off by the club members, I lightheartedly told him, "Nothing." I said the lock had worked fine for me that morning, a little stiff in the tumblers but otherwise fine. I explained that I had used the same combination the other club members had used, but I did notice that the lock had a little dirt or sand in it, and maybe the tumblers had jammed when the lads trying to leave the club had attempted to open the lock. I suggested that he retry the lock with the 1-2-3-4 combination and I was sure it would open. I said, "One thing that works for me is that I push hard on the lock strap when I try to open stubborn locks and then tap them a couple of times, and that usually loosens up the tumblers."

He said he would try again and grumbled, "It had damn well better work, or else." Or else what? I thought, but before I could carry on the conversation he abruptly hung up on me.

The next day I went back to the Zarrelli Duck Club, and sure as hell the gate had been unlocked even though it still lay broken and bent to hell alongside the road. I went in to see the gamekeeper, and it was an interesting meeting. He said, "Terry, the lock worked as you said it would. Somehow I know you got to us on this one, but I am not quite sure how. I am sure of one thing, though; this little game of cat and mouse just can't continue. You are constantly out here underfoot, and the club members are really beginning to groan with all the weight you are putting on them. Besides, many of them can't stand the public's knowledge of their game-hog status after you catch them." With a sigh he said, "Would you like a key or the combination to all our gates? If so, let me know, and in addition I will try to keep our club members in line regarding the laws so we don't have a repeat of what happened out here on Wednesday. I am tired of trying to stay one step ahead of you. I surrender, and I really mean just that. Once I give a man my word, it is good."

Looking him square in the eye, I said, "It's all a matter of fair chase. These critters don't really have any odds in their favor, and most end up dying without making a sound. The only voice they have is mine, and I intend to be heard. I think your club members can attest to that." I paused for a moment, then said, "I accept your offer," and with that shook his hand in such a manner that he knew there would be more to come on the field of battle if his word was not gold. Then I left with a lighter step, knowing that part of the battle had been won for now.

From then on the club stuck to the letter of the law as long as I worked in the valley. The fun was that they never did figure out what I had done to their lock. I did what I had to do to preserve the migratory bird resource for the sake of that resource and those yet to come. It was that simple. Somehow I think that over the years the ducks understood and appreciated my efforts. I hope so. I know I certainly enjoyed the fruits of my labors — and the fair chase that occurred at least one-two-three or four times every month.

12

A Dangerous but Generous Friend

MY TIRED OLD DODGE patrol truck eagerly ran the muddy roads as if it were glad to be out and about again. Every time I came to a mud hole or a puddle, I would hit it with a little more speed than necessary to ensure that the mud and water were flung to the far corners of the truck, letting me *really* know I was finally back in my element and my truck looked the part. Thank God you never lose the kid in you, I thought as I went into a really deep mud hole with gusto and the flying mud ended up clear on the top of the cab. Excellent; now I truly looked the part of a real working federal game warden, I chuckled.

I had just spent a solid week in the office typing up at least a zillion case reports on previous investigations. Before that unfortunate episode — unfortunate because now was the time to be in the bush chasing the violators — I had been running day and night catching hunting folks violating the regulations of the Migratory Bird Treaty Act. This was the Sacramento Valley in the fall, home to millions of migrating waterfowl and thousands of waterfowl hunters, including the elusive night hunters, both of the commercial and noncommercial ilk, all killing many thousands of those fall migrants. It was also home to numerous state Fish and Game wardens and one game management agent. However, most agencies run on paper, and mine was no different. It wasn't until my boss, Jack Downs, finally caught up with me in the muddy rice fields and told me to get some case reports into his office to show I was earning my keep that I abandoned my free-spirited and rather fruitful pursuit of my fellow humans.

During my week of "detention," I had typed up at least 150 closed-case reports on everything from hunters using unplugged guns to numerous lads taking over-limits of ducks and geese. With my administrative work finished until my supervisor "caught" me again, I was once more on the prowl, and the bad guys had better stay clear, I mumbled to myself. Those lads marching on the other side of the law had had a week to really test their skills. Now it was my turn because I figured they had killed enough during my absence. I had to chuckle, though, because there were still another 150 closed-case reports waiting to be filled out. Jack hadn't known about those, so until we met again, I was off the administrative hook and on the run, hopefully making violators do the same.

It was late fall in north-central California and the air was filled with millions of migrating waterfowl. It was one of those typical Sacramento Valley days with a bright blue cloudless sky, the pungent smell of burning rice straw hanging in the air, sticky alkali mud underfoot, and duck hunters everywhere taking rice-fed ducks and geese from their aerial home for the table and a wonderful repast, as humankind had done for centuries. Not having anywhere in particular to go that day, I just drifted to the sounds of the guns and figured I would let the devil work his magic with the gunners while I "batted cleanup."

Driving north on a Sacramento River bypass levee on the east side of the Terhel Farms duck club, south of the Colusa-Gridley highway, I heard a shot to my left and spotted a duck out of the corner of my eye falling into the decoys near a blind in the center of a flooded rice field. The duck had a lot of light gray on it, and since the season was closed on canvasback ducks (lots of light gray on the back, especially the males; hence the name), I slowed the truck for a better look. The duck had dropped in a diked, flooded rice field approximately one hundred acres in size, with a rice check dividing the field almost equally in half. This rice check ran from the banks on one side of the flooded field to the other, and a partially sunken duck blind was located on top of the rice check smack-dab in the center of the field. This made for easy on-foot access via the rice check walkway and was as good a place as any to place a duck blind, I thought.

Ducks, especially the pintail and canvasbacks, liked large open bodies of water (after being shot at so much, this late in the season the open-water scenario was more to their liking) with lots of decoys. This shooter certainly had the advantage on those accounts, I thought.

Since I had nothing better to do and my instinct was letting me know this situation was unusual and might be a good one to check, down went my wheels. Since I was still rolling slowly along the levee road in front of God and everybody like any lame-brained duck hunter, I nosed the Dodge into a convenient stand of trees and brush just off and below the levee and set up shop. My new position was just barely in line of sight of the suspected duck blind. The old tan Dodge, with black hood primer to reduce the glare of long hours in the sun, was almost invisible when ditched in the brush and weeds, and the hunter paid no attention to the jumble of metal that had just been added to the undergrowth directly across from his shooting area.

After a few moments the shooter stood up, looked around to see if the air held any other nearby flying ducks, and, seeing none, left his blind, walked into the decoys, picked up his duck, and walked back to his blind. Even with my sixty-power spotting scope I could not positively identify the species of the duck because he carried it on the far side of his body next to his leg. Needing some exercise anyway, I prepared to walk out and make a firsthand inspection of not only the duck and hunter but the layout of the blind itself, since it was a new one to me. Quietly stepping out of the truck and making every effort not to be seen, I broke through the tangle of brush and stunted cottonwood trees and quickly crossed over and down the side of the levee facing the rice field. Being dressed in camouflage hunting clothes and hip boots, I figured I could get pretty darn close before the lad in the blind even realized he had company.

I stood up as I approached the grassy edge of the flooded rice field, because I was near enough that the lad in the field had no escape route, and headed for the rice check walkway. All at once a dark-skinned man about six foot five inches tall who had been

sitting unseen in the unharvested water grass and rice at the edge
of the field stood up, almost blocking my access to the rice
check, and squared off with me in a purposely deliberate and offensive manner. He moved with the grace and speed of a cat,
which illustrated not only his excellent physical condition but
his apparent resolve as well. My brain quickly changed gears
into a more alert mode. Seeing that I was continuing my trek toward the dike undeterred, the stranger strode the last few steps
to the edge of the flooded field, effectively blocking my access,
and said in a quiet voice, "Who the hell are you?"

Ignoring this unfamiliar challenge by an obvious nonhunter
and without breaking my stride, I said, "Federal agent."

The lad continued stubbornly blocking my access to the rice
check. "The hell you say. What do you want?" he demanded.

Since my business was not with him, I used my best German
manners and responded, "It really is none of your damned business, but if you must know I am going out to check that hunter,
his ducks, and his hunting license!"

Without a moment's hesitation, all the while still blocking me,
he asked, "Where did you say you were going?" The coldness of
his manner and tone told me to be even more on the alert; this
chance meeting between two rather large, equally determined
chaps in the field was no drill.

Looking him right in the eye, I said, "I am going out to that
blind and check that hunter. I am a federal agent with the U.S.
Fish and Wildlife Service; checking hunters taking migratory
waterfowl is within my scope and authority, and that is what I
intend to do, you or no you." I stepped off the dirt berm surrounding the edge of the rice field and into the flooded area,
preparing to walk around the lad and up onto the rice check behind him.

He quickly said, "Oh no, you're not," and made another of
those catlike moves to block me again.

Having had a gutful of that kind of behavior, I stopped and
said with a tad more steel in my voice, "Look, I don't know
what your problem is or who the hell you are, but I identified

myself to you as a federal officer when I didn't have to and made my intentions clear. If you insist on keeping me from the performance of my duties, I will slap your ass in irons and pack your miserable carcass off to the county jail so you have some time to think about using some better manners next time!" At that point I'm sure the chill in my voice and changing blue in my eyes conveyed the sense of a gunfighter pressed to the limit. I was trying to figure out what the hell was going on with this chap and what I had stepped into besides the soft mud of a flooded rice field.

The imposing chap backed off a few feet and opened his hunting coat. In plain view were two Colt .45 semiautomatic pistols in cross-draw shoulder holsters. Looking me coldly in the eye, he said, "Your move."

Damn, this duck hunter–checking business was *really* getting to be serious crap! I thought. I was still not really worried about what I had gotten myself into, but running on the high end of caution, I decided I would ignore this fellow with the cross-draw holsters—carefully, but ignore him I would. About that time, I looked over his shoulder at the duck blind only to see smoke coming out of it, like the smoke from a small cooking fire. This whole event was starting to get bizarre! Realizing that it was my move, and having chosen to ignore his obvious challenge, I said to the large, ominous chap before me, "I am going out to check that fellow, and if you want to come, be my guest."

Backing off his challenging tone, as if he had given in to my stubborn determination, he asked, "Are you armed?"

I pointedly said, "Yes."

Without missing a beat he said, "Give it to me" and held out his hand for my weapon. The one thing I have learned over the years is that I don't ever give up my sidearm. I told him to go to hell, stormed around him before he could move, and headed out onto the rice check toward the smoking duck blind. I hadn't taken four steps before my sizable adversary was hot on my hind end. He said, "I am right behind you. If you make a move for your piece, I will blow your goddamned head clear off, do you understand?" The way he said it, I knew he was all business now, as if he hadn't been before. Ignoring him, figuring I would deal with him later, I continued walking to the duck blind, getting madder all the time. About thirty yards from the blind I noticed another fellow about the same size as the hind end walking behind me standing in the tall grass on the opposite side of the pond by the rice check walkway, and he had what appeared to be a small submachine gun cradled in his arms. Damn, I thought, this was sure getting a long way from the routine checking of ducks with a lot of gray on them. The smoke continued to curl up out of my suspected duck blind, as well as out of my ears, as I continued my approach, but now I was a hell of a lot more cautious. If the chap in the blind was anything like these two goons behind me and on the opposite side of the rice field, then I had one hell of an afternoon in store.

At the blind I met a reddish-haired older gentleman, somewhere in his late sixties or early seventies, who bade me a pleasant "Good morning." Well, the greeting here was certainly warmer than the one I had received at the edge of the rice field, I thought. I identified myself and asked to check his hunting license, duck stamp, shotgun, and any ducks he might have. "No problem," was his calm reply as he handed me his shotgun so I could check it for the number of shells it carried (no more than three allowed). As he busied himself with the other tasks laid out to him, I had a chance to look around in this unusual blind. The source of the smoke was a little charcoal fire under a pan holder, and in a cooking pan, covered with what smelled like cooking wine and spices, were two duck breast halves bubbling away like there was no tomorrow. The fellow in the blind saw my look of disbelief, laughed, and said, "A gooda Italian always takes advantage of the freshness of gooda food. It is luncha time, I hada the gooda food and wine, so I cooka da food." With that came a hearty laugh, backed by a merry twinkle in his steel-cold blue eyes, and then he continued the conversation in perfect English.

The man's name was Art Patino, and he was from the Bay area according to the address on his hunting license. His shotgun was plugged (held only three shells), he had a current hunting license and federal duck stamp, and the duck that had started this mess, upon examination, turned out to be not a canvasback but a drake redhead, a species that looked somewhat like the restricted canvasback but could legally be taken. He must be some sort of cook, I mused as I looked around his blind. It also contained a small gas stove, bottles of spices, bottles of wine, and other assorted foods. This guy was some sort of nut, I thought, but being a cook of sorts myself, I had to admire him. There is nothing better than taking something right out of the wild and within a few moments having it cooking away for the wonderfully fresh and wild taste it will bring to the palate.

After I finished the business at hand and declined an invitation to stay for lunch, we sat in his duck blind and discussed several favorite recipes for duck from our personal cooking libraries. Art appeared to be a gifted and intriguing man, based on his speech and knowledge of just about any topic we covered that morning, and the men I had finally deduced were his bodyguards made him appear to be of great, if not questionable, importance. Yet there was something about him I couldn't put my finger on. He had a ready smile and laugh, but there also seemed to be something held back behind his pleasant facade. I couldn't figure it out except to think this might be a person one would not want to cross or irritate. His cold, steel-blue eyes were just how I imagined a set of eyes from a gunfighter of old. His bearing was distinguished, and a sense of power permeated his presence that told anyone with any powers of observation that he was clearly the boss. His bodyguards' display of loyalty was another indicator of his stature. Finishing our cooking conversation and bidding Art good-bye, I turned to leave and ran smack-dab into dark "man mountain" still stuck to my hind end like an abalone.

Turning back to Art and figuring I would confirm my thoughts, I asked, "Who are these two?" pointing to the dark fellow and the unknown lad at the edge of the pond still watching me intently.

"Oh," Art said slowly, "they are just two close friends, very close friends." His eyes never left mine while he uttered those words.

Looking right back at him, though I am sure without the same intensity, I said, "They sure are." A little puffed up with self-importance and still pissed at what I perceived as interference, I said, "You might tell them to show a little more respect to a fellow twice their size, three times the shot they are, and a federal agent to boot."

I felt a whole lot better at having defended my high government position until Art quietly retorted, "No matter who or what you are, if they did not want you here, you wouldn't be." That statement was followed by another warm smile, which told me I was in weird company at best. Art continued, "Both of these men have orders to care for me and have licenses issued by our government to carry the weapons they have. I have cooking to attend to, and if you have nothing more for me, Mr. Federal Agent, I will attend to that matter."

Really baffled now, I lamely said, "No, I am done with the business at hand; enjoy your hunt, Mr. Patino." I turned and walked back to my patrol vehicle, tailed closely all the while by the confrontational fellow. Without looking back, I scrambled up the levee and headed for my truck. Getting into my vehicle, I looked back to see that both men had again disappeared into the grass alongside the pond as if nothing had happened and the smoke was still drifting from the blind and circling lazily in the windless sky.

Well, I had had enough of that cat-and-mouse game, and now I wanted some answers. I checked with Terrill Sartain (a local duck club owner and landowner, may God rest his soul) to find out what he knew about the red-haired man. Terrill knew little except that the man seemed to have lots of money, supposedly owned a string of liquor stores (thirty-seven if I remember correctly), flew to the hunting area in a twin-engine Cessna airplane, always brought along the two men I had met in the field and several high-class hookers from the San Francisco Bay area as well, and always paid his bills on time. Other than that, Terrill

could offer no insight into the fellow called Art. That was a start,
I thought. Next stop, the Colusa County sheriff's office. There
my questions produced very little because I had so little information about this crew of unknowns for them to go on. Figuring I had just met a bigwig businessman with bodyguards and
having a ton of work lined up to do that day, I let the matter
drop for the moment and then, as is usually the case, forgot
about it.

Months later I was banding mourning dove on the Terhel
Farms foothills ranch in western Colusa County. It was a large
old-time cattle ranch that had been around since the late 1800s.
It was sixty-six thousand acres in size, covered with cheat grass
and millions of scrubby oaks, not to mention some of the best
black-tailed deer populations in the state. Terrill Sartain had
made this area a big-game hunting club for his duck club members as part of a package deal, and it was not unusual to find various hunters on the ranch during the July deer season. The ranch
had a deputized Colusa County officer named Cliff Fulton
(God rest his soul) who was also a deputy Fish and Game warden for the state of California. When I was working on the
ranch, Cliff would help me band dove behind the ranch's locked
gates and I would help him catch deer poachers in the evening, a
very workable situation because I enjoyed doing both activities
and also appreciated Cliff's good company. Snuggled up against
the hills overlooking Lee's Valley and many thousands of acres
of the ranch's holdings was the old two-story ranch house, in
which we stayed. It was a typical ranch house from that era,
built to last and near a source of good water. Other than that, it
was pretty primitive. I remember that the walls of the place were
filled with honeybees and so much honey that some of the wall
boards were all pouched out from the weight of the honey and
comb. The bees never bothered us, nor we them. When we slept
in this old ranch house, we could hear the buzzing of the bees all
night as they tried to maintain a cooler temperature for the hive's
inhabitants. The old ranch lacked any indoor showers, and when
the days turned hot (110 in the shade), as was typical in a Colusa

County summer, it was 110 in the house as well. Not to be out-done by fancier places, we showered outside in a creek just under the fig trees with a gravity-fed hose, cooked our meals in an old ramshackle kitchen on a huge gas stove at the back of the house, and *loved* it, isolation, honeybees, rattlesnakes, and all. The old placed burned to the ground many years later, and with it went the history of the land and the honeybees.

One late summer morning, after working deer spotlighters all night (and catching three), Cliff and I awoke about ten A.M. It was already hot, but I was in the mood for a great brunch, so I hollered over to where Cliff was lying on his bed, "How about a real man's breakfast?" Even if Cliff didn't want such a breakfast, he couldn't say no for fear of me calling him a wimp. Besides, he really liked my cooking and was an eager eater, and I enjoyed cooking for him. Cliff agreed, and off I went to the kitchen (wearing only my underpants) to cook up a meal fit for two kings who were living the *great* life. Out came the sliced turkey breast that had marinated in clam juice in the refrigerator all night (fortunately, we did have electricity). When rolled in cracker crumbs and fried in real butter, as I was now doing, the turkey tasted exactly like abalone, only more tender. Into an-other large frying pan went plenty of sliced zucchini with butter, onions, and lots of garlic, and soon that aroma also filled the kitchen. Into another twelve-inch cast-iron skillet went more butter, sliced potatoes, onions, celery, and sliced jalapeño pep-pers. On went the coffee, and out came a loaf of my bride's world's best homemade bread, along with one of her super pumpkin pies. The homemade crust on that pie was so perfect that it had to be held down by the pumpkin pie mix or it would drift off into the air. ... And taste, it was beyond what most mortals ever live to experience. I was blessed with that woman, I thought as I scurried around the old ranch kitchen on the pitched wooden floors. God, this was a hard life!

As the old kitchen filled with great smells, I heard a twin-engine airplane fly low over the house, which was a prearranged signal for Cliff to go down to the small dirt airstrip in front of the ranch house and pick up some deer club hunting members. Cliff drove off in his open-air Jeep to pick up the people arriving in the plane, followed by my hollered instructions: "Breakfast in twenty." Usually Cliff would take the hunters to the equipment barn, which was adjacent to the ranch house, outfit them with a military Jeep and a map to the ranch's vastness, give them keys to the gates, and turn them loose to chase the wily black-tailed deer. I heard Cliff arrive back at the ranch house shortly after he left and assumed he had dropped the plane's occupants off at the barn to get on with their deer hunting. The next thing I heard as I stood facing the busy stove was footsteps entering the kitchen and a soft, phony-accented voice saying, "For a federala agent, you don't looka so tough. In fact, I don't thinka your pistola would do you mucha good righta now."

I whirled around from my cooking chores, and there facing me with a big grin and a box of groceries in his arms was Art Patino, the man I had checked in the duck blind as he was cooking a freshly killed duck the past hunting season. Feeling somewhat embarrassed at my current state of undress, I was quickly put at ease by Art's ready smile and hearty correct English that followed the rotten Italian: "Do you have enough food for three more?" What a dumb question, I thought; I always cooked for a marine regiment no matter how few showed up to eat. Matching his smile with mine, I said, "Sure. How are you doing, Mr. Patino?"

He quickly said as he set down his box of groceries, "Art is fine for such an elegantly dressed federal agent and gentleman." He extended his hand and I shook it warmly. We both laughed at my outfit, and, leaving the kitchen to my Italian cook counterpart, I went to the bedroom and put on a pair of jeans. Back at the kitchen I found Art examining my culinary delights with a face only cooks wear when trying to figure out another's secrets. "Damn, this sure smells great; what have you done here?" he said, pointing to my skillet filled with frying spuds and everything else. Recognizing a real cook's interest, I explained what I had done in the detail required for sharing recipes. Art said little, just listened and exclaimed now and again as he discovered a new trick or two I had used in my cooking efforts.

I turned to reset the table for three more only to come face to face with the dark-complected, sour-faced, and ill-tempered lad from the previous winter's flooded rice field. He didn't look any better now than he did then, I thought as I felt my demeanor changing. He was not wearing a jacket this time because of the temperature, and his two .45 Colt semiautomatic pistols in cross-draw holsters were readily apparent. For a moment our eyes met, and no one blinked. Art came over to us and, putting a hand on each of our shoulders, said, "Jumo, this is Terry Grosz. Terry, this is Jumo Gallenti." We stood looking at each other for a moment, then extended our hands. Jumo's handshake was firm, and I made sure he got the same message from mine. The doorway was then darkened by another man, and Art introduced him as Dante Gottini, his pilot and "another close friend." I recognized Dante as the lad who had been on the other side of the pond during my first meeting with Art in the duck blind. Art's quick acceptance of me, for whatever reason, had a magic effect on the attitudes of his two "friends." It was obvious that they still didn't trust me, but the boss was at ease with me, so they followed suit. That was fine with me, but why did Jumo wear the two .45s all the time? Only time would tell, and just to be on the safe side or until I figured out what the hell I had by the tail, I would start wearing my .44 magnum everywhere I went while these folks were in town, just in case the bullets started flying.

Over the next couple of days, Art and I started to really enjoy each other's company, and that friendliness was reflected in Jumo's and Dante's attitudes as well. We did a lot of cooking together, shared cook's lies, and drank a lot of excellent wine furnished by Art. One thing I did notice was that every time I cooked, Art would take his plate of food and hand it to Jumo. Jumo would give it the taste test and then hand it back to Art for his enjoyment. I thought that strange, almost as if Art expected me to put poison in the food.

The days passed, and with two freshly killed deer, the three put their twin-engine plane back into the air and with one last pass over the ranch house disappeared to the west. Cliff and I stood there in the cooling evening watching the plane disappear until it we could hear and see it no more. Turning to Cliff, I said, "What the hell is with that crew?"

Cliff said, "I don't know, but those two bodyguards never took their eyes off anything that even looked like it might be a menace to that guy Art!"

"He must be worth a lot of money," I naively said as I headed for one of my traps to band some more recently captured dove.

I forgot that summer's episode with Art as fall approached and prepared for another round of the waterfowl wars with the human populace. One November morning my phone rang just as I was leaving the house. Answering it, I was surprised to find Jumo on the other end. Jumo said, "Terry, the boss wants to talk to you." Figuring that meant Art, I waited, holding the phone.

A moment later I heard Art's familiar voice. "Terry, how are you doing?" he asked.

"Fine," I said.

Art said, "What are you and Donna doing this Saturday?"

I was somewhat surprised that he knew my wife's name but dismissed the thought as a possible slip of the lip during the past summer over the excellence of her pumpkin pie. "I'm probably working pheasant hunters," I responded, "and for Donna, I don't know."

There was a pause, and then Art asked if I knew a good safe place where he could hunt pheasants. I said, "What do you mean 'safe'?"

He said, "Oh, you know, just someplace where we can hunt alone and won't be bothered by other hunters, or anyone else for that matter."

I said, "Sure; you can hunt on my deputy's place, a fellow called Tim Dennis."

"Yeah, I know about him; that sounds good," Art replied. "What time should I be at your house for breakfast for one of those cheese-and-seafood omelets you keep talking about all the time?"

Damn, I was even more taken aback. Now, how did he know Tim? In addition, to just invite himself up like that was a little bold. But, being the cook I am and having found someone who liked to eat my food, I dismissed any thoughts of caution, gave him a time, and hung up. That Saturday at three A.M. sharp, Art showed up in a limo with Jumo and Dante. They entered my home, and I introduced the bunch of them to Donna, who was busy cooking for the lot of us, including Tim Dennis, my deputy. Donna served an outstanding buffet-style breakfast, with a hot apple pie fresh out of the oven, and all of us dove in except Art. He patiently waited until Jumo tasted everything and then dove in as well. The clouded look that flew across my bride's face told me I had some mending of fences to do regarding her cooking and another man having to eat it before Art did! I tried to explain during a quiet moment in the kitchen but saw that I wasn't succeeding in consoling her about someone having to taste *her* cooking to make sure it was all right.

At that unfortunate moment Art came by and complimented Donna on her food, especially her homemade bread and pie (which truly are the greatest). Donna looked Art right in the eye and in a tone of voice meant for his personal attention said, "In the future, you eat what is set before you without the taste test or you and yours can eat somewhere else." I think the steely blue in Art's eyes was more than matched by my wife's that morning!

Art was somewhat taken aback by her frankness and intense blue-eyed stare but recovered quickly and said, "You are right, Donna; I am among friends. If I am invited back, you have my word that is how it will be done."

Donna softened and asked Art if he would like some more coffee, and he smiled at having escaped and replied, "Yes, please." I grinned from ear to ear, knowing I had a great wife but needed to be reminded occasionally. Hell, I should have had her out on that rice check last year, I chuckled to myself.

The pheasant hunt went like clockwork, and everyone had a great time except the pheasants. Over the next few months Art and his crew were guests at our house several times, and he was always the perfect gentleman. He was very good to my kids and treated Donna with the utmost respect. I think he felt that to do otherwise would get him crossways with the boss of the house, and that would cost him any further home-cooked meals.

I later discovered that Art had a nice double-wide house trailer at Terrill Sartain's duck club. When I knew he was around, I was a frequent visitor there as well. He always would meet me at the door and say, "Come ona in and havea some gooda wine anda cheese" in his fake Italian accent. I would sometimes have lunch with him, and it always consisted of many choices of good Italian meats, cheeses, sourdough bread, and wine. Talk always turned to hunting and such things, but nothing was ever said that explained where Art was from or what he did for a living. He didn't offer, and I didn't pry. We had developed a good relationship, almost that of a father and son, and I didn't want that to be interrupted, so I held my questions and he the answers needed between us.

One day the following spring, about three in the morning, I couldn't sleep, so I got up and went to work, as a game warden does. Most seasons were now closed, so I slowly worked along a series of canals in the dark, checking for fishermen or froggers just to pass the time, when I happened to notice a wildly swinging light beam bouncing off the water in a canal to the north. Moving to where I could see and not be seen, I saw three men in a boat who appeared to be frogging. I watched them for about twenty minutes and, satisfied that they had quite a few frogs by the fast way they were catching them, moved quietly to where I could intercept them in case they wanted to toss the evidence before I could get control of the situation. Their small duck boat approached my hiding place in some willows alongside the canal, and as the three got out and prepared to portage the boat over the road across the canal they had just been in, I stepped forward.

"Good morning, federal game warden," I said. "How is the frogging?" They damn near died in their skins, I scared them so badly. They had not expected to be checked at that time in the morning, especially by a man who silently rose up right next to where they were standing. After things were under control and their hearts started working again, I requested and checked their fishing licenses. I then commenced to check their sacks of live bullfrogs and discovered the contents to be way over the limit. Once I sorted everything out regarding who had done what, a chap whose last name was Jeno, who allegedly owned a major hotel in south San Francisco, was the proud possessor of 198 live frogs, a tad over the limit (which was 25 in those days). After taking several pictures, I released the frogs back into the canal, issued Mr. Jeno a state citation for 173 frogs over the limit, and, satisfied with my catch and the $500 fine that was to come, went home and found sleep pretty easily. Lying there in bed, I thought of Jeno before I drifted off to sleep. He had accepted the ticket without fanfare, but I could tell from his red face and the rapidly pulsing veins on the side of his neck that he was pissed. *Really* pissed! However, I had run across that type before and knew that as long as you kept them in front of you, usually nothing else happened. Little did I know that the morning's episode was just the start of another chapter that was almost the last one in the life and times of yours truly.

A knocking at my front door around nine A.M. ruined any chance of sleep, so I sat up and waited to see if Donna would answer the door. Realizing that she had already gone to work, I slipped on a pair of jeans and walked down the cool tile hallway to answer the incessant knocking. I was confronted by two well-dressed chaps who asked if I was Terry Grosz. I said, "Yes," whereupon they identified themselves as federal agents and asked if they could come in and talk to me. Not knowing what the hell was going on, I said, "Sure, come on in," and turned to let them enter the house. We went into the living room, and the lads got right down to business. After a few pleasantries, they laid out seven photographs on the coffee table and asked me if I knew anyone in the pictures. Looking them over, I said, "Sure, that one is Jumo Gallenti; that one is a fellow named Dante Gottini; and the last one on the right is a man named Art Patino. I have no idea as to the identity of the others."

The agents looked at each other, and the lead investigator asked, "Do you really know who these fellows are or what they do for a living?"

I said, "Not really. I suppose they are some sort of businessmen, and Dante is Art's pilot."

The agents looked at each other again, and then one said, pointing to one of the photographs, "That is Art Patino, a high-up member of Murder Incorporated who we believe to be a hit man, and these other two are his personal bodyguards, none of which I would want to screw with!"

I couldn't believe my ears. Murder Incorporated was allegedly a Mafia organization whose main function was to kill folks who had left the Mafia or were going to or who planned to testify for the government against their former colleagues. Goddamn, the thought that they were a group of lads one didn't want to screw with kept running through my mind. Looking at the agents, I told them, "Boy, that is not like the Art I know. He has been a model human being around me and my family. In fact, he never ever took advantage of me or my family, or even tried."

I was brought out of my bewildered daze by the question, "How well do you get along with Art?"

"Pretty well," I said. "He is almost like a father to me in a lot of ways."

The tall agent said, "That's good; we would like you to watch him for us and report to us on anything he does. Would you be willing to do so?"

Still finding it hard to believe what I was hearing but remembering who I was, I said, "Sure; just tell me what you want done and who to report to." Lots of mob history, activities, and instructions took up the next several hours, and then the agents left me to my thoughts. My tiredness had vanished with the revelation that my friend was really not a very nice person. In the end, since I was a federal agent bound by oath, not to mention my own personal ethics, I decided I would be open, do what I had to do, and ... carry my .44 magnum everywhere I went from then on, period. As I was now working for another branch of the federal government and aware of their reputation for leaks, I knew it wouldn't be long before I would be called on the carpet, and I sure wasn't disappointed.

A week after my meeting with the two feds, I received a call on my vehicle's mobile radio from the Colusa County sheriff's office informing me that a person on trailer lot 28 on Terhel Farms Gun Club wanted to see me. I responded that I was en route and about forty-five minutes later pulled up in front of Art's trailer, which was located on lot 28. True to form, Art met me on the porch with his phony Italian spiel about coming in "fora gooda wine anda cheese." I called him a name and got one in return as I entered the trailer. After shaking hands, we exchanged small talk as Art got out the usual samplers of meats, cheese, bread, and wine. We talked ducks, pheasants, and other aspects of hunting, and then things got quiet and serious. Art's soft-colored eyes turned to that steely look he always exhibited when he was on high alert, and then he asked, "What did the feds want?"

I was taken aback by the directness of his question and for a moment just looked at him. Then I let a large smile develop on my face, hoping for the correct interpretation, and said, "They want me to watch you like a hawk."

Art continued to study my face, and then he slowly said, "Are you going to do what they want?"

Not letting my eyes leave his for a second I said, "Sure."

He paused for a moment and then said, "Good; now that I know the ground rules, let's havea somea more gooda wine anda cheese." We both laughed, and I sensed that all would be well between us—just as long as we both understood the ground rules.

Several weeks later the ringing of my phone brought me back from some much-needed sleep and into the reality that accom-

panies that weather-beaten world of a public servant. Picking up
the phone, I said, "Good morning," and the excited but recog-
nizable voice of Tom Ishige, my good friend and informant,
flooded over the telephone lines: "Misser Grosz, Misser Grosz,
don't start your truck, don't start your truck; it will blow up!"
Tom continued with more of the same until I got a chance to
calm him down.

"Tom," I said, "what the hell are you talking about?"

"Misser Grosz, Misser Grosz, there is a contract out on you
by the Mafia. Your truck will blow up if you try to start it.
Don't start your truck!" Now, what kind of crapola is this? I impatiently thought. I finally settled Tom down and managed to
get from him that Jeno, the fellow I had pinched for the gross
over-limit of frogs, had, according to Tom's sources, a $25,000
contract out on me for the inconvenience and embarrassment I
had caused him.

I said, "Tom, are you sure?"

"Yessir, Misser Grosz," came the familiar reply. "That Misser
Jeno is a high-up member of the Mafia in the San Francisco family, and you really embarrassed him when you took those frogs.
Misser Jeno was supposed to have some more high-up Mafia
people over for a frog-leg dinner, and you ruined that. He lost
his face," Tom added.

"Tom," I laughed, "don't worry; no one is going to kill a federal officer over some frogs."

"I think you be wrong, Misser Grosz; you be wrong."

Thanking Tom for the information and trying to make him
feel better, I promised I would be careful and check the engine
on my vehicle every time before starting it. I could tell that made
Tom feel better, and after some other conversation concerning
fishing on the Sacramento River for striped bass, we parted
ways. As I hung up the phone, one thought kept moving
through my mind. Tom had never been wrong in the information he had brought me; never! He was always accurate, many
times even down to the exact time an event was to occur.

I cleaned up, dressed, ate some breakfast, and headed out to meet the day by going to my office to do some paperwork in order to keep my boss, Jack Downs, happy. Opening the door of my patrol truck, I slid in and started to turn the key in the ignition, but Tom's words came back to me again. Shaking my head in disbelief, I got out and looked under the truck's frame and checked the engine and starter motor to see if I had been "wired." All was clear. After driving to my office, the first thing I did was call my fed contact and share Tom's news with him. He said he would check into it, asked for information on Art (which I shared), and we both went on our merry ways, I to not worry about the contract (stupid) and the fed on his way to follow up on my information. I called Jack Downs next to let him know about the threat, and like me he didn't feel that anyone in the Mafia would kill a federal officer over a few frogs, so he just dismissed the issue outright. More relaxed now that I knew my boss, a man I considered to be one of the very best in the business, concurred with my thoughts on the matter, I headed out the door and went to see what the world had to offer a young (read dense sometimes) game management agent.

Several weeks later I received another radio call from the sheriff's office to tell me that the occupant of trailer slot 28 at Terhel Farms Gun Club wished to see me. Recognizing Art's number, I responded, "I have an individual to interview and after that will make contact with the lad in slot 28." Several hours later, after finishing my interview, I pulled into the parking spot next to Art's trailer. Hearing my truck arrive, Art came to the door and said, "Terry, come on in for soma gooda wine anda cheese."

"Sounds good to me; you ground-sluicing any ducks lately?" I asked with a grin.

He told me to go screw myself and then repeated his invitation: "Come on in, some good wine first," following it with the words, "Then we have some business." Figuring that the business concerned my contact with the feds, I prepared to discuss the issue with Art without revealing anything I had told them regarding his activities. We busied ourselves with the preparation of food and the good times that always followed when the two

of us got together. After about half an hour of visiting and eating, Art's good humor and light laughter turned instantly, as
they were wont to do, to stone-cold serious. No matter how
well I thought I knew him, I was always surprised at how
quickly he could turn from a normal human being to one who
appeared deadly in all aspects. His eyes turned that steely blue
again and he said, "I hear there is a contract out on you."

Relieved that it wasn't the business with the feds, I said,
"Yeah, I heard that also, but I am not paying much attention to
it."

Art stood up and coldly said, "That is the trouble with you
dumbshit, I-will-live-forever cops. You need to pay more attention to what happens in life, especially if it is coming from a sec-
tor like this one. What the hell do you think would happen to
Donna and the kids if you got your ass eliminated? You stupid
bastard, the next time you hear that a contract is out on you, you
damn well better pay attention." Art's coldness and harsh language caught me by complete surprise and validated the fact that
I *really* had a problem regarding that contract! Art stood looking down at me for a few moments and then yelled over my
head, "Jumo." I whirled around, thinking maybe Jumo would be
the one executing the contract while simultaneously dropping
my hand to the comforting butt of my .44 magnum, steeling myself to the fact that Jumo was at least going with me on this ride
if that were the case!

Jumo came out of the back room of the trailer pushing a very
badly beaten man in front of him. It took a few moments because of the mess made of his face, but I soon recognized the
man I had pinched for the over-limit of frogs, Mr. Jeno. Jeno
rushed forward, fell to his knees, and grabbed me by the legs, all
the while pleading for forgiveness. He mumbled through split
lips, "I didn't know you was Art's friend; I didn't mean to put
out a contract on you; I will never do it again; anytime you want
to use my hotel and services free of charge, just ask and it will be
yours," plus other things I don't remember. I was thunderstruck
and didn't know what to do. I had never been in such a situa-

tion! My daze was broken as Art started around the table, his body language indicating that he was going to kick Jeno in the ribs as he knelt at my feet. I reached out and grabbed Art by the upper arm to stop him, only to feel the cold steel of a gun barrel stuck in my neck. The cocking of a hammer told me to let Art go, which I did. Fire flashed in Art's eyes as I released him, then softened as his senses returned and he realized it was I who had grabbed him, and now I figured I had a real problem.

Art told Jumo, "Back off and put that thing away right now!" The cold metal left my neck, as did the wind from my sails.

I told Art, "If you had kicked him, that would have been a felony and I would have had to arrest you for it." Art's instant cold look told me that would be next to impossible, and I now noticed Dante quietly filtering into the room with the rest of us. I decided in that instant that Art would go with me if the shooting started. One round from a .44 magnum, 240-grain bullet will fairly take the juice out of anyone's carcass, and I was bent on his destruction if the shooting war was to start. As the northern Cheyenne Indians used to say on the battlefield before we destroyed them and their culture, "Today is a good day to die." That saying kept whirling around in my head as I calmly faced what the dawn was about to bring. I had already decided I was going to die in that trailer in the next few moments for grabbing Art by the arm, but surprisingly, I was not afraid to die. I just wanted to take at least one of the lads with me, all the while wondering what it would be like and what was waiting for me on the other side of the great divide.

Art, sensing the gravity of the moment and the cold look that had to be emanating from my eyes toward him, projecting his personal destruction, quickly lightened the moment. "Jeno," he said, "get your ass out of my sight. Get your butt back to San Francisco, and if I ever hear of you threatening any of my friends in the future, you won't live to see another sunrise." Jeno staggered to his feet and bolted out the door, down the steps, and across the parking lot until he was out of sight among the other duck club residences. Art turned back to me and coldly asked, "Would you have done it?" The frankness of his question and the fact that he had intuited that I was planning to shoot him took me by surprise, but I quickly recovered, remembering who he was and how he lived.

"Yes," I said, still looking him straight in the eye.

"Do you think you could have gotten a round off?" he said.

"I don't know," I said, "but it would have been hard to kill a friend."

There was a moment of silence before he slowly said, "Yes, it would have." Art's eyes softened and he said, "How about some morea gooda wine anda cheese?"

I answered, "Sounds pretty damn good to me as long as you are buying."

Art just grinned at my comeback. "Besides," he continued, "anytime anyone comes close to death and escapes, his appetite for sex and food really increases, yes?" His eyes never left mine.

Staring right back, I said coldly, "You aren't pretty enough to go to bed with, so I will choose the wine and the cheese."

Art continued to stare for a second and then threw back his head and roared with laughter. He walked around to get some more wine and thumped me on the back as he headed to the wine rack. Well, I said to myself, things are at least returning to seminormal. I quietly removed my hand from the butt of the .44 magnum and managed a thin smile at Jumo, who had yet to take his fierce, dark eyes off me or his right hand off the butt of one of his semiautomatics.

When I left Art's trailer that day I went straight to my office and called my federal contact to report what had occurred. My contact said, "So, that contract was for real, huh?"

I said, "What? You son of a bitch, didn't you guys even run that lead down?"

There was a pause and then the lad said, "No, we didn't feel it was a valid concern, especially over a few frogs, so we didn't run it down. Sorry."

I said, "Sorry, my ass. Go find someone else to treat like shit and do your work for you; I'm out." I slammed down the phone and spent the next several hours in the outback trying to cool off. I would never have treated an informant as poorly as they treated me, I thought. And their chances to do so again were nil.

Art and I didn't see much of each other for some time after that. I was busy in my district with a lot of eagle-killing problems in the Pacific Northwest and, never seeing or receiving a call from Art, figured he had his hands full as well doing what he did. The next time we met was the September evening of my going-away party in Colusa in 1974, just before I left for a senior resident agent's position in North Dakota. About halfway through dinner Joel McDermott, the Colusa County undersheriff who was sitting next to me at the head table poked me in the ribs and pointed toward the front door of the building where the party was being held. Standing in the doorway, or rather filling it, was good old Jumo. McDermott must have recognized Jumo and leaned over to ask me if I wanted him removed. Joel was a big lad and had the heart of a lion, but I was afraid that the prospect of fifteen slugs from Jumo's twin .45s would have been a bit much even for him, so I said, "I will handle this." Walking to the front door and facing Jumo, I said, "Evening, Jumo, can I help you?"

Jumo said, "The boss wants to see you," then turned and went out the door to a waiting gray limo. I followed and got into the back seat of the limo at Jumo's direction. Art was sitting there and said, "Congratulations on your promotion. Does that mean you will no longer be in charge of this area?" Before I could answer he said with a chuckle, "Good; now I can shoot over-limits of ducks."

Without batting an eye I said, " You shoot an over-limit and your hind end is mine, and you know it."

He laughed easily and then reached into a large paper sack and handed me a beautifully wrapped gift. "Your going-away gift," he mumbled. I was really touched as I removed the paper wrapping to discover a solid wood gift box holding an Eagle model German Lugar, .45 caliber! I could not believe my eyes. I had

only read about these experimental guns, and if I remember correctly, there were only about nine in existence.

I looked lovingly at my gift and then turned to Art and
thanked him for being so thoughtful but told him, "I can't accept such a present."

I saw the hurt flash across his tired old eyes, older than I remembered from our past days, and he asked, "Why?"

I said, "Art, it is too magnificent a gift. I just can't accept
something like this from you or anyone; government policy."

"Terry, only you and I would know."

I said, "That is right, only you and I would know, and both of
us know that a gift of this caliber, although speaking to the scope
and degree of our friendship, just can't morally be accepted by
me or any federal law enforcement officer." With that I handed
him back the cased weapon. Reaching out, I took his gnarled
hand, shook it firmly, and said, "Good-bye, my friend, and I do
truly mean that," as tears welled up into my eyes.

Not wanting to embarrass myself, I started to leave the limo,
whereupon Art said, "Wait. I want you to take this." He reached
into his shirt pocket and handed me a business card that just
said, "Art Patino" across its face. He said, "Turn it over," which
I did to find a single phone number written across the back.
"Anytime you get into trouble, *any* kind of trouble, call that
number. It will always be a valid number to call no matter what
happens to me." His intense blue gaze was back, I observed, and
with that came the serious realization of the gift he had just
given me.

I said, "OK, it's a deal," shook his hand warmly again, and
left. The limo drove off and with it Art Patino, out of my life
forever, as I reentered the going-away festivities ... or so I
thought.

I moved to Bismarck, North Dakota, to continue my career in
1974. Art Patino was assassinated in 1978, his killer unknown.
Jumo is also dead, as I found out from another federal source,
but I don't have a clue about Dante.

From 1978 to the date of this writing, I have received a phone call from an unknown man every year on or about January 5th through the 15th, asking in a monotone if I need anything. The unknown caller tells me that Art's wish is that "the Eagle" have no worries in life and that *anything* I need is to be granted. ... I am also told that the phone number given to me by Art is still valid and to call if need be. Then the line goes dead. But this story doesn't end there. On January 13, 1999, as I sat in front of my computer editing this story, my phone rang. That wasn't unusual because Chester Hamilton had just been chosen assistant regional director for Region 6, the law enforcement management position I had recently vacated, and as a result many friends had been calling all day to inform me of the selection. Picking up the phone, I said, "Hello."

The voice on the other end said, "This call is from Art. Does 'the Eagle' need anything?" I was stunned! I had forgotten all about the annual call I receive from whomever, and how ironic that it came just as I was editing the very story in which I was telling of meeting Art! I held the phone for a second as my mind's eye ran back through the annals of time regarding this man. I said, "No," and thanked him for calling. *Click* went the line. ... Needless to say, it had been quite a day.

13
Ain't She a Beaut?

IN THE EARLY FALL OF 1972 I still hadn't learned that to work alone at night in the Sacramento Valley chasing commercial-market hunters and duck draggers was somewhat problematic. It wasn't that I hadn't learned the dangers, but every time the birds came into the fields to feed or rest, I felt it was my job to be out there with them and provide what protection I could, scarce as it was because of the vastness of the territory that needed to be covered. If by some chance it meant taking another load of number 4 shot in the back as I had in 1967, then so be it, I grimly thought. They hadn't killed me the first time, although during the healing process it had certainly felt at times like I was dying, especially if I forgot and stretched my back too far and reopened the still healing sores where the shot had penetrated. In fact, as a result of that experience I had became a better night-working officer and survivor. So, like it or not, I was back in the blackest part of the wildlife wars, namely, trying to gain the attention of those in the business of extinction, more commonly known as commercial-market hunters, or tracking down the illegal night-shooting individuals trying to fill their freezers with plump rice-fed ducks and geese. No matter how you cut it, I had my hands full in a three-thousand-square-mile area of the valley loaded with waterfowl as well as those eager to snuff out the lives of those critters with the pull of a trigger.

Ever since modern-day humans first inhabited the Sacramento Valley with their firearms and became familiar with the great hordes of wintering waterfowl, their desire for the birds as a food item or for the money to be gained through the sale of ducks and geese reigned supreme. With a little practice one could learn how to quietly sneak up on thousands of packed waterfowl (as many as fifty thousand in a flock) as they fed in the fields in the night hours (sometimes during the day as well) and, with a number of well-placed shots from a shotgun or series of shotguns firing in sequence, achieve a bounty that was sometimes beyond their wildest dreams. I have heard tales from the old market hunters in towns such as Maxwell and Princeton and from some of the more successful duck draggers (people who shot to fill their freezers and their friends' freezers and occasionally for the market) that if they hit it right, three shooters with "Long Toms" (shotguns with magazine extenders holding anywhere from eight to thirteen shells) could kill up to 650 ducks in a shoot!

Before 1918 (when passage of the Migratory Bird Treaty Act outlawed such practices) these birds from the Sacramento Valley would then be taken by wagon, steamship, or train to middlemen or buyers in the cities, who would purchase the fruits of these harvests to resell to stores, butcher shops, and restaurants, primarily in the San Francisco, Oakland, and Sacramento areas. It was not uncommon for these Sacramento Valley birds to find their way into markets as far away as Las Vegas, Chicago, Reno, and places in Oregon. In fact, if I correctly remember the oral histories narrated by some of these old shooters, ducks, geese, and other wildlife were openly sold in these markets out of open pushcarts around 1916 for as little as $.25 for ducks and $.35 for geese. This practice was very common, and as the old-timers told me, the top-dollar birds in the 1930s and '40s (now illegal to sell) were the mallards, pintail, and canvasbacks, which went for $1.25 to $1.50 each. All the other species of ducks, mainly because they were less known for their excellence as table fare or because of their smaller size, went for $.75 or less in the marketplace.

When I left California in 1974, I heard of prices as high as $5 each for mallards and pintail, unpicked and uncleaned, and the buyer would take all the chances in picking up the birds, in some cases from where they lay stacked in a dry ditch in a rice field, all to be utilized in the restaurants and markets, particularly in China Town in the San Francisco Bay area! So you can plainly see the profit in a few hours of hard work with a little thrill thrown in, especially if the law got on your trail. Bottom line, for a small expenditure in gasoline for the getaway and transport vehicle and several dollars' worth of shotgun shells, a gross of $125 to $600 per night was not unusual for the dedicated gunner in the 1930s and '40s! Those figures become even more meaningful when one considers that most salaries during those years ranged from $3,000 to $10,000 per year for the working man. A whole lot more money could be garnered by selling mallards and pintail at $5 apiece in the 1970s.

As time marched on, along with seasonal droughts followed by reduced waterfowl populations and public hue and cry over the slaughter, game laws were passed to stop such barbaric night shooting and selling of waterfowl as well as for other less flagrant violations. These practices were barbaric not only because of the huge numbers of birds killed but more importantly because for every bird killed, as many shooters used to comment to me, anywhere from two to three were wounded and died from their wounds hours or days later, adding further to the gross waste of the resource.

With the passage in 1918 of these federal game laws protecting migratory birds came a few hardy folks whose souls were truly ahead of their time. These first few law enforcement officers, limited in resources of every kind and hampered by the ingrained night-shooting tradition, politics, lenient court systems, and social ostracism of them and their families, attempted to stem the illegal killing and return the fields to their rightful role as feeding places, not places where large-scale butchery occurred on a nightly basis. However, traditions died hard, and so did the practice of night shooting. Some of the old-timers who would talk to me, a "law dog," during my days in the Sacramento Valley told me that there were about one hundred men engaged in commercial-market hunting in the valley in the 1930s and '40s, years after the passage of the Migratory Bird Treaty Act. Not all of these shooters lived in the valley; many came from the Bay area, but to the best of the old-timers' recollection, this large number plied their trade for many years, law enforcement officers or not. For about five months of the year these lads would be killing for the waterfowl market whenever they had the opportunity. The rest of the year the members of this hard core of commercial-market hunters were either lying low to avoid detection or killing any other kind of wildlife that would provide a few pieces of silver. So for many years after the passage of protective laws, the killing and selling of waterfowl (selling now being a felony) continued along its lusty way.

A group of such shooters usually comprised anywhere from three to five gunmen, with four being the norm. One lad would drive the vehicle, and one or more would be responsible for scouting out the area to be shot. The driver of the vehicle usually dropped the others off and picked up the exhausted, sweaty shooters later, often in a different location, unless they had been jumped by the law. In that case the shooters usually left their shotguns in the field and walked home or to a friend's place to avoid capture. The shooters, both historically and when I worked the valley, were dressed for speed and in my experience usually wore a light shirt, Levis, and a set of fast running shoes and carried a shotgun capable of firing anywhere from five to thirteen shots. If the season was on and the folks planning the drag were commercial hunters, they generally carried numerous lengths of twine looped through their belts that had been precut in lengths long enough to wrap up a limit of ducks once the shoot was over.

The "Long Tom" was a fairly simple killing tool used by many dedicated market hunters. It was usually a Model 11 Remington 12-gauge with a homemade extension magazine that was often longer than the barrel of the shotgun itself! In order for this system to work, the magazine cap on the traditional shotgun was removed, as was the original magazine spring. Then the lad would screw his homemade magazine extender, made from a piece of steel similar in size to the original magazine, onto the still-in-place original shotgun magazine. Finally he would insert another, longer magazine spring into the now modified magazine so as to properly feed the extra shells onto the loading tray, then screw the magazine cap onto the end of his homemade extender—and there you had it, a shotgun capable of shooting anywhere from eight to thirteen shots!

Now, you might think these lads would freeze in the winter weather, being so lightly dressed. No way! They were moving all the time and pumped up with adrenaline, so cold was really not an issue. But then look at your friendly game warden or game management agent positioned in the fields to catch such shooters. A heavy jacket with other weighty clothes and long handles (an old-fashioned name for long johns, woolen and warm), usually made up one's attire. A pair of clumsy hip boots rounded out the outfit. The law enforcement officer had to be on site early to avoid detection and many times lay for hours in the mud or on the cold ground to avoid scaring the feeding ducks nearby or alerting the stalking shooters. Even then the officer's problems were not over. After lying for long periods on the damp ground, your extremities got fairly cold owing to inactivity. Then, if you had to get up quickly and run after a shooter, all that cold blood would flow into the vital organs, creating an uncontrollable shaking until you warmed up. Well, when you're shaking like a dog passing peach pits, speed is not one of your strong points! It doesn't take long to see that the odds stacked up in favor of the shooter.

Many shooters continued this now illegal practice of slaughter to feed their families, to save their farms during the Depression, for the money it supplied, or for the pure pleasure and thrill of the killing. As this practice continued in the face of the ever-increasing law enforcement presence, reputations and egos became built into a Sacramento Valley "red badge of courage." It became quite the thing to literally blow up the ducks under the nose of the law and escape to do the same another day. However, it was a different story to be caught by the law. The embarrassment and ridicule that followed when anyone was apprehended for this type of violation, at least in the upper Sacramento Valley, always led me to protect the names of those so unlucky just as long as they paid their dues to Uncle Sam. I did this because I soon discovered that my sensitivity would lead to some unique friendships, not to mention a bit of grudging respect for what I was attempting to do. In some cases, lads who were historical killers hung their shotguns up for the duration. In other cases, those I apprehended turned information over to me that led to further apprehensions, including, in some instances, family members. So I quickly discovered that I had much to gain if I kept my mouth shut rather than letting my mouth become a brook of information for all who would listen.

Moving into the Sacramento Valley, first in the late '6os as a state Fish and Game warden and then later as a game management agent for the U.S. Fish and Wildlife Service, I managed to catch just the tail end of this piece of bloody history. Even at that late date after the wildlife law enforcement community had been hunting the lawless for years, some of the stain still remained on Mother Nature's kilts. Many of the old guard were gone or too old to continue their bloody trade, and the commercial taste for duck dinners was waning, but in many cases their well-taught offspring (my age or older) were attempting to carry on this blood sport, and it was those folks for the most part whom I now chased as my predecessors had their fathers and grandfathers.

With this history in mind, I often felt that I was the only voice the poor damn critters had in the rice fields at night, and for the most part that was true. The truth of the matter was that not many law enforcement folks, state or federal, preferred to spend their evenings in the damp winter rice fields of the Sacramento Valley, night after night, trying to keep the night hunters separated from the feeding waterfowl. This was especially true in light of the workload associated with all the other hunting seasons and the whole fall waterfowl hunting picture. There was only so much candle you could burn at both ends before your carcass, no matter how young or tough you were, just flat gave out. So many a night found more than a few of the Sacramento Valley officers off somewhere else rather than lying in the cold water and mud of the rice fields protecting the feeding water-fowl.

There was another factor: the mood and temperament of a lot of folks up and down the length and breadth of the Sacramento Valley, farmers as well as townspeople, who were still living the times of the good old days when commercial-market hunting was in full swing. Hell, there was still a pile of the old-time mar-ket hunters and duck draggers living in and around the valley, along with their families, and such times die hard. With that kind of atmosphere, it often seemed that wherever I looked I was crossing swords with those who didn't give a damn about any-thing but filling their wallets or their freezers with plump, rice-fed waterfowl. Throw in all that was happening illegally to the striped bass, salmon, sturgeon, pheasants, bullfrogs, catfish, and deer in the area at the same time, and you had a workload matched only by the gold badge and the stout ethics of the man behind it.

I saw a lot of officers during that period who shouldn't have been carrying the badge. I also saw a few who carried it well, re-gardless of the odds, and to those I take my hat off, as should the American people. What they did, many times at great sacrifice of their personal health and their family life, was preserve some of the heritage all of us enjoy to this day. But those officers were few and far between and the conflicts between humankind and the critters seemed to be in a deadly constant that came from every corner. I hate to think back on how many times I, or a few like me, was the only law out there amidst the constant carnage in the Sacramento Valley. And for the ducks alone, this period of life and death ran from August of any given year until around March 1 or when the birds began migrating back to where they had come from.

The American people will never realize how bad it was and is, or how much of their national wildlife heritage they have lost or are losing because of their overall complaisant attitude and lack of knowledge. It is just amazing! Think back to the days of the bison. A few chaps on the plains wiped out many millions of those animals, and that was back in the days of black-powder guns and very few shooters. In so doing, they not only almost exterminated a species of wildlife but basically eliminated many nations of peoples and their ways of life forever as well. That cause and effect alone should wake up the American people, but it hasn't to this day. The American people just don't seem to learn from their history. Come to think of it, all great empires, past and present, are in the same boat.

Leaving my home one evening as I had so many times in the past, I decided to work an area between Two Mile and Four Mile Roads, just north of the Colusa-Maxwell Highway on the northwest side of the Link Dennis place, not far from the town of Maxwell. Link was one hell of a good man and an excellent manager of the land. I always found him to be an exceptional human being and interested in the resource, even though the ducks sometimes plundered his crops, causing substantial financial losses. I knew he would have no problem if I staked out the ducks on his land, so, quietly and without lights, I sneaked my patrol vehicle in on the back side of his rice farm and then hid it from those prying eyes I meant to apprehend if they were on site pursuing their dirty business.

Loading up with my night-vision gear and other optics, I walked across several rice fields that had recently been harvested toward a swirl of ducks coming in to feed from Delevan National Wildlife Refuge to the northeast. Lying alongside a rice check to catch my breath, I surveyed my field of battle for the evening with my high-light-gathering naval binoculars. I carefully examined every rice check in the area for anything suspicious, especially the silhouette of another human being also watching the swirling mass of feeding ducks. Satisfied that I was alone except for the ducks in the darkening of the night, I walked, stooped over and using a watergrass-covered rice check for cover, for another hundred yards and again repeated my check for company other than the waterfowl. Still clear, I thought as I lowered the binoculars and took another hard look at the now closer noisy mass of feeding ducks.

Ah, the joy of it! Being that close to a wildlife event, actually being part of it, leaves memories that are forever burned into my soul. A cool, darkening evening with a light breeze; the smell of the rice field mud, dead crawdads, and curing grasses on the rice check; and a quietly quacking, occasional wing-striking mass of wildlife resembling a living tornado. All of this was accompanied by the rush of wings of those landing among their brethren already on the ground, or rising to leapfrog their buddies for a better feeding opportunity, and the subtle wind on my face a few seconds later from tens of thousands of madly flapping wings still arriving. The air was full of ducks coming in from every quarter, being drawn to this great living tornado like cannon shot, often flying only a few feet above the ground. The area was happily full of life, as it had been eons ago and was supposed to be. The energy of such a moment was so great that many times I actually had to force myself back into awareness of what had brought me here, namely, the dark side of humankind.

Crawling the last hundred yards, I picked a central spot near the feeding frenzy with the wind at my back and the ducks before me, put my gear on top of the rice check for handy retrieval, and settled as well as possible on the soft, damp ground with my charges. Darkness found me sitting quietly with my back resting against the rice check, watching ten or fifteen thousand mallards, pintail, and the rest of the "kitchen sink" in the waterfowl world greedily feeding in the poorly harvested field. That winter the rains had come and kept coming. As a result, the rice farmer north of Link's property had been able to get only a portion of his crop out because of extremely muddy conditions and his inability to completely drain many of the fields' lower ends. In fact, I had seen him earlier in the season more than once with his Hardy Harvesters sunk to the tops of their huge crawler tracks, almost out of sight, as he struggled to wring some sort of payback from his muddy rice fields. Ultimately he left at least a third of his crop on the ground, and the ducks, in typical hungry

ducklike fashion, were making short work of this naturally provided buffet opportunity.

I had sat partially hidden along that rice check for maybe
forty or fifty minutes watching the moon starting to come up
when all of a sudden I noticed the faintly visible, bent-over figure of a lone individual with a shotgun stalking my group of
feeding waterfowl. I thought, God-o'-Friday, here we go again.
Crouching even further down in my stand of watergrass, I
thought, Last time I saw an easy mark like this one, some son of
a gun shot me three times in the back with a load of number 4
shot before I could take three steps to make the grab. A cold
shiver went down my back, but so did a feeling of excitement.
Without moving more than a whisper, I took a long, slow look
around through my binoculars to see if I might again have unexpected company arriving from the rear to cover the other lad. I
had just enough moonlight to make a good read. No one, nothing. Using an old trick I had learned in the rice fields, I positioned the top part of my binocular lens so it just caught the bottom of the moon. Keeping that sliver of moon at the top of my
field of view, I again scanned the ground around me with the
lower portion of the lens, looking for any souls who might have
some sort of madness in their mind like shooting at me. Nothing, still all clear, I thought. It looked like the lad to my left was a
"singleton" on a mission of destruction all his own. With that realization, the smile on my tired face got even wider. I always
loved a good one-on-one challenge, and this would be another
great opportunity to put that old concern in the back of my
mind about working the rice fields alone at night to bed. The
shaking I was now beginning to feel, an old friend of many times
past, was not from the cold and wetness of the rice field but
from something more primal.

The shooter sneaked cautiously up to the ducks in a low,
bent-over stance, walking most of the way in a deep harvester
track in the mud and then dropping to all fours to crawl the last
forty or fifty yards to a rice check that led upwind to the duck's
feeding location. When he was finally in position, he wasn't

more than forty yards from where I lay hidden alongside my rice check. That was good, because if you were farther than that from any commercial-market hunter or duck dragger, you would never catch him and often would never even see him again after he shot and became aware of your presence. Plain and simply, most of the lads pulling an illegal duck shoot had a "jackrabbit" gear and knew how to use that and the dark of the night to make good their escapes. To say they could "motor" when the law was on their hind ends was an understatement! And racing across harvested rice fields at full tilt, in the semidark of the night, could carry many surprises, some unpleasant, such as running through a skunk, and others more deadly.

The lad, apparently not satisfied with his position, began to crawl along the back side of the rice check toward where I lay. Little did he know that he filled the entire field of view of a pair of binoculars silently trained on him. Good, I thought; get as close as you can, mister, and make my job easier. Even if he crawled right up to me, can you imagine the surprise and what that would do for one's inner calm before the shooting storm? After all, one didn't have to kill the critters to learn a damn good lesson through a test of character like crawling right up to a law enforcement agent in the dark. If that were to happen, I planned on saying more than just "boo."

For some reason the ducks started to get nervous, as indicated by their instantly becoming quiet, and the lad stopped crawling and melted into the ground. For the next twenty minutes as the darkness deepened, nothing happened other than the ducks recommencing their feeding, and I began to get antsy. Not knowing what the hell was going on and no longer able to see the lad at the level he had sunk down to, I started a slow, silent crawl on the opposite side of the rice check toward where I had last seen him. Before I started moving, however, I looked over my shoulder one more time to see whether he had a "drop-off" who was watching his backside and would shoot me from behind once I made my grand appearance.

All was still clear, so I continued my praying-mantis crawl toward the last known location of the object of immediate interest. When I drew close enough to spot him again, I saw that he had settled in next to the rice check and was quietly watching the ducks. He had no idea I was even in the county, much less right next door. With him in my sights, so to speak, I stopped crawling and lay down in a harvester furrow next to the rice check to see what his next move would be. We waited like that, not twenty yards apart, for about twenty more minutes until the partial moon rose higher over the Sutter Buttes. In the pale moonlight I still could not make out who the lad might be but felt pretty certain he was a local just by how he had worked his sneak up to the ducks. No muss, no fuss, just straight to the flock without disturbing them and then quietly waiting for the best shooting opportunity. I thought this lad knew his business and had to be one of my locals. With that, I quietly and slowly divested myself of some of my heavy clothing and gear for the run for the roses I knew was to follow. Colusa County had its share of "rabbits," and I was positive this lad, once he shot, would be as fleet of foot as the rest of the rascals prone to shoot ducks at night and then not have the etiquette to stand and take their medicine.

The ducks turned like a big moving blanket into the slight breeze now coming from the northwest as they eagerly fed and began moving toward this fellow as he lay in deadly wait behind the rice check. The birds fed to within a few yards of his location, and then I heard a soft whistle. Instantly ten thousand heads were up and the happy feeding noises whispered away to quiet, droning concern. I saw the shooter, on his knees, rise up with the shotgun already at his shoulder and begin shooting rapidly into the raised heads and bodies of the massed waterfowl. What had been feeding happiness moments before now turned to abject terror as thousands of ducks tried to rise into the air and escape the gun. As they lifted from the ground, the rapid shooting seemed to be continuous, tearing large circular holes in the "sheet" of bodies fleeing the scene. I quit counting the shots at ten as I lay there spellbound! This was the first time

I had gotten this close to a shooter using a "Long Tom," and needless to say, I was beyond fascination. This was history for me, and I couldn't wait to play it out.

As duck bodies fell to the earth, they were replaced with others, who, being in the path of the gun and its lethal message, also fell to earth, eventually replacing the former living carpet with one of inert and crippled, crawling forms. As the shooting stopped and I knew his shotgun was empty, I jumped up from my hiding place and made a beeline for the shooter, just as if he was the opposing quarterback on a Saturday afternoon during my college days as a defensive tackle. I had already formed an idea of how hard I was going to tackle this lad and how I would find the pieces of his body thereafter so I could bring him before the federal magistrate, thereby allowing the ducks their day in court. Suddenly the chap realized someone was barreling down on him like a freight train, and, springing up like a man possessed, off he went like a shot. I was truly amazed at just how quickly this lad went "from zero to sixty"! Maybe it was my bellowed words, "Federal agent, hold it right there!" that ignited his booster, but whatever it was, the man went from kneeling to full tilt like an explosion! The race was on. He wasn't a very big guy, kind of tall and lanky, but by God, he sure could move. Terry, I thought, it may take a while before the hand of Thor rests on this fellow's shoulder.

We ran north across this big rice field, heading for Canada, or at least so I thought by the way this chap's legs ate up the ground. Actually, we were closer to Newhall Farm headquarters, but I bet the thought of Canada crossed my lad's mind in light of the thing lumbering along behind him. I wasn't far behind, and he knew it, so both of us ran like the devil for five or six hundred yards, knowing full well what the rewards were for the winner and loser of this race. At the end of this sprint across muddy rice fields both of us were really winded, and as if by unspoken agreement we stopped running as if on cue and commenced walking as fast as we could. We walked rapidly like this just a few yards apart for a few hundred yards without any words being spoken. I could feel the sweat starting to run down my back and forming on my legs under my pants, which were covered by my hip boots. But this lad was catchable, and both of us knew it. I could imagine that he was sweating even more, knowing I was so close behind and staying there!

Getting back our winds for the moment, off we both went again like a shot, as fast as we could go. After another four of five hundred yards of this running like a couple of goofy schoolkids, we once more quit running as if by mutual agreement and walked as fast as we each could, one to escape and the other to apprehend. Again, neither of us said a word, just ran and walked as hard as we were able. Hell, neither of us could have said anything anyway, as winded as we were. This little drama went on for at least half an hour, and for at least five hundred miles, or so it seemed to the larger one chasing the lanky one as we zigged and zagged across the moonbeam-drenched rice fields. But youth was winning. I noticed that at the end of each little sprint I was gaining a yard or two on my prey, just enough to encourage me not to let up at this point or all would be lost. For the lad before me, the heavier-sounding footsteps foretold a moment that would not be pleasant if he didn't pick up the pace. So as the moon rose higher in the sky, it was greeted by two crazies running and then walking like hell across what felt like a million miles of harvested muddy rice fields. The man in the moon had to smile, though, because for once, instead of seeing a bunch of lads illegally dragging a mess of dead ducks from the field, he saw the law hot on the trail of one foolish enough to pull the trigger right next to the game warden. Throughout this run through the rice I kept one thing in mind: his shotgun! My eyes never left that or the center of his back as we moved across the ground. I knew he hadn't had time to reload after the shoot, so he was carrying an empty shotgun. However, if he tried to load it on the run and I felt he had been successful in that endeavor, it would be for only one reason. ... If that happened and he turned to face me, well ...

As we continued our run north, I became aware that we were

fast approaching a twenty-foot-wide, ten-foot-deep, semidry canal that ran at right angles to our exhausting footrace. It was more than likely empty except for six or eight inches of soupy dead-crawdad and dead-carp "juice" in the bottom. I knew I was fast running out of gas, and if I was to make my move it would have to be pretty damn soon or never. A man built like me just wasn't designed to run as hard as he could for thirty minutes across a wet rice field, wearing hip boots, chasing a guy half his size in tennis shoes who was running like the wind.

I figured this chap was going to hesitate a second when he hit the canal levee in an attempt to quickly survey the scene before he decided which way to go. At that moment I would make my last sprint and try to close the last few yards separating us. As if on cue, I could see the berm fast coming up in the soft moonlight. I could also see the head of my chap swiveling rapidly as he approached it, looking for the fastest way through this new obstacle. Not finding any, he ran straight to the edge of the canal, hoping to his answer when he got there. He hit the berm, and sure as hell he hesitated for just a split second before making his jump into nothingness and what awaited him at the bottom. I lunged forward with my last bit of energy. Hearing me coming and not having quite made up his mind about the impending drop into the black canal, he started to turn to meet my charge. That was his second major mistake of the evening. I put a right-shoulder tackle on him that would have made my coach proud had he been there. *Oooffph* was my runner's comment at the unexpected contact as my right shoulder dug into the center of his back with a crunch and my arms clasped around him in a picture-perfect flying tackle. In the driving impact of the collision, we both sailed over the bank and into the blackness, hitting the slop and slime at the bottom of the canal a microsecond later with a loud *ploosh*. Brother, rotten carp and crawdads, old tires, and many other things that smelled in the night were our company in the bottom of the ditch. Face first my lad went into nature's concoction, with my weight on top to make sure he got to the very bottom of this essence. Quickly rolling off him and lurching to my feet in the slime, I reached down and grabbed his still half-buried, wriggling carcass by the back of the shirt collar. With the iron-hard grip of a blacksmith, I forcefully lifted him right up out of the slop, turning him until I could look right into his muddy, blowing and gagging, swamp-water-covered face.

As soon as he got his breath, instead of surrendering or anything, he wiped the slop off his face, proudly looked me right in the eye, stuck a very muddy Model 11 Remington shotgun with a homemade magazine extender up where I could see it, and said, "Terry, ain't she a beaut?" From the sound of the voice, I recognized the fellow I'd been chasing as none other than my old friend Albert Toscanni from Princeton, California, a man who was seventy-four years old. Damn his miserable, moth-eaten hide for making me run so damn far to catch him, I thought.

I said, "Al, you know better than this."

"I know, but I am getting so old, I had to kind of try her to see if I still had it in me," he said. "Plus I wanted to show those damn kids of mine I was still the man I used to be." Forgetting the trouble he was in and the carp juice in which we were standing, he again looked at his muddy shotgun in the moonlight and exclaimed, "Jesus, ain't she a beaut?"

I said, "Well, yeah, it is," and it was, the way he had built the extender and fixed it to beautifully fit his shotgun, not to mention its earlier performance blowing up the ducks. Anyway, enough of the pleasantries; I still had a job to do and started by taking his shotgun as evidence.

He said, "I suppose you have to take her, eh? That was a gift to me many years ago from my grandfather, who used it dragging ducks until he could afford a Model 12 Winchester. I must've had that gun since 1913 or '14."

"Al, you don't really give me any other option; you know seizure of the evidence goes with the turf. Friendship aside, I have a job to do, and that now includes picking up all the dead and dying ducks we can find that you just blew up on the backside of Link Dennis's property."

"I guess you have to do what you have to do," he said, "but I sure as hell hate to lose that shotgun; it is a piece of my family's history." There was a long pause in our conversation as we navigated around several pools of standing water in the canal, and then Al said, "You aren't going to tell anyone about this, are you? My sons will be really pissed if they find out I was out here, not to mention the ribbing I will take from the rest of the clan."

Knowing the shame anyone in that area felt about being apprehended by the "duck cops" for dragging ducks, I said, "Not unless you do. I plan on filing late-shooting, unplugged-gun, and over-limit charges on you, and for the most part, unless there is name recognition, most everyone won't know up from down on this matter."

He seemed satisfied with that response, knowing my word was good, and we crawled up out of the canal and walked the rest of the way back to the place of the shooting mostly in silence. I was silenced by the fact that I was saddened to catch an old friend, in fact, one of the first I had met when I arrived in the valley in 1967. He was saddened because he knew that at his age he had reached the end of an era: his.

We finally made it back to the spot where he had blown up the flock of happily feeding ducks. We spent the rest of the pale dark and part of the morning quietly picking up the dead, dying, and mostly crippled ducks. Once we had that done, I left Al with the ducks, walked out to where I had hidden my pickup, and brought it closer so we wouldn't have to carry the ducks any farther than we had to.

The ducks, only sixty-three of them, were loaded into my truck, and Al and I headed back to my house for a friendly breakfast. I was surprised that he hadn't killed more than sixty-three with the thirteen-shot extender on the shotgun. Other old-timers had told me it was not unusual to kill up as many as three hundred with that kind of extender in the old days. Then it dawned on me. Al had been very quiet since he got into my truck for the ride back to my house. Maybe he too was thinking about killing only sixty-three ducks with his new thirteen-shot extender. His silence made me believe he really felt out of it now if that was all he could kill with a storybook drag. My sorrow for that old man and the history he represented deepened even further.

Donna had already gone to work, so I fixed the two of us a hearty breakfast and tried to cheer him up. Even with the good food and several slices of her great homemade bread, I could see that something was really eating at Al, and cheer was not on his menu that morning no matter how hard I tried to make light of his bad situation. After we had eaten, I issued the usual citations for late shooting, over-limit, and unplugged shotgun (he had his hunting license and federal duck stamp). Hoping to lighten his mood a bit, I returned his shotgun but kept his homemade extender. There was no need for me to keep the gun as evidence because I knew where he lived and, after taking a picture of it, knew that would suffice in a court of law. Besides, given his violations, he probably wouldn't have to forfeit the weapon, so why keep it? It had belonged to his grandfather, who had been a big duck dragger, and I knew it meant a lot to Al.

I could tell Al was pleased by the return of the muddy shotgun, but something was still eating at his insides. Not feeling comfortable, even with our friendship, at trying to help him through his concerns, I finally let it alone and took Al back to his hidden vehicle on Newhall Farms property. With a wave, he loaded up and left for his home in the Princeton area. I made a mental note of his vehicle's hiding place in case I might be able to use it myself at a later date and then left to take a shower and rid myself of a rather pungent smell.

Al never appeared in court, just paid his $1,500 fine and settled up with the legal world as far as the two of us were concerned. The part I still carry in my heart today happened several days later. I was working around the Lurline Road area checking duck hunters when the Colusa County sheriff's office called me on the radio and asked if I could be at my house in fifteen minutes to meet someone. I said yes and headed the old Dodge for home. When I arrived I discovered Al quietly sitting in his Chevy one-ton truck waiting for me. Swinging into my driveway, I got out of my truck and was met by Al with his shotgun. My hand went slowly and instinctively to my pistol side in a manner not readily discernible and I said cautiously, "Good morning, Al." I was suddenly rethinking the gesture I had made in returning his shotgun and hoping we had been friends long enough for him not to do something rash or foolish.

He walked over to me, and it was obvious that he had been crying. He said, "Here," and handed me his Remington shotgun with an all-too-clear resignation of spirit.

I said, "What the hell are you doing?"

He said, "It's yours," his eyes downcast and never looking at me.

"What do you mean it's mine?"

He said, "When a man lets another man catch him breaking the law, that's bad. But what is even worse is when you let a game warden who is four times your size run you down and catch you from behind. That is terrible. I can't hunt anymore knowing that. Besides, the gun belongs in your hands instead of mine because you finally stopped the killing that has been going on all these years by me."

"Al, that is ridiculous hogwash," I said. "Here, take it back."

"Nope; keep the gun. It's yours; you caught me fair and square," he said. "I found out the other night I am no longer the man I thought I was. I'm a worn-out old man not worth anything to nobody. If my kids knew of our little meeting, I would be relegated to sitting on the porch. You know the history of my family; we didn't give in to nobody. Even when some of the clan went to jail in the early days, we still held our heads high and killed the duck. I can't do that any longer, so I have to stop before I make a fool out of not only myself but those of my family. I am done, Terry. I am done!" I could hardly look into those tear-filled eyes and just turned away.

Needless to say, I didn't keep the gun. I made him take it back but said, "I will keep the extender I seized the other night for a wildlife museum somewhere down the line if that is all right with you." He agreed, shook my hand, and slowly turned and walked back to his pickup. I could plainly see he was just crushed, and even I was starting to feel bad about the situation.

As he started to drive away with tears running down his face he said, "My duck dragging days are over. No longer can I enjoy what I used to do as a boy. My days are over. In fact, I think the days of the duck are over as well. They just aren't around like they used to be, and I think I might have been part of the problem." With that, he drove away down the lane. I never told anyone about that night's episode until this story, and to my knowledge no one ever found out either. He was a good old man to me and didn't deserve having his name dragged through the mud. I think the mud he got in the ditch that night was enough. ...

I left Colusa for another duty station in Bismarck, North Dakota, in 1974. I was later saddened to learn that Al had died in 1975 after a long bout with lung cancer. He never did hunt again. He hung his shotgun up, and that was that. It was kind of sad because he was a piece of Americana, as were the ducks he shot. Looking back on the situation today, I can see why he cried. I cry inside now knowing that the birds are forever gone, as well as Al and that time in market hunting history that he represented. I know the practice of dragging ducks was not good, but not all history is. However, it was part of the way people lived in that area, and in a lot of people's eyes a very large and important part. Farms and ranches were held together during the Depression by the sale of the ducks, families were fed during hard times, and the valley communities benefited economically during the market hunting era. But, like the bison, passenger pigeon, and market hunter of old, things disappear and times change. I wonder who or what is next?

I know one thing: I will carry to my grave that look Al gave me the day he tried to give me his family shotgun. He was letting go of not only the shotgun but something even more important. With the fall into that stinking ditch so long ago came the realization that life as he knew it was at an end, and the real end came shortly thereafter. You know, even with lung cancer he damn near outran me.

14
The Fence

IN THE FALL OF 1972, during the height of waterfowl season in the Sacramento Valley, I ventured forth one morning into one of the valley's typical howlin' mad winter rain- and windstorms. As I stepped from my garage into the elements about three in the morning, I noticed in the illumination of my house lights that the wind was so strong, the rain was flying horizontal to the ground. Standing on the lee side of my truck, I found my legs getting wet from the calves down while the rest of my body remained dry. Putting my Labrador retriever Shadow into the cab on the passenger side, I took a few moments to enjoy the wrath of the elements. The few stinging drops that reached my face told me today would be one of those wet ones no matter what I wore. And it also told me the hunting for my fellow man would be good as well.

Now, in a storm of that magnitude the ducks and geese have to walk to get around and the chickens with square faces just stay home. Bear in mind that to fly at forty miles per hour in such elements with your eyes open and the rain stinging the eyeballs is difficult at best. To avoid that kind of discomfort the waterfowl will try to set down just as quickly as they can, and many times that will be their last waking moment on this planet if the lads shooting at them from below have their way. It had rained hard all night and was now starting to slack off, but the wind was still screaming and the low, dark clouds were scudding back and forth under the start of a full moon as if they were jet-engine driven. There was still the promise of more moisture to come, so I threw in an extra change of dry clothes just in case. With weather like this, one carrying a badge had to be out and about in order to keep the peace. This kind of day meant water-fowling at its best, and you could bet a month's paycheck that every lad who could escape from work that day would be out in the fields and duck clubs attempting to take advantage of the good hunting the lousy weather provided. The problem that ran along with such weather was the temptation to take more than the law of the land allowed for one day's bag limit.

This was the first such storm of the season and up to now the lads had done only so-so in the duck-killing department. Blue-sky days in the Sacramento Valley usually didn't produce heavy duck kills except on some deep-water duck clubs or for the night shooters, or draggers, so when weather of this type came along, it brought many lads out from under their rocks and into full daylight. When hunters of this type emerged, their urge to kill was seldom guided by the state and federal conservation laws or good sportsmanship. It seemed that the prevailing atti-tude for these folks was, "I've killed hardly any ducks this sea-son because of the unusually good weather, so let's make up for that today." That attitude applied to many of the wealthy duck club members as well. They had paid a pretty penny to hunt on these clubs, and my experience had shown that many figured this type of day was the time for payback. This was why bad weather brought with it gross over-limits, double trips (killing one limit, taking it home, and then coming out for more as if you were making your first trip), and late shooting (shooting after legal shooting time—sunset for migratory waterfowl).

The *real* late-shooting occurrences in the Sacramento Valley in those days, however, were those based on unusual light condi-tions caused by the area's many well-lit farming communities during stormy weather patterns. The low clouds reflected the lights of the many valley towns and created an atmosphere that stayed light longer than normal, allowing the late shooters to carry on their trade long past legal shooting hours, with deadly effect on the low-flying waterfowl. In this reflected light it was possible to see the ducks well enough to shoot sometimes as long as six hours after sunset, even longer if one was shooting over a pond or other water that reflected the light back into the heavens. During my valley career I made probably fifty or sixty late-shooting cases in which I apprehended shooters up to eleven P.M., or six-and-a-half hours after legal shooting time had ended! Many late shooters felt safer in dark, windy conditions, thinking it would be more difficult for the wardens to locate and apprehend them, which was true to a degree. I am sure many of them also thought that in such weather the wardens would stay home in front of the fire and television. That may have been true in some cases as well, but many of us carrying the responsibility of the silver or gold are hunters of humans, and we have no seasons or bag limits! We have a tendency to go where the getting is good, and if that means a wet field under less-than-ideal weather conditions, then so be it. ... Enough musing, I thought as I started up the patrol truck and drove off into the rainy, windy black of the morning like a large land crab with a single purpose in mind.

Daylight found Shadow and me sitting west of Delevan National Wildlife Refuge in anticipation of the ducks lifting off and flying to the area west of Interstate 5 and into the recently harvested rice fields. They were not long in coming, and neither was a group of hunters out of the small town of Williams just to the south, whom I recognized because I had pinched them two weeks before for early-shooting waterfowl—that is, shooting more than half an hour before sunrise. Hidden in a small copse of trees under my camouflage parachute, I was pleased to see the lads park their truck in a grove of cottonwoods alongside a machine shed, get out, and immediately begin looking all around through several pairs of binoculars. One of the lads, just to make sure he hadn't missed anything, stood up in the back of the pickup to get an even better view. Anytime anyone looked around with binoculars immediately after getting out of the vehicle, it meant they were seriously looking for ducks, maybe even a game warden, or both. Either way my smile betrayed the possibility of a better moment to come if the ducks cooperated and these lads were able to do what was on their minds.

I didn't have long to wait as the birds began to trickle into the area. Soon the air in the rice fields before me began to fill with small groups of mallards, pintail, and wigeon looking for a good feeding spot for breakfast. They soon picked a rice field not one hundred yards from my place of concealment and began to land as if every one of them had a problem with the big guts eating the little guts because they were so hungry. My three fellows from Williams, seeing the start of a funnel cloud of ducks roaring into the rice field, began to put on their hunting gear, loaded their shotguns, and walked toward the now feeding and flying ducks. I watched them until they began to crawl to avoid detection by the now rapidly growing flock of ducks and soon disappeared from sight in the tall grasses on the rice checks. With that, I woke up Shadow, and we got out of the patrol truck and began to sneak down a rice check that would put us directly behind my Williams shooters if they got close enough to shoot the now rapidly growing flock of feeding ducks.

Twenty minutes later the dog and yours truly were almost directly across from and behind the hunters, hidden from view by the rice check. As luck would have it, the rain began to fall in sheets, and I could tell the fellows had not really dressed for the occasion. Through my binoculars I could see that they were really miserable and getting damper by the moment. In addition, the ducks were starting to feed away from them. I figured that if they shot at all, it would be soon because of their discomfort and the fact that the ducks would soon move out of shotgun range. Then it happened. All three of the lads, as if on cue, disassembled their Browning AL-5 shotguns, removed the plugs from the magazines, and reaffixed their magazine caps. Keep in mind that when hunting migratory game birds, state and federal laws prohibit the use of shotguns capable of holding more than three shells. By removing the plugs, the lads had increased the shell capacity of their shotguns from three to five. It wasn't a violation yet, but if they used those guns on the ducks, they were going to have a problem with the lad and his dog watching them from behind.

Sure as God made little green apples, all three stood up in unison from their hiding place on the rice check and discharged their shotguns into the mass of feeding ducks, creating one hell of a "hoorah." Fortunately for them and the ducks, the range was a bit far and not much damage was done ... yet. The three men put their shotguns down on their rice check and bailed over the top to pick up their dead, dying, and crippled booty. With that, Shadow and I sailed over our own rice check, raced the thirty or so yards to their rice check as the culprits were chasing their ducks down in the other direction, and hid behind it right next to the three shotguns. Peering over the top of the rice check, I could see the lads scrambling around in the rice field grabbing every flopping duck they could. I could also see that their ground sluice of the feeding ducks, because of the extreme shooting range, had not been really successful. Not that they hadn't killed a pile of ducks, but they hadn't taken the great numbers they could have if the ducks had cooperated by feeding closer.

I just lay there watching as the shooters ran down every duck in sight, gathered them up, and excitedly headed back to their hiding place. The first lad tossed his two handfuls of ducks over the rice check and jumped over it as well to hide. Unfortunately, his ducks landed on my unsuspecting dog, who immediately jumped up and grabbed the first duck within reach. Sailing over the rice check just behind his ducks, the lad almost landed on Shadow and let out a surprised, *"Hey!"* He wasn't half as surprised as his two buddies right behind him, who jumped over the rice check and landed on either side of me.

"Holy crap, what are you doing here?" yelled Gordon.

"Oh no," wailed Danny, his partner, once he also got a look at the rather large smiling lump lying by the shotguns behind the rice check.

"Morning, boys," I said as I stood up to get better control of the situation. "Licenses, duck stamps, and shotguns, please."

The lads, still in shock, sat there in the downpour as if someone had hit them with a baseball bat. Then Gordon said, "Where did you come from?"

"Been here all night," I stated calmly. Sometimes a little white lie goes a long way in keeping the dark side of the hunting community off their feed and in line. If these lads went back and told all their buddies that the crazy damn game warden had lain out all night in a driving rainstorm to protect the ducks, well, that might just make me a few feet taller in the eyes of some of the locals. It might also telegraph to them that only a crazy would go to those extremes, and either way it would have a telling effect on some of the illegal activity. I could tell from the look on their faces that they were in abject shock. To have pulled off such a clean sneak on the ducks and made their shot, only to find the local game management agent smack-dab in their midst, was just too much.

I repeated my request for the licenses and other materials, and this time the lads produced them. I knew they would be properly licensed, having checked them just weeks before, but the shotguns would be another issue, as would the recently killed ducks now scattered up and down the rice check. Taking my time, I slowly checked the unplugged shotguns for effect. Of course, finding them unplugged, I had to comment to that effect for each lad's benefit. They were not only glum but quiet as well. Then we counted the ducks they had ground-sluiced, and lo and behold, they had exactly a legal limit each! Not that they could keep the ducks, mind you, because they had taken them by an illegal means, but they didn't know that yet. There were smiles of relief all around until I called Shadow to my side and invited the lads to follow me into the field that moments before had held several thousand happily feeding ducks. There wasn't a duck lying in the harvested rice field, nor did I expect to see one. The boys had seen to that in their race to gather up the ducks in the direct field of fire. But the adjacent weed-covered rice checks were another matter. In just a few moments Shadow had retrieved six fresh cripples and was still working up and down the remaining rice checks. In about fifteen minutes she had retrieved another dozen cripples, putting each lad exactly six over the limit.

When one shoots ducks in this fashion, there will always be lots of cripples because when the shooting starts the ducks attempt to flee in the direction away from the shooting. This puts their bony backs toward the flying shot, and many times the hits are not instantly fatal. Many times those so crippled will quickly crawl off into the weeds and hide. It was those birds my dog was now finding, but the boys all protested that the cripples Shadow was picking up were not theirs. They figured someone else had shot the field earlier, and those birds must belong to those mysterious other shooters.

I looked long and hard at the boys and said, "Do you fellows really believe that?"

They all lowered their heads, and finally David said, "No." Hearing no other comments from Danny and Gordon, I told them it appeared that they were going to get citations not only for the unplugged shotguns but for over-limits as well.

"Any problem with that, gentlemen?" I asked.

"No," came the collective halting reply. "Are you going to tell our dads?" Gordon asked.

"No," I said, "Every one of you lads is over eighteen, and what you tell your fathers is your business. However, it always seems that things like this get out, and if I was any one of you lads' father and you hadn't told me about this matter, I might be a bit disappointed in my son." I let that thought sink in and commenced to write out the information on a pink-slip field report form. I then had the lads replug their shotguns and, after seizing their ducks because they were over the limit and had taken them with unplugged shotguns, gave them evidence receipts for the ducks. With that, I sent them on their way after explaining the judicial process so they knew what to expect (not that they hadn't gone through this exact same process several weeks earlier for their early-shooting episode). As it turned out, all of them forfeited bail and did not appear to contest the charges. So I not only made a total of $600 for the government that morning ($50 for an unplugged shotgun and $25 for each duck over the limit) but probably was responsible for a few lessons not only in good sportsmanship but in being careful what they did in the future in my enforcement district.

When the lads had returned to their vehicle and disappeared out of sight, I filled up the game bag in my hunting jacket and, carrying the rest of my evidence on my duck strap (a leather strap designed to carry ducks and geese while thrown over one's shoulder), returned to my hiding place. Once there I gutted all the birds so they could be donated in good shape, and as I did, Shadow happily ate all the still warm guts! Since she hadn't eaten her breakfast earlier in the morning in the excitement of going somewhere with the boss, I didn't begrudge her the snack, questionable though it was. However, I would regret that generosity later for what she did in the closed confines of the truck!

Late afternoon found me standing beside my patrol truck at the edge of a Newhall Farms harvested rice field. I wasn't wearing a hat, and, though I was wet and cold, the rain and wind felt good on my tired face and neck. The air was heavy with the typical scent of moisture, dead crawdads, wet earth, and recently burned rice stubble. Thanking the good Lord for my senses and the day's blessings, I slowly let my eyes sweep the adjacent rice fields, looking for anything out of place in and among the swirling, feeding hordes of ducks not more than forty yards from where I stood. Delevan National Wildlife Refuge was behind me, and a quick glance in that direction confirmed that a tornado of ducks was still funneling off the refuge and climbing vertically to about five hundred feet into the air (out of shotgun range as they crossed over the road) before heading off in long skeins and jumbled yet determined bunches into the rice fields to feed. As far as I could see through the stinging, wind-driven raindrops, I had ducks moving out toward every quadrant of the compass. There seemed to be an urgency about their actions, almost as if they sensed that more storm was to come and the wise thing to do was get a full crop now and avoid the bad weather later. Whatever the reason, I had ducks in numbers like the days of old, when humankind was still in a primitive state and life was easier for the winged ones.

Hunching my shoulders even deeper into my camouflage hunting coat against the moisture-laden chill, I thought that with the weather as it was and the current activity of the birds, this would be one of those unique nights that presented excellent conditions for late-shooting waterfowl or dragging the ducks. Once night fell the low clouds would reflect the lights of the many nearby towns into the fields, artificially illuminating them with an almost iridescent glow. My mind rambled back to times when, with the same kind of weather conditions, I had apprehended lawbreakers wing-shooting ducks just south of Willows up to six hours past legal shooting hours! I guess they felt that since the ducks flew all night in their peregrinations, they could shoot all night as well. Their only problems were the laws prohibiting night shooting and a rather large chap prowling the fields along with the ducks, riding shotgun, so to speak. Tonight the wind would diffuse any sounds of the illegal shooting, making my job even more difficult than usual.

With those thoughts in mind, I determined that I would work the late-shooting violators and then slip into the harvested rice fields to work the really big boys, the local duck draggers or their commercial-market hunting counterparts. A grim look flitted across my face as I thought of the work and long, wet night ahead of me. Then, as if sent from on high, the sweet, fluting call of a flock of pintail passing close overhead lightened that load considerably and changed my expression to a smile of appreciation. It was almost as if the ducks had called to me to let me know they would be out for a while feeding and hoped I would find some way to protect them. Damn, I thought, Mother Nature is a hard boss to work for. With that, I slid into my patrol truck and, with both windows down so I could hear better, waited for whatever tonight's adventure was to bring. Hearing nothing out of the ordinary in my immediate vicinity for the next twenty minutes, I decided to leave that spot in favor of a roaming patrol. I cranked up my pickup, and we headed, slipping and sliding, out of the muddy rice field and up onto the gravel of Four Mile Road.

As I drove north on Four Mile Road not more than two hundred yards from my rice field, I spotted two hunters walking along a levee road about sixty yards to the northwest. All at once they paused, raised their shotguns, and shot at a bird rising from an adjacent grassy ditch that just didn't look like a duck with the quick look I had gotten. Quickly parking my truck alongside the road near a broken-down piece of farm machinery so I would look like a farmer fixing the machine, I got out my binoculars for a better look. I had no sooner stopped to look at my chaps than I chanced to hear several shots farther to the north. Locking those in my memory bank with the knowledge that legal shooting time was now over, I continued to watch the two chaps I now suspected of shooting a pheasant during the closed season. One of these lads walked over to where the bird had fallen and, after a careful look all around, stooped over and picked up a dead hen pheasant from the grass. He quickly pulled out the long tail-feathers and then stuffed the carcass down into the front of his chest-high waders. Then the two of them turned and continued walking toward the Four Mile Road, probably heading for their parked car, as if nothing out of the ordinary had occurred. My hunch had been right, and just as they reached their car I started to drive down to where they were standing beside their vehicle.

The hunters were busy getting out of their wet coats and unloading their shotguns, so they didn't pay a whole lot of attention to me as I drove up in an unmarked truck. That changed, though, once I stepped out of the truck, flashed my badge, and requested their cooperation in checking their hunting licenses, duck stamps, and shotguns. I could tell they were trying to be normal but guarded in their actions, and as usual I was relishing the forthcoming moment in regard to the bird of suspected pheasant lineage. Once finished with my checking chores, I asked the lads if they had any game, and they answered they had shot at a few ducks but hadn't gotten anything. I told them to go ahead and finish getting out of their wet gear; I was going to stand there for a moment and listen for any other shooting going on around me.

The two men gave each other a funny kind of look and then, realizing that they were trapped, began to get out of their waders as if everything was all right. Watching out of the corner of my eye so as not to be too obvious, I saw them sit down on the tailgate of their pickup and slide down their chest-high waders. They both did this carefully, making sure they didn't roll their waders down over their legs, as is normally done, but just slid them straight down and then wriggled their feet out of the boot portion. They were clearly hoping that any illegal game hidden in the waders would stay undetected.

After they had gotten out of their chest-highs and put on some dry shoes, I turned and said, "Why don't you lads just hand me the pheasants." It was as if I had struck them with a large stick. They just stood there for a moment and looked at me as if I was a ghost. I figured that if both had shot at the one pheasant, the chances were good that they had been hunting for some time before I had seen them kill that bird. I figured they both might have birds, so I might as well go for the whole basket of eggs and see if I broke any in the process. I continued, "Lads, pheasants don't like to fly in the wet weather, but when they do they usually flush very close and are so damn wet they are an easy, slow-flying, tempting target." Still no movement or words from the lads, but their eyes and body language told it all. By now there should have been a spate of denials under normal circumstances, but these men were novices and had let some sort of critter apparently eat their tongues.

Figuring I had them cold, I gave them the second barrel. "I watched you lads shoot and hide the birds, and it is now time to give them up and face the music," I said and matched those words with a level, all-knowing gaze. Of course, I hadn't seen them shoot and hide any birds but the one, but they both had a few wet pheasant feathers on their shirts and pants that they hadn't noticed. Since I had, I figured I would make a run at them and see where it led.

Finally, the short, dumpy lad squeaked out, "We didn't kill any pheasants." He was so funny I almost laughed. This man looked just like a cat that had eaten the canary and still had feathers on his lips, only in this instance, it was hen pheasant feathers.

"Gentlemen," I said in an almost fatherly voice, "dig them out of the chest-high waders, please." These lads were so terrified it may have been the very first time they had done anything illegal. As if hit simultaneously with a cattle prod, both of them grabbed their waders and tipped them upside down, shaking them vigorously. Damn, out tumbled four hens and two rooster pheasants, all illegal because of the closed season.

The rest was pretty mechanical, and moments after issuing them state citations for their violations I again heard the *thump-thump* of a shotgun about two miles north. This was not uncommon. I was in the heart of some of the finest waterfowl hunting country in the world, and the urge to continue shooting after legal hours, when the skies were filled with low-flying ducks and geese looking for a place to feed, was just too much of a temptation, especially if the shooting had been poor until that moment. Seizing the pheasants and placing evidence tags on them, I thanked the lads for their cooperation and trotted back to my waiting dog and patrol vehicle.

Opening the door, I paused to see if the shooting to the north was going to continue and if not to make up my mind where I should go next. I was not disappointed. The shooting that had my gut instinct running in high gear continued with three more shots in rapid succession. The shooting was in the same general location as earlier and was still only one gun that appeared to be stationary. Instinct told me that this lad was settling in for the duration, which was bad for the ducks and geese but good for a hunter of humans like me.

Cranking up my rig and driving north on Four Mile, I stopped every few minutes to listen and echo-locate the next set of shots. I would fix a landmark in the direction where the shots appeared to be coming from, then proceed in that direction posthaste, stopping after half a mile or so to repeat the procedure. This was always a sure-fire method of working in on a chap late-shooting waterfowl. Also, it gave me the opportunity to grab others near the spots where I stopped to listen to the late shooter if I happened to hear anyone else doing the same thing.

About a half mile north and just east of the Sacramento National Wildlife Refuge, I located my shooter. It was one hour past legal shooting time as I quietly moved my vehicle, which I was running without lights, into a hiding spot south of a big dairy farm just north of the Colusa County line, which meant I was moving into Glenn County not far from Lambertville, a large duck club housing complex. Stepping out of my rig, I heard three more shots just north of me, near the east boundary of the national wildlife refuge, maybe three or four hundred yards away. I could see the snow geese pouring off the refuge by the tens of thousands, heading out to feed in the rice fields. As they passed over a big grassy pasture adjacent to the refuge, the sound of shots again rang out. Those last shots were all I needed for a final location on my shooter.

Telling Shadow to stay in the truck, I took off at a fast trot, heading for those big pastures with my pistol and binoculars banging on my hip and chest, all the while trying to be careful where I placed my feet so as not to twist an ankle. It was a fairly long run, but the continuing shots at the low-flying snow geese gave me the energy to keep going at a pretty good clip. Swinging into the pasture, I crawled over a fence and paused inside the enclosure to get my breath and let my heart settle down for the chase that would inevitably follow if I successfully closed with my late shooter. I took off my heavy coat in order to be able to run faster, quickly checked the chambers of the .44 magnum revolver hanging on my hip, and reholstered the weapon, making sure the hammer snap on the holster was secure. I didn't want to get into a foot chase or fight and have the weapon come out of the holster, so a few last-minute checks were in order. It wasn't as if I didn't know the weapon was loaded, but the first order of law enforcement business is to come home every night, and I damn well didn't want to violate that rule because my weapon came out of the holster and the bad guy got hold of it. Hence the extra caution every time I went into the unknown, especially in the dark against another human being who was armed, as this shooter was.

Using my binoculars, I found that I was still a fair distance away from my shooter, who was still firing at the geese. Every time he shot at the low-flying birds, I could see the flashes from the end of his shotgun barrel as it pointed skyward. I could also see the snow geese rise up over him, stop calling for a second or two, and then continue on calling as if nothing had happened. I started walking cautiously toward the constant shooting, under a living sheet of snow geese passing overhead, providing me with top cover by the constant din of their excited calls. I could not believe that the shooter had not let up on the geese and continued to pound them almost constantly as they flew out of the refuge. Damn, I thought, usually late shooters in circumstances like these would shoot once or twice and then let off and look around to see if they had been discovered. Not this lad; he was killing for all he was worth. As I got closer, I could hear him working the action of his pump shotgun when he shot at the geese and the characteristic *whump* as their inert bodies, broken by the lead shot, slammed to Mother Earth.

The snow geese continued to pour off the refuge by the tens of thousands, unfazed by the noise or flash of the shotgun below. There were so many in the air that the din of their calls and the excitement of flight, coupled with the expectation of a cropful of rice, made the explosions and the birds falling from the numerous formations when they passed over the shooter a nonevent in their goose world. There would be a lessening and quieting of their thousands of calls when a shot was heard, and then all would start up again as they passed overhead. However, it sure as hell wasn't a nonevent to one game management agent on the ground fast approaching the "apple of his eye." The shooter was totally unaware that he was being stalked with just as much determination as he was showing in his preying on the overflying flocks of geese. More geese, illuminating the black sky with their white bodies, fell to earth, completing their dance

with death as my stalk continued. The frequency of this spectacle of living white against the black sky and then nonmoving
white against the ground hurried me along. There was no doubt
about it, this guy could shoot and must have had in his mind that
he'd better get all he could before the Mexicans and Texans got
his share when the geese migrated south.

I quietly moved to within fifteen yards of my target, who was
facing in the opposite direction looking up at the hordes of flying snow geese. Then I knelt down in the wet pasture and scruti-
nized him. He was about six feet tall, stocky in build and weighing at least two hundred pounds (which meant he wouldn't be a
fast runner), and was shooting a 12-gauge pump shotgun. There
were dead snow geese scattered all around him on the ground,
and off to his left I could see a pile of twenty or more (the legal
limit was six in those days—if lawfully taken) that had been
killed earlier and nicely stacked for carrying home once the
geese quit flying for the evening.

I continued to sneak on all fours to within about ten yards of
this chap; then all of a sudden he sensed something was not
right. I guess he saw that the "pitcher's mound" right next to
him, which hadn't been there moments before, had moved.
Damn! I thought. I had hoped to get close enough to just reach
out and grab him and his shotgun all at the same time. That way
there wouldn't be a dangerous foot race in the dark or the
chance of someone getting shot. He turned and said, "Who's
there; who's there?" The second time he called out, I could tell
by the tone and tenor of his voice that he was seconds from
flight, so I stood up and started to run toward him. The lad froze
and said, "Who are you?"

Without slowing down, I mumbled, "Bob."

He said, "Who?"

That was a big mistake on his part, asking questions and all,
because it gave me three more steps on him. Suddenly he yelled,
"Game warden," whirled, and sprinted for the refuge. He was
only about forty yards from freedom. If he could make it into
the national wildlife refuge, there was a half-mile-long and -wide

stretch of the densest growth of tules I had ever seen. Once in there, I would lose him like a shot. He knew it, and I knew it, and that was all it took to lend wings to both our sets of feet. I dropped my binoculars and five-cell flashlight by the geese in order to free my hands and, running as fast as I could, called on every possible ounce of speed. We both were moving pretty damn fast. Even as large as I was, I could run pretty quickly in those days (in college, I could run one hundred yards in eleven seconds flat in a football uniform) and in fact was gaining on my quarry. I got on the tips of my toes, which allowed me to hit my fastest speed, and poured it on. I was reaching for this fellow's shoulder, which was just inches away, when all of a sudden I heard a loud, metallic *yorrrrch!*

The good old refuge people. When they strung a refuge fence, they strung it tight as an E flat piano wire, and this one was no exception. In the heat of the stalk and chase I had forgotten that the refuge boundary fence was so close to that part of the field and the lad I was chasing. Big error on both our parts, as the next few moments were to tell. That sound was my shooter, madly racing full out for his life and freedom toward the tule patch, smacking into the unyielding steel of the fence. Completely stunned by the impact, the shooter went limp as the momentum of hitting the fence at such a high rate of speed rebounded him backward. Now, that created a major problem because a three-hundred-pound game warden was bringing up the rear, just in the process of reaching for the shoulder of this lad, also moving forward at a *very* high rate of speed. Now, owing to his collision with the fence, the first lad was limply hurtling in the opposite direction at the same speed at which he had been moving forward moments before. Unfortunately, there was a "freight train" coming right up his hind end, with more than a slight head of steam built up. Needless to say, the field of mice, rats, shrews, and all the other little people in the immediate vicinity got to observe a physics lesson in heavier bodies and lighter bodies taking place right before their surprised eyes.

There was a tremendous *thud* that probably measured 5.6 on

the Richter Scale as approximately five hundred–plus pounds met at a high speed under less than pleasant circumstances. ... Then the heavier object, me, propelled the lighter object, him, back toward whence he came, namely, the piano-wire fence, only this time with a weight that was truly worthy of attention attached to his rear. The fence was up to the challenge and shredded the lad like a salami going through a meat slicer. *Yorrrrrrrrch* sounded the now loudly complaining fence. A little bit was good, but a whole lot more was severely testing the work of the fencing crew as the closest two steel fence posts bent almost to the ground under the force of the joint trainlike collision.

Fortunately, the shooter's body kept me from hitting the barbed wires and being injured. We hit that fence so hard and at such an angle that I slid under the bottom strand onto the refuge property and flew for another eight feet before coming to rest among twelve thousand years' worth of goose shit and tule roots. I hurriedly got to my feet and ran back to my prize, who was hanging on the fence as if a shrike had placed him there. Standing over the inert and groaning lad, I could see that there was no need to hustle at that point. My shooter was almost out like a light and firmly tangled up and bleeding badly in the barbed wire. Meanwhile, the hordes of snow geese continued to pour off the refuge, regardless of the drama being played out beneath them, and for their benefit, I might add. That's snow geese for you.

I dragged the man off the fence and then realized that his entire front was sticky with blood. He had been basically cut to ribbons, as were his clothes (including his Levi jeans) when he hit the fence. I'm sure the second impact put the finishing touches to the living fresco he now represented. I eventually brought him around, and after I identified myself and collected his shotgun, we slowly walked back to his previous position in the pasture where he had had so much fun late shooting waterfowl earlier in the evening. Every step the lad took was followed by a groan, and it was obvious that his interest in a goose dinner had dropped clear to the bottom of his life list. Picking up my binoculars and flashlight, which was still turned on when I dropped it, I finally got a good look at the other fellow. What a mess. He looked like a stuck hog. There were cuts and welts clear across his face and, all the way down to his shins. His clothes were in such tatters that they did little to soak up the bleeding from all the open wounds across his chest and rather large belly. He had a four-inch gash across his chin and a smaller one on his neck and was damned lucky in my opinion that he hadn't cut clear through his throat to his carotid. It was plain that Refuge Manager Ed Collins and his fencing crew had won the battle of the charge of the heavy brigade.

I could see that my shooter wouldn't die or need immediate medical attention, so I took the time to pick up all his empty shotgun shells for evidence. Picking up those shell casings, I could see that they represented a lesson in and of themselves. He had shot fifty-one times, all long after legal shooting hours. Between the two of us, we picked up forty-one dead snow geese and made several trips to my pickup before my friend ran out of gas and had to sit down because his wounds were starting to stiffen up. I left him in the care of my dog and went back into the field, picked up the last of the snow geese, and trudged back to my truck. As I loading the last geese, I thought, Damn, forty-one geese with fifty-one shots, and in the dead of night! Brother, I was glad I got to him before he killed everything that left that refuge en route to the rice fields that night.

It turned out that he was a local dairyman who had figured he would go out and kill enough geese to fill his freezer for the year. He was of German extraction and said he possessed several very good sausage recipes from his grandfather. His plan was to kill a ton of snow geese, grind them up, and make enough sausage to last him for a year. He had plans for the goose livers as well. Well, what he got was a faceful of fence and a hind end full of game management agent, neither of which were sausage-making materials. I finally loaded him into my truck and took him down to the hospital, where they patched him up with forty-six stitches. While there, I made good use of my time writing him state citations for late-shooting waterfowl, taking an over-limit of geese, use and aid of an unplugged shotgun, no federal duck stamp, and hunting without a license. His citation payload came to $960 dollars and the loss of his hunting rights for one year. Come to think of it, his doctor's bill ran pretty high as well.

I don't remember ever seeing that chap out hunting again the rest of the time I worked in the Sacramento Valley. I think he kept to the tending of his milk cows and left the late shooting to others fleeter of foot and with a better understanding of the terrain, not to mention Newton's third law of physics.

Today, when the wind gets to ripping through the heavens, it takes me back to the time when the man hit the refuge fence and came springing back at me to the ringing sound of E flat, which joined in with nature's call of the wild chorus of whistling wings and excited snow-goose claxons.

Ah, youth. It occurs only once in a lifetime and passes at about the same rate as two fast-moving bodies hitting a slow-moving fence.

15

The Parachute Flare

THE HEAVY RECOIL followed by the thundering report of the 30-06, 03A3 bolt-action rifle as I steadied the stock on the ground and the orangish-red trail of flame arching skyward told me my parachute flare was airborne. I watched the orange eye of the rifle flare arch upward into the inky black of night and waited for the flare portion of the device to go off, which would illuminate a rice field literally crawling with feeding ducks. The twenty thousand or so ducks feeding just yards away, upon hearing the report of the rifle, didn't wait around for the fireworks to follow but were lifting off from this and every surrounding harvested rice field just as fast as they could. The constant roar of thousands of fleeing wings did not drown out the resounding *boom* of the flare as it exploded into green brilliance high over the thousands of waterfowl, freezing them in the black of the night, tinged for a microsecond with a lime-green glow. For that instant the night was changed into day as the flare, dangling below its parachute, drifted slowly earthward, lighting all below for the world to see. And what a sight it was as the carpet of remaining frightened ducks rose in unison in the greenish light and scattered to all 360 degrees of the compass in an attempt to get away from the brilliantly shining object in the sky.

Satisfaction with this first use of my new toy and its ability to disperse feeding waterfowl, in the process making them very nervous and hard to approach by the errant local duck draggers or their commercial counterparts, turned to dismay as I saw two unmistakable human forms in the adjacent rice field, not more than one hundred yards away, running to get out of the flare's light. I hadn't even had an inkling those lads were in the neighborhood and by setting off my flare had pretty well ruined their night, not to mention my chances of catching them. Swearing under my breath, I quickly worked the rifle bolt, indexing another blank cartridge into the chamber, and attached another flare to the launching device at the end of the rifle barrel, using the aid of the dimming light from the first flare to help me complete my now frantic task. Since the lads were some distance away now, I lowered the trajectory of the rifle barrel a bit and let her go! Another explosive report and hard thumping recoil told me my second parachute flare was away. I was hoping it would go off close to the lads who were running across the rice fields as if the devil himself was chasing them, and I got my wish. By pure damn craphouse luck, the flare went off low above the ground and almost right over the fleeing figures. For a second after the flare ignited, because of its explosive brilliance, I lost all sight of the running duo. I chuckled with the realization that the flare had gone off not more than thirty or forty yards from the nearest lad, taking care of any residual night vision they might have had, not to mention a real hurt being put on two already tested pairs of shorts. I would bet those two chaps weren't chuckling about their current state of affairs! With the second explosion and the flare's brilliant ignition more or less right in their laps, I bet their sphincters slammed shut.

When the brilliance of the flare died down a bit, I could see that the lads were running in two different directions now at an even higher rate of speed, as if they had been shot from a cannon. Seeing the havoc I had caused my two hopeful night-feeding-duck shooters, mixed with the flying hordes of ducks going every which way but loose, scared crapless by the light of the flares, I lay back in the rice straw and laughed until tears came to my eyes. Moments like that just had to be thoroughly appreciated for their instant good, and I was enjoying this one for all it was worth. It is not often that one wearing the badge can catch his prey with their pants down, if you get my drift. Finally my laughter ended, as did the brilliance of the last flare, returning the night to its natural state of darkness, so I stood up to review what was left of my once quiet domain. Needless to say, the ducks were now more than alerted for a mile in every direction, and my two lads were likely still moving like the wind to escape the light of day recently created just above their hind ends (I imagined they thought for their benefit). I was sure the stories they would later tell of their supposed hairbreadth escape would make for a more than priceless moment.

Standing there silently in the valley's cold winter air, I waited until the darkness was once again punctuated by the sound of whistling wings overhead, telling me the world of waterfowl was starting to return to normal and that in a moment the feeding ducks would again rule the harvested rice fields. I could tell by their calls that the air was still full of confused ducks, but it would be only a matter of time before they would land in a place safer than the area they had just vacated. In addition, owing to the shock and disturbance they had just undergone, no one was going to sneak up on any of these goosey ducks for the rest of that night!

Gathering up my gear and taking one last quick look around the area, I started walking out to where I had hidden my pickup, all the while keeping a casual eye on the direction I had last seen the lads running. I was hoping, without much confidence, that I would see their headlights or taillights leaving, which might give me a clue as to what farm access road they had used and possibly shed some light on who the lads might be or where they were going. No such luck, however. The night remained black and clueless. I tiredly loaded my gear into my well-camouflaged truck, cranked it up, and headed for home and a few hours of much-needed sleep before my next visit to the cold rice fields of Colusa County and another evening with its hundreds of thousands of feeding ducks and geese. On the way home I again kicked myself for the lost opportunity in apprehending the night-shooting lads but also had to chuckle at their two speed gears, one after the first rocket went off and the second after the last rocket blew up just off their sterns.

The next evening found me in roughly the same area of the

county but in another rice field starting to fill with feeding mallards and pintail, waiting for the dark of night to fall and the fortune or misfortune it would bring. That evening I had gotten antsy during a wonderful dinner my bride had fixed her tired fellow, and a feeling that something needed looking after in the outback had drawn me earlier than usual to my home away from home, the rice fields. An early arrival always meant the risk of discovery by human predators eyeing the fields as well, but I figured I had slid in without being discovered and was pleased. Stepping out of my rig, I carefully covered it with my camouflage parachute and threw a couple of dead tree limbs on top of the whole mess to further add to the spirit of concealment. It looked good, so I took out my navy binoculars and began a patient 360 degree swing around the horizon. Other than a few farm vehicles messing around and skeins of ducks on the move, all seemed quiet.

Putting the binoculars down, I lit up one of my strong Parodi Italian cigars, lay back against a cottonwood tree, and enjoyed the quietness of my natural domain. The evening sky, with its mare's tail cloud formations, foretold a weather change, and as I patiently waited in my hiding place just northwest of the intersection of the Colusa-Maxwell highway and Two Mile Road, the air continued to fill with hungry waterfowl heading for their rice fields of dreams on every side of me. What a view they made for me to enjoy. There is something deeply moving in a quiet evening accented with a moisture-laden soft breeze predicting change and hundreds of thousands of God's winged creatures carrying out their dance with the fortunes of life. For untold eons this dance had taken place without change. Then in a short period of time, as far as time goes, modern humans made their appearance, and the dance hasn't been quite the same since. A degree of predictable deadliness had entered the scene with results that were acceptable only to those pulling the triggers and gathering cash upon sale of the ducks to the ever-hungry illegal commercial markets.

I truly felt my smallness that evening looking at all that magnificence on display in the world of waterfowl and realizing how little I could actually contribute toward its survival. The spectacle overhead brought home the fact that I was the only one working the entire county that evening, with literally hundreds of thousands of feeding waterfowl in numerous bunches scattered throughout the valley to protect. The previous evening's futile parachute-flare gesture brought back to me the odds I was truly facing. Yet here I was again, giving up my family and all the enjoyment it held, trying to save a torn piece of this fabric called national heritage for the American people, who for the most part didn't seem to know what the hell was going on in the trenches, or give a damn if they did. In these kinds of situations, to win was everything, to lose was all, especially when one lost what belonged to all the others. Sometimes that is all the driving force one in our profession needs. Plain and simply, there is honor in a fight if it is for one's children and their children. Damn history anyway; it never forgives, and humankind always forgets. These thoughts whirled around in my head as I speculated grimly about my odds and began quietly trudging across one of the endless rice fields in the now dark of the night in my quest to preclude another duck slaughter by my adversaries.

Darkness, aided by increasing cloud cover from the northwest, settled in like a velvet blanket, as did thousands of ducks quietly settling into the blackened, previously harvested and burned rice fields for hundreds of acres around me. Forty minutes later the now total cover of darkness and continual soft whirring of wings overhead were my cue to begin the evening's events. Gathering up my gear from my first resting place, out farther into the field walked one tired, lone U.S. game management agent on a mission—a warrior in a battle he knew could not be won but one that had to be fought regardless over many nights until the threat was gone for another year and the birds had migrated back to the arctic. A battle always fought on the adversary's ground but fought nevertheless.

Moving quietly yet quickly, using the cover afforded by a large watergrass-covered rice check, I alternately walked stooped over and crawled to within thirty yards of about twenty thousand swirling, feeding ducks. More birds were arriving all the time, having tuned in to the feeding activity below them as they passed overhead, and soon I was surrounded by ducks in every direction. The air overhead was full of sailing bodies looking for a better place to feed, while others on the ground happily discussed the day's events as they fed back and forth and felt that life was good. Starting to now spook up small bunches of feeding ducks, I decided I was close enough to the main feeding flock, and to avoid scaring them off as well I selected a nice grassy spot on the rice check and settled in for the duration.

Sitting there watching the darkened blur of events unfolding around me, I couldn't think of a better place to catch those killing ducks illegally than right smack-dab in the middle of the "marketplace," so to speak, and I was pleased with my position. Then my thoughts went back to the time at Gold Beach in Redwood State Park, Humboldt County, when I did the same thing in the dark of the night, only that time among a herd of Roosevelt elk that were being poached at night on a regular basis. When the poachers' bullets started flying that night the elk ran over me like a bunch of furry freight trains. When I awoke after being knocked out by an 850-pound elk, I no longer thought that placement of my carcass among the "decoys" was such a good idea. Then I recollected the time in the winter of 1967 when I sat guarding a bunch of ducks, and when three lads blew them up and I started to chase them for the error of their ways, I ended up with several loads of 12-gauge number 4 lead shot in my back. As those black thoughts crossed my mind, the soft whirring of my two guardian angels' wings (I have two because of my size) could be heard as if to dispel those negative memories. With that ethereal reminder, my youthful belief in my own immortality returned.

I had just laid my tired back against a rice check and started to really take in the sights and sounds under the cloudy sky when, as if on cue, the entire field of feeding ducks grew instantly silent. I instinctively froze, pulled my head down into my chest, anticipating shots from unseen night hunters flying over my head, and quickly searched with my eyes and ears for any clue to the ducks' behavior. In an instant thousands of wings explosively took to the air, the wind of their flight hitting my face several seconds later. Still expecting shooting at any moment, I crouched even lower alongside my rice check in the hope of avoiding any flying lead pellets that were sure to follow if this was going to be a shoot. However, I was still ready to move in any direction toward the sound of the guns and shooters if I got the opportunity.

The air was now filled with the roar of thousands of wings but not the roar of shotguns. What the hell, I wondered, was causing this panicky exodus? Hastily turning on my Starlight scope, I scanned the field that moments before had held thousands of happily feeding ducks. The eerie green-tinged view through the Starlight scope showed thousands of flying ducks rapidly vacating my field as well as the rice fields all around me. Damn, I knew I had not scared the birds even with my Robert Redford looks, so what the hell? I continued to scan the area around me until it grew quiet with the departure of all the ducks. Not a sound was to be heard except the faint rustling of the rice straw beneath my legs as I continually changed positions in my quest for anything that may have spooked the ducks.

Then, there it was! Off to the north I spotted the hurrying darkened figure of a moving vehicle. A pickup, possibly a light-colored Ford, was moving across the upper end of that field about a quarter of a mile away. It was moving pretty fast for rice field travel and appeared to be heading toward Interstate 5, Colusa County's north-south interstate. What dingbats! I marveled. If one was going to poach feeding ducks in the rice fields at night, one didn't use a pickup and drive it right out to where God and everybody could see it! Then the vehicle stopped near the intersection of several rice checks, and I saw two figures get out and commence throwing what appeared to be bundles of ducks into the bed of the truck. Closer examination with the Starlight confirmed in my mind that that was exactly what the lads were doing, pitching numerous bundles of ducks into their pickup. Many appeared to be pintail males from the vast amount of white that showed on their bellies as they were heaved skyward into the back of the truck. Damn, I thought! No one had shot the field that evening since I had been there, so what was this little operation all about? Then it dawned on me. They had to be loading ducks from a previous day's or night's shoot. They must have shot the birds, let them lie to make sure they weren't being watched or pursued, and then picked them up the very next opportunity. It was cold in December in the Sacramento Valley, and the birds could sit for a little while before they spoiled.

I was too far away to run them down, but that didn't stop me from making a determined move toward the lads, hoping I would get to them before they left the field. Taking one more long look and hoping that the way they were pitching ducks into the back of that pickup meant they might be there a while, I made ready for the run that was sure to come. Stripping down to my running gear and leaving all my heavy gear except the Starlight scope and flashlight on the rice check, I took off like a slow-moving flash. Moving slowly at first in order to limber up and not tear something, I picked up speed after the first hundred yards and then, as I began to get a feel for the terrain underfoot, upped my speed again. Realizing that to go straight at the lads would make for a longer run, I cut an angle toward them, aiming for a point I figured they would cross if they left in their vehicle and where, with a little luck, I might just be able to surprise them. With that interception (if it happened), I could shine my flashlight in their eyes and identify them if they were locals and chose not to stop (as was more than likely) or get the license plate number and visit the lads later.

It was a great plan, but it didn't happen. I wasn't a world-class runner going through those muddy rice fields with hip boots, and I fell hard twice as I stepped into unseen harvester tracks that were at least two feet deep. The furrow I made upon falling was even deeper than that! When I was about one hundred yards from my quarry, I heard a motor start up, and a quick, chest-heaving pause to look through the Starlight scope confirmed that fact. The vehicle was on the move again, and in the opposite direction from my position just south of them. Damn, I thought, instead of moving to one side or the other so I could intercept them, they were moving directly away from my tired old carcass. I could only stand there in frustration and watch them drive off into the night, eventually turning toward the interstate and disappearing into the darkness. In that frustration, I thought it was at times like this that I believed God had to be a poacher. My rapidly beating heart and burning lungs told me I was still very much alive, so I told myself not to push it with that "God-poacher" thing, and I didn't (I didn't want a blind, night-flying mallard smacking my head at forty-five miles per hour). Even I wasn't a total fool, although running around in a rice field all night by myself would certainly lend credibility to that thought.

Moving over to where their truck had been parked in the hope that I might find some clues to the identity of the lads, I came to another dead end. All that was left in the faint light of my flashlight streaming through my partially opened fingers were tire prints exactly like those of most farm rigs in the area, lots of duck feathers, and one bunch of eight drake pintail they had overlooked in their haste to load up and get the hell out of there. The bunch of ducks had been field dressed (entrails drawn), which further explained why they had been left in the field apparently overnight without the thought of spoilage. That gutting maneuver in the field was a little strange, I thought, as I had not run across that particular activity in the past, but nothing surprised me anymore in this line of work. I figured the lads were either cooler than all get-out or were new to the game and dumber than posts. The safest way to illegally take ducks for the market or home use was to kill quickly and get the hell out of the area with your ill-gotten gain or to let your buyers come and get the birds at a later time. It was not a good idea to take the time to gut them in the area in which you had just created a noisy "hoorah." With all the time it would take to dress all your kill, you were just creating an extra opportunity to get caught.

A little more checking around to examine the footprints in the area led me to discover about eighty pounds of duck guts tossed into a shallow ditch by where the lads had been parked. That quantity spelled out the fact that these lads had killed quite a few ducks. Very unusual, I again thought, to clean the ducks in the field and then leave them overnight. That is, unless the lads pulling the triggers lacked almost all fear of being apprehended. Maybe that was it, I thought. Maybe they weren't dumb as posts but dumb like foxes. That idea made me grind my teeth even more in frustration. To have that kind of coolness in *my* district, if that were what it was, told me I needed to pick it up another notch until I had someone's hind end in tow for the error of their duck-killing ways.

The field was starting to fill up again with swirling masses of hungry ducks, so I stopped worrying about my "beating," moved back to my original spot, dug in against my favorite rice check, and held my ground for the better part of the evening. Soon there were again thousands of ducks, having lost their fright, feeding all around me. Not as many as I had before the scare from the vehicle moving across the field, but a respectable bunch to sit on just the same, so I did. Off to the south about a mile away, I heard a ragged string of shots, which told me someone had just gotten into a mess of ducks in that area as they fed on the ground. Mentally marking the spot as best I could, I continued to sit on my feeders in the hope that if someone shot into them I would be close enough at hand to teach the shooters a lesson. No such luck, as my night in that spot passed uneventfully, but in other areas at some distance from me, the lads were active. That night I heard a total of what I thought must be three commercial shoots or large drags, none of which were even close to my field. In each case I heard fifteen or twenty rapid shots from multiple shotguns, then total silence. About three A.M. my ducks finished feeding and began to filter out of the field and head for home in numerous small bunches, home being one of the several national wildlife refuges that dotted the area to the north, south, and almost due east.

Lying back on the rice check in the dark, I had a quiet moment to plan my strategy for the coming night. Most of the shooting I heard that evening had come from the south, probably south of the highway connecting the Sacramento Valley towns of Colusa and Williams. Realizing that the lads doing the shooting might not be back that night, I decided that would nonetheless be the area of my attention after getting a little sleep. I knew the birds were there, and the local warden responsible for that area was not prone to spending his nights in the damp, cold rice fields with the ducks all that frequently. Knowing that and guessing the night hunters had learned the warden's less-than-stellar working habits long ago, I figured I would give the local Williams warden and his ducks an unexpected hand.

I began to realize how tired I was after coming down from my earlier adrenaline high, so I decided to call it quits. Gathering up my gear, I took one last quick look around to keep a handle on the weather, and off I went for what I hoped would be a warm bed and some well-earned rest. Tromping across the burned rice fields back to my truck, my only surprise was when a red fox with a duck in its mouth, hearing something large coming, suddenly emerged from a ditch at a high rate of speed and ran directly into my right leg. With a quick whirl on its hind legs, it was gone just as quickly as it had appeared. I only hope no one saw my own whirl when the fox, without warning, ran into me.

Arriving at my truck, I took another careful look around the fields with the Starlight scope and then removed and stored my parachute for another day. I began unloading my gear into the bed of the truck so that, relieved of that burden, I could take off my heavy clothing. When the metal gear of the cased Starlight scope hit the bottom of the truck bed, it made a soft *plop*, not the expected sound of metal hitting metal. What the hell? I thought as I turned on my flashlight and directed its beam into the truck bed to see what the dickens I had hit. There before me in two large piles were about a hundred pounds of fresh duck guts! I couldn't believe my tired eyes! Somehow the commercial-market hunters or draggers had spotted my hidden truck, or me hiding it, and after I left had driven over and poured several piles of fresh duck guts into it as a show of their prowess and contempt for the laws and me as an officer and individual. I could feel my jaw hardening and my determination to catch those bastards hardening to match. To challenge the lion in his den with a truckload of duck guts was stepping the battle up a notch, and I was just the chap to accept that challenge!

Quickly checking the area, I discovered a set of tire tracks that appeared to match the tracks of the truck I had seen earlier where the two men had loaded numerous bunches of cleaned pintail as I tried to head them off at the pass. The tracks had swung within feet of my hidden truck, and I could see several sets of footprints in the soft ground leading back and forth from their truck to mine. Both sets of footprints appeared to be size 10 or 11, and I kept that in mind because there were no other clues to go on. I cleaned the guts out of the bed of the truck with my hands and put them in an adjacent ditch full of water so the skunks, crawdads, and other critters could make some use of the "grits." With each double handful of guts that went into the ditch, my jaw got tighter and tighter until my teeth hurt. This quantity of duck entrails represented a lot of ducks, not to mention a tremendous loss to the gene pool from those birds in the next breeding season, I thought. There was only one way to square this sail, and unfortunately for the lads doing the placing of the guts, they had found just the lad to do the squaring—especially after this particular poke in the eye with a sharp stick.

Leaving my not-so-secret hiding place without the use of any lights, I headed for home. Once I pulled onto the Maxwell highway, I turned my lights on and tried to run my plans for tomorrow night through my mind. It was no good. I was still pissed and tired at the same time and just drifted toward home without being aware of much going on around me. When I turned into Princeton Lane, which led to my home, my headlights illuminated another smaller but still considerable pile of duck guts in the middle of the road. It was obvious that someone knew where the "law" lived and had placed the guts there for effect. Stopping there and just sitting looking at what was before me in the head-lights did nothing to alleviate the anger and frustration I had felt since my discovery of the gut piles in the back of my truck. I asked God to give me the extra strength and wisdom to do what needed doing and with that, leaving the guts as a reminder, went the few remaining yards to my home and turned in for some much-needed rest. Then, sitting there in my pickup, I found my jaw getting tight again over the last hour's events. Somehow it just didn't seem right for me to go to bed while the ducks were paying a rather high price for my sleep. That did it! I thought. To bed? No. I showered to wake up, changed my sweat-soaked shirts, socks, and pants, and took a long drink of cold, icy tea my wife always kept handy for me.

It was before Donna normally had to get up and go to her teaching job in Williams, but there she was when I stepped out of the shower. She had two frying pans going, one full of heavily spiced side pork and the other full of mashed potatoes from the dinner table the night before. I grinned, saying nothing about her going back to bed (it would have done no good) as I dried myself off and dressed for the day's events. In a few moments I sat down to fresh homemade bread, fried spuds cooked with onions, garlic, green pepper, and the like, and about a pound of crisp fried side pork. Man, that woman could not only cook but cook what was needed for me to last for the long haul. For one pounding out mile after mile in the marshes and muddy rice fields sixteen to eighteen hours per day, that kind of meal was just the ticket, pure fuel for a furnace that might not see another meal for the next fifteen hours because one didn't quit in the middle of any action to go get something to eat—at least I didn't. And neither did that little stinker I married! Donna poured me a quart of ice-cold milk and, sitting across the table from me, intently looked at me with those beautiful, deep blue eyes. I knew the look; it was none other than an examination of the man she loved to see if he was all right. Getting up from the table without saying a word, I walked over to her and gave her a great big bear hug and a kiss to put her concerns to rest. Then I returned to my breakfast with relish. Seeing that I was OK, she got up, gave me a kiss, and went back to bed. God doesn't make many women like that one, I thought as I discovered a large slice of homemade blueberry pie behind the huge plate of steaming side pork. Man, if I ate all this I wouldn't be able to move or catch any of the bad guys, even if they were only walking to get away from me. Nonetheless, there was nothing left at the breakfast table when I finished! Donna knew my limitations and knew food was not something that would slow me down.

Then back out I went to the southwest of Colusa just at daylight to watch the ducks returning from their fields of choice so I would know exactly which field I wanted to sit in during the next go-around with Mother Nature and the knotheads hanging on to her skirts. I ran across several local outlaws from Grimes, a small town to the south, known for their night shooting of ducks. They appeared to be driving around trying to find where the ducks had fed the night before as well. Because ducks and geese will often return to the fields in which they just safely and successfully fed, it is a simple matter to be there waiting there for them when they return if you want a good legal or illegal shoot. I stopped the Grimes lads and, on a hunch, let them know how much I had enjoyed the duck gut presents and, since they more than likely knew who the mysterious gift givers were, asked them to thank them for me as well. I also told the lads that within thirty days, after I contacted my informants, some of those involved in placing the duck guts would be going to the federal lockup in Sacramento for their night hunting activities, so they should be prepared. In short, Christmas was going to come early for those who had been bad. It was more false bravado and frustration than actuality, but it made me feel better.

The men only grinned and said they were just out riding around waiting for the coffee shop to open so they could go visit some friends. My hard, cold stare told them to try again because that dog wouldn't fight. With nervous grins they left the rice fields and drove off toward the town of Colusa. Once they arrived at the local coffee shop, I was sure my words of warning would reach the right ears, exactly according to my now forming plan. I didn't realize just how hard my jaw had been set until I had to relax it after they left to put in a chew of tobacco! It was all I could do to get half of the pouch of Redman into my maw. I guess you could say I had stuck my lance in the ground. Mindful of history and the usual historical fate of those who stuck their lances in the ground, I decided that trend was about to end in the battlefields of Colusa County as far as the duck wars were concerned! At least, I hoped so.

For the next few days I left the valley rice fields alone and began to press all the known markets and buyers in the habit of buying or moving ducks for any information that might lead to my targets. I contacted many "friends" on the other side of the law and called in every bit of credit I had. Another agent in my squad and several surrounding game wardens with the California Department of Fish and Game wrung out their sources of information as well, and slowly but surely a picture began to develop. A lot of ducks had recently been brought into the markets for the buyers in Olivehurst, Yuba City, Marysville, and the small town of Sutter. A fair number of these ducks were reported to be always field dressed so that a higher price could be garnered, and most of those ducks were pintail. Finally one of my oldest and most trusted Asian informants in Yuba City, Tom Ishige, let me know that the two lads I was after were possibly from Williams, but he would tell me no more out of fear of reprisal. He apparently worked part time on one of the farms where these lads sometimes worked and was pure and simply deathly afraid of them if they discovered he was talking to me, especially if they were the topic of the discussion. Little did he realize what he had really told me. I had suspected two fellows from Williams but had very little to go on other than gut instinct, some raw intelligence, history, and their individual newfound wealth in the form of two brand-new Ford three-quarter-ton pickups. The fear shown by Tom told me the lads in question must be mean fellows, and it just so happened that the lads I was interested in were, especially that when they were on drugs, into their booze, or felt they had been ratted on.

Spotting one of these lads' new, light-colored pickup on the streets of Colusa one afternoon, I casually walked by and looked into the bed for any telltale signs or clues that might lead me to conclude that this chap had been transporting masses of dead waterfowl. The usual amount of junk associated with farming and a wide, bloody smear like a pile of duck guts might make sliding across the plywood sheet in the bottom of the bed greeted my eyes. Lodging that bit of information in the recesses of my mind, I kept walking so as not to arouse any suspicion in the owner or anyone else who might have seen me saunter by.

Later that day I got another break from an old friend named Joe Willow. Joe owned the Willow Garage in Colusa, and as his mechanics were fixing a short in my brake light–taillight cutout switches on the patrol vehicle, he offhandedly remarked that one of the fellows I suspected had just had a similar device put into his new Ford pickup. I pretended to not really hear what Joe had said so my interest wouldn't become community property in the mouths of the mechanics listening nearby for my reaction, but you can bet your bottom dollar I mentally registered that bit of information.

Running my mental camera back over the night I had seen the truck driving across the field, I thought its outline could have been that of a boxy-looking Ford. The lightness of that truck as seen through the Starlight would also fit. Then I remembered that the rig should have had to brake several times crossing numerous harvester track ruts scattered throughout the darkened field, and I had not seen any taillights during that whole episode! That would explain the cutoff switches. I was still not dead-on sure of my quarry, but I was picking up enough of the gauntlet that had been thrown down in the form of the duck guts that I was now getting dangerous and close if they were the fellows I was after.

I went to the Colusa County sheriff's office and asked several of the deputies I trusted to keep an eye out for the travels, direction of travel, dates, and times my suspected lads ventured forth from their residences, and they agreed to cooperate. In the meantime, I continued working every night and just enough during the days on the duck clubs to keep all the other duck hunters off their feed in their normal hunting activities during the ongoing waterfowl season.

God had given me a body with tremendous recuperative powers, and I sure put it to the test over the next several weeks. He had also given me a very understanding wife along with a mom who had passed on enough German stubbornness to carry me through just about anything. With those advantages and my two long-suffering guardian angels, what more could I want? But even with those odds, I was being sorely tested.

Soon I had a handle on most of the ducks' nightly feeding patterns, especially in the areas on both sides of the valley known to be frequented by my two lads from Williams. I had also located every field I could find where ducks were feeding now or were known to feed in Colusa County at that time of the year that would allow the easy escape of a pickup from the field onto any state or county highway. If they had put switches on their rig to cut out their lights, that meant they were going to use the truck in the fields for fast loading and transport of the ducks after their shoot. That would be a weak point, I figured, and I meant to exploit it if I had the opportunity.

Several nights into the third week of my intense effort to capture these lads, I got my first real opportunity. Working south of State Highway 20, which connected the towns of Colusa and Williams, I was sitting in the middle of about five bunches of feeding ducks that came to a total of maybe 100,000 birds. They made such a racket that it was no small wonder every market hunter and local duck dragger looking to fill his freezer with rice-fed duck dinners wasn't gathered there like ants at a picnic! I had moved into the fields shortly after dark with my Starlight scope, trusty 03A3 with two flares, and some deer meat sandwiches for my dinner that had been sat on by my trusty dog, Shadow. In no time flat I was surrounded by hordes of feeding ducks, all happily making like there was no tomorrow as far as the rice seeds went. The evening flew by as I was constantly thrilled by the ebb and flow of the thousands of feeding ducks all around me. Several times they got so close and were so numerous that they walked right over my inert, canvas-covered form lying by the rice check as the feeding frenzy forced them into the next rice field for additional feed.

About two-twenty A.M. during one of my Starlight scope area sweeps, I saw a darkened light-colored vehicle pull off a secondary blacktop highway into a harvested rice field about half a mile away and stop. Then nothing. I had a break in the feeding masses of ducks before me, so I crawled through that area and, once out of sight of the ducks, started walking along a rice check that more or less led toward my vehicle target. The Starlight scope kept me up to date on the vehicle's activity as I crept right up to the truck without the lads inside seeing me. Once I reached it, I stood undiscovered at the rear and listened to the two men inside. Their talk was muffled, and soon their heads disappeared from view. I didn't see them for about ten minutes, and then the driver's-side door opened and out came a pair of legs without any pants on them! Damn, I had intruded upon a pair of local gay folks doing what comes naturally! Recognizing one of the excited voices as that of one of Colusa's biggest businessmen, I turned and slipped off into the dark of the night, thankful that they hadn't seen me. Whew, I was sure glad I hadn't barged in on that affair. It would have more than ruined everyone's day, I thought as I crunched back across the stubble in the rice field!

Because the ducks had changed their feeding locations, I was unable to go back the way I had come without scaring them. So I headed over to a large dry feeder ditch covered with tall grass and started to walk down it to the area of my feeding ducks. It was darker than all get-out in that ditch, and after about a dozen or so yards, *wham!* I walked into something huge, metallic, and unmoving. My barked shins and knees certainly let me know about that last fact! Turning on my flashlight and letting the light beam shine through my partially closed fingers to avoid anyone else seeing the light, I saw a new Ford three-quarter-ton pickup in all its glory. Goddamn, it was the shiny new Ford belonging to one of my suspects from Williams, good old Randy himself! I checked the license plate, with which I was familiar, and it was his truck all right. I put my fingers through the grill and discovered that the engine was still warm. In the front seat were several boxes of shotgun shells and other junk, and sure as hell this was one of the rigs I was looking for. But what was it doing hidden in this ditch? It didn't take this bullheaded German more than a few seconds to figure that one out. Quickly checking the tire tread, I discovered that it matched the one I had found in the field at the start of this "hoorah" several weeks earlier. I checked around the two doors and found that the footprints in the soft mud were either size 10 or 11 *and* both had the same tread designs as those I had found around my hidden pickup several weeks earlier! Even in the dark I could feel the start of a smile on my face.

The lads were out in the field stalking my feeding ducks right now, I thought. If they successfully pulled off a shoot, they would come back to the rig and either leave the critters in the field overnight or pick them up and leave after gutting them. Damn, my head spun. What to do? Looking over the rig on the off chance that the bed would already be full of ducks, I was disappointed to only find one dead pintail, several fuel cans, spare tools, cans of oil, rags, chainsaw parts, and the like. As I started to walk away to scan the field of feeding ducks with my Starlight scope for the two lads, the devil in me took over my normally God-fearing soul for the umpteenth time. Without a moment's hesitation, I walked back to the truck, grabbed that pintail from the back, removed its entrails, and stuck them under the wiper blade on the driver's side of the windshield. That small gesture of defiance would sure as hell let the lads know who was now on their trail and had identified them as the gut-pile bandits! I would bet a month's paycheck that when they saw those guts on the windshield, they wished they hadn't put those guts in the bed of my truck or on my driveway. Damn, it felt good to be in the driver's seat once again. Now all I had to do was catch them in the act, and my night would be complete. Yeah, that was all ...

Crawling back up on the dike, I looked all around with my Starlight scope for any sign of action. None, except that now the feeding ducks had split and were gathered on both sides of a nearby north-south farm road in the middle of several rice fields. That was fine and dandy except that the ducks on the east side of the road had a six-foot-deep canal with water flowing in it as a barrier between them and those on the west side. Since that was where most of the ducks were heading in their night on the town, I sneaked alongside the canal just above the water line for about one-quarter of a mile to a crossover point. Crossing the canal and careful not to alert the ducks or anyone else, I continued back down the other side of the canal toward my feeding ducks, keeping a sharp lookout for my suspects through the Starlight scope. All the while I kept thinking, This really makes it awkward for me, especially if the shooters end up shooting into the smaller bunch of feeding ducks on the west side of the canal while I am stuck over here on the opposite side. That would mean a long, fast trot or a cold swim to get back across that canal in order to catch them.

Second-guessing myself, I thought I could wait back at the truck, but if they showed up without their shotguns and ducks, as I suspected they were wont to do, I would have nothing. Hence my desire to catch them in the field after the shoot, possibly when they took the time to gut out the ducks. The idea of these lads gutting out the ducks in the field kept sticking in my craw. Almost every other night hunter took the ducks to a deserted barn or garage and gutted them out at their leisure, not in the field. Oh well, to each his own, I guessed.

About that time the smaller bunch of ducks across the canal exploded into the air. It was obvious that something had spooked them big time! Trapped by the canal, all I could do was watch the area with my scope and listen for any shots. Then it hit me! Terry, your job is to preserve as well as protect; get with it! Grabbing my rifle, I hooked one of my parachute flares onto the launching device on the end of the barrel, stuck the rifle stock on the ground (by placing the stock on the ground I avoided a murderous recoil had it been placed against my shoulder), and aimed it high over the ducks now fleeing the area. *Whoomp*, the rifle went as the rocket carrying the flare arched skyward. *Roar* went the wings of the thousands of ducks on my side of the canal that I had forgotten about in my haste to get a rocket airborne. Oh, well, let's have a circus while we're at it, I thought. Hurriedly reloading, I again set the rifle butt down, and *whoomp* went my second and last flare as the first flare exploded at that very moment over the scene. Damn, it was great! The Fourth of July in December. Ducks were going everywhere, the bad guys, wherever they were, had to be on the run, any other outlaws eyeballing the ducks in this area had to be pissing down their legs at the moment, and the two gay men I had discovered in the truck earlier probably had eyes as big as their sexual ideas had been.

Now that I had woken up the entire neighborhood, I headed back down the canal road at a ground-eating trot toward my crossing point. Once on the other side I headed back toward the hidden pickup to see the reaction of the lads when they discovered the surprise on their windshield. I arrived just in time to see the darkened shape of the truck leaving the area. Cranking up my Starlight scope, I could see that the truck held two occupants. They sped across the darkened field up onto a farm road out to Lone Star Road, turned north, and drove out of sight, never turning on their lights. Again a large smile was slowly forming on my face. True, I didn't have the lads as of yet, but I could smell a catch coming sometime soon!

Since every duck within a mile of my location had a bad case of the "big eye" after my earlier activity, there was no use staying in those fields any longer, especially in light of the departure of my Williams chaps. I was sure any other chaps that had ideas about blowing up the ducks were now long gone as well. So I packed up my gear and, with a lighter step, headed for my hidden vehicle. I wasn't upset at not catching my lads. Not one bit. I was on their trail, they had to know I was on their trail, and as far as I was concerned it was just a matter of time. Out of arrogance and probably financial need to pay for their new Ford trucks, they would almost certainly continue their night-shooting field escapades. They had chosen to play in my arena and now it was time to see who had the most pluck.

Arriving back at my vehicle and looking into the bed, I was pleased at not finding anything out of the ordinary. I loaded up and drove out of the area without lights, heading for home and maybe a well-deserved breakfast, this time with my bride. That thought brought a smile came to my muddy face, and somehow the gas pedal was pressed even further down toward the floor.

A week went by, and then I received a call from Tom Ishige, my friend in Yuba City, who notified me that his boss's supplier of wild ducks for the market had been forced to place several deliveries on hold. It seemed that his main suppliers had gotten cold feet and were going to have to be extra careful because they felt the local fed was on to them. It seemed that they had dumped duck guts in his truck, and the fed had in turn put duck guts on their truck windshield, as he had gotten the story. Bingo! I now knew for sure who my targets were, and with a little help from the sheriff's office on these lads' nighttime activities, it was just a matter of time. As I said earlier, don't beard the lion in his den unless you are prepared to mingle with the rest of the pride!

Thanking Tom, I headed over to the sheriff's office to make sure the deputies were really dogging my two lads from Williams and keeping good records of their movements. The information that they had accumulated to date showed that the two men had a pattern of leaving home and driving south one night and then going north the next. Checking their schedules against the known illegal night-shooting events I had recorded, I found this information to coincide with some of the nighttime field shooting I had heard. Also, the lads would be home all day sleeping, since neither held a real job at that time of the year, preferring their all-night sojourns in the rice fields and the money from the sale of their ill-gotten gains.

With that intelligence, I worked out an arrangement with the Williams deputy that he would let me know when both fellows were sleeping in the early afternoon. That should tell me they planned to hit the ducks that evening. Going on their schedule of hunting north and then south on successive nights to throw me off, I would be in the correct quadrant ahead of them, working and waiting. Then it would be up to me and my knowledge of the area, endurance, and understanding of the habits of feeding ducks to try to bring us all together as one big happy family. Those were all the odds I would need, plus the fact that they seemed to always shoot just the large bunches of ducks, which would help me narrow the field of battle even further. Most old-time commercial-market hunters avoided the really large bunches of feeding ducks because they felt that the feds always baby-sat concentrations of that size. Since my lads were working over the very largest of the bunches, guess which duck concentrations I would choose to sit on? I was now beginning to lose the frustration I had felt earlier and regain that old feeling that one gets from hunting one's fellow human and knowing that the catch is not far away.

One Friday soon afterward, Deputy Del Garrison, a big-hearted bear of a man, called me on the telephone and relayed a message from the Williams officer that the lads were sleeping. I checked the schedule and saw that the lads were due to hunt north that evening, so north I went. That worked out really well because I had been covering the whole north end of Colusa County throughout the previous night, and the only really big bunches of ducks were just south west of the Terhel Farms headquarters. The only concern I had was that these large groups of ducks were feeding nowhere near the areas previously frequented by my two shooters. Then a thought hit me. It wasn't a big problem to locate the ducks as they fed in the fields at night because they really telegraphed where they were going. What if these lads had changed their hunting pattern and were now working the east side of the valley to throw me off the trail? I know I would move my theater of operations if someone was hot on my trail; why wouldn't they?

The more I thought of it, the more I thought I ought to change my own work habits and drift to where the resources were located in the greatest numbers. That would be the east side of the valley, and by damn, that is where I was going to give her a try. If these lads were indeed changing their shooting patterns, boy, wouldn't they be surprised if I was there as well? I was certainly not concerned about locating the hordes of feeding ducks on the east side of the county either. I would guess there had been at least seventy-five thousand ducks feeding in that area over the past few evenings, so they would be easy to find even after dark because of the noise they would be making. With my mind made up, I was set to go. Loading up another supply of parachute flares from a munitions container in my garage, I grabbed some sandwiches made from my wife's great homemade bread and off I went. I knew exactly where I was going to hide my truck and wanted to get there early to avoid the kind of wreck that could be caused by not planning well enough, as had occurred the time I found the duck guts in my truck.

Hiding my truck in a dry swale next to several stately oaks, I dragged my camouflage parachute over it and then crawled over to a mound of dirt next to the trees by my rice field of choice and set up to study the are and further plan my operations. I had my usual gear: 03A3 rifle with flares, Starlight scope, grub enough for a man my size (that is, a lot), five-cell flashlight, binoculars, and on my feet for the first time a pair of tennis shoes instead of the usual hip boots or heavy leather Redwing boots so I could fly like a bird, or at least run faster. One of the Williams lads had gone to the state track meet one year, and I knew that if I hooked up with him I would have to be fleet of foot, or at least be able to outlast him. Speed was not my forte, but endurance was. Having carried three hundred or more pounds for so many years, I had developed a good set of strong legs and a great set of lungs. I figured those factors would have to serve me well if I had to chase this speedster. However, with use of drugs and booze and the resulting abuse of his body, which I knew about from his police record, I figured I might have the edge. The other lad would be no slouch in the speed department either, especially because the fuel that comes from being chased has a tendency to lend wings to many a lad's feet.

The evening started off pleasantly enough with fairly nice weather, no wind, and at least a thousand acres of harvested rice fields in front of me for the ducks to feed in. There was zero human activity until just about dusk. Then the ducks began to arrive from the Butte Sink, at first just a few pairs, then several small flocks, and finally ducks by the zillion. The air over the Butte Sink began to fill with mallards, pintail, and all the other members of the duck community adding their happy voices as if there wasn't enough noise already. Here they came, looking for the evening chow line. The air was filled with winged cannonballs at every level and from every point on the compass. Punctuating this mess of wildlife were the ever-calling wood ducks, adding their melody to this symphony of sounds. God, it was great to be alive and experience this mass of wildlife energy.

A few vehicles drove by on the high levee roads separating the huge rice fields, but none were the type I was looking for. Then, hello—a nice new light-gray Ford pickup, like the one Randy owned, moved slowly up a levee road from the south and drove without stopping the length of Terrill Sartain's land, looking over the swirling masses of ducks in the dimming light, and then left, turning east on the Colusa-Gridley highway. Dark settled in for the night, and on went my trusty Starlight scope. I still had to figure how to sneak up on the lads after they had pulled their shoot, but now that I knew where they would probably hunt that night, I figured they would likely drive in from the treeline to the north on a seldom-used equipment road and around a cable gate in order to get into the field after the shoot in order to pick up their ducks. The noose was not yet complete, but my chances were getting better—*much* better! I figured if they still had the guts (no pun intended) to pull a shoot and then draw the ducks on site, I would have time to get close enough to cut them off and grab them. That plus my new winged feet with the tennis shoes made this detail a snap, or so it appeared.

About one A.M., I noticed a vehicle running west without lights on the Colusa-Gridley highway stop and then turn into the north end of Terrill's rice fields. The rig was still at least half a mile from the ducks, which did not appear alarmed by the new arrival. I watched the darkened rig slowly make its way across an empty harvested rice field toward the still feeding ducks on the equipment road I had suspected would be used. The vehicle appeared to cross several dry, shallow ditches in the process, and then the damn thing just disappeared! What the hell? I thought. A truck can't just disappear right in front of my eyes! I continued to search for several minutes, but the truck was no more to be seen. Damn, I needed to locate that vehicle in order to see which direction the lads were going into the fields around me, but the truck and its shooters had been swallowed up by the earth, or so it seemed.

By now the entire area was covered with bunches of feeding ducks. It doesn't take long for that many ducks to feed out an area, and by their feeding sounds I could tell the ducks were bound and determined to eat everything in sight that evening if possible. There were four main bunches of ducks now. Gathering up my gear, I left the comfort of my dirt mound and headed northeast for the middle ground between all of them. It took a long time crawling and walking slowly stooped over to avoid scaring the ducks, but finally I was more or less in the middle of the rascals and just south of where I had last seen the truck before it disappeared. Damn, what a din: whistling bodies flying through the darkened sky like cannon shot, quacks everywhere, and the flowing-water sound of a zillion bills happily scooping up the rice grains left after harvest. If it hadn't been for the lads on the other end of the field, it would have been a night to remember for its cheerful beauty. As it turned out, it was a night to remember for other reasons!

Quiet reigned for about thirty minutes after I got into place;

then a ragged volley of fifteen or so shots erupted about two hundred yards north of me, as did thousands of fleeing ducks. There she goes, I thought as I spun around and focused my Starlight scope on that area in a vain attempt to see what was going down. All I could see in the field of green within the scope were the black blurs of thousands of escaping waterfowl in the air and those on the ground still getting up like a giant green-tinged carpet. Other flocks of feeding ducks, alarmed at the disturbance, were also getting airborne, and that had a synergistic effect on all the rest until the entire group of ducks was airborne and milling about. Damn, what a mess of critters. I was always amazed at how many ducks there really were in an area like this once they all took flight. You never saw them all arrive because they filtered in in small numbers at different times from every point of the compass, but boy, when they took off all at once, there was no missing the fact that you had a hatful!

Straining my eyes through the Starlight scope, I waited for the appearance of the lads who had pulled the triggers, and it didn't take long. On one of my many slow sweeps, I finally saw two men as they rose up out of a rice field and just stood there looking about. One was using what appeared to be binoculars and was scanning the field for any evidence of wardens approaching. I hoped he wasn't using a device like my Starlight Scope. If he was, he would be able to see me using mine (one could see the purple glow of a scope in use if one was using another similar scope), and the jig would be up. The lad continued to look the area over with his optics and didn't seem to notice mine, which was locked right on them. Good, I thought, I still have the edge.

They stood there for about ten minutes until they were finally satisfied that no one was after them, then lay down their shotguns and started gathering up their kill. From all the white patches and movement still going on on the ground before them, they had killed the hell out of the ducks. Good, I thought, it would take them some time to clean up the mess, and that would give me time to move in on them for the moment I had been waiting for! I had a way to go, and with the gear I was going to take with me until I got close I knew it would be slow going, so away I went.

I found the tennis shoes great for the flat ground, but they sure didn't offer any ankle support when I stepped into an unseen harvester tire rut in the soft clay fields. I kept plowing on, though, because I had worked too hard to catch these lads, and they did need catching. Pausing every forty yards or so, I would turn on the scope and watch them to see if everything was all right, then continue on. About the third time I turned on the scope, I could see that they were starting to haul their ducks to an area where several rice checks came together in a corner. I was now about eighty yards away from the lads and breathing hard from carrying the heavy, awkward load of gear. Shifting my gear around, I took my mind off the walking on the uneven field (sliding my feet along the ground instead of taking steps off into nothingness) until I suddenly stepped down into a two-foot-deep rut made by one of the rice harvesters as it slid around a wet corner in the field while harvesting rice. The instant sharp pain was so bad it almost made me cry out. Goddamnit, did I ever turn my right ankle. Automatically dropping all my gear, I grabbed my ankle in abject pain. At first I figured from the pain level that I had broken it! Those goddamned lousy tennis shoes may have made me faster, but without the correct ankle support they had caused one hell of a wreck!

In a few moments, the agony subsided from a constant sharp stabbing to a painful throbbing, the kind that makes your eyes water no matter how tough you think you are. Grabbing my scope by groping around on the darkened ground and turning it on, I could see that the lads still didn't know I was there. Once this pain subsides I will be off and after them like a slow flash, I thought. However, that was not to be. Instead the pain just got worse. Feeling my swelling ankle, I could tell I had really screwed it up. The damned thing was twice as large as the other ankle, more than filling my shoe, and trying to put much weight on it was out of the question. The two times I tried to walk, my efforts were rewarded with sharp, crashing pain from the ankle to my hind end! It was fast becoming obvious that I was not going to apprehend any duck shooters that night. Damn, I was angry with myself for not holding up physically, and just when I needed it too! Trying one more time to put weight on the ankle, hoping against hope that it would work, I was rewarded by an even worse pain telling me not to do that again, *ever!* There I sat in the soft mud of a rice field while not many yards away the two shooters I had been after for weeks were making off with the ducks they had just shot.

I thought of trying to crawl up on the lads and somehow hold them at bay with voice commands but soon dropped that idea. These were bad men, and a stunt like that may engender a worse reaction than I would be prepared for. In addition, I had to somehow grab these lads in the act, preferably with the load of ducks in their vehicle, in a pile at their feet, or in their hands. Anything less would mean a long court battle, and what I had at this point, namely, my testimony about what I saw through a fuzzy Starlight scope at eighty yards, would not be enough evidence. Damn, I thought, so close and yet so far. What I would have given to have been wearing my boots that evening!

Watching the shooters through my night scope from my now painful sitting position, I could see them running bunches of dead ducks from the field to what appeared to be a deep, dry rice canal some yards away from where the shoot had occurred. Their vehicle was still not in sight. It was obvious that I would not be chasing these fellows for their deed, but I couldn't just sit there and let them escape scot-free! Scrambling around in the dark, I retrieved my 03A3 rifle with the rocket launcher and three rifle flares. Attaching a flare to the launching device, I chambered a blank 30-06 cartridge, stuck the stock into the mud by where I sat, took aim, and let her go! *Boom* went the shot and high into the air went the orange eye of the rocket fuel propelling the flare. Dropping my rifle, I grabbed my binoculars to watch the forthcoming events. *Kapow* went the flare, and the instant green light froze the two men in their tracks. One had a large bunch of ducks in his hand and the other had been busily gathering up more from the ground when someone turned on the lights. Even with that burst of illumination, I still couldn't see their faces well enough to take them on in a court of law. Damn, talk about frustrated! They remained frozen for a moment, and then I heard one of them shout something like, "Run!" I hurriedly loaded another flare and let it go just over them so they could hear the *whoosh* of the flare as it passed within feet of their heads. It was a dangerous thing to do, but at that point I wanted these lads to run clear across two counties before they stopped, and this was one sure way to do it. *Boom* went the low-flying flare as it sailed past their heads and blew up about a hundred feet off the ground and fifty yards in front of them near the place where all the rice checks came together.

By now there was abject panic in the field and in the air. I could hear feeding ducks from a long distance away taking to the air in every other field around me, and a look at my lads through the binoculars showed that they were doing the one-hundred-yard sprint across the rice field in 10 seconds flat. That wasn't fast enough, though; the parachute flare could do the hundred in 9.9! Grabbing my last flare, I let it go high overhead for maximum light and then just sat there with my throbbing ankle for company, cussing my stupidity and watching the show. Every duck in the area was leaving, as were my two lads. They had run across their rice field and were showing no inclination to reduce their pace until they got clear across the county! As they ran out of the light of the flare I noticed that the second, low-trajectory burning flare had dropped right into the ditch where they had been taking the dead ducks for storage. Damn, how ironic, I thought. If the lads had stayed, the local federal would have helped them load their ducks with the aid of his flare.

The flare had dropped into the ditch and out of sight, but I could still see a faint light as it continued to burn itself out. Turning on my Starlight scope, I watched the lads run into a grove of oak trees to the north and out of sight. Damn, I thought. I had just lost the chance of a lifetime to catch two lads who sure needed catching. In this case, instead of my kingdom for a horse, it was my kingdom for a sound ankle and a good pair of boots!

Satisfied that the lads were gone for the ages, I turned my scope toward where they had pulled their shot in the field so I could mark the location exactly, come back in the morning with a taped-up ankle, and at least retrieve the birds they had left behind in their haste to escape. Swinging the scope around to the rice checks where the lads had carried several bunches of ducks to hide them for later retrieval, I was surprised to see a large glow at ground level. The parachute flare had started a fire in the dry rice straw in that ditch, and now it was burning like holy blazes. I watched the ever-growing fire for a few moments and finally quit worrying about it because the fire wasn't going anywhere except maybe down a dry ditch bank. The farmers would burn that rice field and ditch later anyway, just as they had the one I was sitting in.

Grabbing my gear, I started to slowly, and I do mean *slowly*, hobble across the field back to my patrol vehicle. It took a long time, and as I crept across the field using my rifle stock as a crutch, I thought I could hear faint shots going off in the distance, far to the north. Without giving it a second thought because of the pain, I just concentrated on getting back to my truck without clanging that damn sore ankle on anything. Once at my truck, I turned as I loaded the gear and was again surprised at the now very large glow back at the ditch where the still burning parachute flare had dropped. There was a huge blaze there now, fairly well centered in the ditch. Oh well, if it burned up some of the ducks in the ditch that would be OK because there were a jillion that they had not picked up lying about in the field, so I still had plenty of evidence. Right now my throbbing ankle told me to get to a doctor, if for nothing else then to get some painkillers so I could continue working. I planned to see the sawbones in Colusa, get the ankle wrapped, get some painkillers, and then go back out to the field and pick up the ducks.

Starting up my truck, a four-speed, I gingerly worked the clutch, brake, and throttle with my left foot as I drove out and headed down the River Road toward Colusa and some much-needed medical help. I hadn't gone more than four or five miles south when I noticed an oncoming patrol car with all its emergency lights flashing roaring toward me. As it passed through my headlights, I noticed the driver was Eloy Zaragoza, a city of Colusa police officer. What the hell was he doing clear out here outside his jurisdiction? A few moments later I noticed another police car coming my way with all its lights flashing. As it passed me, I saw that this one was a Colusa County sheriff's car driven by the undersheriff, Joel McDermott. Damn, I thought, something really bad is going down. Since these lads were always there for me, I decided I was going to give them a hand, bad ankle or not! Spinning my truck around and almost blacking out as I hit my ankle on the edge of the brake pedal, I recovered amidst a hatful of swearing and tearing eyes and began following the fast-disappearing flashing lights ahead of me.

As I sped north I wondered why I had not heard anything on the radio. I found I had turned it off earlier so any random transmission would not give me away if I happened on any bad guys. What a dingbat, I thought as I turned it on and, as it warmed up, thumbed the mike button so I could call the sheriff's office and see what was going on. Once I got Colusa County on the air, I was surprised to find that the lads were scrambling to save me! What the hell? I asked for more information. It seemed that someone had reported to the Colusa Police Department that shots were being exchanged between me and several market hunters in Terrill Sartain's rice field. How the hell anyone knew I was there at that time of night, much less in a shootout, was beyond me, but the call had come in all the same. The caller would not identify himself, but I sure as hell did!

"Colusa," I said, "this is me, Terry. I sure as hell am not being shot at; in fact, I was coming into Colusa to get some medical attention for a damn well-turned ankle!" I told Colusa to slow the lads down from the Code 3 run they were making because there wasn't any need for such a maneuver that could be dangerous, especially if they hit one of the large deer coming off the river after getting a drink of water. I said I would meet the lads shortly if they would slow down a bit because I was just a few miles behind them on the same road. The Colusa dispatcher said he would let them know, and a few moments later called and asked me to meet Eloy and Joel on the first north-south Terrill Farms levee road just off the Gridley highway. I agreed, and in a few moments was parked alongside my two very good but anxious friends. They were surprised to see me all right after receiving the phone call alerting them to my "shootout." It later turned out that the caller hadn't said I was involved in the shootout but just that a shootout was in progress in the field across from where we were parked and now observing a damn good fire. How the hell the mix-up occurred was beyond me.

There were lots of questions as to why I was limping like a smashed cat, and I had to explain my harvester track–tennis shoe episode. Being the good friends they were, they didn't stop with the questioning until they were satisfied I was all right. Then all our eyes turned to the burning object in the middle of Terrill's rice field. Putting my binoculars to work, from the elevated position of the levee I could see what appeared to be a burning pickup blazing away in the same rice field I had worked earlier that night. But there sure as hell hadn't been any pickup out there when I was there except that of the bad guys, which they had driven in earlier in the evening, the one I had lost sight of. I was sure their pickup had been located farther to the north! Oh well, turning my binoculars back to the action at hand I could see that the pickup in question was burning like all get-out, and we could hear the shotgun shells exploding and glass tinkling even from where we stood several hundred yards away. The three of us stood there watching the spectacle in the field for a few moments, and then the pain in my ankle warned me that I had better get some health care or more pain was to come.

I told Joel that since the fire wasn't going anywhere we should let the damn pickup burn, and once I got my foot fixed I would come back with my four-wheel-drive pickup and take him out there for a look-see. Joel agreed, whereupon the three of us returned to Colusa, letting the pickup burn harmlessly to the ground since there wasn't anything we could do at that point to stop it, nor could the fire department by the time they could have arrived.

On the way back to Colusa I couldn't help but think about that pickup and how it had gotten into the very rice field I had been sitting on almost all night long without me seeing it. Then the pain in my ankle pushed those thoughts out of my mind until I got it wrapped and put some painkillers to work. Then the thoughts came back. I tiredly got back into my patrol truck and swung by the Colusa County sheriff's office to pick up Joel. We had a lively discussion about how the pickup could have gotten into that rice field, how the fire had started, and who the owner might be but came to no conclusion. When we arrived at the rice field I carefully picked my four-wheel-drive way across the semimuddy ground to the still smoking pickup truck. Joel and I stepped out and walked (or in my case hobbled) over to what used to be a new Ford 4x4 pickup that was now in a terrible state of disrepair. Boy, was it ever! The truck had literally burned to the ground, tires and all. Then came the dawn: this looked like Randy's truck! A quick look at the license plate confirmed my thoughts. It was Randy's brand-new Ford truck all right, the one he had recently purchased with the profits from the illegal sale of waterfowl, according to my informant Tom.

My mind was whirling now. The truck was in a shallow ditch, just deep enough to hide the silhouette of a truck at night. I hobbled a few yards to the south side of the ditch containing the still smoking pickup, and a scene of carnage met my eyes. Piles of dead and dying ducks littered the ground. Letting my eyes rise, I could look directly at the very place where I had hidden earlier in the evening and where I had sprained my ankle. Turning, I could see two sets of footprints leading all over the field, made by people picking up ducks, then leading over to the ditch (where many ducks were piled), and then returning. The footprints matched those I had seen earlier. Walking to the rear of the burned-out truck, I could see about sixty dead ducks piled on the ground awaiting loading. In the bed of the burned truck were the remains of another forty or so ducks, all badly charred.

It all came together. The lads had hidden their truck in the shallow ditch shortly after they arrived under the cloak of darkness. No wonder I had lost sight of them. They had driven into that ditch and then walked down the ditch, out of sight, about fifty yards toward the feeding duck concentrations. The ducks had been feeding in this area for several days, and it didn't take a rocket scientist to realize that all one had to do was sneak in without scaring the ducks and then pull off one's shoot. After that, it was just a simple matter of carrying the ducks fifty or so yards, loading them into the truck, and driving home. All very simple, except that something had gone badly wrong.

Returning to the burned-out shell of what used to be a brand-new pickup, Joel and I looked for clues to the origin of the fire. There wasn't anything out of the ordinary. The burned-out truck bed was full of oil cans, gas cans, pipe, dead ducks, farm trash, and *a spring-and-wire contraption that looked like the frame of an umbrella used to hold open a parachute flare after it had exploded*. There it was! Was this the clue we were looking for? What the hell was part of a parachute flare doing in the back of these chaps' truck? My thoughts ran like wildfire. Running the previous evening's events through my mind, I mentally retraced my actions with the parachute flares. Then it hit me! The parachute flare that had gone off at too low an altitude and had drifted, still burning, into the ditch behind the two chaps. Damn! Now it rang a bell. The flare had drifted straight into the back of Randy's pickup, which had been parked in the ditch. It must have landed among the oil and gasoline cans and set them off. That fuel set the entire truck on fire and burned it to the ground as the two shooters sprinted for the trees in the opposite direction! God, what irony. By a fluke of nature and a little wind drift, God had again lifted His hand and made it difficult for the lads on the other side of the fence to enjoy their trade or the fruits of their illegal labors. Maybe God had been a game warden after all, huh?

I pointed out the remaining parts of the parachute flare to Joel and the possibility that it may have caused the fire. He carefully examined the wire contraption that was used to snap out and hold open the small parachute as it drifted to earth. Without a second thought, he said, "Doesn't look like it to me; looks like an ordinary piece of farm junk. Case closed. They must have left a burning rag in the back or the like."

"Joel," I said, "I was in these fields earlier and shot several parachute flares in this direction at two fellows who had just blown up the ducks. Maybe one of my parachute flares landed in the back of this truck and set it afire."

Joel looked at me and said, "Tiny, the way you shoot, you got to be kidding. There is also welding equipment in the back of the truck, and maybe that was the fire's cause." I felt differently, but he was the undersheriff and crime-scene investigator, so I just went along with his conclusion. It was obvious that the owners had gotten a little carried away with the harvest of the ducks, and Joel just grinned at the turn of events and said, "He shouldn't have been here. Old Man Sartain would have a fit if he had caught these folks dragging his ducks on his property."

"Yeah, he wouldn't have been too happy with them," I agreed. Joel called in the license-plate number on the burned truck and told the sheriff's office dispatcher to call the owner and let him know the condition and location of his truck.

Satisfied that the burning of the pickup had been an accident (no matter how it happened), Joel suggested that he give me a hand, and we picked up the remaining seventy-seven ducks lying on the ground behind the pickup and scattered throughout the rice field. I also loaded a few not-so-badly-burned ducks from the center of the pile in the back of the pickup and photographed the rest with the truck's license plate in view (what was left of it), and we left the scene. Randy, I later found out from Joe Willow at the garage and wrecker service, had the wreck of a truck towed to a local farm, where his farmer friend stored it for several years. It eventually went to a junkyard in Yuba City for scrap metal.

Driving back to Colusa, I again let my mind wander over the evening's events. Now I knew why the fire had been so large as I hobbled out of that rice field. It wasn't the rice straw in the ditch burning but the damn truck. I also now knew why I kept hearing "shots" behind me. It wasn't illegal hunters in the rice fields to the north but shotgun and rifle ammunition left in the truck exploding as it burned. Now it all made sense. A smile crossed my tired lips as I laid further plans to torment my commercial-market hunters who now had one brand-new pickup less in their inventory. The bad guys had to have a lather up by now, I thought. They had not yet fully paid for these new trucks. Now one of the trucks was gone, and they had to be getting nervous about the game management agent hot on their tails. This would slow them down in their killing, and that would make paying for those two trucks, since they didn't have real jobs, even harder.

With one more ace up my sleeve, I headed for those places known to harbor duck buyers in the Yuba City area and through my friend Tom began to spread the word (falsely) that an undercover buyer was working the duck trade as in the days of the "peanut salesman" (a federal undercover agent who had used that as his cover in the 1950s and had captured a lot of market hunters in the Sacramento Valley, many of whom went to prison). I made sure my group of informants told everyone they had better be extra careful who they purchased their ducks from because it might be the undercover agent. Boy, you talk about paranoia. It ran through the illegal duck-buying and -shooting community like a bad case of pinkeye in Mrs. Jones's third grade class! With that bit of psychological warfare going on, I knew that making payments on that remaining new Ford would be difficult, and the owner might even need to default.

Two weeks later I met Randy in the street and struck up a conversation. Just being seen in public with a federal caused a lot of people to sweat in those days, and Randy was no exception. All he wanted to do was get on down the road and away from

me. Realizing the spot I was putting him in by being seen together on the streets of Colusa, I just hung in with the conversation. "I understand you lost your truck the other night," I said.
Randy just nodded and mumbled something I couldn't understand. "You know, Randy," I continued, "there were a lot of
dead ducks in the back of that truck." He just looked at me,
wishing for a place to crawl off to, but I had my hooks in him
and was going to play my last ace or else. "Randy, I hope you
don't turn that burned-up truck into your insurance company
for them to pay off as an accident."

"Why not?" he asked sharply.

"Because that truck and whoever was driving it were involved
in illegal activities at the time of the fire, and I'm sure the insurance company wouldn't be very happy to hear about that. Also,
keep in mind that to turn in a false insurance claim is to commit
a felony. Have you thought of that?" Randy just looked at me as
that thought now crossed his mind. "I do intend to notify your
insurance company of the pending federal investigation, and if
you file a false insurance claim, they might very well prosecute
you." I could see the blood draining from Randy's face and neck
as he realized he was trapped into paying for a truck that no
longer existed. "I also know you didn't file a stolen vehicle report within the required forty-eight-hour period, Randy, so you
can't use that as a ruse to cast the blame at this late date as an insurance payment justification either."

Randy looked like he was going to vomit. Now, four-wheel-
drive vehicles could be had in those days for about $3,000, not a
lot by today's standards, but still a sizable chunk of change to
those who didn't choose to work at steady jobs. I had him, and
he knew it! "Next time you and Paul go duck hunting, keep it
legal and don't throw the duck guts anyplace where a person
might take offense." He now knew for sure that I knew, and
Randy was just frozen in place. I went on, "If you do, who
knows, that person might put some ducks guts on your windshield wiper as a warning of worse things to come if you don't
cease and desist." With that, Randy blanched, whirled, and

stormed off, calling me every name in the book and a few others that weren't there.

I found out later that Randy withdrew his false insurance claim on his truck and had to eat the payments. Paul's new Ford was repossessed three months later because he was not able to kill and sell enough ducks to keep up the payments owing to my "undercover agent working the valley" ruse. Apparently my rumor war with the illegal duck buyers worked so well that few ducks were being purchased from anyone except well-established, old-time hunters with solid reputations. Since Randy and Paul were new to the market hunting business, they were among the first shooters to be dropped by the paranoid buyers.

I never caught sight of those lads again in the fields at night or shooting ducks illegally. I know they probably did to pay for their drug habits, but large-scale work in this arena did not appear to be their can of worms after that little episode. That is what this profession is all about. If you can prevent the illegal events from occurring, it's better than having to catch the perpetrators after they have pulled the triggers. It is always better to put the resource back into the environment at the top end rather than carrying the wildlife out in body bags at the bottom end, no two ways about it.

I never had duck guts put into the back of my patrol truck or driveway again during the rest of the years I worked the Sacramento Valley. Word got out, I guess. I never again wore tennis shoes into a field of battle and still carry a sometimes painful (if I step on it wrong) and weak right ankle to this day. However, it is good to have a constant physical reminder of one's mortality and to carry the resulting thought of what one can do and the hurdles that can be overcome when one puts one's mind to it, many times making the difference between wining and losing! A win was certainly scored that night in Terrill's rice fields for not only me but the nation's fabric in the form of its ducks.

History never really forgives. But with any luck, we won't forget.

About the Author

TERRY GROSZ earned his bachelor's degree in 1964 and his master's in wildlife management in 1966 from Humboldt State College in California. He was a California State Fish and Game Warden, based first in Eureka and then Colusa, from 1966 to 1970. He then joined the U.S. Fish & Wildlife Service, and served in California as a U.S. Game Management Agent and Special Agent until 1974. After that, he was promoted to Senior Resident Agent and placed in charge of North and South Dakota for two years, followed by three years as Senior Special Agent in Washington, D.C., with the Endangered Species Program, Division of Law Enforcement. While in Washington, he also served as a foreign liaison officer. In 1979 he became Assistant Special Agent in Charge in Minneapolis, and then was promoted to Special Agent in Charge, and transferred to Denver in 1981, where he remained until retirement in June 1998 (although his title changed to Assistant Regional Director for Law Enforcement).

He has earned many awards and honors during his career, including, from the U.S. Fish & Wildlife Service, the Meritorious Service Award in 1996, and Top Ten Awards in 1987 as one of the top ten employees (in an agency of some 9,000). The Fish & Wildlife Foundation presented him with the Guy Bradley Award in 1989, and in 1995 he received the Conservation Achievement Award for Law Enforcement from the National Wildlife Federation. His first book, *Wildlife Wars,* was published in 1999.

Terry Grosz lives in Colorado with his wife, Donna, who teaches fourth grade and makes the best pies in the world. They have three grown children.